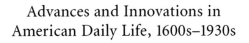
Advances and Innovations in
American Daily Life, 1600s–1930s

ALSO BY ERNIE GROSS

This Day in American History, Revised Edition
(McFarland, 2001)

This Day in Sports
(McFarland, 2001)

Advances and Innovations in American Daily Life, 1600s–1930s

by
ERNIE GROSS

McFarland & Company, Inc., Publishers
Jefferson, North Carolina, and London

Library of Congress Cataloguing-in-Publication Data

Gross, Ernie.
　　Advances and innovations in American daily life, 1600s–1930s / by Ernie Gross.
　　　　p.　cm.
　　Includes bibliographical references and index.
　　ISBN 0-7864-1248-8 (softcover : 50# alkaline paper) ∞
　　1. United States— Social life and customs.　2. Technological innovations— United
States— History.　I. Title.
　　E161 .G76 2002
　　973 — dc21　　　　　　　　　　　　　　　　　　　　　　　　　　2002007474

British Library cataloguing data are available

Cover art ©2002 Index Stock

Manufactured in the United States of America

*McFarland & Company, Inc., Publishers
Box 611, Jefferson, North Carolina 28640
www.mcfarlandpub.com*

Contents

Preface 1

1. Agriculture 3
2. Art 14
3. Business and Finance 21
4. Clothing 39
5. Communications 42
6. Education 49
7. Energy 65
8. Entertainment 73
9. Food and Drink 87
10. Health 97
11. Labor 117
12. Law 121
13. Manufacturing 124
14. Military 147
15. Music 151
16. Public Service 161
17. Publications 166
18. Religion 182
19. Science 198

20. Shelter and Domestic Furnishings 209

21. Social Welfare 218

22. Sports 223

23. Transportation 244

Index 275

Preface

American daily life keeps changing and improving as it has for nearly 400 years. We accept the changes and put them to use, usually helping make life easier, more productive and more enjoyable.

Many of our current activities rest on methods and equipment that go back to our beginnings in the new world; many more developed through the nearly 400 years of life in America as our needs and knowledge increased.

Our national beginnings in Jamestown (1607) and Plymouth (1620) rested on colonists adapting their lifestyles learned in Europe to the needs of the new American life. This book tries to show the gradual evolution of all our activities of life; the beginnings are fairly clearly marked but, in many cases, this evolution continues. It is hard to say that something started here and ended there, when in most cases we have not reached an end. Nevertheless, much of what we think of as the American lifestyle still relies on technology and products that were well established by the 1930s, and this book covers most innovations until roughly that era.

Dedicated to describing beginnings, this book does not attempt to carry these activities through their entire development to modern times.

1. Agriculture

When English colonists began arriving in North America in the 17th century, they brought with them some materials, tools, cuttings and seeds and their skills in farming. They also learned or borrowed from the Spanish, who had come earlier, and from the native Indians.

The settlers were able to borrow much farming knowledge from the Indians—the soil and their cultivation methods, primitive though they were. The colonists rarely planted more than 100 acres because clearing the forested land was a major undertaking.

Soon the settlers were growing grains and fodder, fruits and vegetables, raising cattle and other farm animals and developing cash crops such as cotton, rice, and tobacco.

Almost all settlements quickly developed grist and sawmills, breweries, bakeries, cooperages and tanneries. Bakeries were exceedingly busy providing bread for residents and for export. Coopers were fully occupied with making barrels and casks for fish and salt pork.

Agricultural Education and Associations

The growth of American agriculture was aided by various forms of education.

The Philadelphia Society for the Promotion of Agriculture, organized in 1785, numbered George Washington and Benjamin Franklin as members. Similar societies followed in South Carolina 1785, Maine 1787, New York 1791, Massachusetts 1792, and Connecticut 1794.

The first specialized school of agriculture was the Gardiner, Maine, Lyceum (1821); the state appropriated $1,000 for the school (1823), probably the first state school aid.

The first professor of agriculture was Samuel L. Mitchill (1764–1831) at Columbia College (1792).

Agricultural education was started by 1840 in many states. Colleges of agriculture began in the 1850s — Michigan Agricultural College (now Michigan State University (1857); Farmer's High School (became Pennsylvania Agricultural College, now Penn State University) (1859), and Maryland Agricultural College (now part of University of Maryland) (1856).

Liberty H. Bailey (1858–1924) organized the first college horticultural department at Michigan State University (1884). He organized the New York State Agricultural College at Cornell (1890), serving as its dean until 1913.

Another avenue of agricultural education was the experimental farm. The first such farm began in 1735 on ten acres in Savannah, Georgia. A botanist collected seeds of drugs and dyes which might do well in Georgia. With the help of private funds, Connecticut established the first state agricultural experiment station at Middletown (1875).

Some leaders in agricultural education and experimentation were:

Orange Judd (1822–92), editor and publisher of *The American Agriculturist* (1856–83).

Samuel W. Johnson (1830–1909), agricultural chemist, founded agricultural regulatory work.

Wilbur O. Atwater (1844–1907), largely responsible for creating the Middletown, Connecticut, Station, he became director of the Agriculture Department's Office of Experimental Stations (1888–1907). Atwater published tables of caloric content of foods in 1906, which are still in use.

An early source of agricultural education was the fair. Colonial towns held market days which later gave rise to annual and semiannual fairs. Annual cattle and hog fairs began in 1641 in New Amsterdam and in Philadelphia in the 1680s. An early fair featuring farm animals and produce was held in Washington (1810) and President and Mrs. James Madison attended.

Elkanah Watson (1758–1842), a retired banker, organized a "cattle show" with his neighbors in Pittsfield, Massachusetts (1812). He helped organize the Berkshire Agricultural Society (1813), which staged an annual county fair where farms exhibited their livestock and crops and their wives showed homemade foods and handiwork. The idea spread and has become an enduring institution.

The farm demonstration program — the county agent — was an additional source of education for farmers. Seaman A. Knapp (1833–1911) designed the program to disseminate news of agricultural discoveries and technologies, then it was expanded to include home demonstration programs for farm women and 4-H clubs.

Research helped spread new technologies and crops. Among the research leaders were Luther Burbank (1849–1926) and George Washington Carver (1864–1943). Burbank developed 90 different varieties of vegetables and hundreds of varieties of fruits and flowers. Carver, head of agricultural research at Tuskegee University, developed more than 400 byproducts of peanuts, soybeans and sweet potatoes. He helped shift the South out of its one crop (cotton) economy.

Added to these agricultural education sources were various publications. The first agricultural book was *The Husbandman's Guide* (1710), a 107-page reprint of an English book. The first American agricultural book was *Essays Upon Field Husbandry in New England* (1759) by Jared Eliot (1685–1759), a Congregational minister. Another early book was *The New England Farmer*, the first American agricultural dictionary (1790), prepared by the Rev. Samuel Deane (1733–1814). Deane, a Congregational minister in Portland, Maine, farmed nearby during the Revolution and conducted many farm experiments.

One of the first scientific treatises on agriculture was *A Muck Manual for Farmers* (1842) by the chemist Samuel L. Dana (1795–1868).

The farm press also provided some agricultural education — *The Agricultural Museum*, the first farm publication, edited by Rev. David Wiley (1768–1813), was published monthly in Washington (1810–12). *The American Farmer*, the first continuous American farm periodical, founded in 1819 and continued under various names until 1897, was published weekly by John S. Skinner (1788–1851) in Baltimore; *The Plough Boy* in Albany (1819–23) and *The Cultivator* (1834), the first to achieve national circulation.

An educational resource of another sort was a major farm organization, The National Grange of the Patrons of Husbandry, better known as The Grange. Founded in February 1868 by Oliver H. Kelley (1826–1913) and six associates, it was very popular in the 1870s and 1880s, particularly in the South and Midwest with 20,000 granges.

Animals

The early settlers brought their domestic animals from England because the Indians had only dogs. Cows were landed at Jamestown (1611) and in New England (1624), where they were imported by Edward Winslow (1595–1655), who later became governor of Plymouth Colony. Cows were first raised principally for their hides, secondly for meat, and only incidentally for milk. Every farmer raised hogs to help feed the family and some salt pork was exported. Sheep were imported (1609) by Jamestown colonists and the first horses arrived for Mathewe Cradock, governor of Massachusetts Bay Colony, in 1629. Colonists' efforts at cattle ranching and sheep raising benefitted from the experience of the earlier Spanish settlers.

Richard King (1825–85), a steamboat operator on the Rio Grande River, bought 15,500 acres of grazing land (1852) for less than two cents an acre. He kept adding to his Texas holdings and by 1825 controlled more than 600,000 acres. His heirs continued to expand the King ranch, which eventually grew to nearly one million acres.

One of the earliest big cattle ranchers was John E. Chisum (1824–84), who developed a ranch near Roswell, New Mexico (1873), which had almost 100,000 head of cattle.

Crops

Corn growing, which the settlers learned from the Indians, was the first successful colonial crop. Spaniards arriving in Cuba (1492) found a grain the Indians called "mahiz" and during the sixteenth century explorers found Indians growing the crop.

Originally the colonists grew corn for fodder, especially in the Delaware Valley, but it soon became a valuable food crop. By the mid–1800s, corn was widely grown in the United States with the heaviest concentration in the Middle West.

Corn was easy to raise, requiring only about 50 days of a farmer's year, and the yield was high. The entire plant was used for food and other needs. Wheat and rye supplanted corn in the Delaware Valley, with wheat the dominant crop after 1640. A federal plant pathologist, Mark A. Carleton (1866–1925), who brought grain crops from foreign countries for American use, introduced Kubanka wheat from Russia in the 1890s. This led to the start of the American durum wheat industry.

The Spaniards brought alfalfa to their settlements in Peru and Mexico and from there it spread to the southwestern United States. The strain now used in the North was introduced by German immigrants about 1880.

In the South, rice became a major crop thanks to earlier Spanish experiments and the work of some later agriculturists. Trial plantings in America began in the 1620s. Legend has it that a Captain J. Thurber was sailing from Madagascar with a shipload of rice (1685), when a storm damaged his vessel and he found shelter in Charleston, South Carolina. He expressed his gratitude by giving residents a small quantity of seed rice, which flourished.

Robert F. W. Allston (1801–1864) built a system of drainage ditches and embankments on marshland of his family's South Carolina plantation. This made rice growing possible on such land beginning about 1830. Seaman A. Knapp whose work later led to the Federal County Agent program, headed a large colonization experiment at Lake Charles, Louisiana (1902–1910), and helped develop the rice industry there.

In 1740, Eliza Lucas (later Mrs. Charles Pinckney) (1722–93), one of the first American women entrepreneurs, successfully introduced indigo growing in the South and marketed the first crop (1744). (Indigo was the source of blue dye popular with clothmakers but had only a brief life as a colonial crop.) As a teenager, she assumed management of her father's plantation near Charleston, South Carolina.

Columbus found cotton growing in the Bahamas (1492) and by the 1500s it was grown throughout the world. Cotton growing was limited by the difficulty of removing seeds from the cotton by hand. This changed radically when Eli Whitney (1765–1825) invented the cotton gin (1791) and production skyrocketed from 10,000 bales (1793) to a million bales (1835).

Sugar also succeeded because of earlier experience by the Spaniards. Columbus took sugar plants from the Canary Islands (1493) to Santo Domingo; it then spread throughout the Caribbean. The first sugar mill was built (1509) in what is now the Dominican Republic and in Cuba (1511). Then on to Mexico, Peru and Brazil.

Sugar cane was brought to Louisiana by Jesuit priests (1751) from Santo Domingo. The first American sugar mill was erected in Louisiana (1758) by Joseph Dubreuil and the first shipment of sugar to France was made in 1765. The commercial success of refined sugar (1795) was due to the efforts of a pioneer sugar producer, Jean Etienne Boré (1741–1820). He first planted sugar cane in 1794 and harvested the first crop the next year.

Tobacco was another crop for which the Spanish deserve credit. Explorers in the New World found Indians using tobacco and introduced it in Spain and Portugal (1550).

The first Virginia tobacco (1612), grown from seeds obtained from the Spanish, was planted by John Rolfe (1585–1622). (Rolfe is remembered as the husband of the Indian chief's daughter, Pocahontas). The plantations around the Chesapeake Bay then became the world's largest producer of tobacco. Settlers were planting tobacco even in the streets of Jamestown, Virginia, by 1617. Tobacco became so plentiful that by 1629, Virginia limited the annual production to 1.5 million pounds. Ten years later Virginia ordered half the crop destroyed.

Cigars and cigarettes came much later and were originally produced by hand. Simeon Viets opened a cigar factory (1810) in West Suffield, Connecticut, and the F. A. Kinney Co. in New York City imported Polish and Russian cigarette workers (1868) to teach American girls how to roll cigarettes.

W. H. Pease patented a tobacco shredding machine (1860) but it was not until rolling machines were invented that use of tobacco in cigarettes was increased substantially. Albert H. Hook patented a machine (1876) which could turn out 100,000 cigarettes daily (equalling the production of 50 hand rollers) and costs dropped from 80 cents to 30 cents per thousand. During this period, James B. Duke (1856–1925) and his brother, Benjamin N. Duke (1855–1929), opened their first tobacco factory (1874) in Durham, North Carolina, which grew into the American Tobacco Company (1890).

Cigars were handrolled until 1883 when Oscar Hammerstein I (1847–1919) patented a cigar-making machine.

Opposition to tobacco use began when Benjamin Waterhouse (1756–1846), a prominent physician, published a popular book, *Shewing the Evil Tendency of the Use of Tobacco* (1805), which went through five editions.

Fruit growing began fairly early in American life. Almost every farmer planted an orchard, usually apples and peaches. Massachusetts Governor, John Winthrop (1588 – 1649), imported apples from England (1629). The first large apple orchards were planted near Boston by William Blaxton, who moved to Rhode Island (1635), where he again started orchards.

According to legend, John Chapman (1774–1845) — better known as Johnny Appleseed — began in about 1800 to carry apple seeds from Pennsylvania to Ohio to create apple orchards.

John J. Dufour (1763–1827) established a 630-acre vineyard outside Lexington, Kentucky, (1798). A pioneer viticulturist and founder of Swiss vineyards in the United States, he called his place "The First Vineyards." Later he built successful vineyards at Vevay, Indiana.

Nicholas Longworth (1782–1863), a leader of American grape culture, began experimenting with wine grapes and strawberries in the early 1800s. John Adlum (1759–1836) had a 200-acre farm in Georgetown (now part of Washington, DC) where he developed the Catawba grape. Ephraim W. Bull (1806–95) developed the Concord grape (1853).

Bananas were first imported from Cuba (1804).

Citrus fruit got started in California in the mid–1800s and one of the earliest growers was Thomas A. Garey (1830–1909), author of *The American Fruit Culturist* (1864). David Lubin (1849–1919), a California grower, organized fruit growers and an International Institute of Agriculture (1910) to help share information. William Kenrick (1768–1834), who carried on the nursery organized by his father (1790), helped lay the foundation for the present-day fruit industry.

Most garden vegetables were not grown in early colonial days, except pumpkins, beans, and squash which were grown with the corn. New England was the original American source for cabbage, turnips, onions, carrots and parsnips. The Dutch began growing beets, spinach, endives, leeks and some herbs and melons. Pennsylvania Germans started asparagus and cauliflower. Sweet potatoes were indigenous to the Virginia and Maryland Eastern Shore, and white potatoes were grown farther south.

The English and Dutch imported bees (the Indians called them "English flies") for honey. The Indians taught them how to tap sugar maple trees and boil the sap to make sugar.

Dairy

The dairy industry received a big boost when Stephen M. Babcock (1843–1931), considered the developer of scientific dairy processes, devised a simple method to measure the butterfat content of milk. This led to the elimination of the common practice of watering and adulteration of milk.

The modern dairy industry was a development of the 1870s–80s. One of the founding contributors was William D. Hoard (1836–1918).

He edited *Hoard's Dairyman*, considered a foremost agricultural journal, circulated throughout the country and abroad. He was also active in forming dairymen's associations.

During the early days butter was made with wooden churns on farms. The first commercial creamery is believed to have been built in Orange County, New York (1856), by R. S. Woodhull.

Farm Machinery

Producing crops became less difficult as machines were developed. Early farm implements were of wood — harrows had teeth of hickory or oak — scythes were later equipped with wooden "cradles" to catch the cut stalks. Other wooden tools were rakes, pitchforks and flails for threshing. Most farmers used two-wheeled carts pulled by a yoke of oxen.

Cultivation of the land until the 1670s depended on the hoe, shovel, and mattock, all made of wood. Then with the arrival of strong oxen and horses, plows began to be used.

The first patent for a plow was issued (1797) to Charles Newbold, a farmer in Burlington County, New Jersey, who produced the first cast iron plow. It did not become popular because farmers feared the iron would poison the soil. Two new cast iron plows appeared in 1819 — Jethro Wood (1774–1834) patented one which was distinguished by the shape of the wooden moldboard and Stephen McCormick (1784–1875), another that had detachable and standardized parts. Both designs were widely copied and McCormick's plow was popular in the South, Wood's in the North. Then John Lane (1789–1855), a Chicago blacksmith, made a plow (1833) with a wooden foundation covered with metal strips to clean the plow of the black loamy Midwestern soil. His son, John (1824–97), made improvements on the plow. John Deere (1804–86), another blacksmith, developed a steel plow (1837). He built a plant in Moline, Illinois (1847), arranged for steel shipments from a mill and by 1857 was turning out 10,000 plows a year. James Oliver (1823–1908) began producing a chilled cast iron plow (1868) that revolutionized plow making.

Similar efforts were made to develop a reaper to harvest wheat and rye. Robert McCormick (1780–1846) spent many years trying to develop a mechanical reaper. He developed one (1809) which worked fairly well with straight grain but was useless if the grain was bent or fallen.

The first reaper that worked was invented (1826) by Henry Ogle and five years later Cyrus H. McCormick (1809–84) succeeded where his father had failed. The basic design of this McCormick reaper has remained. He continued to make improvements, moved to Chicago where the machine proved more efficient in flat country. At almost the same time, Obed Hussey (1792–1860) developed a grain reaper (1833) and a fierce rivalry between the McCormick and Hussey machines began. McCormick won by incorporating improvements, heavy advertising, offering credit and developing labor-saving devices for his factory.

Additional improvements in grain harvesting included a binder patented (1850) by John S. Heath; a harvester that bundled grain (1859) by Charles W. Marsh (1834–1918), and a knotter and twine-binder developed(1878) by John F. Appleby (1840–1917).

William Deering (1826–1913) introduced the first self-propelled farm machine, combining a grain harvester and the Appleby twine binder (1900). The Deering operation became part of International Harvester Company. After the grain was harvested there remained the task of separating the grain kernels from the straw, which was done by hand and the fanning mill.

Jerome I. Case (1818–91) invented an improved threshing machine (1844) and by 1857 was producing 1,600 machines a year and mechanical threshing became standard. Hiram A. Pitts (1800–60) and his brother, John, of Winthrop, Maine, patented a combined portable threshing machine and fanning mill (1837). They continued to improve it in the next 15 years and the Pitts machine became the model for most modern threshers.

Planting traditionally was sowing seeds broadcast. Believing it would be more economical to sow in rows, Jethro Tull (1674–1741) developed a horse-drawn seed drill about 1701, the first such machine to operate successfully. He developed a horse-drawn machine about 1715 to cultivate between the seeded rows. Henry Burden (1791–1870), who developed an improved plow, invented the first American cultivator (1820).

The development of machines to replace horses and oxen began when Gideon Horgan patented the first steam-driven tractor with tracks (1850), followed by W.P. Miller (1858) and by Thomas S. Minnes (1870). The first successful gasoline tractor was built by John Froelich, an Iowa farmer and blacksmith (1892). Ten years later, the Case company built one, and C.V. Hart and C.H. Parr of Iowa City, Iowa, built the first exclusive tractor factory (1905), later becoming part of the Oliver Co.

Steam tractors reached their peak by 1912 and in the next 12 years were discontinued with the arrival of economical, durable internal combustion engine tractors.

Fences

Early in colonial days, wandering cattle endangered growing crops. Virginia had a law calling for a four-and-a-half feet high post-and-rail fence to contain cattle and other states followed suit. In New England, fields were surrounded by stone walls or post-and-rail fences.

Joseph F. Glidden (1813–1906) invented barbed wire (1873), which more than anything else helped tame the West and made homesteading possible.

Fertilizer

Edmund Ruffin (1794–1865) developed various methods in Virginia of restoring soil fertility, including adding calcareous earth (marl) to the soil.

James J. Mapes (1806–66) received the first patent on an artificial fertilizer (1859) and developed a nitrogenous superphosphate, probably the first complete artificial plant food.

Edmund M. Pendleton (1815–84), a successful doctor and Georgia plantation owner, produced fertilizers for the public and his own use.

Forestry

Forestry in the United States got a late start and a prime mover was Bernhard E. Fernow (1851–1923), a Prussian forester who came to the United States in 1876. He became manager of a commercial forest in Pennsylvania and began writing articles on the subject. Fernow played a major role in forming the forerunner of the American Forestry Association (1882). He was named chief of the newly-organized Forestry Division of the Agriculture Department (1886). He also organized the New York State College of Forestry at Cornell University, the first such American school, and similar schools at Penn State University and the University of Toronto.

Gifford Pinchot (1865–1946), after studying in Europe, introduced scientific forest management and promoted conservation. He conducted one of the first American programs of systematic forestry in North Carolina (1892–98). Pinchot succeeded Fernow as head of the Forest Service (1898).

In 1891, federal tree planting began in western Nebraska and the first national forestry reserve was created in Yellowstone Park. New York opened the first state reserve (1885).

Along with the start of forestry came the beginning of tree surgery. Englishman John Davey (1846–1923) came to Kent, Ohio (1872), and opened a successful landscaping-gardening business. Davey, regarded as the founder of American tree surgery, wrote the popular *The Tree Doctor*.

Soil conservation came when farmers began to see the effects of continuous plowing and planting. Hugh H. Bennett (1881–1960) first drew attention to the problem (1928) and served as the first director of the Agriculture Department's Soil Conservation Service (1935–52).

Seed Business

William Prince (1752–1802) began growing seedlings for sale on Long Island. He advertised a variety of fruit and ornamental trees and bushes. David Landreth (1802–80) inherited a seed business begun in Philadelphia (1784) and started publishing the *Illustrated Floral Magazine* (1832). Grant Thornton (1773–1863), a grocer, painted some pots for sale and put plants in them. Soon there were inquiries for seeds and about 1803 he founded a successful, long-lasting seed business. He issued the first American seed catalog, *The Gentleman and Gardener's Kalendar* (1812).

Washington Atlee Burpee (1858–1915) of Philadelphia became the first to establish a successful mail order seed business (1876), which became one of the world's best known and was continued by his family.

2. Art

Art Education and Associations

Art in the schools began in the 1840s when drawing was introduced in the schools of Boston, Philadelphia and Baltimore. Harvard became (1874) the first American college to have a course on art history. Princeton followed (1882) and by the mid-twentieth century about 200 colleges were giving courses in art history.

The oldest permanent art association is the Pennsylvania Academy of Fine Arts, founded in Philadelphia (1805), that began as a private art school (1791). An earlier group (Academy of Sciences and Fine Arts) was formed in Richmond, Virginia (1786), but did not last and the New York Academy of Fine Arts existed from 1802 to 1841.

Design

In the field of design, two names stand out — Norman Bel Geddes (1893–1958) and Raymond F. Loewy (1893–1986). Geddes became a successful stage designer (1918) and was involved in directing and producing 200 operas, plays and films. He changed the concept of scenic design from the ornamental to a clean, functional effect so that the audience would not be conscious of the scenery or background. He began to apply his design concepts to industry (1927) and created a huge design organization, which became the foremost proponent of streamlining.

Loewy was a fashion illustrator for magazines and a display designer for New York City department stores. He began designing industrial products (1929) and his organization became the world's largest industrial design firm. Loewy designed numerous electrical appliances and he became a leading designer of buildings, including department stores.

Galleries

The first American art gallery was created in New York City (1832) by Luman Reed (1787–1836), a retired wholesale grocer. He gave the gallery to the New York Historical Society upon his death. Reed's action helped make American art collecting fashionable and eventually led the way to great museums founded by Henry C. Frick (1849–1919), Andrew S. Mellon (1855–1937), Charles L. Freer (1856–1919) and William Corcoran (1798–1888).

Illustration

Matthew Pratt (1734–1805) is considered the first successful commercial artist, known for his signboards.

Charles D. Gibson (1867–1944), creator of the "Gibson girl," was the leading American illustrator and his creations set American fashions between 1890 and 1910. Norman Rockwell (1894–1978) was a popular illustrator, best known for his *Saturday Evening Post* covers (averaging ten a year from 1916 to 1969). Two other prominent illustrators were Newell C. Wyeth (1882–1945) and Rockwell Kent (1882–1971).

In American lithography, Currier and Ives stand out, producing more than 7,000 prints from 1840 to 1890. Nathaniel Currier (1813–88) opened his shop in New York City in 1835 and was joined by James M. Ives (1824–95) in 1857.

Painting

Jeremiah Dummer (1645–1718), a silversmith, is believed to have been the first native-born painter in the colonies.

The most common type of painting in the colonies was portraiture, and the best known portrait artists were Peter Pelham (1695–1751), John Smibert (1688–1751), Robert Feke (1705–50) and John S. Copley (1738–1815).

Pelham was one of the first to use the mezzotint technique of engraving. Smibert came to the colonies on the promise of a teaching position in a college to be built in Bermuda. The college never materialized and he settled down to portrait painting and selling art supplies and prints by famous artists. By selling copies of European masters, he made a significant contribution to the art education of colonial Boston.

Feke, one of the better portrait artists, shows the influence of Smibert, who may have been his teacher. Copley learned painting and engraving from his stepfather (Pelham) and became an accomplished painter by age 18. He painted numerous portraits, became wealthy and is considered the first great American painter.

Charles Willson Peale (1741–1827) was a leading portrait artist after the Revolution. Gilbert C. Stuart (1755–1828), a portrait painter, was best known for his portraits of George Washington.

Washington Allston (1779–1843) is credited with introducing the romantic painting style to the United States.

Among the early landscape painters were members of the Hudson River School of landscape painting, the first native American movement in painting. Thomas Cole (1801–1848) was a leader in forming the school, assisted by Asher B. Durand (1796–1886), a master of steel engraving, among others. George Inness (1825–94) was one of the last and most talented members of the school.

In the early twentieth century, a trio of regional artists appeared, representing a truly American style — Thomas Hart Benton (1889–1975), John Steuart Curry (1897–1946), and Grant Wood (1892–1942).

John LaFarge (1835–1910) became an unrivaled muralist after painting murals for the Trinity Church in Boston (1876–77). He invented an opalescent glass that he used in windows of his own design.

Modern art in America dates from the 1913 Armory Show in New York City. The Association of American Painters and Sculptors, formed in 1911, staged the show February 15 to March 15, giving Americans the first glimpse of European modern art movements. Arthur B. Davies (1862–1928), head of the Association, was largely responsible for staging the Armory Show and an earlier exhibition by young American artists rebelling against the National Academy.

Among the Americans represented in the Armory Show were Robert Henri (1865–1929), John F. Sloan (1871–1951), John C. Marin (1872–1953), and Maurice B. Prendergast (1861–1924).

Some of them came to be called the "Ashcan School" because of their use of such motifs as backyards and garbage cans. Included were Henri, Sloan, Prendergast, Davies, George B. Luks (1867–1933), William J. Glackens (1870–1938), Everett Shinn (1876–1953), and Ernest Lawson (1873–1939).

Abstract painting began to emerge in the United States after World War II and gained wide influence and acceptance. Arthur G. Dove (1880–1946) is generally considered the first American abstract artist. Among the leaders of the American abstract school were Jackson Pollock (1912–56), Willem DeKooning (1904–97), Mark Rothko (1903–1970), Arshile Gorky (1904–48) and Barnett Newman (1905–70). Pollock played a major role in developing American abstract expressionism with his colorful "drip" paintings. He worked on whole rolls of canvas from which portions were cut and shown as individual paintings.

Charles Demuth (1883–1935) was a leader in introducing the cubist technique to the United States and was recognized as one of the first watercolorists of his time. Roy Lichtenstein (1923–97), a controversial pop art painter, was inspired by comic strips. Robert Rauschenberg (1925–) produced what is considered the first American pop art painting in 1958 — a semi-abstraction with a hole into which he inserted four Coca-Cola bottles.

Other contributors to American art developments were: Benjamin West (1738–1820) spent much of his life in England but taught many young Americans to become great painters (Copley, Stuart, Peale). John L. Krimmel (1789–1821) was one of the few early American painters to chronicle events of his day. James A.B. Whistler (1834–1903) spent his adult life in England and is best known for his mother's portrait. Mary Cassatt (1844–1926) has often been called America's greatest female painter. Edward Hopper (1882–1967) was renowned for realistic scenes of contemporary life. George W. Bellows (1882–1925) is best known for his work in sports and urban scenes. Andrew Wyeth (1917–) is known for his photographic style. Frederic Remington (1861–1909) was the leading documentary artist of the American West.

Photography

American photography got its start in the 1840s with John Plumbe (1809–57) and Mathew B. Brady (1823–96). Plumbe began in Philadelphia (1840) and five years later had 13 branches across the country. He developed the Plumbeotype, a reproduction of daguerreotypes on paper.

Brady learned about daguerreotypes from Samuel F.B. Morse (later of telegraph fame) and opened his first New York gallery in 1844. A year later, he was photographing portraits of important people. Brady spent his entire fortune of almost $100,000 to hire and equip a corps of photo teams to produce a photographic history of the Civil War. Brady had to sell everything and died in an alms ward of a New York City hospital.

A tintype camera was patented (1856) by Hamilton L. Smith.

Timothy O'Sullivan (1840–82), a Brady apprentice, pioneered in photographing places of beauty and interest; William H. Jackson (1843–1942) was an early photographer of the American West; Edward Weston (1866–58) did many nature studies.

David Bachrach, Jr. (1845–1921), was a pioneer portrait photographer (1868) in Baltimore and co-invented a half-screen engraving process to improve tone quality of a photograph.

Edward Steichen (1879–1973) and Alfred Stieglitz (1864–1946) helped make photography a fine art. Dorothea Lange (1896–1965) was one of the first photo journalists, best known for pictures of migratory farm workers during the depression.

Eadweard Muybridge (1830–1904) was a pioneer in motion pictures. He had been hired to photograph a running horse to prove that at one point the horse had all four feet off the ground. Muybridge invented a praxiscope (1878) to reproduce moving pictures on a screen.

The first celestial photograph was a daguerreotype of the moon taken (1840) by a scientist, John W. Draper, who did much to improve daguerreotype plates. The first aerial photographs were taken October 13, 1860, by J.W. Black from a balloon 1,200 feet above Boston. The first photograph of a solar eclipse was taken August 7, 1869, by Edward C. Pickering, a physics professor.

The first photographic patent was issued (1840) to Alexander S. Wolcott for "a method of taking likenesses by means of a concave reflector and plates so prepared that luminous and other rays will act thereon."

The first light meters were an actionmeter devised by J.F. Soleil; an extinction light meter by C.F. Albinus (1844), and an exposure photometer by J.F. Taylor (1866).

John Carbutt (1832–1905) developed a photo-collotype process, becoming the first American producer of gelatin dry plates and standardized the size of photographic lantern slides.

Frederic E. Ives (1856–1937) perfected a half-tone process for making line photo-engravings. Ives pioneered in color photography and developed a process (1914) for motion pictures in natural colors.

George Eastman (1854–1932) perfected a process (1880) for making dry photographic plates and developed a paper-backed film sold in roll form four years later. Eastman introduced the Kodak, a simple, inexpensive fixed-focus box camera (1888). The user could take pictures, send the camera to the factory, and then receive developed pictures and a reloaded camera.

This changed photography from being difficult, expensive, and time-consuming into a hobby accessible to millions. Eastman built a new plant and the company dominated the market by 1927.

Edwin H. Land (1909–91) made discoveries about polarized light while still a student and opened a laboratory (1932) to make polarized filters for cameras and polarized sunglasses lenses. Land developed a technique (1941) for producing three-dimensional photographs and introduced the Polaroid camera (1947) in which a finished picture was produced inside the camera within a minute after exposure.

Other contributors to developing photo equipment and processes include:

> Victor Animatograph Co. Inc., of Davenport, Iowa, introduced the first portable motion picture camera (1923).

> David H. Houston of Cambria, Wisconsin, patented roll film for cameras (1881); Hannibal W. Goodwin (1822–1900), an Episcopal clergyman, patented the first celluloid photographic film (1898), and two Kodak employees (Leopold Mannes 1899–1964 and Leopold Godowsky 1870–1936) invented Kodachrome (1935).

> William F. Folmer (1862–1936) had many inventions, including the first high speed multiple-split focal plane shutter for cameras (1898), one of the first serial cameras and the Graflex camera.

> Henry H. Snelling (1817–97) published the *Photographic Art Journal* (1851) and several books on photography, including *A Dictionary of the Photographic Art* (1854).

Sculpture

William Rush (1756–1833), considered the first native American sculptor, created many ornamental ship carvings and figureheads. He also did a number of other sculptures including a life-size George Washington in Independence Hall.

Horatio Greenough (1805–1852) was the first American sculptor to receive a commission from the American government. However, his importance rests on art essays outlining the basic theory of functionalism, which had much influence, especially on modern art.

The first full-length bronze statue was done by English-born Ball

Hughes (1847) depicting the figure of Nathaniel Bowditch, the astronomer, which was erected in Mt. Auburn Cemetery, Cambridge, Massachusetts.

In 1853, the bronze equestrian statue of Andrew Jackson was unveiled in Lafayette Park across from the White House. The statue by Clark Mills (1815–1883) was the first equestrian and largest bronze statue done in the United States.

Gutzon Borglum (1867–1941) became a popular English painter and sculptor and then returned to the United Sates (1901) to concentrate on sculpture. He was commissioned to prepare a Robert E. Lee memorial at Stone Mountain, Georgia. Work was interrupted by World War I and then Borglum resigned during a dispute over the handling of funds. In 1927, he was commissioned by South Dakota to prepare a state memorial on Mt. Rushmore. It became a national project two years later and, when completed, showed the faces of Washington (unveiled in 1930), Jefferson (1936), Lincoln (1937) and Theodore Roosevelt (1939) carved into the rock mountain.

Robert Laurent (1890–1970) influenced the development of modern American sculpture and Claes Oldenburg (1929–) was a leader in pop sculpture. Alexander Calder (1898–1976) originated the mobile, the first successful attempt to incorporate movement into sculpture. The mobile moved with the aid of air currents and its own delicate balance.

3. Business and Finance

After the American settlers built shelters and began to produce food and clothing, they started producing and consuming goods and services.

In the Southern states tobacco, rice, and cotton became early cash crops. The New England states depended on the lumber industry, shipbuilding, whaling and the growing of wheat and corn. Lumber, which was in short supply in England, was the first American export. Ships bringing settlers from England returned home with lumber.

The first American business publication was the weekly *New York Prices Current*, begun in New York City (1795) by James Oram. The first economics magazine was the *Quarterly Journal of Economics*, started in 1886.

In Boston, merchants began to meet for an hour each working day "for the more convenient and expeditious dispatch of Merchants Affayres." The first American chamber of commerce was organized in New York City (1768) with the purpose of "promoting and encouraging commerce, supporting industry, adjusting disputes relative to trade and navigation and producing such laws and regulations as may be found necessary..." (the present United States Chamber of Commerce was founded in 1912; the Junior Chamber of Commerce in 1915).

The first American commercial corporation was the New York Fishing Co., chartered in 1675.

Accounting

New York became the first state (1896) to regulate public accounting with the title of Certified Public Accountant (CPA) granted after passing a professional examination. Pennsylvania followed (1899) and by 1923 all states and the District of Columbia had such laws.

The first accountants society was the Institute of Accountants and Bookkeepers, organized (1882) in New York City. It later became the Institute of Accounts (1886). The American Association of Public Accountants was organized in New York City (1886).

Advertising

On May 1, 1704, the first American paid advertisements were printed in the *Boston News Letter*. Three ads occupied four inches in a single column — one offered a "very good fulling mill" at Oyster Bay, Long Island, for sale or lease; another offered a reward for the capture of a thief and return of wearing apparel and the third was a notice of the loss of two anvils.

By 1771, all 31 papers in the colonies carried advertising. At first, news dealers accepted ads for any American paper and received 30% commission. Advertising agents often held out until near the paper's deadline and the publisher would lower the rate so as to be sure of the ad. Many early newspaper ads were for patent medicine which tended to give advertising a bad name.

When Benjamin Franklin was publishing a Philadelphia paper, he began to make ads more readable by using more white space around an ad as well as boxes.

Volney B. Palmer, an editorial writer and later on the advertising staff of the *Pottsville* (Pennsylvania) *Miner's Journal*, opened in Philadelphia what is considered the first American advertising agency. He was primarily an agent for the publishers, receiving 25% commission.

George P. Rowell (1838–1908) opened an agency (1865) in Boston, moving to New York in 1867. He contracted with many weekly papers for a column of space for a certain length of time and then offered space to advertisers at less than the going rate — offering "an inch of space a month in 100 papers for $100." He issued the first newspaper directory (1869) which flourished until it was absorbed by the N. W. Ayer directory (1908) and founded *Printer's Ink*, an advertising journal (1888).

The first modern advertising agency, N. W. Ayer and Sons Inc., was founded in Philadelphia (1869). Francis W. Ayer (1848–1923), who borrowed $250 to start the agency, introduced the commission system in the 1870s when the agency kept the difference between the discount and full price for the space used. He revolutionized advertising methods and standards; pioneered in the use of trademarks, slogans, and other now common advertising practices; did much to establish advertising as a necessary and reputable adjunct to business. He put the agency's service to advertisers ahead of selling space; from then on agencies expanded their services to include preparing copy and art services.

Bruce Barton (1886–1967), who gained fame later as an author, held several magazine editing and sales management jobs for a publisher and then he and two partners organized an advertising agency (1919), which he headed. He reorganized the company (1928) to become Batten, Barton, Durstine and Osborne Inc. (BBDO) which became a giant in the industry.

William Benton (1900–73) and Chester B. Bowles (1901–86) founded an ad agency (1929), Benton & Bowles, which became a leader in the field. James Walter Thompson (1847–1928) worked for an ad agency buying space from magazines and retailing it to merchants. He bought out the agency (1878) and formed the J. Walter Thompson Company, which became the most successful of its time.

The first neon tube advertising sign was installed on the marquee of the Cosmopolitan Theater in New York City in July 1923.

The first flashing electric sign was placed on the New York Times Building in New York City to show election returns November 6, 1928; the sign was invented by Francis E.J. Wilde of Meadowmere Park, New York.

The first animated cartoon electric sign was displayed by Douglas Leigh April 28, 1937 on a building on Broadway in New York City.

Banking

The Bank of the United States was incorporated as a national bank in 1791 with a 20-year charter and capital of $10 million. There was no central bank in 1811–16 and the Second Bank, which operated for 20 years, was not renewed in 1836. Without a central bank there was much speculation and many local banks were formed. The boom was short-lived and there were many bankruptcies. The federal currency was in dire shape from 1837 to 1863. It is reported that banks at that time issued about 10,000 different kinds of notes.

President Lincoln signed a national banking act in 1863 that created the Office of the Comptroller of the Currency and established a system of uniform notes of standard denominations that circulated at par everywhere. The nationally-unified banking system created in 1863 had some defects in managing the volume of currency, not responding to the changing needs of business.

The National Monetary Commission (1912) proposed various changes, including the creation of the Federal Reserve System, which began with the opening of 12 Federal Reserve banks (1914).

The first American commercial bank, the Bank of North America, opened in Philadelphia in 1782. Organized by Robert Morris (1734–1806), the bank's original depositors and stockholders included Thomas Jefferson, Alexander Hamilton, Benjamin Franklin, James Monroe, John Jay and Stephen Decatur.

The first American savings banks— the Bank for Savings in New York City and the Provident Institution for Savings in Boston — both opened 1819.

The first building and loan association, the Oxford Provident Building Association, was organized 1831 in Thomas Sidebotham's tavern in Frankford, Pennsylvania, (now part of Philadelphia).

The first bank clearing house, the New York Clearing House, was organized by 38 New York City banks at 13 Wall Street (1853).

Some leading bank figures were:

Alexander Brown (1765–1834), who, after becoming the largest importer of Irish linen in North America, founded the first investment banking house in the early 1800s, Alexander Brown & Sons. The business was carried on by his sons and the New York branch became Brown Brothers Harriman & Co.

August Belmont (1816–90), enroute to Havana (1837) to handle Rothschild banking house interests, started his own business in the United States instead and immediately prospered.

John Thompson (1802–91) founded two New York City banks, First National (1863) and Chase National (1877).

Junius S. Morgan (1813–90) founded a private banking firm that was carried on by his son, J(ohn) P. Morgan (1837–1913), who formed Drexel, Morgan & Co. (1871) with Anthony J. Drexel (1826–93). The firm became J.P. Morgan Co. (1895) and a world leading financial organization.

A(madeo) P. Giannini (1870–1949), a retired produce dealer, founded the Bank of Italy (1904) in San Jose, California. It was the first regional banking operation. Within a year, the bank doubled in size through mergers and by 1948, now known as the Bank of America, had become the nation's largest bank.

John Moody (1868–1958) founded a number of financial publications, *Moody's Manual of Railroads and Corporation Securities* (1900), the monthly *Moody's Magazine* (1905), and the annual *Moody's Analysis of Investments* (1909).

As the early settlers prospered, they began seeking investment opportunities. As soon as the *Boston News Letter* began publication (1704), advertisements appeared by a gentleman who had money "to lend out at Interest upon good Security."

Charles Gayler (1820–92) of New York City patented a "fireproof iron chest" (1833) and the first safe deposit vault was opened (1865) by the Safe Deposit Co. of New York at 140 Broadway.

The first Christmas club was started (1909) by Merkel Landis, treasurer of the Carlisle (Pennsylvania) Trust Co. and traveler's checks were devised (1891) by Marcellus F. Berry, general agent of the American Express Co.

Alphonse Desjardins, who organized the first credit union in Canada (1900), helped form the first American union association (1908) in Manchester, New Hampshire.

The first drive-in bank began at the Exchange National Bank in Chicago (1946). The "auto bank" consisted of ten teller windows protected by bulletproof glass and corrugated steel with automatic slide-out windows.

The first armored car was placed in service (1918) by Brinks Inc. in Chicago.

The Postal Savings Bank system went into operation in 1911 and ended in 1966.

The first bank robbery occurred March 19, 1831, when burglars used duplicate keys to enter the City Bank of New York City and made off with $245,000. They were quickly captured and most of the money was recovered.

The American Bankers Association was organized in 1875.

A four-day bank holiday was declared March 6, 1933, by President Franklin D. Roosevelt. The Federal Deposit Insurance Corp., guaranteeing bank deposits up to $500 started on June 16, 1933.

Business Technology

The growth of business and finance was accompanied and greatly aided by the development of business machines.

CASH REGISTERS

John Ritty (1836–1918), a restaurant operator, and his brother patented a "cash register and indicator" (1879) and five years later, John H. Patterson (1844–1922) bought the company (National Manufacturing Co.) and its Dayton, Ohio, plant with 13 employees.

A day later, Patterson offered to return the company plus $2,000 to get out of the deal. He was turned down and set to work to improve the machine and the company. Patterson changed the name to National Cash Register Co. (NCR) and concentrated on marketing — sales conventions and schools, exclusive sales territories, large sale commissions, large well-trained service staffs and many employee benefits.

WORD PROCESSING

Joseph Smith Duncan (1858–1926) of Sioux City, Iowa, invented the addressograph machine (1892), patenting an improved model in 1896.

William A. Burt (1792–1858) patented the first American mechanical writing device, the "Typographer" (1829), a forerunner of the typewriter. The machine looked like a soapbox, an arm on top could be turned to a desired letter to be pressed down and printed.

In 1843, Charles Thurber (1803–86) of Worcester, Massachusetts, patented a printing machine (the "Chirographer") with letters actuated by the press of a finger. It had a movable carriage (platen) and the paper could be turned when the line was completed. The machine worked well but slowly and there was no demand for it.

John B. Fairbanks received a patent (1850) for a "phonetic writer," the first to have a continuous paper feed. Oliver T. Eddy (1799–1868) of Baltimore patented a typewriter (1850) that had a piano keyboard and an inked ribbon.

John Pratt (1831–1900) patented a machine (1866) called a "Ptereotype," the forerunner of the Hammond typewriter. Pratt patented an improved machine (1882), which he sold to James B. Hammond (1839–1913), who had patented his own machine two years earlier.

Christopher L. Sholes (1819–90), with the help of two co-workers,

Carlos Glidden (1834–77) and Samuel W. Soule, patented a machine (1868) that eight years later became the Remington typewriter. (Sholes sold the patent rights to Remington Arms Co. for $12,000 because he could not afford to improve the invention.) The machine was the first to feature a modern standard arrangement of keyboard characters.

John T. Underwood (1857–1935) formed his typewriter company in 1895. The four Smith brothers manufactured the first L.C. Smith typewriter in 1904 and the Royal first appeared in 1906.

Electric typewriters appeared in the early 1900s, although Thomas A. Edison (1847–1931) received a patent for one in 1872. Application of power to the typewriter did not occur for about 30 years.

Computers

The calculator or adding machine goes back to two machines which were patented but proved impractical — one by DuBois D. Parmelee of New Paltz, New York, (1850) and the other which printed totals and subtotals, by Edmund D. Barbour of Boston (1872).

Then Frank S. Baldwin (1838–1925) patented a calculator, the Arithmometer (1902), but had difficulty getting it produced. He met Jay R. Monroe (1883–1937) and they founded the Monroe Calculating Machine Co. (1911) and redesigned the machine.

Dorr E. Felt (1862–1930) patented the first accurate adding machine, the Comptometer (1887), the first wholly key-operated machine. William S. Burroughs (1855–98) patented the first practical adding machine (1888). It was the first to be successfully marketed.

Tabulating machines date back to Herman Hollerith (1860–1929), a Patent Office employee who experimented with mechanizing record data. Hollerith patented a system using punched cards (1889) and it was used for the 1890 census and later in other countries. After numerous improvements, the Hollerith system tabulated the 1900 census in 19 months, compared to eight years of manual tabulation in previous years.

Hollerith organized the Tabulating Machine Co. (1896) which, after merging with two other firms, became the Computing-Tabulating Recording Co. (1911). Thomas J. Watson (1874–1956), general sales manager of the National Cash Register Co., was named president of Computing-Tabulating (1914), which ten years later became the International Business Machine Company (IBM).

A differential analyzer was invented (1930) by Vannevar Bush (1890–1974) and other engineers. This was a machine for solving differential equations and led to an early form of the analog computer.

Howard H. Aiken (1900–73), faced with a large number of computations in his graduate studies, planned an automatic computer (1937). The Navy and IBM backed Aiken who finished the machine, the Mark I, in 1944. It was able to make computations 100 times faster than manual operations. The computer contained more than 750,000 parts, was 57 feet long, and weighed five tons.

John W. Mauchly (1907–80) and John P. Eckert, Jr. (1919–95), developed the first general purpose digital computer (1946) using punched cards. In 1951, they developed the first commercially available computer, the UNIVAC, which was built by Remington Rand.

Copiers

Edison also developed a mimeograph machine (1876) ushering in reproduction machines and Albert B. Dick (1856–1934) began manufacturing mimeograph machines in 1887. The first photographic copying machine, the Photostat, was made by Eastman Kodak in 1910.

Chester F. Carlson (1906–68) worked in a New York electronics plant which needed many copies of documents. Carbon copies and photostats were not good and Carlson developed a dry process (xerography) in 1940 using no chemicals, with the key being the photo-electric effect.

Carlson couldn't interest more than 20 companies in his invention and he signed agreements with the Battelle Development Corporation (1944) and Haloid Company (1947) for its commercial development. The Haloid-Xerox Co. (later Xerox Corp.) introduced the first commercial xerographic copying machine (1959).

Credit

In the field of credit and credit rating, Lewis Tappan (1788–1873) founded the nation's first credit rating firm, the Mercantile Agency (1841). A short time later (1849), John M. Bradstreet formed the Improve Mercantile Agency in Cincinnati, Ohio, which became the Bradstreet Company (1876).

Robert G. Dun (1826–1900) joined Tappan's agency, became a partner in 1854 and took over sole ownership in 1859. R. G. Dun & Co. merged (1933) with the Bradstreet Co. to form Dun & Bradstreet, Inc.

Another early credit protective group was the Merchants' Vigilance Association, formed (1842) by New York City importers and commission houses.

Copperthwaite & Sons, a furniture retailer, was a pioneer in the credit field when it introduced consumer installment purchases (1907). Franklin Bank of New York introduced the credit card (1951).

Currency

Soon after the American settlers arrived, they began to trade with the Indians and it wasn't long before they began to make glass beads (Jamestown 1621, Salem 1639) to conduct that trade.

Massachusetts Bay Colony established a mint in Boston (1652), with the pine tree shilling the most noted of its coins. After the Revolution, Congress created a national currency based on the decimal system, with the dollar as the nation's monetary unit. The first mint was established (1792) in Philadelphia and began issuing cents and half cents (1793), half dimes, half dollars, and silver dollars (1794), and dimes and quarters (1796). The nickel was not authorized until 1866.

The currency system adopted in 1785 is credited to Robert Morris, financier of the Revolution and later superintendent of finance. He was assisted by Gouverneur Morris (1752–1816), no relation.

The motto, "In God We Trust," was first used in 1864 on the short-lived two-cents piece. It was restored to coins (1908) and to coins and currency in 1955.

The first trading stamps were the S & H (green) stamps, originated in 1891 by Thomas H. Sperry of Bridgeport, Connecticut, who formed the Sperry Hutchinson Co. in 1896.

Economics

Henry C. Carey (1793–1879), a publisher, became called the founder of the American school of economics because of his three-volume work, *Principles of Political Economy* (1837–40). John B. Clark (1847–1938) dominated American economic theory for a decade as a professor and founder of the American Economics Association (1885).

Francis A. Walker (1840–97) led in modernizing and broadening the character and scope of economics and supervised the 1870 and 1880 United States census.

Wesley C. Mitchell (1874–1948) was a pioneer in economic studies and became the world's foremost authority on business cycles. Wassily W. Leontief (1906–93) originated and developed the input-output analysis used in economic planning and in forecasting output and growth requirements. (He won the 1973 Nobel Economics Prize.) Simon Kuznets (1901–85) came to the United States as an economics student, then joined the newly-formed National Bureau of Economic Research. He developed the concept of the Gross National Product (GNP), now the accepted measure of a nation's wealth, for which he won the 1971 Nobel Economics Prize.

Roger W. Babson (1875–1967) developed the use of statistics and charts in business and investment. He set up a newspaper syndicate to provide economic predictions and founded three business schools— Babson Institute, Wellesley, Massachusetts, (1919), Webber College for Women, Polk County, Florida, (1927), and Midwest Institute, Eureka, Kansas, (1946).

Exchanges

The first securities exchange opened (1791) in Philadelphia. In that same year the New York Stock Exchange began informally when 24 merchants met in the shade of a buttonwood tree on Wall Street.

The New York Exchange was organized in 1792 and formally chartered in 1817. The Chicago Board of Trade was organized (1848) and incorporated by a special act of the Illinois legislature. A clearing house for stocks and bonds was organized in Philadelphia (1870).

Hotels

American hotels began as inns at the seaports, then followed the rivers and post roads inland. One of the earliest was the Blue Anchor in Philadelphia, where William Penn stayed upon his arrival in 1682. The discovery of mineral springs led to the start of resort hotels, such as those at Yellow Springs, Pennsylvania (1722), and York Sulphur Springs, Pennsylvania (1790). By 1830, others followed — Saratoga Springs, New York,

Hot Springs, Virginia, White Sulphur Springs, West Virginia, Niagara Falls, New York, and the New Jersey shore.

The world's first luxury hotel was the 170-room Tremont in Boston, which opened in 1819. The daily rate was two dollars, including four meals. Guests could have single rooms with their own key and wash bowl, a pitcher, a free cake of soap and running water in the eight basement "bathing rooms."

The first fireproof hotel was the Palmer House in Chicago which opened 1873, two years after the first Palmer House was destroyed by fire. The first hotel exclusively for women was the Martha Washington in New York City (1903).

Ellsworth M. Statler (1863–1928) opened the first modern commercial hotel in Buffalo (1904). He built the first hotel (1901), a temporary building with 2,100 rooms to house visitors to the Pan-American Exposition in Buffalo. Statler's commercial hotel was the first to provide running ice water and a private bath in each room. He also originated the practice of placing the morning newspaper at the guest's door.

Conrad N. Hilton (1887–1979) entered the hotel business in Texas (1919) after he failed to gain an interest in a bank. He bought several hotels and then built a new hotel in Dallas (1925). After the depression, he acquired large established hotels in major cities. The Hilton Hotel Corporation was formed (1946) and gained control of the Statler hotels (1954).

Insurance

The first American life insurance company, founded in 1759 in Philadelphia, was the "Corporation for the Relief of Poor and Distressed Presbyterian Ministers and of the Poor and Distressed Widows and Children of Presbyterian Ministers."

The first commercial life insurance company, also in Philadelphia, was the Pennsylvania Company for Insurance on Life and Granting Annuities (1812).

Insurance began to grow with the development of mutual companies in which a company was able to provide protection without investing large sums of money. Eight present companies stem from that period.

The first American fire insurance company, The Friendly Society for the Mutual Insurance of Houses Against Fire, was formed in Charleston, South Carolina (1735). Five years later, fire destroyed half the city and the company.

The Philadelphia Contributorship for the Insurance of Houses from Loss by Fire was formed in 1752. The insurance business in Hartford, Connecticut, began when a fire insurance policy was written in 1754.

John Copson, of Philadelphia, was said to be the first marine insurance agent. He advertised in the *American Weekly Mercury* May 5, 1721, that he was opening an office for insuring vessels, goods and merchandise. The first agency was that of Israel Whelan in New York City (1804) representing the Phoenix Fire Office in London.

Travelers Insurance Company was the first accident insurance company, chartered in Hartford (1863). The first policy, for $1,000, was issued in 1864 to James Botter, but it only covered the period he spent walking between the postoffice and his home; the premium was two cents. Travelers also issued the first automobile insurance policy to Dr. Truman J. Martin of Buffalo. The premium was $11.25 and covered liability of $5,000–$10,000.

The beginnings of other types of insurance were: *unemployment—* State of Wisconsin (1932); *health—* Massachusetts Health Insurance Co. (1842); *state health insurance—* Rhode Island (1942); *workmen's compensation—* federal (1908), state (Wisconsin 1911); *group life—* Equitable Life Assurance Society (1912) covering 3,000 employees of Montgomery Ward; *group hospitalization—* Baylor U. Hospital (1929); *boiler—* Hartford Steam Boiler Inspection and Insurance Co. (1866); *credit—* US Credit System Company (1889); *title—* Real Estate Title Insurance and Trust Co. (1876).

Massachusetts adopted compulsory auto insurance (1927), the first of its kind. New York founded the first state insurance department (1860). New Hampshire created the first state insurance board (1851).

Insurance rate standardization was begun (1866) by the National Board of Fire Underwriters, composed of 76 insurance companies.

Early leaders in the insurance field include:

William Bard (1778–1853), who organized the New York Life Insurance and Trust Co. (1830), the first company to make life insurance its primary business.

James G. Batterson (1823–1901) founded Travelers Insurance, the first accident insurance company (1863). The idea was ridiculed and opposed but within two years about 70 such companies were in existence.

John F. Dryden (1839–1911) helped found the Widows and Orphans Friendly Society (1873) and five years later it became the Prudential Insurance Company, which he headed for 30 years (1881–1911).

George W. Perkins (1862–1920) began as an office boy at New York Life when he was 15. He rose to First Vice President and during his career reorganized the company and the insurance industry. Originally insurance companies turned over policies to general agents who hired soliciting agents. The often underpaid solicitors were faithful to the general agents, not the company. Perkins dispensed with the general agents in 1892 and hired local solicitors. This resulted in a force of well-trained, loyal salesmen who were paid on the length of service and amount of policies written.

An actuary of Mutual Life, Sheppard Homans, published the first important mortality tables based on 1868 United States data. These figures guided the industry until 1941 when new tables were issued by the National Association of Insurance Commissioners.

Lottery

Another potential source of government income is the lottery. Private lotteries to dispose of goods and property were popular in the 1730s until they were outlawed. The first important American lottery was held (1614) by the Virginia Company with a 4500 crowns first prize. Other colonies had similar lotteries to raise money for public improvements and to assist in financing colleges, among them Harvard, Columbia, Dartmouth, and Williams.

Congress adopted a national lottery (1776) to help pay for the war. After the Revolution, lotteries were popular throughout the country and fraud was common. New York State had weekly drawings in 1830, with prizes exceeding nine million dollars. Legislatures in Massachusetts, Pennsylvania and New York outlawed lotteries (1833); the next year they were joined by Ohio, Vermont, Maine, New Jersey, New Hampshire and Illinois.

After the Civil War, Louisiana began a successful lottery and former Confederate General Pierre G.T. Beauregard (1818–93) managed it from 1870 to 1888. President Benjamin Harrison denounced the lotteries and Congress passed a law forbidding use of the mail system in lotteries.

Louisiana outlawed the lottery in 1892 and they were generally illegal nationwide from then until 1963 when New Hampshire created a state lottery and was quickly followed by others.

Mail Order

The first mail order house was established by (A.) Montgomery Ward (1843–1913) in Chicago (1872). Ward worked as a traveling salesman for a St. Louis wholesaler and saw the problems of farmers who had to pay high prices for a limited selection of products. He had the idea for a retail outlet which bought at wholesale and offered the products by mail at a small markup. Ward issued his first catalog — a single sheet price list of 30 items without illustrations — in 1872; by 1874, it grew to eight pages and the firm prospered.

Not far behind was Sears Roebuck. Richard W. Sears (1863–1914) obtained the right to sell a shipment of watches left abandoned at the railroad station in Redwood Falls, Minnesota (1886). He promoted the watches by letter, offering them at a bargain price, and quickly sold out. He ordered more watches, advertised in the papers, and got excellent results. Sears then founded a mail order watch business that same year in Minneapolis and hired Alvah C. Roebuck to fix any returned watches. They formed Sears Roebuck (1893) in Chicago and the first catalog offered a choice of 25 watches. From watches they expanded into a variety of products.

Watches were also the basis for the success of another mail order business. Robert H. Ingersoll (1859–1928) began a small business (1880) in New York City making and selling rubber stamps, then developed a large line of notions and novelties. With his brother, Charles (1865–1948), Ingersoll opened a large chain of retail outlets and developed a mail order business. They bought 1,000 watches (1895) from the Waterbury Clock Company that became very popular at a price of one dollar each. The watch name was changed to Ingersoll and by 1919 more than 70 million had been sold. It became known as "the watch that made the dollar famous."

J(ames) C. Penney (1875–1971) began as a clerk in a Hamilton, Missouri, store (1895) at a pay of $2.27 a month. As store manager, he bought a one-third share in a store in Kemmerer, Wyoming, for $2,000 to start his chain (1904). Remembering his opportunity, Penney made it possible for all store managers to buy stock in the company; later all employees had the opportunity to share company profits. The 500th Penney store opened in Hamilton (1924), the site of Penney's first job. At the time of his death (1971), the chain had 1,660 stores.

Among the pioneers in the dry goods business was Marshall Field (1834–1906). He began as a traveling salesman and clerk in a Chicago store (1856), became general manager five years later and partner the next year. With Potter Palmer (1826–1902) and Levi Z. Leiter (1834–1904), he formed Field, Palmer and Leiter (1865), which later became Marshall Field and Company. Field was responsible for many merchandising innovations, such as displaying prices of all merchandise, liberal credit and the return of goods within a reasonable time. He was the first to locate a restaurant in the store.

Benjamin Altman (1840–1913) opened a dry goods store on Third Avenue, near 10th Street, in New York City (1865). He led the move of business uptown (1906), locating his store on Fifth Avenue and 34th Street. By 1914, the store occupied an entire city block. Altman was among the first to provide employee benefits.

Edward A. Filene (1860–1937) and his younger brother assumed management of the dry goods store in Boston founded by his father (1891). Filene introduced the bargain basement and promoted employee welfare.

One of the earliest department stores was founded (1858) by Rowland H. Macy (1822–77) in New York City. It later became the property of the Straus family. Lazarus Straus and his son, Isidor (1845–1912) came to the United States in the early 1850s and formed a partnership which took over the pottery and glassware department of Macy's (1874). Two other Straus brothers, Nathan (1848–1931) and Oscar (1850–1926) joined the firm (1881). Isidor and Nathan became Macy partners (1888), then sole owners (1896), developing the world's largest department store.

John Wanamaker (1838–1922) and his brother-in-law, Nathan Brown, opened a men's clothing store in Philadelphia (1861). It later became a department store called the Grand Depot. Wanamaker invited merchants with other lines to lease space in the store. When they failed to do so, Wanamaker established small specialty shops in the store. Wanamaker later took over New York City's largest retail store, the A.T. Stewart Company. Wanamaker pioneered a number of merchandising methods, notably use of newspaper advertising, the system of offering full refunds to dissatisfied customers and establishing employee welfare and training systems.

Alexander T. Stewart (1803–76) opened a small dry goods shop (1823) on lower Broadway and Chambers Street in New York City that by 1850 had become the world's largest dry goods establishment. Stewart built the world's largest retail store (1862), occupying an entire square block (Broadway and 4th Avenue, between 9th and 10th Streets).

Another early department store was founded by Brigham Young

(1801–1877) soon after the Mormons arrived in Salt Lake City (1868). The Zion's Cooperative Mercantile Institution was originally a group of separate stores featuring different products; a year later all were housed under one roof.

Isaac Gimbel (1856–1931) and his brother, Jacob (1850–1922), after running stores in Milwaukee and Philadelphia, founded Gimbel's Department Store in New York City (1910), which became one of the world's largest.

Public Relations

Public relations or promotion began as early as 1641 when Harvard College made what was probably the first systematic fund raising effort by sending three clergymen to England on a "begging mission." Columbia College was possibly the first institution to issue a press release, announcing its commencement in 1758. The *Federalist Papers* in 1787–89 were written as public relations documents to gain approval of the Constitution.

A pioneer in public relations was Amos Kendall, who was Postmaster General (1835–40) and conveyed the ideas of President Jackson to the Congress and the nation.

Ivy L. Lee (1877–1934), a New York City reporter, was named press agent for the Democratic National Committee (1904). He went into public relations and successfully developed it into a recognized profession. He handled numerous accounts, including John D. Rockefeller, Sr.

Edward L. Bernays (1891–1995) and his wife founded (1919) the first American public relations consulting firm serving government, industry and labor organizations. His lectures at New York University and writings did much to define the field of public relations.

Retail

Expanding populations in and around towns provided a growing market for retail shop goods. Retailing began early in the colonies, with the majority being small groceries, followed by dry goods stores, specialty shops and book stores.

George Hogg (1784–1849), a manufacturer and merchant, may have been the first to operate a chain of stores. He had a large wholesale dry goods business in Pittsburgh and a large wholesale grocery. As the business grew, Hogg established 15 mercantile houses in Ohio, a forwarding house in Sandusky, Ohio, and 61 stores in Pennsylvania and New York.

John Jacob Astor (1763–1848) entered the fur business in 1786 and his American Fur Co., organized 1888, became the first American business monopoly. He established Astoria, Oregon, (1811) as a depot for his western fur trading.

The first shopping arcade, the Philadelphia Arcade, opened in 1827 on a site enclosed by Chestnut and Carpenter streets, and 6th and 7th streets. The land cost $42,500 and construction $112,000. Cleveland opened an arcade of 112 stores (1890), the forerunner of today's shopping malls.

In the field of five-and-dime stores, Frank W. Woolworth (1852–1919) was the trailblazer. While working in a Watertown, New York, store (1878) he convinced the owner to set up a special counter where all items would sell for five cents. It was very successful and the merchant backed Woolworth in opening his first dime store in Utica, New York (1879). The store failed in four months and Woolworth moved to Lancaster, Pennsylvania, where the venture was a success. He kept adding stores and founded the F.W. Woolworth Co. in 1912; there were 1,000 stores worldwide by 1919.

J. J. McCrory founded his five-and-dime store chain in Scottsdale, Pennsylvania (1882). Samuel H. Kress (1863–1955) followed in Memphis (1896), and S.(ebastian) S. Kresge (1867–1966) opened his chain in 1899. Kresge began with McCrory with stores in Memphis and Detroit. Kresge took over the Detroit store (1899) to start his chain, which in 1961 became K-Mart discount stores.

Chain groceries began with the Greater Atlantic and Pacific Tea Company. George B. Hartford (1833–1917) opened his first store (1859), a tea store, in New York City, and another the next year. These became the Great American Tea Company and ten years later, the A & P. The Piggly Wiggly chain, which began in 1916, was the first to feature self-service.

Leaders in drug stores were Charles R. Walgreen (1873–1939) and Louis K. Liggett (1875–1946). Walgreen began as a pharmacist in a Chicago drugstore, which he bought in 1902. He added stores until he retired (1934), and by then there were more than 500 Walgreen stores. Liggett founded (1903) and headed the United Drug Company, which began as a central buying agency for drug stores, and was board chairman of the Liggett chain.

The door-to-door sales business was typified by Alfred C. Fuller

(1885–1973). He began as a salesman for a brush company (1905) and a year later formed his own company in Hartford, Connecticut. He made brushes at night and sold them door-to-door during the day, using a corps of independent dealers. Sales by the "Fuller brush man" reached $12 million annually by 1920.

Taxes

The first federal income tax went into effect in 1862, imposing a three percent tax on incomes of more than $800. The tax was increased (1864) to five percent on incomes between $641 and $4,999 and up to 10% on incomes higher than $10,000. This tax lasted until 1872.

A proportional two percent tax was adopted in 1884 but the Supreme Court ruled it unconstitutional. Soon after the 16th Amendment went into effect in 1913 an income tax was imposed. A tax of one percent was levied on incomes higher than $3,000 for unmarried persons and higher than $4,000 for married persons. A surtax ranging from one to six percent was levied on incomes in excess of $20,000. There also was a corporate tax of one percent.

The pay-as-you-go (withholding) income tax devised by Beardsley Ruml (1894–1960), president of the Federal Reserve Bank of New York, went into effect July 1, 1943.

Four states tried imposing income taxes in the 1800s but they were not successful. The first state income tax to last was the 1911 Wisconsin tax, which was followed by more than 30 states.

Various other federal taxes have been imposed, such as the cigarette tax which began in 1864 and gasoline (one cent per gallon) in 1932. States have tried to impose similar taxes. Iowa began a cigarette tax ($1 per 1,000) in 1921. Gasoline was taxed in Oregon (one cent per gallon) in 1919, and in West Virginia, the first state sales tax was implemented in 1921.

4. Clothing

Ebenezer Butterick (1826–1903), a tailor, developed the first mass-produced patterns for garment making. He and his wife marketed their first patterns in 1863. Six years later they began a monthly fashion magazine (*Metropolitan*, later *Delineator*), to promote pattern sales which rose to six million a year by 1871.

The first recorded American clothing factory opened in 1831 in New York City. Bloomers were introduced at the women's rights convention in Seneca Falls, New York, July 19, 1848, by feminist Amelia Jenks Bloomer (1818–94). Edna W. Chase (1877–1957), editor of *Vogue*, which she developed into a leading fashion magazine, organized the first American fashion show (1914). Dacron men's suits were introduced (1951) by Hart, Schaffner & Marx. Sanford L. Cluett (1874–1968), vice president of the family shirt and collar business, invented the sanforizing process (named for him). Earmuffs were invented by Chester Greenwood of Farmington, Maine (1873).

Accessories

The first hat factory is believed to have been established in Danbury, Connecticut (1780), by Zadoc Benedict and the first straw hats are credited to a 12-year-old, Betsey Metcalfe. The first derby hats were manufactured (1850) by Henry Knapp of South Derby, Connecticut, who sold them to New York jobbers. The first soft felt hats for women were introduced (1851) by John N. Genin (1819–78) in New York City.

Rudolph Eickemeyer (1831–95) and George Osterheld patented the first hat blocking and shaping machine (1866). The original machine, which was improved over the years, folded edges of leather bands and sewed them into the hat.

John B. Stetson (1830–1906) opened a hat factory in Philadelphia (1865) and got off to a very slow start. Stetson then launched hats with new styling — wide-brimmed and high crowned — which became known simply as "Stetsons" and were very popular. By 1900, Stetson was operating the largest hat factory in the world.

The first manufacturer of gloves in commercial quantities was Talmadge Edwards (1747–1821) of Johnstown, New York. He had been invited to Johnstown to teach glove makers his process for dressing leather. Edwards hired young women to cut out the gloves and farmers' wives to sew them. This was the beginning of the glove industry. Edwards took a few dozen pairs of gloves with him on a horseback trip to Albany (1810), where he sold all the gloves quickly.

Pants

Levi Strauss (1829?–1902) set out from New York City as a young man to seek his fortune in the California gold rush. A friend complained to him about the quality of work pants. Strauss made a pair for him from tent canvas. Strauss then began to make pants which miners called "levis." There was an endless demand for the pants and Strauss made only two changes in the first 20 years— using dyed material for uniformity and added copper rivets to reinforce pocket corners. The pants became the most popular work pants in the West among the miners and cowboys, then spread throughout the country.

Shirts

Detached collars were first made in Troy, New York (1825), by Hannah L. Montague, who was tired of washing her husband's shirts when only the collar was dirty. At about the same time, Ebenezer Brown (1795–1889), a retired minister who became a dry-goods merchant, heard of Mrs. Montague's work. He began manufacturing detachable collars in various sizes (1829). Brown left the business to Mrs. Montague's husband, Orlando, and Austin Granger, who opened a plant in Troy to manufacture linen collars and shirt bosoms. Walter Hunt, inventor of numerous items (including the safety pin), patented a disposable paper collar (1854).

The first important shirt factory was established (1818) in Boston by Oliver F. Winchester (1810–80), better remembered for his later operation of a rifle plant.

Shoes

The first American shoe manufacturer was Thomas Beard, who arrived on the *Mayflower* and began turning out shoes in 1628. The tanning of leather was begun by the Indians and the first known white tanner (1623) was Experience Miller of Plymouth, Massachusetts.

Samuel Preston invented a machine to peg shoes and George H. Corliss (1817–88) patented a boot-stitching machine (1842).

Lyman R. Blake (1835–83) co-invented a shoe stitching machine (1859) which revolutionized shoe manufacturing. At first, parts of the shoe were cut and given to shoemakers, who worked on them at home. Then sewing machines were used on the upper parts until 1858 when Blake devised a machine to sew the entire shoe. Gordon McKay (1821–1903) bought Blake's patent for the machine and improved it.

William H. McElwain (1867–1908) started a shoe factory with $10,500 in Bridgewater, Massachusetts (1894), designed to turn out attractive men's shoes for two dollars a pair using quantity production methods. Within five years, he was successful and built several new plants. McElwain's factories turned out five million pairs of shoes in 1908.

Thomas C. Wales of Dorchester, Massachusetts, received a patent (1858) for waterproofing boots and gaiters and Seth Boyden (1788–1870) developed a process for making patent leather. Jan E. Matzeliger (1852–89) patented a machine (1883) which could produce an entire shoe in a minute. His patent was acquired and developed by the United Shoe Machinery Co. Humphrey O'Sullivan of Lovell, Massachusetts, patented the rubber heel in 1899.

5. Communications

Radio/Television

The earliest demonstration of radio was made by Nathan B. Stubblefield in Philadelphia (1906). He gave a public exhibition of his invention in Fairmont Park and his voice was heard a mile from the transmitter. Stubblefield received a patent on his wireless invention (1908) but did nothing to promote it. He expected to make much money from the invention and would not divulge details until after receiving his patent, depriving himself of deserved fame.

Reginald A. Fessenden (1866–1932), a chemist/electrician, was the first American to transmit the human voice (1900). He used a spark transmitter and a 50-foot antenna mast to transmit speech to a station a mile away. The sound quality was poor but it marked the start of radio-telephony.

Fessenden patented a high frequency alternator (1901), which generated a continuous wave to enable broadcast of speech. He built a station at Brant Rock, Massachusetts, where, on Christmas Eve 1906, he made the first broadcast of voice and music — including two songs, a poem and a short talk. The program was heard by wireless operators aboard ships within a radius of several hundred miles. Fessenden made the first telephonic connection between the United States and Scotland, a two-way conversation between Brant Rock and a station in Machrihanish, Scotland (1907).

Lee DeForest (1873–1961) patented many devices important to radio, telephone, television, radar and movies. These included the triode electron tube (1906) called an audion. DeForest made the first radio broadcast March 5, 1907 (the "William Tell Overture"), from Telharmonic

Hall in New York City to Brooklyn and the first live music broadcast in 1910 (Enrico Caruso at the Met).

David Sarnoff (1891–1971), a telegraph operator with Marconi Wireless, gained fame when he picked up the distress signals (1912) from the sinking *Titanic* and stayed in contact for 72 hours. Sarnoff rose rapidly with the company, becoming commercial manager (1919) when RCA took over Marconi Wireless, president in 1930 and chairman of the board 1947–70. Sarnoff insisted on founding National Broadcasting Co. so that buyers of RCA radios would have something to hear.

Edwin H. Armstrong (1890–1954) invented the regenerative or feedback circuit (1913) which revolutionized early radio. During World War I, he developed a superheterodyne circuit which became the basic design for AM (amplitude modulation) radio and developed a super-regenerative circuit (1920) which was used in short wave radio. Armstrong also demonstrated frequency modulation (FM), a system which eliminated static interference.

Ernst F. W. Alexanderson (1878–1975) worked with Fessenden and helped develop the high-frequency alternator (1901), which made possible transoceanic communication. He invented the modern radio tuning device (1916) and transmitted the first transatlantic facsimile message (1924). Alexanderson also developed a television receiver (1927) and a complete television system three years later.

The first radio news broadcast was August 31, 1920, by WMJ, Detroit, and the first daily news program began September 1, 1922, on WBAY, New York City.

Radio broadcasting to homes began when Frank Conrad (1874–1941), a Westinghouse engineer, began a series of broadcasts (1919) from his garage near Pittsburgh. A department store advertising radios mentioned Conrad's broadcasts and sold out all their radios. Westinghouse heard about the ad and Conrad's broadcasts and thought the company could use some of its idle facilities to make radio receivers.

Westinghouse gave Conrad a transmitter, set up a station in the plant, announced a broadcast schedule and Station KDKA was born. On November 2, 1920, the station broadcast presidential election returns and on November 30 began regular evening broadcasts. Station WMJ in Detroit also broadcast the 1920 presidential election returns.

Other radio firsts include: Presidential radio broadcast, President Harding on June 21, 1923, dedicating the Francis Scott Key Memorial in Baltimore over WEAR (now WFBR); first commercial radio broadcast complete with ads, August 21, 1922, over WEAF, the ATT experimental station; first coast-to-coast radio hookup, February 8, 1924, when John J. Carty, Bell research director, spoke in Chicago; first network in operation, National Broadcasting Company on November 25, 1926, with 24 stations; Federal Radio Commission created February 23, 1927; later became Federal Communications Commission on June 19, 1934.

Among the early television researchers was Herbert E. Ives (1882–1953) of Bell Laboratories, who transmitted pictures (1921) by electrical signals over telephone wires, greatly improving the quality of pictures sent over long distances.

Allan DuMont (1901–65) made significant contributions to developing a commercially practical cathode ray picture tube. Charles F. Jenkins (1867–1934) began the broadcast of silhouette pictures from his Washington, DC, laboratory (1925). General Electric laboratory in Schenectady began daily tests on the experimental station W2XAD (1928).

Philo T. Farnsworth (1906–71) developed a design and basic principles for a television system (1926) and Philco provided financial backing in the 1930s. World War II ended Farnsworth's efforts. By war's end, Vladimir K. Zworykin (1889–1982) had perfected a different approach.

Zworykin, an RCA engineer, demonstrated a crude television system (1923) and the kinescope picture tube a little later. He invented the iconoscope, the first practical pick-up tube for television (1931), making possible the all-electronic television system.

NBC, owned by RCA, began regular television service with the opening of the 1939 New York City World's Fair. The first official American network television broadcast was February 1, 1940, when an NBC program in New York City was picked up and rebroadcast by Station WRGB in Schenectady. Columbia Broadcasting System presented the first television newscast December 7, 1941, reporting the Pearl Harbor attack. The war slowed television programming but by 1948 there were 36 stations on the air, 70 under construction, and about one million sets in use.

Other television firsts include: First demonstration April 7, 1927, when Commerce Secretary Herbert Hoover in Washington was seen in New York City; first transcontinental television broadcast, September 4, 1951, when President Truman spoke at the Japanese Peace Treaty Conference in San Francisco; first transmission of television signals between the United States and Europe occurred via Telstar I on July 10, 1962; first community television antenna system, Astoria, Oregon, in December 1949 with three subscribers; pay television demonstrated January 11, 1951, by Zenith Corp.; first political convention on television, Philadelphia

1940; first commercial television license issued to Station W2XBS in New York City July 1, 1941 (became Station WNBT); first educational television station, KHUT, Houston 1953.

Telegraph

The earliest venture into the telegraph was an electromagnetic system (1831) devised by Joseph Henry. He was able to transmit signals with the electromagnet through more than a mile of wire. He never put the invention to practical use. The real movement began with Samuel F. B. Morse (1791–1872), who, after a conversation (1832) about electromagnetism, had an idea for an electrical device that would transmit information. He had a working model by 1838 and developed a dot-and-dash code that bears his name.

Public interest was difficult to stimulate. Alfred L. Vail (1807–1859) helped Morse by demonstrating the telegraph (1838) at his father's Speedwell Iron Works near Morristown, New Jersey. Morse received a patent on June 20, 1841. Vail, Morse and Hiram Sibley (1807–88) convinced Congress (1843) to build a demonstration telegraph line between Washington and Baltimore.

Ezra Cornell (1807–74) developed a machine to lay pipe for the telegraph line but when the wires could not be insulated in the pipe, Cornell developed an insulation and put the wire on poles. The line, which ran along the Baltimore and Ohio railroad tracks was completed May 24, 1844, and Morse, in Washington, tapped a message on the telegraph — "What hath God wrought?"— which was received by Vail in Baltimore. A great deal of litigation followed until Morse's claim was upheld by the Supreme Court (1854).

Royal E. House (1814–95) designed and built a printing telegraph (1844) capable of printing more than 50 words a minute. Over the years several successful House telegraph lines were built but the system was gradually displaced by the Morse lines.

Sibley and Cornell combined a number of telegraph lines to form the original Western Union (1856) which in 1881 was expanded by consolidating three companies.

John W. Mackay (1831–1902) helped found Commercial Cable Co. (1883) which laid two cables in Europe that were not successful. In an effort to break the Western Union monopoly Mackay founded Postal Telegraph (1996).

Congress authorized construction of a telegraph line from the Mississippi River to the Pacific Coast (1855).

Morse laid the first cable, an insulated copper wire, between the Battery and Governor's Island in New York (1842) and the first practical submarine telegraph cable was laid by Cornell between Fort Lee, New Jersey, and New York City three years later.

Cyrus W. Fields (1819–92), a retired businessman, became interested (1854) in the possibility of a transatlantic cable. After three failed attempts, the cable was successfully completed (1858) but broke down after three weeks. Repair work was delayed by the Civil War and finally completed in July 1866. The line ran from Valentia, Ireland, to Heart's Content, Newfoundland. The Pacific cable went into operation in 1903, connecting San Francisco and Hawaii.

Various inventions over the years improved the telegraph — David E. Hughes (1831–1900) developed a type-printing telegraph instrument (1856) which was immediately successful and widely-used in foreign countries; Michael I. Pupin, a system of multiplex telegraph (1894); Patrick B. Delany (1845–1924), a multiplex telegraph by which six messages could be sent at the same time over one wire and a rapid machine telegraph system capable of recording 3,000 words a minute over a single wire; Stephen D. Field (1846–1913), multiple call district telegraph box (1874), a dynamo telegraph (1879), and a rapid speed stock ticker (1884).

Others firsts in telegraphy: First singing telegram, July 18, 1933 (after 1950 all singing was done by phone); first telegraph company, Majestic Telegraph Company (1847); first telegraphic ticker installed in a brokerage office, David Groesbeck and Company, New York City (1867); first transcontinental telegraph line completed October 24, 1861, with the first telegram received by President Lincoln from Sacramento.

Telephone

Alexander Graham Bell was a student of acoustics following his grandfather, Alexander, an elocution teacher. His father, Melville, also an elocution teacher, invented "visible speech," a written code showing the exact positions of the throat, tongue and lips during speech. The "visible speech" was originally designed to help people learn foreign languages but it became useful in teaching deaf people to speak.

The Bells moved from Scotland to Canada (1870) and the father continued teaching. Young Bell went to Boston to substitute for his father before a group of teachers of the deaf and stayed there teaching his father's system. In October 1872, Bell opened a speech school in Boston and then met Gardiner G. Hubbard (1822–97), a wealthy lawyer whose daughter was a Bell pupil. Bell and the daughter fell in love and she inspired his work in experimenting with a "harmonic telephone" that would transmit musical notes. Bell switched to human speech and came upon the principle of the telephone in June 1874.

Bell developed patent specifications for the telephone which Hubbard filed on February 14, 1876, a few hours before Elisha Gray (1835–1901) filed a "caveat" or a warning to other inventors of a speaking telephone. Bell patented a multiplex system (1875) using tuned reeds and on June 3, 1875, transmitted a barely comprehensible message to his assistant, Thomas A. Watson (1854–1934). Then on March 10, 1876, Bell spoke his famous "Mr. Watson, come here, I want you."

A year later, the Bell Telephone Co. was founded, becoming in turn the National Bell Telephone Co., American Bell Telephone Co. and finally the American Telephone & Telegraph Co. (1899). Independent telephone companies sprang up, beginning in 1894, with the first in Noblesville, Indiana. By 1957 there were 5,000 companies and they formed the National Independent Telephone Association. A great deal of litigation followed Bell's patent and the stiffest competition came from Western Union, which had purchased Gray's patents. Bell finally won on November 10, 1879.

John J. Carty (1861–1932), chief engineer of ATT (1907), consolidated all research activities into what became Bell Laboratories, and directed research into attaining transcontinental and transatlantic service.

Charles J. Glidden (1857–1927) built the world's first telephone exchange at Lowell, Massachusetts (1879) with 50 subscribers. Glidden discovered that female voices carry better over the phone than men's, resulting in female operators. Late in 1879 telephone subscribers began to be designated by numbers rather than names. A local physician, during a measles epidemic, pointed out that if the four Lowell operators were stricken, inexperienced substitutes would have trouble learning which name went with each of the 100 jacks on the switchboard and service would be paralyzed.

Telephone firsts include: First phone installed in the home of Charles Williams in Somerville, Massachusetts, in April of 1877; first automatic telephone switching system developed by Almon B. Strowger (1889) and installed in LaPorte, Indiana (1892); the first transcontinental conversation took place on January 25, 1915, by Bell in New York City and Watson in San Francisco, with the call costing $20.70 for the first three minutes, $6.75 for each additional minute; first transatlantic call between New York City and London was January 7, 1927, and 31 calls were made that day at $75 for three minutes.

First switchboard or exchange began May 17, 1877, at 342 Washington Street, Boston, where Edwin T. Holmes operated an electric burglar alarm system. It operated as an exchange by day with the first woman operator, Emma B. Nutt, and at night it served as an alarm system. The first commercial switchboard was run by George W. Coy in New Haven January 28, 1878, with 21 customers; the first directory issued February 21, 1878.

The coin telephone was invented (1881) by William Gray (1830–1901) of Hartford and was first installed in the Hartford Bank (1889); mobile phone service was inaugurated July 17, 1946, by Southwestern Bell Telephone in St. Louis.

6. Education

Puritan leaders, most influential in colonial education, were determined that children be literate in order to read the Bible. Formal education of children came early in the American settlements. The Latin Grammar School was founded in Boston (1635) and concentrated on classical studies and preparation for college, serving as a model for later schools.

The first compulsory education law was enacted in Massachusetts (1642) requiring all parents to teach their children to read and to ply a trade. Five years later, Massachusetts passed a law requiring a community with 50 households to maintain a school and every town with 100 householders to maintain a grammar school.

In the middle colonies education was controlled by church parishes, not civil authority as in New England. In the South, education was an obligation of the family and home, and settlers there were able to provide traditional education with tutors.

Benjamin Franklin started a new type of secondary school, the Academy for the Education of Youth in Philadelphia (1751), which was followed by many similar schools—public but not free. These schools attracted non-college bound students from all religious faiths and marked an important step in the development of American education away from religious and classical education into more practical and democratic channels.

The teaching of evolution brought about a famous trial. John T. Scopes (1900–70), a Tennessee high school teacher, was arrested (1925) for violating the state law banning the teaching of evolution. Scopes was found guilty and fined $100, but the decision was later overturned.

Business education received its formal American start when the

Wharton School of Finance and Commerce at the University of Pennsylvania became the first collegiate school of business (1881).

Home economics by various names was taught in several schools beginning in the early 1870s at Iowa State University and Kansas and Illinois. By 1895, ten Midwestern schools had such courses. In the East, specialized classes and schools emphasized cooking, gardening, and school feeding.

Organizations related to learning and education date back to the mid-eighteenth century. The first American learned society was founded (1743) after Benjamin Franklin published "A Proposal for Promoting Useful Knowledge Among the British Plantations in America." This led to the American Philosophical Society, with Franklin as the first secretary and later president (1769–90).

This was followed by the American Academy of Arts and Sciences (1780), Academy of Natural Sciences (1812), New York Academy of Science (1827), American Association for the Advancement of Science (1848), and the National Academy of Sciences (1863).

The first local educational association was the Middlesex County Association in Connecticut (1799). The first national education association was the American Institute of Instruction, formed in 1830.

Parent-teacher groups began with the National Congress of Mothers (1897), which became the National Congress of Parents and Teachers.

Adult Education

Adult education in the United States began (1826) with the founding of the American Lyceum by Josiah Holbrook (1788–1854) in Milbury, Massachusetts. By 1834, there were some 3,000 town lyceums meeting weekly "for the mutual improvement of their members and the common benefits of society."

Then came the Chautauqua Movement. The founders were John H. Vincent (1832–1920), a Methodist minister who founded the monthly *Sunday School Teacher* (1865) and established a widely-used Sunday School curriculum, and Lewis Miller (1829–99), an agricultural machinery manufacturer. In 1874, they created a Sunday School teachers institute at Lake Chautauqua, New York. Four years later, it was broadened into the Chautauqua Literary and Scientific Circle with lectures on various subjects. The idea caught on and similar centers were set up throughout the country.

Along with this movement, a large number of government agencies and a growing number of volunteer organizations became concerned with educating adults. Private and public educational institutions began correspondence courses; New York State created a University Extension Division (1891), the University of Wisconsin widened its correspondence courses (1906) from academic and cultural subjects to include areas concerned with problems of the people and the state. The Federal Government began providing funds (1914) to supplement state money and created a cooperative agricultural extension service.

Colleges/Universities

Early American colleges regarded themselves as centers to educate men for the church. By 1740, less than half the graduates entered the ministry; by 1775, only a quarter. Lawyers and doctors, after basic college education, got the rest of their training from handbooks and working with established professionals.

Some states tried to convert private colleges to state schools but that effort was ended by the Supreme Court (1819) when it held that the charter of Dartmouth College was a contract which could not be changed by the state alone. Private colleges flourished and states began to create state universities.

Here are some of the early major colleges and their leaders:

Harvard — The first American college was founded (1636) in Cambridge, Massachusetts, when John Harvard (1607–1638), a resident of Charlestown, Massachusetts, left half of his estate (about 780 pounds) and his library of about 400 books to the college, which opened in 1638. His bequests more than doubled the school's resources and the Massachusetts General Court named the college in his honor (1639).

Henry Dunster (1609–59), a clergyman, became Harvard's second president (1640), replacing an ineffective first president. Dunster, an able administrator and fund raiser, launched the college on the path it followed for 200 years. Dunster was forced to resign (1654) when he adopted certain Baptist views.

Charles W. Eliot (1834–1926) was president of Harvard for 40 years (1869–1909) and completely reorganized the school by grouping all undergraduate studies in the college and established a graduate school (1890). Elective courses were introduced into the college, the schools of law and medicine were improved. His influence reached into the secondary schools because Harvard raised its admission requirements, a move followed by other colleges, requiring higher standards in the secondary schools.

William and Mary — James Blair (1655–1743), a Virginia Anglican rector, got the colony to petition the crown for a college, which he presented to the King and Queen (1691). A charter for the College of William and Mary was granted two years later and Blair began his 50 year presidency of the school.

The college was closed during the Civil War and its president, Benjamin S. Ewell (1810–94), led the rebuilding, spending his own money until he received government help. Ewell rang the chapel bell periodically to keep the charter in force and the college reopened in 1888.

Yale — The school began (1701) as the Collegiate School of Connecticut at Killingworth, then moved (1716) to New Haven, where it was renamed in honor of its English benefactor, Elihu Yale (1649–1721). The first president (actually rector until 1745) was Abraham Pierson (1645–1707), who served six years until 1707. The declared purpose of the institution was to prepare youth "for Publick employment both in Church and Civil State."

Princeton — Samuel Davies, a colonial preacher who founded the Presbytery of Hanover in Virginia, helped raise funds in England and Scotland to build the College of New Jersey (now Princeton). It opened in May 1747 in Elizabeth, New Jersey, and moved to Princeton in 1752. Jonathan Dickinson (1688–1747), the foremost colonial Presbyterian clergyman and co-founder of the college, served briefly (1747) as first president; Davies served from 1759 to 1761.

Pennsylvania — Benjamin Franklin helped found the William Penn Academy and the College of Philadelphia (1751). Forty years later, the schools formed the basis for the University of Pennsylvania.

Columbia — King's College (later Columbia) opened (1754) in New York City, with Samuel Johnson (1696–1772) as first president (1754–63). He began teaching eight students in Trinity Church and the college moved into its own quarters in 1756. It was closed during the Revolution and reopened (1784) with its name changed to Columbia.

Nicholas Murray Butler (1862–1947) served as Columbia president (1902–45), changing the school from a provincial college to a university of world renown.

Dartmouth — Eleazar Wheelock (1711–79), a Congregational minister, founded Moor's Charity School (1754) in Lebanon, Connecticut. The school of Indians and whites failed in 1768. Wheelock was invited to New Hampshire (1770) to operate a school and he and 30 students founded the town of Hanover and Dartmouth College, which he headed (1770–79).

Other college heads who influenced American higher education were: William Rainey Harper (1856–1906), first president of the new University of Chicago (1891–1906); Timothy Dwight (1752–1817), president of Yale (1795–1817) and an intellectual leader of the country; Francis Wayland (1796–1865), headed Brown University (1827–55), where he introduced electives, developed the library and emphasized science teaching; Daniel C. Gilman (1831–1908), first president of Johns Hopkins University (1875), who helped found the Johns Hopkins Hospital (1899) and its medical school (1893) and Thomas Hunter (1831–1915), who organized the first evening high school (1866) and the New York City Normal College, which he headed (1870–1906) that later became Hunter College (1914).

The first city college was chartered (1785) in Charleston, South Carolina. The first Catholic college was Georgetown (now University) in Washington, DC, chartered in 1789, opened in 1791. The first nondenominational college was Blount College (now University of Tennessee) in Knoxville, chartered 1794. Oberlin (Ohio) Collegiate Institute opened in December of 1833 as the first American coeducational college. Women were admitted only to the preparatory department until 1837 when four women were enrolled as full students. Three of them graduated and were the first women to receive bachelor's degrees equal to those given men. Under the leadership of Horace Mann, Antioch College in Yellow Springs, Ohio began coeducation in 1852.

The first Negro land grant college was Alcorn Agricultural and Mechanical College at Rodney, Mississippi (1871) and the first Negro university began as the Ashmun Institute (1854), later becoming Lincoln University, in Chester County, Pennsylvania.

Illinois Wesleyan University began a series of undergraduate and graduate courses to be done by correspondence (1874). Forty courses were required for a bachelor's degree with a final examination at the university. It was discontinued in 1910.

The Chautauqua Movement began a correspondence school of languages (1879), headed by William Rainey Harper. Three years later it became the Chautauqua home study program. Harper, when he was University of Chicago president (1891), created home study courses there.

Private correspondence courses were begun by Thomas J. Foster (1843–1936) to prevent accidents at the mines. His Colliery Engineering

School of Mines grew into the International Correspondence Schools of Scranton, Pennsylvania, in the 1890s.

William College was the founder of the first general alumni organization (1821).

The first fraternity, Phi Beta Kappa, was formed December 5, 1776 at the College of William and Mary as a secret social group, later becoming an honor society. The first modern social fraternity was Kappa Alpha at Union College (1825) and Sigma Phi, also at Union, was the first to establish chapters at other schools (1831). The first sorority was Pi Beta Phi (1867). The first professional fraternity was Theta Xi, an engineering and science group, formed at Rensselaer Polytechnic Institute (1864).

Junior colleges were considered in the 1850s in discussing two year colleges. Dr. Harper at the University of Chicago (1896) set up the freshman and sophomore classes as a separate division, which he called a junior college. The idea grew slowly but by the 1980s there were more than 1,200 junior and community colleges.

Education for the Physically Impaired

Education for the physically impaired dates back to 1817. Thomas H. Gallaudet (1787–1851) graduated as a minister but poor health kept him from following that career. He became interested in teaching the deaf and a group of Hartford men formed a society (1815) to instruct the deaf, raised $2,278 and sent Gallaudet to Europe to learn teaching methods. Gallaudet returned from France with Laurent Clerc, a deaf teacher for the deaf. With Clerc's help, he opened a free school for the deaf in Hartford (1817), the Connecticut (later American) Asylum, the first such school in the United States. Gallaudet enlarged the school and taught other teachers who later established schools.

His son, Edwin M. (1837–1917), and Amos Kendall (1789–1869), former Postmaster General, founded the school for the deaf in Washington, DC (1857), the National Deaf Mute College, which later became Gallaudet College.

Another of his sons, Thomas (1822–1902), an Episcopal rector, established a Bible class for the deaf in his church and later was rector of St. Ann's Church for Deaf Mutes in New York City.

An early effort to help the deaf goes back to 1677 when Philip Nelson in Cowley, Massachusetts, tried to teach a deaf mute. Another was when Francis Green (1742–1809) of Boston who had a deaf son, directed a census of the deaf (1803) in Massachusetts and was one of the first Americans to write about the deaf.

Other early efforts included Rev. John Stafford, who was an almshouse chaplain, found several deaf children in New York City's almshouses (1810) and tried to teach them. His efforts resulted in the founding of the New York Institution for the Deaf (1818). John Braidwood began to teach deaf children in Virginia (1812) and later established a school. All of these programs used the manual system for teaching the deaf.

Harriet B. Rogers (1834–1919), a pioneer oral teacher of the deaf, became the first principal of Clarke School for the Deaf in Northampton, Massachusetts (1867), the first such school in the country. This school was followed by the Lexington School in New York City.

Dr. John D. Fisher (1797–1850) pioneered in education of the blind. After a trip to France (1825), he convinced some influential friends to start the New England Asylum (later the Perkins Institution) in 1829.

John D. Russ (1801–81) was co-founder of the New York Institute for the Blind (1832). The school began with three pupils and Russ was the teacher.

The first state school for the blind was the Ohio Institution for the Blind which opened in the Columbus Presbyterian Church with five pupils (1837).

The Seeing Eye Dogs was incorporated (1828) in Tennessee, moving soon thereafter to Morristown, New Jersey.

Educational Leaders

A leader of American public education was Horace Mann (1796–1859), secretary of the newly-created Massachusetts State Board of Education (1837–1849). He helped make numerous changes in the state — promoting normal schools, higher salaries for teachers, new schools and a minimum school year. He began annual educational conventions in every county. Mann's actions and reforms affected education throughout the country.

Other early leaders of American education were: Henry Barnard (1811–1900) was Rhode Island's first Commissioner of Public Schools (1848–49), Connecticut school superintendent (1849–58), then head of the University of Wisconsin and St. John's University. He became the first U.S. Commissioner of Education (1867–70).

Francis W. Parker (1837–1902), a leader of progressive education, began to reform Quincy, Massachusetts, schools (1875). He attacked learning by rote and introduced techniques to make subjects more meaningful. He headed a normal school in Chicago (1883–1899) and founded what became the University of Chicago School of Education (1901).

John Dewey (1859–1952) founded the University of Chicago Laboratory School for testing his progressive education theories (1896). He moved to Columbia University (1904), where he helped its Teachers College become a leading school of education, stressing student-centered, rather than subject-centered, schooling.

Martha M. Berry (1866–1942) launched a pioneer work-study program with her school and college in Georgia. Poor mountain children paid their tuition by part-time work on a school farm or in the school workshops.

Three successful businessmen assisted education with their gifts—Peter Cooper founded Cooper Union in New York City (1859), which provided free education for adults; Anthony J. Drexel founded the Drexel Institute in Philadelphia (1892), which offered technology classes for all regardless of race, religion, sex, or social class, and Matthew Vassar (1792–1868), a successful brewer, endowed Vassar College.

Two men led the way in teaching penmanship — Austin N. Palmer (1859–1927) for his widely-taught Palmer method, and Platt R. Spencer (1800–64). John R. Gregg (1867–1948) developed a shorthand system in England (1888) and five years later brought it to the United States, where it spread rapidly.

Industrial Schools

Industrial schools began (1819) in Derby, Connecticut, when Josiah Holbrook, who later gained fame as founder of the lyceum movement, established the first. This was followed (1824) by an agricultural seminary and the Rensselaer Polytechnic Institute in Troy, New York, founded by Amos Eaton (1776–1846).

Several mechanics institutes were founded in the larger industrial centers — General Society of Mechanics and Tradesmen in New York (1820), Maryland Institute in Baltimore (1825), Franklin Institute in Philadelphia (1824), and Ohio Mechanics Institute in Cincinnati (1829). An industrial school for girls was organized in Leominster, Massachusetts (1854).

Charles Pratt (1830–91), a successful producer of illuminating gas, endowed the Pratt Institution in Brooklyn (1887) to train skilled artisans, designers and draftsmen.

Libraries

Libraries in the United States began soon after the settlers arrived. The first public institutional library began at Harvard when John Harvard left his collection of nearly 400 volumes to the college (1638). Other colleges were not far behind — William and Mary (1693), Yale (1701), Pennsylvania and Princeton (1755), and Columbia (1757).

About 1700, through the efforts of Rev. Thomas Bray (1656–1730), parish libraries for ministers and parishioners were created in some Anglican parishes, especially in the South.

Charleston, South Carolina, created a library (1698) and Benjamin Franklin founded the first subscription circulating library, the Library Company (1731). Fifty persons contributed 40 shillings each for buying the first books and paid 10 shillings in annual charges. By the time of the Revolution, there were about 64 similar libraries in other cities.

The first free public library was the Juvenile Library in Dublin, New Hampshire (1822).

College libraries were small until the twentieth century and then they expanded rapidly. Some have developed great libraries to support their research programs and there are now more than 35 college libraries containing one million or more volumes.

The Library of Congress began (1800) with the purchase of 740 volumes for $508, then became the national library and one of the world's greatest.

Libraries have been frequent objects of philanthropy. Industrialist Andrew Carnegie was one of the outstanding examples with donations of about $43 million and James Lenox (1800–1880), whose rare books collection formed part of the founding collection of the New York Public Library.

The first time government funds were contributed to a library was for the Bingham Library for Youth in Salisbury, Connecticut (1803). Taxes to support public libraries began when Petersborough, New Hampshire, established a town library (1833). Michigan, in its 1838 constitution, provided for public libraries and New Hampshire appears to have been the first state to pass specific library legislation (1849).

The first children's department in a library was begun by John C.

Dana (1856–1929) in the Denver library (1894). The first bookmobile was a book wagon started at the Washington County Free Library in Hagerstown, Maryland (1905). A Mr. Thomas, the library janitor, drove a wagon through the county three times a week. There were shelves on the outside of the wagon so that the books were easily visible.

Among the leaders in library work, the most noted was Melvil Dewey (1851–1931), who prepared the decimal system (1876), a simple, comprehensive way of cataloguing books which is now used throughout the English-speaking world. He created the first school for librarians at Columbia University (1887), which was moved to Albany the next year and became the New York State Library, with Dewey as director.

Other notable library figures were:

Richard R. Bowker (1848–1933), a literary editor and publisher of bibliographic material, who helped organize the American Library Association (1876) and founded the *Library Journal*, which he edited for 30 years.

William F. Poole (1821–94) originated the *Index to Periodical Literature* (1848).

Charles A. Cutter (1837–1903) developed the dictionary catalog for libraries.

Herbert Putnam (1861–1955) as Librarian of Congress (1899–1939), developed what had been a congressional reference library into a great national library equal to those of Great Britain and France.

Justin Winsor (1831–97), superintendent of the Boston Public Library (1868–77), contributed much to the creation of a profession of librarianship.

Military Institutions

Private military schools in the United States began with Alden Partridge (1785–1854), who founded the American Literary, Scientific and Military Academy in Norwich, Vermont (1819). The school later became Norwich University.

The United States military academies started with the Military Academy at West Point, New York, which opened July 4, 1802 with five officers and ten cadets. The others in order of creation were the United States Naval Academy, which began as the Naval School (1845–1850); United

States Coast Guard Academy, which began as the Revenue Cutter School of Instruction (1876) in New London, Connecticut; United States Merchant Marine Academy at Kings Point, New York (1938), and United States Air Force Academy at Colorado Springs, Colorado, which began (1955) at a temporary site at Lowery Air Force Base in Colorado. The academies were opened to women students in 1975.

Museums

Museums in the United States began in a limited way in the 1700s — Harvard and the American Philosophical Society each had a cabinet of curiosities. The Library Society in Charleston, South Carolina, began a natural history museum (1773), the first in America, and Charles Willson Peale's scientific and historical museum in Philadelphia opened in 1785.

Local societies sponsored museums, most of which experienced hard times in their early years and then began to prosper. The Buffalo (New York) Society of Natural Sciences established the educational role of museums. In the 1860s, eminent scientists gave lectures there, the society's director became a public school science teacher and began a trend of bringing his students to the museum. The society sponsored evening lectures at the high schools (1876) and the staff began weekly natural history talks for children in the museum after school.

The first building in the United States constructed for use as a public museum was Pilgrim Hall in Plymouth, Massachusetts (1824). Among the important contributors to developing museums were Frederic W. Putnam (1839–1915), curator of the Peabody Museum at Harvard for 41 years, and Carl E. Akeley (1864–1926). Putnam revolutionized museum practices from merely buying collections to sending out expeditions that pioneered in exploring Southwest American and Central American archaeology. Akeley, a taxidermist, invented a cement gun used to create animals for museum habitat groups and a motion picture camera considered the best for naturalists. His sculpture helped usher in a new era of museum exhibition.

Schools

The first evening school opened in New Amsterdam (1661) and St. Mary's Church in Philadelphia established the first American parochial school (1782).

New York created its Board of Regents (1784) to supervise education and five years later Massachusetts created school districts. New York established a state school superintendent (1812) and by 1850 most northern states had done so; by 1860 most states had boards of education.

Over the years, governments have played a significant role in the growth and development of education through legislation and financial aids. The courts in several decisions defined the roles for education and the rules to control actions. The United States Supreme Court in the famed Dartmouth case (1819) ruled that a school's charter was a contract which a state could not change unilaterally. The Court ruled similarly (1954) against segregating black and white students in separate schools. The Michigan Supreme Court affirmed the power of a community to levy taxes to support secondary schools (1874), a principle that was followed in other states. Massachusetts, in 1852, required children eight to 14 to attend school 12 weeks of each year, six of them consecutive.

Between the Revolution and the Civil War, the United States turned from private sectarian schools to a system of common schools, free and open to all. New York created the first free public school system (1867).

The first American high school was the English Classical School (later English High School) which opened in Boston in May, 1820. Massachusetts required a high school in each community of 500 families (1827). The first commercial high school opened (1868) in Pittsburgh and the first junior high schools were the McKinley and Washington schools in Berkeley, California (1910).

Mrs. Carl Schurz (1833–76) opened a German-speaking kindergarten (1855) in Watertown, Wisconsin, the first kindergarten in the United States. The first American kindergarten was opened in Boston (1860) by Elizabeth P. Peabody (1804–94). Susan E. Blow (1843–1916) opened the first American public kindergarten in a St. Louis suburb (1873) and the following year opened a training school for kindergarten teachers. The first free kindergarten opened in Florence, Massachusetts (1876). The first nursery school was established (1827) in New York City by the Infant School Society.

The frontier strengthened liberal elements in a growing nation and paved the way for new educational outlooks. Academies and private schools offered subjects useful in trade and commerce, moving away from religious and classical education to more practical and democratic channels.

Teacher Training

The growth of schools required expansion of teacher training, which began when Rev. Samuel R. Hall (1795–1877) created the first American normal school in Concord, Vermont (1823), and James G. Carter (1795–1849), a pioneer advocate of normal schools, set one up at Lancaster, Massachusetts (1839).

Calvin E. Stowe (1802–86), husband of Harriet Beecher Stowe, led in founding a teachers college in Cincinnati (1833). Three years later, Ohio named him education commissioner and sent him to Europe to study public school systems. His report was used in several states to create school systems.

Another early effort occurred (1839) when Henry Barnard held the first teachers training institute. It was attended by 26 men for six weeks. Elizabeth Harrison (1849–1927) established a teachers training school (1887), serving as its head until 1920.

The first state teachers convention was held (1831) in Utica, New York; the first national convention (1857) in Philadelphia, with the founding of the National Teachers Association (later the National Education Association [NEA]). The American Association of University Professors was organized in 1915; the American Federation of Teachers in 1916.

Textbooks/Teaching Aids

The early American schools concentrated on reading, Latin and religion. The most prominent textbooks were the hornbook and the *New England Primer* (1690), which reflected the Puritan interpretation of the Bible. *The Primer* was the most frequently used textbook during the first 150 years when millions of copies were distributed.

The hornbook was a wooden paddle on which was pasted a sheet of paper with the alphabet, the Lord's prayer, verses from the Bible and religious poetry, all covered by a sheet of transparent horn.

Ezekiel Cheever (1615–1708), master of the Boston Latin School (1670–1708), prepared a Latin textbook which was the standard for New England schools for 100 years.

Noah Webster (1758–1843) wrote *The American Spelling Book* (1783) — better known as the "Blue Backed Speller" — which became a sensational success, settling and standardizing American spelling. This was the prelude to his major work in 1828 — *The American Dictionary*.

In addition to the very popular Webster and *Primer*, other early textbooks were the first American mathematics text, *Arithmetick Vulgar and Decimal* (1729) by Isaac Greenwood (1702–45); the first algebra book by an American, *A New and Complete System of Arithmetic* by Nicholas Pike (1743–1819) in 1788.

The first textbook printed in America was *A New Guide to the English Tongue* by an Englishman, Thomas Dilworth, in 1740. It was a combined reader, speller, and grammar.

Lindley Murray (1745–1826), called the "father" of English grammar, produced many texts on the subject. His *Grammar of the English Language*, published in 1795, went through many editions by 1864, and sold about two million copies.

Jedidiah Morse, known as the "father" of American geography, prepared the first American text on the subject, *Geography Made Easy* (1784), which went through 25 editions during his lifetime.

A series of books which contributed greatly to shaping the American mind in the 19th century was the *Eclectic Readers* by William H. McGuffey (1800–73). The six readers, published between 1836 and 1867, attained sales of 122 million copies. The readers were anthologies of selections from American and English literature and were a great improvement over textbooks then available to small schools.

Long before the term audiovisual was conceived, teachers were using aids such as pictures, book illustrations, maps and globes, charts, specimens, and models.

In 1905, the first school museum was started in St. Louis and by 1923, many large school systems had departments of visual instruction. The film strip was introduced in the early 1920s and strips with sound appeared in the late 1960s.

Effective educational radio began in 1930 and motion pictures in 1923. The Ohio School of the Air began broadcasting to schools in 1929.

Women/Minority Education

Education for women and racial minorities came slowly. French-born Anthony Benezet (1713–84), a teacher in the Germantown (Pennsylvania) Academy and Friends School for a number of years, operated a school for girls in Philadelphia (1755–66). He was also interested in education for blacks, opening a night school for them and leaving funds in his will for a black school.

The first boarding school for girls in the United States opened in Bethlehem, Pennsylvania (1746); it operated until 1790. One of the prime movers in female education was Emma H. Willard (1787–1870). She launched the Middlebury Seminary for females in her Troy, New York, home (1814), including courses in mathematics and philosophy, subjects then unheard of for women. She moved the school to Waterford, New York, two years later but returned to Troy (1821) and with the help of local citizens established the Troy Female Seminary. Mrs. Willard developed new teaching methods, published textbooks which won immediate recognition and trained hundreds of teachers. Her ardent efforts for women's higher education did much to gain public support.

Almira H.L. Phelps (1793–1884), a sister of Mrs. Willard, taught at the Patapsco Female Institute in Ellicott City, Maryland, (1841–56) and popularized science teaching for girls, promoted physical education, and helped train many young women for teaching.

Catherine E. Beecher (1800–78) established the Hartford Female Seminary, an advanced girls school (1824). She introduced calisthenics as a course and did much to introduce domestic science into the curriculum.

Jacob Abbott (1803–79), author of the 30-volume *Rollo* series for juveniles, founded the Mt. Vernon School in Boston, a secondary school for girls (1829).

Mary M. Lyon (1797–1849), after teaching at various schools, raised funds to start the Mount Holyoke Female Seminary (later College) (1837) in South Hadley, Massachusetts.

Georgia Female College (later Wesleyan) opened in Macon (1839), the first college in the world chartered to give degrees to women. The first vocational high school for girls, the Girls Trade School in Boston, opened 1904 as a summer experiment. Vassar College (1861) became the first women's college with funds sufficient to offer a liberal arts education equal to that of men's schools. The Harvard Annex, which became Radcliffe College, was chartered 1882.

Frederick A. P. Barnard (1809–89), president of Columbia University (1864–87), worked to extend higher education for women in a separate college using Columbia faculty. He inaugurated college instruction for women (1883) and a new college named in his honor opened a year after his death.

In education for racial minorities, two names stand out — Mary McLeod Bethune (1875–1955) and Booker T. Washington (1865–1915). Bethune opened a school in Daytona Beach, Florida (1904), the Normal and Industrial Institute for Negro Girls. The school merged (1923) with Cookman Institute for Men in Jacksonville, becoming the Bethune-Cookman College in Daytona Beach, which Mary Bethune headed until 1942. Washington headed Tuskegee Institute when it was founded (1881) in an old church and shanty with 40 unschooled black students from nearby farms. It grew into one of the world's leading centers for black education. At his death, the Institute had more than 100 buildings, a faculty of 200 or more, 1,500 students, and an endowment of $2 million.

7. Energy

Lumber and water power were the sources of energy in early American industries. Bituminous coal followed, after which came natural gas, petroleum, electricity, and nuclear energy.

Coal and Coke

Explorers discovered bituminous coal along the Illinois River (1673) but commercial mining did not begin until 1745 near Richmond, Virginia, and 1755 in Ohio. Bituminous coal was found in outcropping seams in the mountainous regions of Pennsylvania, Virginia and Maryland. A large seam was found near Barton, Maryland (1810). By the early 1830s, many small companies were operating.

Philip Hone (1780–1851) was active in the Pennsylvania coal business, leading him to pioneer the development of canals and railroads to move the coal. He organized the Delaware and Hudson Canal Co.

Valentine B. Horton (1802–88) was a pioneer in bituminous coal mining in Ohio and shipped coal down the Ohio River. He designed a tow boat which made it possible to return the empty barges up the river.

Anthracite coal was discovered accidentally by a hunter in Carbon County, Pennsylvania, (1791) but for a long time was not widely used because of its hardness and difficulty in burning.

The first beehive coke oven was built in Pennsylvania (1841). The first American byproduct coke ovens were built at the Solvay Process Company in Syracuse, New York, to produce ammonia in the Solvay ammonia-soda process. The coke and gas obtained were used as fuel.

Electricity

Benjamin Franklin, the multitalented newspaper/magazine publisher, diplomat and scientist, developed an interest in electricity about 1744. He devoted the next ten years to experimenting, including his famous 1752 kite flying experiment in a thunderstorm which convincingly showed the electrical nature of lightning.

Thomas A. Edison, whose name is synonymous with electricity, received his first patent June 1, 1869, for an electrical vote recorder. In the next few years, he developed quadruplex telegraphy and the carbon transmitter. After many fruitless experiments in his large new laboratory at Menlo Park, New Jersey, he succeeded October 21, 1879, in making an incandescent lamp in which a loop of carbonized cotton thread glowed in a vacuum for more than 40 hours.

He demonstrated the first experimental overhead line for lighting incandescent lamps on January 1, 1880, by having the main street in Menlo Park lighted on New Year's Eve. He demonstrated the first direct current underground power transmission system November 2, 1880. Transmission of electric power using alternating current came shortly after the introduction of the transformer (1882).

In later years, Edison developed a system of wide and efficient power distribution from central generating stations. He organized various companies to exploit and develop his inventions; these were merged into the Edison General Electric Company (1878), the first company to supply power and light. Edison and Thomas Houston Electric Company joined (1892) to form the General Electric Company. Edison went on to develop early stages of movie making and musical recording.

There were many others who contributed to the development of electricity. William J. Hammer (1858–1934), an assistant to Edison, served as chief engineer for the Edison Lamp Works (1880–81). He established the first central station in the world for incandescent electric lighting in London (1882) for the English Edison Company.

Harry W. Leonard (1861–1915), an electrical engineer associated with Edison in introducing the central station electric system (1884), patented the first electric train lighting system (1889) and electric elevator controls (1892).

Thomas W. Davenport (1802–51), blacksmith, developed an electric motor using four magnets, a battery and a commutator in 1834. He was the first to employ principles that are now universal. He received a patent (1837) but could not get financial backing to produce his motor.

Leo Daft (1843–1922) opened a successful photo studio in Troy, New York (1861). He switched to electricity, concentrating on electrical transmission, and built several power plants and electric locomotives. He built the first complete central power station for Massachusetts Electric Power Company (1884) and the next year, the first electric traction system in Baltimore.

Charles P. Steinmetz (1865–1923), an electrical engineer, contributed much to the development of modern alternating-current power systems. He made three major contributions to electrical science — (1) law of hysteresis, making it possible to accurately forecast losses in electrical apparatus due to magnetism, (2) development of a method to calculate alternating current phenomena and (3) the theory of traveling waves which opened the way to develop lightning arresters to protect high power transmission lines.

Moses G. Farmer (1820–93), an educator with a deep interest in mechanics, invented a model electric train, with a passenger car for children and an engine, but it did not attract any financial support. He and William F. Channing (1820–1901) perfected an electric fire alarm system which Farmer had invented earlier. It was installed in Boston (1852). He made electric lamps with platinum filaments to light his home in 1859, 20 years before Edison. Farmer failed to achieve fame because his experimental inventions were solely to satisfy his own curiosity, leaving commercial development to others.

Joseph Henry (1797–1878), while teaching mathematics and natural philosophy, began investigating electrical phenomena, particularly magnetism. His first major achievement was building a powerful electromagnet (1828). By the next year, he had constructed primitive versions of the telegraph and an electric motor. He independently observed the self-inductance of a current in a coil, in honor of which the unit of electrical inductance was named the Henry. He made many other discoveries, including the electric bell (1831) and laid the groundwork for developing the transformer. (He became the first secretary of the Smithsonian Institution 1896).

Nikola Tesla (1856–1943) discovered the rotating magnetic field as an effective method of using alternating current. He adapted this to his induction motor (patented in 1888) which made universal transmission and distribution of electricity possible. He also invented the Tesla coil and devised the basic circuits and apparatus later adapted for wireless transmission.

Charles F. Brush (1843–1929) devised a system of arc lamps for street lighting and invented an improved dynamo and arc lights which he demonstrated successfully in Cleveland on April 29, 1879.

William D. Coolidge (1873–1975), in the early 1900s, discovered that ductile tungsten was a better material for light bulb filaments and developed a method for production. Such filaments are still in use. He also developed a tube for producing x-rays.

George Westinghouse (1846–1914), inventor of the air brake (1869) that made train travel safer, founded the Westinghouse Electric Corporation (1886). He had become interested in the potential use of alternating current for wide distribution of electricity. With the help of scientists such as Tesla, he worked out a practical transmission system for generating, transmitting and conversion of alternating-current power, which became the almost exclusive electric method. Westinghouse produced dynamos, transformers and motors for alternating-current power systems.

The world's first hydroelectric power station began operating September 30, 1882, at Appleton, Wisconsin, 26 days before Edison's steam electric plant began production on Pearl Street, New York City. The first American alternating current hydroelectric plant was built on the Willamette River near Oregon City, Oregon (1889). The plant was the source of the first long distance transmission of alternating-current power, sending power to Portland, 13 miles away. Five years later, the large hydraulic turbines at Niagara Falls went into production.

The first electric company organized to produce and sell electricity was the California Electric Light Company in San Francisco. It began operation on June 30, 1897.

John Wanamaker's store in Philadelphia was the first store to use electric lights on December 26, 1878.

Numerous electrical appliances were invented after 1859: Dr. Schuyler S. Wheeler (1860–1923) invented an electric fan (1882). Henry W. Seeley, of New York City, invented an electric flatiron (1882). Harvey Hubbell of Bridgeport, Connecticut, invented an electric light socket with pull chain (1896). The Kliegl brothers— John H. (1869–1959 and Anton T. (1872–1927)—created the Klieg light for the motion picture industry (1911). Peter Cooper Hewitt (1861–1921) invented the mercury vapor lamp (1901). Oliver B. Shallenberger of Rochester, Pennsylvania, created electric meters (1888, 1895). George B. Simpson of Washington, DC, invented the electric range (1859) and William S. Hadaway of New York City, the electric stove (1896).

The electric toaster was introduced (1926) by Toastmaster; American Electric and Novelty Manufacturing Company produced the flash-light (1898); and General Electric and Westinghouse introduced the tubular fluorescent lamp (1938).

The first commercial system using alternating-current for transmission was built by William Stanley (1858–1916), inventor of the transformer, at Great Barrington, Massachusetts (1886). A similar plant was built in Buffalo the same year.

The photoelectric cell ("magic eye") was demonstrated for the first time by Westinghouse Electric on October 21, 1925; the first commercial installation was used to open doors at Wilcox's Pier Restaurant in West Haven, Connecticut, June 19, 1934.

Edward Weston (1850–1936) came to the United States (1870) to enter the nickel plating business. He built the first successful dynamo for electroplating. He turned to electrical measurement (1886) and his electric instrument company became world famous for quality.

Elihu Thomson (1853–1937) was co-developer of a successful arc lighting system and discovered the alternating current repulsion phenomenon (1883). This led to his successful production of alternating current motors. He also developed a resistance electric welding process, a high frequency generator and transformer, and a three-coil generator.

Conrad Hubert (1855–1928) patented a battery and small electric lamp (1902), which were the basic patents for today's electric flashlight. He continued to improve his "portable electric light" until 1914.

Francis B. Crocker (1861–1921) was instrumental in establishing American electrical standards and with Schuyler S. Wheeler, inventor of the electric fan, founded an electrical equipment company (1888).

Natural Gas

The first American gas company was the Gas Light Company in Baltimore (1817). Rembrandt Peale (1778–1860) introduced gaslights (1816) in his museum in Baltimore. The city council authorized him to manufacture the gas, lay pipes and contracted with him for street lights.

Natural gas was used for manufacturing in Olean, New York (1870), and at Leechburg, Pennsylvania (1873), in iron and puddle mill furnaces. It was first used as an illuminant in Fredonia, New York (1824).

The first gas street lights were installed in Pelham Street, Newport, Rhode Island (1806), in front of the home of David Melville (1773–1856), a pewterer who patented a process for making coal gas. Gas lights in the White House went into operation December 29, 1848.

The first municipal gas plant was that of Wheeling, West Virginia (1871) after the city purchased the Wheeling Gas Co., which had been incorporated in 1850.

Nuclear Power

Nuclear power dates back to the 1930s. George B. Pegram (1876–1958) of Columbia University helped carry out the first successful American demonstration of nuclear fission on January 25, 1939. John Ray Dunning (1907–75), a nuclear physicist, laid the foundation for much of this early development in nuclear physics by measuring the energy released from uranium fission. In 1940, he and Alfred Nier of the University of Minnesota showed that U-235 would undergo fission and helped invent a gas diffusion system for separating U-235 from uranium ore.

Enrico Fermi (1901–54), while experimenting with neutrons in the 1930s, unknowingly achieved nuclear fission. Fermi, along with Arthur Compton (1892–1960), University of Chicago physicist, Leo Szilard (1898–1964) and colleagues, succeeded in achieving a controlled chain reaction of uranium under the Stagg Field stands at the University of Chicago, December 2, 1942, marking the beginning of the atomic age.

Ernest O. Lawrence (1901–58), University of California physicist, demonstrated his first model of a cyclotron, popularly called an atom smasher in 1930. He completed the first large scale cyclotron in 1933, then larger models in 1938 and 1942, with which he was able to convert many stable elements into radioactive isotopes. Some of these were later used in biological and medical research.

Edwin M. McMillin (1907–91), head of the University of California radiation laboratory, with Glenn T. Seaborg (1912–99), isolated plutonium (1941). McMillin helped establish an atomic energy laboratory at Los Alamos, New Mexico (1942) and after World War II developed the synchrotron, which gave atomic particles much higher energies than earlier accelerators. The Atomic Energy Commission took over the nation's atomic energy program on January 1, 1947, with David E. Lilienthal (1899–1981) as chairman. The AEC became the Nuclear Regulatory Commission January 19, 1957.

The first electric power was obtained from nuclear energy (1951) at the AEC testing station at Idaho Falls, Idaho.

The Manhattan Project was organized (1943) for the production of an atomic bomb with General Leslie R. Groves (1897–1970) in charge. The first atomic bomb was successfully exploded at Trinity, near Albuquerque, New Mexico, on July 16, 1945. The first atom bomb was dropped on Hiroshima, Japan, in August 1945, in the first use of atomic energy in warfare. The first peacetime atomic test of a bomb was conducted on Bikini Atoll in the Pacific Ocean on July 24, 1946.

Petroleum

Early development of petroleum began in the 1850s. George H. Bissell (1821–94) and his partner, J. G. Eveleth, bought or leased tracts of land around Oil Creek, Pennsylvania, and began digging wells and trenches in search of petroleum. The first oil refinery was started (1855) by Samuel M. Kier (1813–74), a Pittsburgh druggist who was using the oil for medicinal purposes. In 1858, Bissell conceived the idea of digging deep wells for oil. His Pennsylvania Rock Oil Company, formed January 1, 1855, was the first American oil company and contracted with Edwin L. Drake (1819–80) to drill for oil. Drake developed the first successful oil well near Titusville, Pennsylvania, August 27, 1859. He struck an oil pool at 69½ feet, producing about 25 barrels of oil and the world's first oil well began operation.

The first commercial refinery was erected by William Barnsdall and William F. Abbey (1819–1901) in Oil Creek Valley, Pennsylvania (1860). Abbey took some oil to New York, where he sold 200 barrels to a drug and chemical manufacturer, probably marking the start of the American petroleum industry. He worked actively to build the first refinery and was a co-founder (1867) of an oil pipeline in Pennsylvania.

Barrows and Company of Oil Creek built the first successful pipeline (1862), running from an oil well to a refinery 1,000 feet away. Three years later, a five-mile pipeline from Oil Creek to Pithole, Pennsylvania, was completed. The world's longest crude oil pipeline (1,341 miles) opened between Longview, Texas, and Phoenixville, Pennsylvania, in 1943.

John D. Rockefeller (1839–1937) formed Andrews, Clark and Co. (1863) in Cleveland to enter the oil refining business as a sideline to his produce and commission business. Two years later, the firm became Rockefeller and Andrews and opened a second refinery.

The firm became Standard Oil Company of Ohio (1870), a joint stock company which gained control of the oil industry by 1878. The

Ohio Supreme Court ruled (1892) the company in violation of the Sherman Anti-Trust Act and the stock company was replaced by a holding company, Standard Oil of New Jersey (1899). This company continued until the U.S. Supreme Court ordered its dissolution in 1911.

The Texas oil boom began (1901) with the Spindletop well near Beaumont and the first important commercial oil well in Oklahoma was found the same year.

Over the years there were many developments in the processing of petroleum. Abraham Gesner (1797–1864), a Canadian doctor and geologist, received a patent in March 1855 for a process to make kerosene by heat distillation.

Henry H. Rogers (1840–1909) devised and patented machinery for separating naphtha from crude oil in 1871. While with Standard Oil he originated the idea of long distance pipeline transmission.

Eugene J. Houdry (1892–1962) developed a process (1922) to produce ethyl gasoline, which was first marketed in Dayton, Ohio (1923).

Charles S. Palmer (1858–1939) invented the basic process for cracking oils to obtain gasoline in 1900 (selling the rights to Standard Oil in 1916).

William M. Burton (1865–1954) developed a chemical cracking process in 1912 that doubled the yield of gasoline from crude petroleum and helped make the automobile a practical machine.

Roy Cross (1884–1917) was co-inventor of a petroleum cracking process and designed a number of gasoline refining plants.

Gustav Egloff (1886–1955) devised the multiple-coil process for cracking crude oil that increased the yield of high-octane gasoline.

Edward Ellsberg (1891–1983) invented improved methods of dehydrating and dewaxing lubricating oils and of cracking crude oil for manufacturing anti-knock gasoline.

Herman Frasch (1851–1914), a chemical engineer, developed a process for desulfurizing petroleum and extracting sulfur from underground deposits (1902). This led to development of the sulfur mining industry.

The first gasoline pump was manufactured by Sylvanus P. Bowser (1885). The first drive-in gasoline station was opened in Pittsburgh December 1, 1913, by the Gulf Refining Company.

The first sea-going oil drill was put in service (1955) by C. G. Glasscock Drilling Company; the first successful offshore oil well was drilled in Santa Barbara County, California, in 1896. Construction began March 9, 1975, of an Alaska oil pipeline and the first oil moved 800 miles on July 28, 1977.

8. Entertainment

Amusement Parks/Rides

The amusement parks were best typified by George C. Tilyou (1862–1914), who developed Coney Island —first laying out Bowery, the "amusement street," and building a theater. He opened Steeplechase Park (1897) with rides, many of his own invention, and fun houses. The park grew to 20 acres and Tilyou built other parks elsewhere. (Tilyou is also credited with introducing the hot dog.)

George W. G. Ferris (1859–96), a steel consultant, entered a competition to develop an engineering work to match the Paris Eiffel Tower which would be unveiled at the 1893 Columbia Exposition in Chicago. Ferris built a wheel 250 feet high, capable of carrying 40 people in small cars. The Ferris Wheel worked perfectly and safely and was the marvel of the fair — and later became a standard ride at amusement parks and fairs. Charles W. Parker of Leavenworth, Kansas, developed carousels with moving horses (1896).

Animation

Animated cartoons were tried as early as 1831 by various Europeans. The first cartoon drawn specifically for the movies was by Stuart Blackton (1875–1941) for Vitagraph, of which he was a founder (1906), called *Humorous Phases of Funny Faces*. He was the first to film drawings frame by frame.

This was followed by Winsor McCay (1871–1934), a noted cartoonist who produced "Gertie the Dinosaur" (1909) and adapted the comic strip "Little Nemo" to film (1911). At about the same time, John R. Bray (1879–1967) of New York City patented certain animation procedures and started his *Col. Heeza Liar* series, the first to be released commercially through movie theaters. With Earl Hurd, he helped revolutionize film animation.

Max Fleischer (1883–1972) introduced his *Out of the Inkwell* series in 1922, the first to combine photography with cartoon characters and made the Popeye screen cartoons (1930).

Walt Disney (1901–1966), who was working as a cartoonist in Kansas City, experimented with animated cartoons and produced a series of films (1923–26), *Alice in Cartoonland*, combining live and animated action. The first Disney efforts failed to generate enthusiasm until he put Mickey (originally Mortimer) Mouse into the film *Steamboat Willie*. More Mickey Mouse cartoons drew worldwide audiences and then came *Silly Symphonies*, with new characters—Donald Duck and Pluto. Disney's first color cartoon was *Flowers and Trees* (1932) and the first feature length animated cartoon was *Snow White and the Seven Dwarfs* (1938), which took four years to make and contained 477,000 photographed drawings.

Circus

Another theater form was the circus. The first American circus was that of John Bill Ricketts, a famous English horseman who opened in Philadelphia and New York City (1792). A building was constructed for the Ricketts company at 12th and Market Streets in Philadelphia. His show featured a rope walker, a clown and riding acts. President George Washington attended a performance April 22, 1793. The first circus parade, heralding its arrival, is believed to have occurred in 1837 in Albany, New York. The steam calliope, a familiar circus sight and sound, was invented (1855) by Joshua C. Stoddard. The first circus to be presented in a canvas tent was that of Nathan Howe and Aaron Turner (1826).

A leading name in the circus was that of P(hineas) T. Barnum (1810–91), a legendary showman. He launched a circus in 1871 and ten years later merged with his chief competitor, James A. Bailey (1847–1906), to form the Barnum and Bailey Circus.

The Ringling brothers— Albert (1852–1916), Otto (1858–1911), Alfred (1861–1919), Charles (1863–1926) and John (1866–1936)—began their careers as the Classic and Comic Concert Company (1882). Their song and dance troupe grew with the addition of animal acts and a band. They formed their first circus in 1884 and bought their first elephant in 1888. They bought the Forepaugh-Sells Circus (1906) and a year later, the Barnum and Bailey, thus creating the legendary Ringling Bros. and Barnum and Bailey Circus.

Dance

Ballet was almost non-existent until Stephen Sicard presented his pupils in a work called *The Congress Returns* (1791). The famous French choreographer Alexander Placide (1770–1812) and his wife produced *The Bird Catcher* at the John St. Theater in New York City the next year. The first formal ballet — *The Deserter* — was presented February 7, 1827, in the Bowery Theater in New York City, featuring Madame Francisquy Hutin.

A steady flow of European dancers followed that performance until the 1840–42 visits by Austrian dancer, Fanny Elssler. A long dry spell followed until the Russian ballerina, Anna Pavlova, made a tour (1910), followed by Serge Diaghilev and Vaslav Nijinsky. Then Russians established ballet schools and companies in the United States.

Augusta Maywood (1825–76) was the first American ballerina to achieve international renown. She made her debut at age 12 in Philadelphia and went on to become prima ballerina at Milan's LaScala (1848).

Nora Kaye (1920–87) was unrivaled as a dramatic dancer and had leading roles in *Pillars of Fire* and *The Cage* by Jerome Robbins (1918–98).

Modern dance began with Isadora Duncan (1878–1927), followed by the Denishawn School (Ruth St. Denis 1877–1968 and Ted Shawn 1891–1972), which introduced Martha Graham (1895–1991), Doris Humphrey (1895–1958) and Charles Weidman (1901–75), the latter two forming their own group. Duncan rebelled against the artificiality of the dance, paved the way for modern expressive dancing and was the first to raise dancing to a creative art. St. Denis and her husband, Shawn, were pioneers of modern dance, significantly raising the stature of American dance. Graham was a major influence on dance evolution and Alvin Nikolais (1910–93) created unique environmental theater, choreographing both movement and decor.

Hanya Holm (1893–1992) as choreographer influenced modern dance and Loie Fuller (1862–1928) was noted for her innovations in stage lighting and her "skirt dances."

Bill Robinson (1878–1949), known as "Bojangles," was one of the great Broadway and movie dancers. Paul Draper (1911–97) established his own dance form, combining elements of ballet and tap dancing.

Vernon B. Castle (1887–1918), and his wife, Irene (1896–1969), formed the leading dance team of the years 1912 to 1918 and developed such dances as the one-step, turkey trot and the Castle Walk.

Games and Toys

One of the earliest American games was "craps" (dice), which was introduced about 1813 in New Orleans from France. The name comes from the nickname of a Creole — Johnny Crapaud — whose name gradually became "craps."

The first game manufacturing company was the John McLaughlin Company of New York City (1828). A leader in the field was Milton Bradley (1836–1911), who in 1860 developed a board game, "The Checkered Game of Life." It was a huge success and led to formation of Milton Bradley and Company (1864).

Joshua L. Cowan (1880–1965) invented the toy electric train (1900), Richard Stieff designed the "teddy bear," named for President Theodore Roosevelt (1903), and Rose C. O'Neill (1874–1944) began to produce kewpie dolls about 1910.

Alfred C. Gilbert (1884–1961) formed the Mysto Manufacturing Company (1909) to produce apparatus for magicians. He developed a new toy, the Erector set (1912). His company became the A.C. Gilbert Company, turning out chemistry sets and other materials for young scientists and builders, and took over the American Flyer Company, maker of electric trains (1938).

The first modern crossword puzzle was prepared by Arthur Wynne and published December 21, 1913, in the *New York World*. The first book of crossword puzzles was published by the *World*. The double crostic puzzle was developed by Elizabeth S. Kingsley (1871–1975) and was first presented in the *Saturday Review* (1934).

The ancient Chinese game of mah-jongg was introduced in the United States in 1922 and quickly became a craze. The manufacture of pinball machines began in 1930 by the In and Outdoor Games Company of Chicago.

Bridge was the outgrowth of whist, an old game brought to the colonies. The first American rule book for the game was *The Whist*

Players Hand Book by Thomas Matthews (1844). The American Whist League was founded by 36 clubs April 14–17, 1891, in Milwaukee, during which the first duplicate whist tournament was held.

The first contract bridge game was played aboard a steamer waiting to enter the Panama Canal November 1, 1925. The players were Harold S. Vanderbilt (1884–1970), inventor of the game, and his friends. The first duplicate bridge championship was held July 9, 1914, at the Lake Placid (New York) Club. The bridge "battle of the century" occurred in 1931 between Ely Culbertson and Sidney Lenz and their partners. The Culbertson team won 77 rubbers to 73.

The first American chess champion was Paul Morphy (1837–84). He became champion after winning a tournament conducted October 6, 1857, by the American Chess Congress in New York City. Morphy toured Europe the next two years defeating all chess masters he met and was recognized as the unofficial world champion. The first American officially recognized as world champion was Bobby (Robert J.) Fisher (1943–). At 13, he was the youngest American junior chess champion; at 15 he won the U.S. Chess Federation title and became the youngest to be named an individual grand master (1958). He won the United States championship (1959–61, 1963–66) and defeated Boris Spassky of Russia (1972) to win the world title.

Minstrels

The first truly American form of stage entertainment was the minstrel show of which Thomas D. Rice (1808–60) is considered the founder. An ambitious theater handyman in Louisville, Rice did a song and dance act impersonating "Jumpin' Jim Crow" (1828). This was very popular and Rice followed it with what he called the "Ethiopian Operas," the forerunner of minstrelsy.

Daniel D. Emmett (1815–1904), a fiddler and song writer ("Dixie," "Blue Tail Fly," "Old Dan Tucker"), and Edwin D. Christy (1815–62) formed the Virginia Minstrels (1842), which were later called the Christy Minstrels. They made their New York City debut April 27, 1846, and in 1847 rented Mechanics Hall on Broadway, where they played for nearly ten years. Emmett and Christy started features which later became standard in all minstrels—variety acts, comedy routines revolving around the end men, Tambo and Bones, and a white-faced master of ceremonies, Mr. Interlocutor. Minstrel shows were popular between 1850 and 1870 and were virtually dead by 1900 because of several factors, including the arrival of vaudeville.

Movies

Early attempts at movies date back to the Civil War and animated cartoons to as early as 1831.

Coleman Sellers (1827–1907), a Philadelphia mechanical engineer, patented the Kinematoscope (1861), which showed a succession of phases of an action mounted on the blades of a paddlewheel, which when revolved gave the effect of animation.

Henry R. Heyl presented his Phasmatrope in February of 1870 before an audience of 1,600 in Philadelphia's Academy of Music. This was a wheel on which were mounted six photographs of a waltzing couple that repeated three times.

Then came the Praxiscope (1873) developed by Eadweard Muybridge, an accomplished photographer. He had been hired by Leland Stanford, former California governor and sportsman, to prove by photography that a running horse has all four feet off the ground at a point in his stride. Using 24 separate cameras, Muybridge proved this to be true and became interested in animal locomotion. Muybridge invented the Praxiscope, which projected pictures rapidly on a screen giving the impression of the original motion. This was the forerunner of the motion picture projector.

Thomas A. Edison applied for a patent on his Kinetograph camera and Kinetoscope viewer in 1891 (granted 1893). He apparently thought so little of his own invention that he failed to pay an additional $150 which would have granted him international copyright, something he would later regret. He showed the Kinetoscope at the Brooklyn Institute (1893) and in the next year he copyrighted the first motion picture — 47 successive frames of Fred Ott sneezing, known as the Edison Kinetoscope Record of a Sneeze. His machine stood idle until 1894, when the first of several Kinetoscope parlors opened in New York City. European inventions forced Edison to develop a projector for his Kinetoscope pictures. In June 1895, Thomas Armat, working with Charles F. Jenkins, invented the Vitascope, which projected motion pictures on a large screen. They sold the projector to Edison and it had its world premiere April 23, 1896 at Koster and Biel's Music Hall at 34th Street and Herald Square in New York City.

Edison built the world's first movie studio, the "Black Maria," near his West Orange, New Jersey laboratory for $637.67. Here acts were brought in and photographed for use in the "movies" parlors. Competition again forced Edison to make improvements and to develop a portable version of his Kinetograph. One of the earliest attempts to tell a story on film took place (1897) when R.G. Holloman produced a Passion Play in three reels with a cast of actors and set designs.

However, the real birth of narrative film occurred (1903) with *The Great Train Robbery*, a single reel (about eight minutes) which contained the first evidence of editing technique. Edwin S. Porter (1870–1941), who directed and photographed *Robbery* produced the first story film, *The Life of an American Fireman* (1899), for Edison. The popularity of the *Robbery* film launched the era of the nickelodeon.

This also was the time when pioneering directors and producers emerged. The Warner brothers— Harry (1881–1958), Albert (1884–1967) and Jack (1892–1978)— began showing films in Youngstown, Ohio, and then moved to New Castle, Pennsylvania (1903), where they opened their first theater. It was called a nickelodeon because admission was five cents. They moved quickly and grew. They formed their own distribution company, then a production company (Vitagraph), and by 1918 studios in Hollywood. On August 5, 1926, they released the movie, *Don Juan*, with John Barrymore and a complete synchronized score.

The first sound film picture, *Phonofilm*, was shown (1923) by Lee DeForest. These movies made no stir until the successful part-talking picture, *The Jazz Singer*, with Al Jolson, was shown on October 6, 1927.

D. W. Griffith (1875–1948) toured with several theater groups and then began writing and acting in one reelers with the Biograph Company. He formed his own company (1908) which included such later notables as Lionel Barrymore, Dorothy and Lillian Gish, Mabel Normand, Mary Pickford and H. B. Walthall. Griffith was responsible for lengthening films to two reels (1912) and four reels (1914). He directed and produced nearly 500 films in 23 years. His first great film was *The Birth of a Nation* (1915), which was a sensation, establishing movies both as entertainment and an art.

Mack Sennett (1884–1960) began working with Griffith (1909) and two years later opened his own studio, Keystone Company. He produced and directed the first feature-length comedy, *Tillie's Punctured Romance*, starring Marie Dressler and Charlie Chaplin (1914). Sennett, who turned out about 1,000 short films, including the "Keystone Kops," was considered the founder of American slapstick comedy.

Cecil B. DeMille (1881–1959) began in the theater at age 19, co-authored a number of plays and then joined with Samuel Goldwyn (1882–1974) and Jesse L. Lasky (1880–1958) to form the Lasky Feature Play Company (1913). The company produced the first full-length film, *The Squaw Man* (1913). DeMille produced more than 70 films, including spectacular historical and biblical films like *The Ten Commandments*.

Other pioneers in the movie industry were:

Carl Laemmle (1867–1939) bought two prospering movie houses (1906) and then went into distributing and making films for other distributors (1910). Two years later he founded Universal Pictures.

William Fox (1879–1952) went into the movie business (1904) by buying a Brooklyn nickelodeon for $1,600, then formed an exhibition and production company, and a chain of theaters. He formed the Fox Film Corporation (1915) and virtually controlled the production and distribution of silent film.

Louis B. Mayer (1885–1957) followed the familiar route of movie house owner, then a chain, and a distribution firm. He formed his own company (1918), which eventually became part of Metro-Goldwyn-Mayer (MGM).

Marcus Loew (1870–1927) developed a chain of nickelodeons by 1905, then added theaters, bought Metro Pictures (1920) and absorbed Goldwyn Pictures four years later. Loew and Mayer joined forces to form MGM.

The first color moving pictures were exhibited at Madison Square Garden Concert Hall December 11, 1907, showing fast-moving pictures through red and green screens. Technicolor was developed (1915) by Herbert T. Kalmus (1881–1963), a chemical engineer, and the first successful technicolor picture was *The Toll of the Sea* (1922). However, color was not considered important until the success of *Gone with the Wind* in 1939.

Some additional movie firsts were: The first motion picture theater, Electric Theater, 252 S. Main Street, Los Angeles, opened April 2, 1902; the first drive-in movie theater, Camden, New Jersey, opened June 5, 1933; the first newsreels were Pathe News in November of 1910.

Robert J. Flaherty (1884–1951) was a pioneer in documentary film-making—*Nanook of the North* (1923), *Moana* (1926), *Man of Aran* (1934). He established standards for all nonfiction filmmakers.

Cinerama, a three-film strip process, was demonstrated September 30, 1952, in New York City and stimulated interest in wide screens. Cinemascope was introduced for the film *The Robe* (1953).

The first Oscars were presented by the American Academy of Motion Picture Arts and Sciences on May 16, 1929, in Hollywood. The first winners were Emil Jannings for best actor, Janet Gaynor for best actress, Frank Borzage and Lewis Milestone for best directors, and *Wings* as best motion picture.

Will R. Hayes (1879–1954) served as "movies" czar (President, Motion Picture Producers and Distributors) from 1922 to 1945.

Louella Parsons (1893–1972) was the first movie columnist, beginning with the *Chicago Record-Herald* (1914).

Parades

The first Mardi Gras celebration was held in New Orleans (1827) by students who organized a procession on Shrove Tuesday. The first decorated floats appeared in 1857. The first Mummers Parade was held in Philadelphia (1876).

Puppetry

A long-enduring form of entertainment was puppetry and the first English-style puppet show in America was *The Adventure of Harlequin and Scaramouche* in New York City (1738) performed by Henry Holt of London.

One of the earliest references to puppetry was an advertisement in the *Pennsylvania Gazette* on December 30, 1742, telling of a performance on Chestnut Street each evening with several scenes including "an agreeable comedy or tragedy by changeable figures of two feet high." During the nineteenth century the format of the puppet show was variety with string puppets.

The start of the twentieth century first saw a revival of puppetry at the Chicago Little Theater (1914). Tony (Anthony F.) Sarg (1882–1942) created his first troupe in 1915, appearing in New York City two years later. Sarg toured the country and set a pattern of shows with high standards, which were carried on by many others he trained, including Rufus Rose (who animated "Howdy Doody") and Bill (William B.) Baird (1904–87).

Showboats

Another area of stage entertainment was the showboat which became popular after the Civil War. The first showboat was probably *Noah's Ark*, with a group of itinerant players under Noah M. Ludlow (1795–1886), a veteran actor. He converted a keel boat and began putting on shows (1817) on the Cumberland, Ohio and Mississippi rivers. The first boat built to be a showboat was the *Floating Theater* built (1851) for William Chapman Sr., a British actor, and his family of six. The theater had a tiny stage, equipped with tallow candle footlights, wooden benches and seats for 200. The most spectacular showboat was the *Floating Circus Palace*, which seated 3,400 and had 100 performers and crew, and 40 animals, plying the Mississippi (1852). Another early boat was Henry Butler's, which traveled the Erie Canal serving as a "museum" by day, a theater at night.

Augustus B. French, a showboat entertainer, at age 45 married 16-year-old Callie Leach and they built their first showboat, *The New Sensation* (1878). In the next 25 years, the French's had five boats, the last being captained by French's widow after his death in 1902. (She had become the first licensed woman boat pilot on the Mississippi, in 1888.) Other showboat operators were Edwin A. Price; Ralph Emerson (1881–1914), who operated nine boats after 1900; Sam Bryant and son, Billy; and the Menke brothers, Bill, Harry, Ben, and Charlie.

Theater

The American theater began in the 1700s with almost exclusively foreign performers. By the 1800s, American settlers began developing their own theater forms and actors. The first performance by non-professionals was given August 27, 1665, in Accomack County, Virginia. The play was *Ye Bare and Ye Cubb* by Philip A. Bruce. The play would not have been remembered "if a puritanic spectator had not felt that such a manifestation of wickedness deserved the condemnation by the law...." After two court hearings the three actors were found not guilty of "sedition" and "the court found nothing corrosive of society" in the play.

The first professional theater troupe was led by Lewis Hallam (1740–1808) with a production of *The Merchant of Venice* in Williamsburg, Virginia, September 15, 1752. This first professional theater production in the colonies was followed by other Hallam productions.

In the next several decades, both Philadelphia and New York City developed their own theater companies, as did several Southern cities. As new cities sprang up, more theaters were built and touring companies visited them. An American theater was built (1718) facing the Palace Green in Williamsburg by William Levingstone, a merchant and surgeon, and operated by Charles Staff, a dancing master, and his wife, Mary. The first formal theaters came after the Revolution in Philadelphia and Newport, Rhode Island (1793), and New York City the following year.

The first professionally-produced play (1759) by an American was *The Prince of Parthia*, written by Thomas Godfrey (1736–63) and shown April 24, 1767, in the Southwark Theater in Philadelphia.

Other early productions included:

William Dunlap (1766–1839), the first American professional playwright, wrote *The Father of an Only Child*, produced in New York City (1789), followed by *Leicester* (1794) and *Andre* (1798), which featured an American history theme.

Royall Tyler (1757–1826) wrote the comedy, *The Contrast*, which was produced April 16, 1787, developing the popular theme of the native, shrewd rural Yankee.

John A. Stone (1800–34) wrote *Metamora* (1828) which introduced the Indian character to American plays and also introduced Edwin Forrest (1806–72), the first native star.

Two other early popular themes of American plays were introduced by Benjamin A. Baker (1818–90), who featured the tough city boy in *A Glance at New York* (1848) and Frank Murdoch (1843–72), who featured the frontiersman in *Davy Crockett* (1872).

Joseph Jefferson (1829–1905), a renowned actor, is best remembered for his adaptation of Washington Irving's *Rip van Winkle*, in which he starred (1859–1905).

Dion Boucicault (1820–90) exerted a tremendous influence on the American stage, writing or adapting more than 130 plays. He is credited with establishing the "long run"— showing a play in New York City then taking it on tour with different actors.

Augustus Thomas (1857–1943) wrote plays (*Alabama, In Mizzoura, Arizona*) which helped develop the popular American theater.

Following Edwin Forrest, many leading contributors to the American stage appeared:

Maurice Barrymore (1847–1905) and his actress wife, Georgianna Drew, launched what became known as the "royal family" of the American theater. He and his wife performed and toured for many years and were joined by three Barrymore children — Lionel (1878–1954), Ethel (1879–1959) and John (1882–1942) — all stars.

Junius B. Booth (1796–1852), an English stage star who came to the United States at age 21, dominated the American stage for 30 years. He was the father of actors Edwin T. Booth (1833–93), considered by some the greatest actor of the nineteenth century, and John Wilkes Booth (1838–65), best remembered as the assassin of President Lincoln.

Richard Mansfield (1854–1907) came to the United States at age 17 with his singer mother and ten years later was a sensational hit in *A Parisian Romance*. He continued as a leading actor for 25 years.

David Belasco (1853–1931), a noted producer, playwright and actor who pioneered extensive and imaginative lighting and the use of realistic props and sets.

George M. Cohan (1878–1942), a member of a vaudeville family, began his career at age nine. He acted, sang and danced, wrote plays and music ("Over There," "You're a Grand Old Flag," "Yankee Doodle Dandy").

Charles Frohmann (1860–1915), a theatrical producer and manager, was largely responsible for the star system.

Florenz Ziegfeld (1869–1932) made a unique contribution to the American theater with his musical revues beginning in 1907. He set standards of taste and artistry that influenced the theater.

Other contributors to the American stage included William Gillette (1853–1937), noted actor best known for his Sherlock Holmes; James H. Hackett (1800–71), the first American actor to win international fame; James W. Wallack (1795–1864), a leading actor and theater manager for 35 years; Charlotte Cushman (1816–76), the first great American tragedienne; and Minnie Maddern Fiske (1865–1932), a pioneer of theatrical realism.

Schools for persons with theatrical ambitions began with the Lyceum

School in New York City, opened 1884 by Franklin W. Sargent (1856–1923). The "school of expression" opened ten years earlier by (James M.) Steele Mackaye (1842–94), actor and playwright. They were succeeded by the American Academy of Dramatic Arts (1888).

Two theatrical designers made unique contributions to the development of the American stage — Robert E. Jones (1887–1954), a pioneer in imaginative staging, and Jo Mielziner (1901–76), who was responsible for some of the finest theatrical sets.

In the reporting and criticism of the theater there was George Jean Nathan (1882–1958), who did much to raise the nation's cultural standards and tastes.

A theater institution, *Variety*, the show business weekly, was founded (1905) by Sime Silverman (1873–1933) with a staff of three turning out 16 pages. By 1933 the weekly had a staff of 225 and issues were often more than 100 pages. The Theater Guild, considered the starting point of modern American theater, was formed (1918) in New York City.

The first actors union was the Actors National Protective Union (1896), which merged with two other groups (1919) to form the Associated Actors and Artists of America.

Steele Mackaye, who ran a theatrical school, also invented an elevator stage and developed artificial ventilation and overhead and indirect lighting for stages.

The first "little theater" was established (1915) by George C. Cook (1873–1924), when he founded the Playwright's Theater in New York City after organizing the Provincetown Players.

Burlesque was brought to the United States (1868) by Lydia Thompson's troupe of "British Blondes," which included a chorus line of girls in tights. Burlesque became a male patronage show and was popular until 1950.

Vaudeville

Vaudeville was the outgrowth of traveling acrobats, singers and story tellers who went to places not reached by formal theater companies. In some larger cities there were so-called museums, such as P.T. Barnum's American Museum in New York City, which added freaks, trained animals and skits.

The Franklin Theater in New York City advertised itself (1842) as the first variety theater, offering programs that came to be known as vaudeville. The Jay Morris Concert and Olio Company of 20 persons offered variety programs at the Franklin, including live models, magic lantern slides, comic lectures and other features.

Tony (Antonio) Pastor (1837–1908) got his early training with circuses and opened a music hall (the American Theater) on lower Broadway about 1862. He sang original songs (he wrote more than 2,000) and was considered the greatest vaudevillian of the time. Pastor dedicated a small theater on 14th Street offering a "straight, clean variety show" (1881).

Benjamin F. Keith (1846–1914) also began with the circus and with Edward F. Albee (1857–1930) opened the popular-priced Gaiety Theater in Boston (1883). It was the first American theater to offer continuous performance variety shows. Keith conceived the idea of a chain of vaudeville theaters, presenting refined entertainment, and convinced many stage performers to appear in vaudeville. Keith and Albee controlled 400 theaters by 1920, mostly in the East.

Their major opposition was the Orpheum Circuit founded (1903) by Martin Beck (1867–1940), who had theaters from Chicago to California and built the New York Palace Theater, which became the outstanding American vaudeville house (1913–32).

9. Food and Drink

Beverages

Archaeologists have discovered portable stills in early Virginia compounds, giving rise to the belief that early American settlers found they could make whiskey from corn. Settlers planted orchards early and could make cider or peach brandy from their fruit. Colonists began to grow malt and hops and beer production followed, with two breweries in Virginia by 1629 and one in Massachusetts by 1637.

Rum was an early popular drink and the prosperity of New England rested on rum used to barter for slaves, gold and ivory. There were some 150 rum distilleries in New England by 1763. The rum was made from molasses, most of which came from the West Indies.

American brewing began when the British brewed beer in their first attempt to colonize in America (1584). Dutch colonists reportedly set up a brew house in 1612 on Manhattan Island. Massachusetts issued regulations (1657) for the ingredients of beer. William Penn (1644–1718) erected the first brewery in Pennsylvania and Francis Perot's Sons Malting Company in Philadelphia was established by Anthony Morris (1654–1721). Only British types of beer were produced until the 1850s and then the German brewer, John Wagner, in Philadelphia, introduced new methods of making lager beer, setting the foundation for the modern American industry.

Adolphus Busch (1839–1913) became president of the St. Louis brewery founded by his father-in-law, Eberhard Anheuser (1861); it became the Anheuser Busch Brewing Company (1879). Busch developed a lighter, drier beer, making it possible to ship it long distances unrefrigerated.

Among the early leaders in beer brewing were the Ruppert Brewery in New York City (1867) and the Schaeffer Brewing Company, which introduced bottled beer (1891).

Early settlers tried to grow European grapes in the East but the climate was unfavorable. Adapting native grapes succeeded when John Alexander in Indiana began a winery (1801) and it flourished for many years. In 1818, Thomas Eichelberger was able to grow commercially successful wine grapes in York, Pennsylvania, and Elijah Fay began his first vineyard in the Chautauqua grape belt of New York. Nicholas Longworth, often called the father of American grape growing, made the first American champagne in Cincinnati (1842).

California wines began with Mission wines for sacramental purposes in the 1600s. Jean Louis Vignes imported French grape vines (1833) but it was not until after the Gold Rush that grape growing began to thrive. After the first transcontinental railroad opened, California wines were able to invade the Midwest and Eastern markets and become leading sellers.

American soft drinks date back to the beginning of the nineteenth century. Benjamin Silliman (1779–1864), a Yale University chemist, began producing bottled soda water on a commercial scale (1807), opening a public establishment for its sale.

Joseph Hawkins invented machinery (1809) with which he produced carbonated water in Philadelphia and John Matthews (1808–70) used machines of his own to make soda water which he sold to drugstores. Introduction of flavors to soda water began early but its exact origin is unknown. Charles E. Hires (1851–1937), a Philadelphia druggist, developed root beer, which was introduced successfully at the 1876 Centennial Exposition in Philadelphia. Hires, while on his honeymoon in New Jersey (1875), was served a drink made of sassafras bark, sarsaparilla root, juniper berries and other roots. After considerable experimentation, he developed a packageable, water-soluble concentrate from which root beer could be made. Asa G. Candler (1851–1929) was a pharmacist who purchased the formula for a soft drink from a patent medicine maker (1887). Candler improved it, named it Coca-Cola and developed a successful manufacturing and distribution system.

William Horlick (1846–1936) began producing malted milk in 1883.

The first license to sell coffee in the United States was issued to a Dorothy Jones of Boston (1670) and the Merchants Coffee House was established in New York City (1737). Charles W. Post developed a substitute for coffee, Postum (1894), which was a huge success.

Almost as quickly as settlers developed liquors, opposition to the use of spirits arose. The Quakers began their warnings in the eighteenth century and farmers in Litchfield, Connecticut, formed a temperance society. Intensive religious revivalism spurred formation of temperance groups and the American Society for the Promotion of Temperance was formed (1826). Massachusetts passed its "15 gallon law" (1828) which limited sales of less than 15 gallons of liquor — but the law was repealed in 1840. Maine passed the first state prohibition law (1846) which it strengthened in 1851. Its example was followed by 13 states by 1850. However, that was a temporary fervor because most of the states soon repealed the laws until a new wave of prohibition set in between 1880 and 1890.

A real temperance movement is said to have started Christmas Eve, 1873, when Eliza Trimble Thompson of Hillsboro, Ohio, led 70 women from a prayer meeting to the outside of a saloon where they sang and pleaded with the owner to close. The National Women's Christian Temperance Union (WCTU) was organized November 18, 1874, in Cleveland with Frances E. C. Willard (1839–98) serving as secretary the first five years and president for the next 20. The Anti-Saloon League began in Oberlin, Ohio (1893), and was the model for the national league formed December 18, 1895, in Washington. The National Prohibition Party was formed (1869) with James Black (1823–93) as its first presidential candidate in 1880.

Prohibitionists gained their first national victory (1913) when a law was passed prohibiting transportation of intoxicating beverages into a dry state. Then came national prohibition (18th Amendment) which went into effect in 1920, lasting until 1933.

Candy

John Hannan began operating a chocolate mill at Dorchester, Massachusetts (1765), which became Baker and Company (1780). Milton S. Hershey (1857–1945) formed a company (1903) to make chocolate bars and the town of Hershey, Pennsylvania, grew around the plant, which became the largest producer of chocolate products.

The first chewing gum ("Maine Pure Spruce Gum") was made in Bangor, Maine (1848), by John Curtis. William Wrigley, Jr. (1861–1932), began making chewing gum (1891), along with soap and baking powder. As the gum business grew rapidly, he dropped the others. Then Wrigley added the flavoring spearmint to the gum (1899).

The Racine (Wisconsin) Confectioners' Machinery Corporation developed a machine (1908) to make lollipops.

The first popcorn was introduced to the Pilgrims (1630) at their first Thanksgiving dinner by the Indians who contributed a deerskin bag filled with corn for the dinner.

Cereals

The first American oatmeal maker was Ferdinand Schumacher (1822–1908), who organized the German Mills American Oatmeal Company (1854).

Will K. Kellogg (1860–1951), operator of a Battle Creek, Michigan, sanitarium with his brother, developed a crunchy breakfast food which was used in the sanitarium and sold by mail order. The mail order business grew and became the Sanitas Food Company (1900), and later the W. K. Kellogg Company. The new cereal, Corn Flakes, revolutionized American eating habits, replacing the traditional heavy, hot breakfast with cold cereals.

Henry Perky of Watertown, New York, founded the Shredded Wheat Company (1893) and Charles W. Post (1854–1914) launched a line of breakfast foods about 1900 after successfully developing a coffee substitute (Postum).

Cookbooks

The first American cookbook, modeled on an English book, was *The Compleat Housewife* (1742). Another of the first American cookbooks (1796) was *American Cookery* by Amelia Simmons. Eliza Leslie (1787–1858) wrote several cookbooks between 1828 and 1854.

A long-lasting popular cookbook is that of Fannie M. Farmer (1857–1915), director of the Boston Cooking School (1891–1902). She operated her own school after 1902 to train housewives rather than servants. Farmer published her first cookbook (1896) making a major contribution by introducing standardized level measurements.

Sara Tyson Rorer (1849–1937), a domestic science teacher and cooking school operator, is believed to have been the first American dietician. The first American cooking school — New York Cooking School — was opened by Juliet Corson (1842–97) in her home on St. Martin's Place (1876).

Dairy

The first American commercial creamery is believed to have been built by R. S. Woodhull in Orange County, New York (1756).

Gail Borden (1801–74) had several failures in trying to prepare dried or condensed foods. Borden lived in a Shaker community in New Lebanon, New York, and succeeded in making condensed milk by copying the Shaker vacuum-pan method of making maple syrup. Borden patented the condensed milk process (1856) and organized the New York Condensed Milk Company which became the Borden Company (1899). The demands of the Union Army during the Civil War made condensed milk a success.

John B. Meyenberg of Highland, Illinois, introduced canned evaporated milk (1884) and Samuel K. Percy of New York City patented dried milk (1872). Stephen M. Babcock developed a simple test for butterfat content of milk (1890) which eliminated the practice of watering milk.

Farmers of Cheshire, Massachusetts, founded a cheese cooperative (1801) and the first cheese factory of consequence was built (1851) by Jesse Williams of Rome, New York. Alfred Paraf of New York City patented a process (1873) for the manufacture of oleomargarine.

Ice cream was probably introduced in the colonies very early from England and ice cream parlors appeared at the end of the 1700s. A Mr. Hall of 76 Chatham Street (now Park Row), New York City, advertised ice cream on June 8, 1786. George Washington's expense ledger showed the purchase of a "cream machine for ice" (1784). A hand-cranked freezer was invented (1846) and the first ice cream factory was built in Baltimore (1851) by Jacob Fussell.

The ice cream soda was invented (1879) and the ice cream sundae is said to have been introduced at the Red Cross Pharmacy in Ithaca, New York, about 1897. Legend has it that Charles S. Menchey, an ice cream salesman, gave an ice cream sandwich and flowers to his girlfriend. He rolled a sandwich layer into a come to serve as a vase for the flowers. The cone was introduced publicly at the 1904 Louisiana Exposition in St. Louis. Christine K. Nelson of Onawa, Iowa, patented the Eskimo pie January 24, 1922.

Flour

The flour rolling mill, invented in 1880 by John Stevens (1820–90) of Neenah, Wisconsin, increased production by 70 percent and improved flour quality.

Charles A. Pillsbury (1842–99) bought a small flour mill (1869) and developed it into the world's largest flour milling company by 1889. Pillsbury took full advantage of new machinery and methods, and skillfully used advertising and promotion of his products.

Sylvester Graham (1794–1851), a health and temperance lecturer, promoted the use of coarsely ground, unsifted whole grain wheat flour, which came to be known as graham flour. He developed the graham cracker.

Theodore Pearson opened a cracker bakery (1792) in Newburyport, Massachusetts, and Josiah Bent (1771–1836) began making hard water crackers (1801) in Milton, Massachusetts. Crackers, almost a household necessity in New England, were made of flour and water and used no salt or shortening.

First shortening made by hydrogenation of vegetable oils (Crisco) was introduced by Procter & Gamble (1911). Compressed fresh yeast was introduced (1868) by Charles Fleischmann (1834–97). His yeast did not attract any interest until the 1876 Philadelphia Centennial Exposition and the yeast became popular. He devised an elaborate system for delivering fresh yeast.

Food Preservation

William Underwood (1787–1864) opened a food preserving firm in Boston (1820). Isaac Winslow began experimenting with canning corn in 1830, patenting his process.

Gilbert C. Van Camp (1817–1900) opened a cannery for fruits and vegetables in Indianapolis (1861).

Henry J. Heinz (1844–1919), while working in his father's brick manufacturing plant, conducted a wholesale business in fresh vegetables he grew on his own land. With a brother and cousin, he founded (1876) the F and J. Heinz Company to make and market pickles, ketchup and baked beans. The firm became the H. J. Heinz Company (1888) and grew to include seed farms, several container factories and many food-processing plants.

John D. Dole began canning pineapple in Hawaii (1903).

George A. Hormel and Company, founded in 1892, produced the first canned hams.

Thomas Kensett and his father-in-law, Ezra Daggett, founded a firm to can salmon, oysters and lobsters in New York City (1819). Twenty years later the glass containers used for canning were replaced by tin-plated cans.

William Hume (1830–1902), his two brothers and a friend began canning salmon in California (1864), then moved to Washington on the Columbia River. By 1881, the Humes had more than a dozen canneries.

Clarence Birdseye (1886–1956) developed a process to freeze foods and founded a company (1930) that began freezing, a mode of food preservation which grew tremendously.

Fruit

Some fruit was brought to Florida by Spanish explorers in the 1500s who used the fruit to trade with the Indians. Soon citrus fruit trees were growing wild near rivers and lakes from seeds dropped by the Indians.

The first seedless navel oranges were grown in the United States by the Department of Agriculture, which brought a dozen budded saplings from Brazil (1872). Jonathan Tibbett got two of the trees (1873) and planted them at his Riverside, California home, starting the industry.

The first grapefruit was planted in Florida (1835) by a Spanish noble-man, Don Phillippe.

Henry Perrine (1797–1840), American consul in Mexico, collected many tropical fruits which he planted in Florida and imported the first avocado (1833), which was planted in California.

Minor C. Keith (1848–1929) went to Costa Rica to help his brother build a railroad. Keith completed the line after his brother died (1894). While there, he began experimenting with banana growing. He acquired several banana plantations and formed (1899) the United Fruit Company, which became dominant in the Central American banana business.

Honey

Lorenzo L. Langstroth (1810–95) became an apiarist (1852) at Oxford, Ohio. His invention of the first movable frame beehive revolutionized beekeeping and his methods became standard in honey production. Amos I. Root (1839–1923) was a manufacturer of beekeepers' supplies and probably did more than anyone to commercialize American beekeeping.

Meat

William Pynchon (1590?–1662) became the first American meat packer in 1636. He was from Springfield, Massachusetts.

Gustavus F. Swift (1839–1903) entered the meat business (1855) when he peddled dressed beef door-to-door. He established Swift and Company (1875) and revolutionized the industry when he began volume shipment of dressed beef in refrigerator cars (1877). Earlier, cattle were shipped to the East where they were slaughtered. Swift also led in finding uses for previously unused animal parts for making soap, glue, fertilizer and other by-products.

George H. Hammond (1838–86) was first to use refrigerated cars to ship dressed beef to the East. In 1868 or 1869, Hammond shipped beef from Detroit to Boston using a car built by William Davis (1812–68). The first shipment was a success and additional cars were built.

Philip D. Armour (1832–1901) entered meat packing and the grain business in 1863. Two years later he guessed that pork prices would fall with a Union victory so he sold barrels of pork at $30 to $40 for future delivery. Armour was right and was able to buy the pork for $18, netting nearly $2 million profit. Three Armour brothers organized the firm (1870) making Chicago the center for pork.

Michael Cudahy (1841–1910) was general superintendent for Armour's Chicago operations and launched Summer meat curing under refrigeration (1870). Meat packing to then had been a winter season business. Cudahy and Armour opened the first meat packing plant in Omaha, which became Cudahy Packing Company (1890).

The Bureau of Animal Industry was created May 29, 1884, to conduct federal meat inspection.

Chop suey was prepared by the Chinese embassy chef in New York on August 29, 1896; the dish was unknown in China.

Restaurants

In the field of American restaurants, several names stand out: Lorenzo Delmonico, Howard D. Johnson, Fred(erick H.) Harvey, and Ray Kroc.

Delmonico (1813–91) joined his uncles in a catering business in New York City (1832) and they opened a restaurant on William Street. It was unusual for its time, being open during the day and offering a wide range of domestic and European foods. He opened a new restaurant (1835) on Broad Street, which was an immediate success and followed by a number of branches. Delmonico led the way in making New York City a culinary center.

Johnson (1897–1972) took over a debt-ridden drugstore and soda fountain in Wollaston, Massachusetts (1924). He built up a large ice cream business serving 28 flavors. The first restaurant bearing his name opened 1929 in southern Massachusetts and its owner named it Howard Johnson to capitalize on the growing fame of the ice cream.

Harvey (1835–1901) offered to open a restaurant if the Santa Fe Railroad gave him space in the Topeka, Kansas, depot. An attractive, clean restaurant (1876) succeeded and was followed by 46 other restaurants, 13 hotels and 30 dining cars. Harvey did much to enhance long distance rail travel.

The lunch wagon was introduced in Providence, Rhode Island (1872), by Walter Scott; the first cafeteria was opened in Chicago (Adams Street between Clark and LaSalle) (1895) by Ernest Kimball; the first self-service restaurant, the Exchange Buffet, opened September 4, 1885, in New York City; the first automatic food vendor, the Automat, was opened 1902 at 828 Chestnut Street, in Philadelphia by Horn and Hardart.

The first penny restaurant (most items were one cent) was opened by Bernarr A. Macfadden (1868–1955) at 487 Pearl Street, New York City, and by 1906 there were 30 in operation.

McDonald's fast food chain was started in 1955 by Ray A. Kroc (1902–84).

Sugar

Sugar was brought to Louisiana by Jesuit priests from the Dominican Republic and the first practical sugar refinery was opened in 1791 in New Orleans by Antonio Mendez.

Jean Etienne Boré successfully granulated sugar and launched the Louisiana sugar industry. Valcour Aime (1798–1867) built the first American sugar refinery and made continuous improvements in sugar manufacture.

Norbert Rillieux (1806–94) made technological improvements in sugar refining including the first practical evaporation pan.

California Sugar Refining Company was founded (1863) by Claus Spreckels (1828–1908) and a brother. He improved the processing of Hawaiian sugar and later added refining of beet sugar. By 1883, Spreckels' firm had a near monopoly of refining and marketing sugar in the West.

Henry O. Havemeyer (1847–1907) merged 15 sugar refineries in the New York City area to form the Sugar Refineries Company (1887). Four years later it became the American Sugar Refining Company and by early 1900s produced about half the sugar used in the United States.

Sugar beets were first grown in the United States about 1830 at Ensfield, Pennsylvania, and E. H. Dyer established the first successful American beet sugar factory at Alvorado, California.

10. Health

Ambulances

The earliest ambulance service was provided by the Commercial (now General) Hospital in Cincinnati prior to 1865. Similar service was begun (1869) by James F. Wood (1813–82), co-founder and chief surgeon, Bellevue Hospital, in New York City.

Anesthesia

Anesthesia was of great importance in the development of medical treatments. Its beginnings lay in dentistry where the value of nitrous oxide was discovered by Horace Wells.

Crawford W. Long (1815–78) is considered to have been the first to use an anesthetic in American surgery. On March 30, 1842, he removed a tumor from the neck of a man to whom he had given ether. By September, 1846, Long had completed eight successful operations but had not published the results. When he finally did (1849), others were claiming the discovery of anesthesia — William T. G. Morton, a dentist who brought it into common use; Charles T. Jackson (1805–80) and Horace Wells. Eventually Long's claim was recognized.

Samuel Guthrie (1782–1848), a chemist, was one of three men who independently discovered the process for making chloroform (1831) and Albert Einhorn synthesized "procain" (novocain) in 1905. Carl Koller (1857–1944) introduced the use of cocaine as a surface (local) anesthetic in eye surgery (1944).

Blood

The discovery of human blood groups (1900) by Karl Landsteiner (1868–1943) led to typing of blood, which, along with the work of Alexis Carrel in suturing blood vessels, made safe blood transfusions possible. Landsteiner received the 1939 Nobel Prize. Others who made important contributions to the knowledge of human blood were immunologist William C. Boyd (1903–83); Edwin Joseph Cohn (1892–1953), developer of a method of separating proteins found in blood; and Philip Levine (1900–87), who, with Landsteiner and Alexander Wiener (1907–76), as the first to recognize the Rh factor in blood (1940).

The first blood bank opened (1937) in Cook County Hospital in Chicago, the first eye bank in New York Hospital, New York City (1944), and the first bone bank at the New York Orthopedic Hospital (1946).

The first blood bank was devised by Charles R. Drew (1904–50), who developed a method of storing blood plasma. He organized programs in the United States and Great Britain during World War II. The irony of Drew's contribution is that the Red Cross refused to accept his blood because he was black. Drew fought successfully to change that policy. Years later, he was injured in an automobile accident in North Carolina, was turned away from a nearby hospital because of his race and died en route to another hospital — one for blacks.

Dentistry

Dentistry in the United States began with the American Revolution when two French dentists, Joseph LeMayeur and James Gardette, came to help the Americans and taught dentistry to several men in the colonial army. Among the trainees was John Greenwood (1760–1819), who began his practice in New York City about 1785. He is credited with having developed a foot-powered dental drill and with introducing porcelain artificial teeth. Two sets of teeth he made for George Washington are still in existence.

The first American-born dentist, Josiah Flagg (1737–95) began practicing (1782) in Boston. The New York City Dispensary for the Poor began providing dental service in 1791—a fee of 50 cents was charged for extractions and silver-lead fillings, one dollar for gold fillings.

Eleazar Parmly (1797–1874) began his career assisting his dentist brother in Boston and then for two years (1817–18) was an itinerant dentist floating an "ark" on the Mississippi and Ohio rivers. After several years in Europe, he began a successful practice in New York City and was a leader in getting recognition for dentistry as a profession.

Horace H. Hayden (1769–1844) and Chapin A. Harris (1806–60), doctors who also practiced dentistry, tried to establish a dentistry department at the University of Maryland. When that failed they founded the Baltimore College of Dental Surgery, the world's first dental school (1839). Harris also founded the first dental periodical, the *American Journal of Dentistry* (1839) and in the same year published one of the most popular dental books, *The Dental Art*. The first American dental textbook was published by R. C. Skinner in 1801, *A Treatise on the Human Teeth*, written to promote his dental practice.

The first school of orthodontia was founded (1895) by Edward H. Angle (1855–1930) in St. Louis. Five years earlier, he had become a specialist, limiting his practice to orthodontics.

Anesthesia was an outgrowth of dentistry. Horace Wells (1815–48), a dentist, watched a demonstration of using nitrous oxide ("laughing gas") in 1844. He persuaded the demonstrator to use the gas on him while another dentist (John M. Riggs) extracted one of his teeth. The extraction was painless and Wells began using nitrous oxide in his practice. About two years later, William T. G. Morton (1819–68), who practiced with Wells and had experimented with ether, made a successful, painless tooth extraction.

John Allen (1810–92) developed a type of platinum denture (1851) which is still in use. Prior to Allen's method, dentures were porcelain teeth fastened to gold plates but there was no way to prevent oral secretion between the teeth. With a porcelain "continuous gum" over the plate, teeth could be set in any arrangement and at the same time be sealed against seepage of oral fluids.

Greene V. Black (1836–1915) developed silver amalgam (1895) for filling cavities and was the first to enlarge the cavities before filling them, a method still in use. John H. Beers, of San Francisco, patented a gold crown (1873); Mahlon Loomis (1826–86) invented a kaolin process (1854) to make artificial teeth, and William H. Taggart, of Chicago, developed a casting process (1907) that made gold inlay fillings possible.

The first dental chair to provide a head rest and position changes was designed by M. Waldo Hanchett of Syracuse (1848); a dental mallet and removable bridge were invented (1875) by William C. A. Bonwill (1833–99); an electric dental drill was invented by George F. Green of Kalamazoo, Michigan (1875); and Frank Abbott (1836–97), dean of the

New York College of Dentistry (1869–97), invented numerous dental instruments (scalers, chisels, excavators, pluggers), some of which are still in use.

The first local dental society was the New York Society of Surgeon-Dentists founded in 1814.

Education

American medical education goes back to 1730 when Thomas Cadwalader (1708–99) opened a private school of anatomy in Philadelphia and to 1750 when John Bard, the first New York City health officer, and Peter Middleton (d 1781), a medical professor at King's College (later Columbia), performed the first recorded dissection of a human body for medical instruction.

Most colonial doctors learned medicine from such popular handbooks as *Every Man His Own Doctor; or, the Poor Planter's Physician* (1743). A few had served apprenticeships in other doctors' offices and much fewer had received medical degrees abroad.

The first American medical school (College of Physicians in Philadelphia) was organized (1765) by John Morgan (1735–89) and William Shippen. It later became the University of Pennsylvania School of Medicine, graduating its first class in 1768. A medical school was created at King's College (1767) through the efforts of Samuel Bard (1742–1821), son of John Bard. It was reorganized in 1811 as a separate institute — College of Physicians and Surgeons — with Bard as president (1811–21).

A major figure in American medicine, Benjamin Rush, introduced clinical instruction at the Philadelphia Hospital and initiated the Philadelphia Dispensary (1786), the first free dispensary.

Nathaniel Chapman (1780–1853), who went on to become the first president of the American Medical Association (1848), founded the first American postgraduate medical school, Philadelphia Medical Institute (1817).

The first specialty medical colleges were: pharmacy — Philadelphia College of Apothecaries (1821); homeopathic medicine — North American Academy of Homeopathic Healing Art, Allentown, Pennsylvania (1835); optometry — North Illinois College of Optometry and Otology (1872); coeducational medical — Boston University School of Medicine (1873).

Elizabeth Blackwell (1821–1910) became the first woman to earn an

MD degree in modern times, graduating (1849) at the head of her class of Geneva (New York) Medical School. After postgraduate work in Europe, she opened a private clinic in New York City (1853), which four years later became the New York Infirmary, staffed entirely by women.

Mary Harris Thompson (1829–95) became the first American woman surgeon (1863) after graduating from the New England Medical College. She founded a hospital in Chicago for widows and poor children (1865).

Medical education was greatly influenced by the Johns Hopkins Medical School, which began in 1893 and admitted only college graduates with a year's training in the natural sciences. Another major influence was the 1910 study and report by Abraham Flexner (1866–1959), of the Carnegie Foundation for the Advancement of Teaching, which called for improvements in medical education. The report forced many schools to raise their standards, about 60 to close and modern medical education dates from that report.

Hospitals

While the Pennsylvania Hospital in 1752 was the first, there were earlier facilities for medical care. In St. Augustine, Florida, settlers in 1565 set aside six beds in a home for the poor. The first secular hospital was established by the Dutch West India Company in New Amsterdam (1658) as a pesthouse for soldiers and sailors (a facility to care for infectious diseased patients). It later became a combination city poorhouse, house of correction and penitentiary, orphan asylum and hospital for the pauper sick and insane.

In 1847, the West India Company formed the foundation for Bellevue Hospital. Similarly, Old Blockley, founded in Philadelphia (1713), went through comparable phases and eventually became the Philadelphia General Hospital. The Urusline Order in New Orleans created an infirmary open to all persons (1734).

The first dispensary to provide free medicine for the needy was established in Philadelphia (1786) by Episcopal Bishop William White and the City Dispensary for the Medical Relief of the Poor opened 1791 in New York City.

Some physicians and surgeons who led in the founding of hospitals were: John Kearsley, doctor and teacher, endowed and founded Christ

Church Hospital in Philadelphia. He also was an architect and designed Christ Church.

The first interracial hospital in the United States was the Provident Hospital in Chicago (1891). The founder was Daniel H. Williams (1858–1931), a surgeon who was not permitted to work in the local hospitals because he was black. Provident also included the first nurse training school for black women.

Joseph B. DeLee (1869–1942) pioneered in free medical care for needy mothers and founded the Chicago Lying-In Hospital (1895) and the Chicago Maternity Center (1932).

Abraham R. Jackson (1827–92) limited his practice to gynecology (1870) and the next year founded the Woman's Hospital of Illinois in Chicago.

James M. Sims (1813–83), another gynecologist, led in the founding of the Woman's Hospital in New York City (1855).

Edward Delafield (1794–1875), one of the first Americans to concentrate on ophthalmology, helped found the New York Eye Infirmary (1820) and the American Ophthalmological Society (1864), serving as its first president.

The first orthopedic hospital was the Hospital for the Ruptured and Crippled in New York City (1863). The first community hospital opened in Elk City, Oklahoma (1929), and the first crippled children's hospital was the Gillette State Hospital in St. Paul, Minnesota (1897).

Laboratories

Physiologist Henry P. Bowditch (1840–1911) founded the first laboratory for experimental medicine (1871) and in that same year Harvard created the first American physiological laboratory for students. Providence, Rhode Island, established the first municipal health laboratory (1888) and Rhode Island created the first state laboratory six years later. The first American pathology laboratory was developed (1879) at the Bellevue Hospital Medical College by William H. Welch (1850–1934).

Literature

Medical publications and books did much to spread news of advances and of developments. The first medical magazine was *The Medical Repository*, published in New York City (1797). The first to publish results of research projects was the *Journal of Experimental Medicine* (1896), published by William H. Welch, a pathologist who developed the first American pathology laboratory at Bellevue Hospital Medical College.

William Brown (1752–92), physician-general of the Continental Army, published the first American pharmacopeia (official list of medicines) (1778); it contained 32 pages entirely in Latin. This was followed by Lyman Spalding (1775–1821), who published the *United States Pharmacopeia* (1820).

Robley Dunglison (1798–1869) published the *New Dictionary of Medical Science and Literature* (1833), which became the standard of medicine. William Osler (1849–1919) wrote *The Principles and Practice of Medicine* (1892), which for 30 years dominated the field and was translated into many languages. The book is credited with inspiring the start of Rockefeller support of medical research.

John Jones (1729–91) wrote the first surgical textbook, *Plain ... Remarks on the Treatment of Wounds and Fractures* (1775).

Medical Devices

Michael I. Pupin (1858–1935), a physician, developed a machine with which he produced the first American x-ray picture (1896) and Francis L. Satterlee (1881–1935), who began taking x-rays at 15, invented a protective shield for x-ray operators.

Philip Drinker (1894–1972) and Louis A. Shaw (1886–1940) developed the first respirator (iron lung), a laboratory model (1927) at the Harvard School for Public Health. A second machine was used at the Boston Children's Hospital the next year on a young girl with polio.

Charles F. Taylor (1827–99), an orthopedic surgeon, developed braces and other types of orthopedic appliances.

Medicine

Physicians were among the first arrivals in Jamestown and Plymouth settlements. Lawrence Bohune arrived in Jamestown (1610) and Samuel Fuller arrived on the *Mayflower* at Plymouth (1620). Bohune returned to England for a visit in 1622 and on the way back to Virginia his ship was attacked by Spaniards and Bohune died in the fighting.

The colonists generally enjoyed good health but they suffered occasional disastrous epidemics— smallpox in nearly every city (Boston 1666, 1678, 1721; New York City 1731–32; Philadelphia 1730, 1732, 1736; Newport 1739); dysentery in New York City (1683), and yellow fever in Charleston (1729, 1739).

John Kearsley (1684–1722) settled in Philadelphia (1711) and his medical office was called the "first college" in the colonies. Kearsley taught and trained many early doctors, among them William Shippen (1736–1808), Thomas Bond (1712–84), and John Bard (1716–99).

Bond, with the help of Benjamin Franklin, founded the Pennsylvania Hospital (1752), the first in the nation. Bond also helped found the medical school at the College of Philadelphia (later the University of Pennsylvania) in 1765. He is credited with devising a splint for certain fractures and introducing the use of mercury in medicine.

New York became the first colony to license physicians (1760) but most states still had no licensing procedure in 1851. In 1776, there were about 3,500 medical practitioners but only about 400 had gone to medical schools.

Philip S. Physick (1768–1837), called the "father" of American surgery, originated or improved several surgical techniques, procedures and instruments.

John C. Warren (1778–1856), a co-founder and first surgeon of Massachusetts General Hospital (1821), performed the first surgical operation using ether as an anesthetic on October 16, 1846.

Zabdiel Boylston (1679–1766) was the first to give smallpox inoculations (at the urging of Cotton Mather). During a Boston smallpox epidemic (1721), despite public opposition, Boylston inoculated 241 persons, including his two sons. Only six died, including four who had the disease before inoculation. Benjamin Waterhouse, a co-founder of Harvard Medical College, introduced vaccination with cowpox vaccine to prevent smallpox (1800). Other pioneers in inoculation were James Jackson (1777–1867) and Elisha North (1771–1843).

Nursing

An integral part of medical care is nursing, which did not gain much recognition until after the Civil War.

Valentine Seaman (1772–1817), a physician at New York Hospital, developed a course of lectures for 24 nurses (1798), the first organized nurses training in the United States. He continued the training until 1817.

At the start of the Civil War, there were no trained nurses. Volunteer women in New York City organized the Women's Central Association of Relief, which later became the United States Sanitary Commission. Most of the nursing during the Civil War was done by untrained volunteers.

A school of nursing was started at Bellevue Hospital, New York City (1873), along with similar schools in New Haven and Boston. The first interracial hospital, Provident, in Chicago, set up a nurses training school for black females (1891).

The first superintendent of nurses, Mary A. Nutting (1858–1948), was named at Johns Hopkins Hospital (1894). She later (1907–25) became the first full-time professor of nursing and head of the nursing department at Columbia University.

North Carolina enacted the first state law (1903) requiring state examinations and registration of nurses. All other states quickly followed.

Lillian D. Wald (1867–1940) founded the Henry Street Settlement in New York City (1895) and organized the first nonsectarian health nursing system in the world. She extended the nursing service to a local public school (1902). It was so successful the city's Board of Health created a city-wide public school nursing program, the first anywhere.

Obstetrics

Gunning S. Bedford (1806–70) founded the University Medical College, New York City (1840), which also included the first free obstetric clinic.

William P. Dewees (1768–1841) was one of the first to specialize in obstetrics at a time when the "man-midwife" was ridiculed. He was very successful and also taught the subject.

Horatio R. Storer (1830–1922), a pioneer gynecologist, founded a gynecological journal, the first publication devoted exclusively to diseases of women.

Charles Knowlton (1800–50) was the first physician to publish a popular tract on birth control (1832). He was prosecuted and jailed for three months in Cambridge, Massachusetts.

Margaret Sanger (1883–1966) opened the first American birth control clinic in Brooklyn (1916). A year later, she founded the National Birth Control League, which became the Planned Parenthood Foundation (1942).

Ophthalmology

The bifocal eyeglass was invented by Benjamin Franklin in 1785 because he was annoyed at having to wear two pairs of glasses. After the invention he wrote: "I have only to move my eyes up or down as I want to see distinctly far or near."

Edward Delafield was the first American to concentrate on ophthalmology and with fellow surgeon, John K. Rodgers, started the New York Eye Infirmary (1820) on Chatham Street, New York City. Delafield founded and headed the American Ophthalmological Society (1864).

Edward G. Loring (1837–88) devised the first practical ophthalmoscope.

Lucien Howe (1848–1928), founder of the Buffalo Eye and Ear Infirmary (1876), was instrumental in getting New York State (1890) to require application of prophylactic drops into the eyes of newborn children. Vermont passed a law (1903) requiring annual eye examinations of school children.

George M. Gould (1848–1922) invented bifocal lens glasses (1888) and bifocal contact lenses were developed by Newton K. Wesley of Chicago (1958). Plastic lenses for cataract patients were first used in 1952 and plastic contact lenses in 1954.

Organizations

Societies and boards grew with the medical profession and helped direct and manage care-giving.

Failure of the province to regulate medical practice led to the formation of a "medical society" in Boston (1736) under the leadership of Dr. William Douglass (1691–1752). Physicians in Connecticut, Massachusetts and New York formed the Sharon Medical Society (1779) and the Medical Society of Massachusetts was founded in 1781. The American Medical Association (AMA) was founded (1847) in Philadelphia.

The Humane Society of Philadelphia was organized (1780) to provide emergency first aid and to recover drowned persons.

Municipal health boards were created in Baltimore (1798), followed by Charleston, South Carolina (1815), and Philadelphia (1818). Two sanitary surveys in Massachusetts (1850) and New York City (1865) sparked interest in public health programs. Massachusetts was the first to create a state health board (1869) and by 1919 all states had health departments and boards.

Elisha Harris (1824–84) was a founder of the U.S. Sanitary Commission during the Civil war and invented a hospital "car" to transport the wounded. He helped organize the New York City Health Board and organized the first free vaccinations in the city (1869).

Charles F. Chandler (1836–1925), head of the New York City Health Board, made a great many contributions to public health, the most notable of which was the flushing toilet. He refused to patent his invention so that it quickly became available to all.

Osteopathy/Chiropractic

Osteopathy in the United States was founded 1875 by Andrew T. Still (1828–1917). He opened the American School of Osteopathy in Kirkville, Missouri (1892). Chiropracty was first practiced in 1895 by Daniel David Palmer (1845–1913) and three years later he opened a school in Davenport, Iowa.

Pediatrics

The practice of pediatrics goes back to Abraham Jacobi (1830–1919), who opened the first free pediatrics clinic in New York City (1860) and was the first American professor of children's diseases.

Thomas M. Rotch (1849–1914) began practicing pediatrics in 1876. He was the first to limit his practice to children.

The first hospital for infants was the Babies Hospital on 36th Street, New York City (1887), with eight beds; the first hospital for children was the Nursery and Child's Hospital in New York City (1854).

Alfred Blalock (1899–1964), chief surgeon at Johns Hopkins, and Helen B. Taussig (1898–1986) developed a successful operation (1944) to save "blue babies," infants suffering from a lack of oxygen. The operation marked the beginning of modern heart surgery.

One of the most popular American pediatricians was Benjamin N.

Spock (1903–99), whose book *Baby and Child Care* (1946) was a best seller for many years.

The first incubator for infants, then called a "hatching cradle," was built (1888) by William C. Deming of New York City and the first baby carriage (1848) in New York City by Charles Burton. There was such criticism of the carriage because it constantly hit passersby. Burton moved to England, where he built a successful business.

Pharmaceuticals

The growth of American medicine was helped by the discovery and development of vaccines and pharmaceuticals. The activities of apothecaries were so well established by the time of the American Revolution that the Continental Congress created an office of Apothecary General, headed by Andrew Craigie (1743–1819).

Harry Plotz (1890–1947), bacteriologist, developed a protective vaccine against typhus; John F. Enders and Hans Zinsser (1878–1940) developed the first anti-typhus vaccine (1930).

Theophil Mitchell Prudden (1849–1924), a pathologist at Rockefeller Institute, was the first to make a diphtheria antitoxin in the United States about 1880.

John J. Abel (1857–1938) isolated insulin in crystalline form (1926) and Jokichi Takamine (1854–1922) isolated adrenalin from the suprarenal gland (1901), the first gland hormone discovered in pure form.

Rene J. Dubos (1901–82) isolated tyrocidine and gramicidin (1929), which were too toxic for internal use but were effective on various external infections.

Percy L. Julian (1899–1975) synthesized physostigmine, used in treating glaucoma, and later synthesized steroids from a soya base.

Edward C. Kendall, biochemist, helped isolate cortisone (1948) and used it clinically for arthritis.

Benjamin M. Duggar (1873–1956), a botanist, discovered aureomycin chlortetracycline, the first broad spectrum antibiotic (1948).

Selman A. Waksman (1888–1973) and his Rutgers University co-workers isolated streptomycin (1943), the first specific agent found to be effective in treating tuberculosis.

John Ehrlich discovered chloramphenicol (1947); it was useful against bacilli unaffected by penicillin.

Ira Remsen and a pupil, C. Fahlberg, discovered saccharine at Johns

Hopkins University (1879). Remsen organized the Johns Hopkins chemistry department (1876) and became school president in 1901.

The first American pharmacy professor was Samuel P. Gifford at the Philadelphia College Medical School (1789).

Pharmaceutical companies made numerous contributions over the years. Edward R. Squibb (1819–1900), while serving as a Navy assistant surgeon (1847), discovered that many of the drugs supplied him were of poor quality or impure. He was permitted to establish a laboratory at the Brooklyn Navy Hospital to produce chemicals and drugs (1851). When the military later refused to provide funds, he resigned and set up his own lab (1858), which prospered during the Civil war. Squibb drafted the first pure food and drug laws in New York and New Jersey.

Among other pharmacy firms were Johnson and Johnson (1886), original producers of adhesive and medicated plasters after Robert W. Johnson (1854–1930) and George J. Seabury (1844–1909) first produced medicated plaster (1874); Albert C. Barnes (1872–1951), who created the antiseptic argyrol (1901); Jacob Dunton, a Philadelphia wholesale druggist, was first to produce compressed pills or tablets commercially during the Civil War; DuPont Company first produced sulfanilamide (1930), and Charles Pfizer and Co. produced the antibiotic tetramycin (1950).

Along with the general medical practice, there also were patent medicine makers and sellers. Especially popular and well-known was the home remedy of Lydia E. Pinkham (1819–93) for women's disorders. The Panic of 1873 caused her to begin marketing her remedy which was widely advertised and purchased even though medical science found no therapeutic value in the remedy. James C. Ayer (1818–78), a doctor and Lowell, Massachusetts, druggist, marketed a reputed remedy for pulmonary troubles.

Physiology

The treatment of many diseases depended on the growing knowledge of the body and its functions. Among the leading physiologists was Anton J. Carlson (1875–1956), who contributed much to the understanding of the body — the heart and circulation, lymph, saliva, the thyroids and parathyroids, the pancreas and immune bodies.

Walter B. Cannon (1871–1945) was one of the greatest physiologists and the first to utilize x-rays in his studies. Detlev W. Bronk (1897–1975) contributed much to the understanding of neuromuscular and nerve physiology.

Psychology

Psychological factors were often important in treating an illness. Abraham A. Brill (1874–1948) is considered the founder of American psychoanalysis, introducing Freudian practice to the United States. Adolf Meyer (1866–1950) directed the psychiatric clinic in Johns Hopkins University (1910–41) and made it the world's foremost psychiatric training center.

Karl A. Menninger (1893–1990) and his father, Charles F. (1862–1953), founded the non-profit Menninger Foundation (1920) in Topeka, Kansas, to study, treat and prevent mental illness. William C. Menninger (1899–1966), Karl's brother, also joined them.

In the field of mental health, Benjamin Rush, a major medical figure, wrote the first systematic American book on mental illness (1812) and led the way toward its rational treatment.

Clifford W. Beers (1876–1943) was the outstanding figure in developing organizations to cope with mental illness. He suffered a nervous breakdown (1906) and was confined for two years in institutions. Beers learned that institutions provided no help to inmates and wrote a popular book on his experiences. He organized the Connecticut Society for Mental Hygiene (1908), the first such organization in the world. Then he led in founding the National Commission (1909), the American Foundation (1918) and the International Foundation (1931).

Another early leader in the field was a teacher, Dorothea L. Dix (1802–87). She was asked to run a Sunday school in prison and was shocked by the inhumane treatment of the insane. She studied the problem in Massachusetts for two years, then convinced the state legislature to enlarge the state asylum. Over the next 40 years Dix inspired the building of 32 institutions in the United States and several in Europe and Japan, staffed with well-trained personnel.

Specialists

Medicine quickly developed into areas of specialty as knowledge of illnesses and cures grew through research and studies.

In 1822, surgeon William Beaumont (1785–1853) had a patient with a gunshot wound which left a permanent two-and-a half inch opening in the stomach. Beaumont was able to study human digestion and the digestibility of foods through this opening. He published a study (1833) which is considered the greatest single contribution to knowledge of gastric digestion.

Calvin B. Bridges (1889–1938), a geneticist, made important contributions to the study of heredity.

Alice Hamilton (1869–1970), a toxicologist, pioneered in the study of industrial diseases and hygiene.

Charles W. Stiles (1867–1941) discovered the hookworm (1902), a widespread Southern parasite.

The first major comprehensive study of sexual behavior was directed by Alfred C. Kinsey (1894–1956), director of Indiana University Institute of Sexual Research.

Thomas M. Rivers (1888–1962) was the American pioneer in studying viruses which he considered distinct causes of disease.

Raymond Pearl (1879–1940), a biologist, began applying statistical methods to biology, laying the foundation for biometry.

Surgery

Among the firsts in American surgery were: Abdominal (ovariotomy)— Ephraim McDowell (1771–1830) performed the first ovariotomy on Christmas Day in 1809 without anesthetics, removing a 20-pound tumor from a Kentucky woman. The patient lived another 20 years. Appendectomy — William W. Grant (1846–1934) of Davenport, Iowa (1885). Caesarean — Jesse Bennett, on his wife, Elizabeth, in Edom, Virginia (1794). Gallstones— John S. Bobb of Indianapolis (1867). Heart — Claude S. Beck (1894–1971) of Cleveland (1935) (angina);Daniel H. Williams of Chicago (1895) (repair of damaged artery); Floyd J. Lewis implant of assisting heart using deep freeze method (1952) at University of Minnesota Medical School. Kidney transplant — Richard H. Lawler (1895–1982) of Chicago (1950). Liver transplant — Thomas E. Starzl (1963). Lobotomy — James W. Watts of Washington, DC, and Walter Freeman (1895–1972) in 1956. Lung transplant — James B. Hardy (1964); lung removal — Everts A. Graham (1883–1957) of St. Louis (1933). Mastoid — Joseph C. Hutchinson of Brooklyn (1859). Hysterectomy — Paul F. Eve (1806–770.

William S. Halsted (1852–1922) performed what was probably the first successful blood transfusion in the United States (1881). Halsted gave his own blood to his sister, who was hemorrhaging after childbirth. He made many contributions to surgery — wearing of rubber gloves, using silk sutures instead of catgut, and injection of cocaine around nerve trunks to block sensation in limited areas (1885). Halsted established the first school of surgery (1890) at Johns Hopkins Hospital.

Other major contributors to surgery include William W. Keen (1837–1932), the first American brain surgeon. Alexis Carrel (1873–1944) developed new methods of suturing blood vessels, making it possible to perform safe transfusions and paving the way for further studies of blood vessels and organ transplants.

George W. Crile (1864–1943) made many contributions with studies of surgical shock and was an early user of blood transfusions.

Harvey W. Cushing (1869–1939), a founder of neurosurgery, developed many new techniques and procedures for surgery of the brain and spinal cord.

Henry G. Davis (1807–96) founded the "traction school" of orthopedic surgery, using continuous traction for providing relief of joint irritation.

Robert Battey (1828–95) was a pioneer in abdominal surgery.

Charles McBurney (1845–1913) pioneered in antiseptic surgery and was an authority on appendectomy.

James M. Sims began using silver wire for sutures (1849). This was followed by catgut and silk, and Roy P. Scholz of St. Louis developed fiberglass sutures (1939).

Heart — Michael E. DeBakey (1908–) pioneer American heart surgeon, was the first to perform now standard operations to correct aneurysms and artery obstruction, and led to the first artery bypass operation (1964). He invented a roller-type heart pump, now a key part of heart-lung machines.

Adrian Kantrowitz (1918–) performed the first American heart transplant operation in 1967, the world's second. He developed several artificial heart devices to help pump blood. With Dr. DeBakey, he implanted an "assisting" heart to help a diseased overworked heart.

The first totally-artificial heart was implanted April 4, 1969, by Denton A. Cooley (1920–) but the patient died four days later. The first permanent artificial heart was implanted in a human being in 1982 and kept the patient alive three months.

Throat

Horace Green (1802–66) was the first American physician to specialize in diseases of the throat and air passages and John Watson (1807–63) is credited with being the first in the United States to perform an esophagotomy (1844).

Treatment of Disease

Scarlet fever — George F. Dick (1881–1867) and his wife, Gladys (1881–1963), discovered the germ of the disease and developed a serum for its cure (1923).

Polio — Thomas M. Rivers pioneered in the study of viruses and was actively involved in the long range study that led to the discovery of the Salk vaccine. Thomas H. Weller (1915–), John F. Enders (1897–1985) and Frederick C. Robbins (1916–) developed the polio virus in tissue culture, making it possible to develop a vaccine. They shared the 1954 Nobel Prize.

Jonas A. Salk (1914–95) developed the first vaccine against polio, widely used in the United States after massive field testing (1954). Albert B. Sabin (1906–92) developed the oral polio vaccine from live virus (1956) and it was widely used in many countries because it was inexpensive to make and could be stored for long periods of time. The vaccine was licensed in the United States (1961) but not widely used because by then polio had been virtually eliminated.

Yellow fever/malaria — Walter Reed, Jesse W. Lazear and William C. Gorgas were the leaders in reducing the number suffering from these diseases. Reed (1851–1902) was an Army physician who headed a commission which determined that a certain type of mosquito transmitted the disease. Lazear (1866–1900), a member of the Reed commission, was convinced the mosquito was the carrier. He allowed himself to be bitten by a mosquito and survived the fever with a diseased heart. Later, he was accidentally bitten and died nine days later. Gorgas (1854–1920) administered effective mosquito control programs in Havana and Panama with sharply reduced incidences of yellow fever and malaria.

Arthritis — Biochemist Edward C. Kendall (1886–1972) helped isolate cortisone (1847) with Philip S. Hench (1896–1965) and they were the first to use it in treating arthritis.

Addison's disease — Robert F. Loeb (1895–1973) made studies of salt metabolism to control the disease and George W. Thorn (1906–) made studies of adrenal cortex which led to treatment of the disease.

Diabetes— Eugene L. Opie (1873–1971) established (1902) that diabetes results from destruction of specific portions of pancreatic tissue.

Diphtheria — Bela Schick (1877–1967), while still in Hungary, developed a skin test (1913) for determining the susceptibility to diphtheria. He was later chief pediatrician at Mt. Sinai Hospital in New York City. Hermann M. Biggs (1859–1923), a pioneer in preventive medicine, introduced the use of diphtheria toxin in the United States (1894).

Infantile paralysis— Simon Flexner (1863–1946), laboratory director of Rockefeller Institute of Medical Research, successfully isolated the infantile paralysis germ.

Appendicitis— Reginald H. Fitz (1843–1913) identified and named the disease (1886) and proposed radical surgery for its cure.

Cancer — William J. Hammer, an electrical engineer who worked with Edison, first suggested using radium for cancer treatment and William Duane (1872–1935), a biophysicist, developed methods and apparatus for using x-rays and radium in treating cancer. Emil H. Grube began x-ray treatment of cancer soon after the 1896 development of the x-ray machine. The earliest users of radium in treating the disease were Robert Abbe (1851–1928) and Howard A. Kelly (1858–1943).

John J. Bittner (1904–61) contributed to the theory that cancer is caused by a virus and Charles B. Huggins (1901–97) discovered the role of hormones in treating cancer of the prostate. Huggins shared the 1997 Nobel Prize.

George F. Papanicolaou (1883–1962) developed the "pap" smear test (1928) for the early detection of cervical cancer. The test was ignored until 1940.

The first cancer hospital was the New York Cancer Hospital at 106th Street and Central Park West, New York City (1887), and the first municipal cancer hospital was the New York Cancer Institute on Welfare Island (1923).

A free cancer home for incurables was established in New York City (1896) by Mother Alphonsa (1851–1926) and later became the Rosary Hill Home in Hawthorne, New York. Mother Alphonsa, who organized the Servants of Relief for Incurable Cancer, was Rose Hawthorne, daughter of the famous writer.

The first cancer laboratory was created by New York State at Buffalo University (1898) with Roswell Park (1852–1914) as director.

Tuberculosis— Channing House in Boston became the first tubercular home (1857) and the first tuberculosis hospital was the National Jewish Hospital in Denver (1899). The first modern tuberculosis sanitarium was begun by Edward L. Trudeau (1848–1915) at Saranac Lake, New York (1884). Trudeau, a doctor and victim of tuberculosis, lived in the Adirondacks and studied the disease. He founded the Adirondack Cottage Sanitarium (now Trudeau Sanitarium), the first American effort of open-air treatment of the disease. The Saranac Laboratory (1894) was the first in the United States devoted to the study of the disease. William A. Park (1863–1939), of the New York City Health Department, developed a tuberculosis vaccine (1928). Emily P. Bissell (1861–1948) designed the Christmas seal (1907) and launched the first sales drive to aid tubercular children.

Pellagra — Joseph Goldberger (1874–1929), a public health surgeon, discovered (1925) that the cause of pellagra was a vitamin deficiency and this led to its virtual extinction.

Heart — Dickinson W. Richards (1893–1973), with Andre F. Cournand (1895–1988) and Werner T. Forssmann (1904–79), perfected a technique to make accurate measurements of heart and lung functions. This became known as cardiac catheterization and opened a new era in heart research.

Veterinary Medicine

The first American veterinary surgeon, John Haslam, arrived from England (1803). Charles C. Grice, an English veterinary graduate, opened the first American veterinary hospital (1820) in New York City. Boston Veterinary Institute was the first veterinary college (1855); Iowa State College was the first state veterinary school (1879).

Vitamins

Casimir Funk (1884–1967), biochemist, first isolated thiamine, later known as Vitamin B-1, in 1912. His work began a revolution in biochemistry and nutritional science.

Elmer V. McCollum (1879–1967) discovered Vitamins A and D and demonstrated the relationship between proper nutrition and good health; Herbert M. Evans (1881–1971) and Katherine S. Bishop discovered Vitamin E (1922); Albert Szent-György (1893–1986) and Charles G. King

(1896–1988) discovered Vitamin C (1932), and Edward L. Rickes discovered Vitamin B-12 (1948).

Edward A. Doisy (1893–1986) isolated what became known as Vitamin K (1939) and developed a method of producing and handling the delicate compound valuable in treating hemorrhages.

Lafayette B. Mendel (1872–1935), physiological chemist, was one of first to show nutritive value of vitamins and proteins. He helped establish the modern science of nutrition. Mendel discovered Vitamin A (1913) and the function of Vitamin C.

Wilbur O. Atwater, director of the U.S. Office of Experiment Stations, published tables of caloric potential of many foods (1896); the tables as still used.

Horace Fletcher (1849–1919), a nutritionist, attributed good health to thorough mastication of food. "Fletcherism" and "to fletcherize" became part of the American language.

Thomas B. Osborne (1859–1929), biochemist, investigated vegetable proteins and discovered vitamins in cod liver oil.

11. Labor

Labor Unions

One of the first American labor unions was the Federated Society of Journeymen Cordwainers (shoemakers) organized in Philadelphia August 1, 1794. When the union struck, a Philadelphia court ruled the strike a "conspiracy" of workers and a criminal act. A New York court held all efforts to raise wages illegal (1834).

Some years later, the Massachusetts Supreme Court ruled that it was not unlawful to strike to gain a close shop. Any illegality of the strike depended on the means used.

Two early strikes occurred in New York City — master bakers walked out (1741) in protest of regulation of bread prices and printers struck (1778) and won a three dollars a week increase.

Early attempts to create a national labor union included William H. Sylvis (1828–69), a member of the Iron Molders Union. He helped found the National Labor Union, which he headed from 1868 to 1869.

The Knights of Labor was organized December 30, 1869, as a secret society with Uriah S. Stevens as its first head. Terence V. Powderly (1849–1924) became the Knights' leader (Grand Master Workman) in 1879 and served 14 years. He was deposed because of his opposition to striking as a weapon and favoring arbitration.

A conference of labor organizations held November 15, 1881, in Pittsburgh resulted in forming the Federation of Organized Trades and Labor Unions, predecessor of the American Federation of Labor.

An early labor leader was Samuel Gompers (1850–1924), a cigarmaker like his father. He reorganized the Cigarmakers Union (1877), introducing high dues, strike and pension funds, and restricting union activities to economic issues. He helped found the Federation of Organized Trades, which became the American Federation of Labor on December 8, 1886. Gompers was president of the AFL until his death (except in 1895).

Gompers was succeeded by William Green (1873–1952), secretary-treasurer of the United Mine Workers, who served from 1924 to 1952. During Green's presidency the industrial and craft unions formed the Congress of Industrial Organizations (CIO) in 1935.

John L. Lewis (1880–1969), a miner since he was 15, joined the United Mine Workers and became a local president. Elected president of the UMW (1920), he became a general field agent for the AFL. He helped form the Committee for Industrial Organizations. The AFL expelled the ten unions represented by the Committee, which became the CIO on November 14, 1937, with Lewis as president. Lewis opposed the third-term effort of President Roosevelt in 1940 and when the president was elected, Lewis resigned as CIO president. Two years later he took the UMW out of the CIO and back to the AFL.

Philip Murray (1886–1952), vice president of the UMW (1912–40), became CIO president after Lewis' resignation, serving from 1940 to 1952.

After Green's death, George Meany (1894–1980), became AFL president and Walter P. Reuther (1907–70), United Auto Workers president, succeeded Philip Murray as CIO head (1952). Meany and Reuther negotiated the merger of the AFL and CIO (1955) with Meany as president.

Some other early labor leaders included:

William B. Wilson (1862–1934), organizer of the UMW (1890) and the first Secretary of Labor (1913–21).

Sidney Hillman (1887–1946), president of the Amalgamated Clothing Workers (1915–46).

Cesar Chavez (1927–93), founder of the California Grape Pickers Union, the first important American farm workers union.

Sara A. M. Conboy (1870–1928), was the first woman national labor union officer (Secretary-Treasurer, United Textile Workers 1914–28).

William D. Haywood (1869–1928), organizer of the Industrial Workers of the World (1905), the foremost American radical organization.

Worker's Rights

Regulation of wages and hours goes back to the early 1800s. Massachusetts enacted a law (1836) forbidding the employment of children under 15 for more than nine months of the year, requiring such children to attend school the other three months. The state set a maximum work day of ten hours for children under ten in 1842.

President Martin Van Buren ordered a ten-hour day for laborers and mechanics working on federal projects without any reduction in pay (1840). The work day was reduced to eight hours for these workers (1868) and in 1906, the eight-hour day applied to all federal workers.

The 40-hour work week with time and a half for overtime was required of all companies with government contracts (1936); it was applied nationally in 1940.

The Fair Labor Standards Act of June 25, 1938, raised the minimum pay in interstate commerce from 25 to 40 cents an hour with time and a half for overtime and prohibited employment of children under 16. The minimum wage has been increased from time to time since then.

The government took other labor actions beyond wages and hours. The first publicly-financed employment offices were established by cities— New York City (1834), San Francisco (1868), Los Angeles and Seattle (1893). Ohio established the first state-directed system (1890). The federal government's action began (1907) when the Bureau of Immigration and Naturalization began to distribute immigrant labor among the states. The Bureau developed the beginnings of a nationwide employment opportunity information system (1914). World War I intensified the need for an organized public employment system and the U.S. Employment Service was established January 3, 1918, in the Labor Department.

Dorman B. Eaton (1823–99) headed the Civil Service Commission (1873–75), which was ineffective. He drafted a National Civil Service Act (1883) and headed a revitalized commission (1883–86). An act was passed (1920) requiring compulsory retirement at 70 and an annuity after 15 years service.

Legislation to cover railroad workers was passed June 27, 1934, upholding their rights to organize and bargain, and created a national Railroad Adjustment Board. The Railroad Retirement Board was created August 29, 1935, to administer railroad retirement and unemployment insurance programs.

Illinois prohibited the employment of women in coal mines (1879). The Bureau of Labor was created in 1884 in the Interior Department.

Four years later, a labor department was created and headed by a commissioner. The Department of Labor and Commerce was created (1903), headed by George E. Cortelyou (1862–1940) as first secretary. The department was divided in 1913 with William B. Wilson as Secretary of Labor and William C. Redfield (1858–1932) as Commerce Secretary.

The first workmen's compensation law went into effect July 4, 1911, in New Jersey and was quickly followed by other states. Wisconsin enacted the first unemployment insurance law January 28, 1932. Maryland was first to adopt a state workmen's compensation law, and California was first to set a minimum wage (two dollars a day) for most state employees (1906).

The Children's Bureau was created April 9, 1912, with Julia C. Lathrop (1858–1932) as first director and a Women's Bureau began in 1920.

Statutory provisions for arbitration of labor disputes began with a general law in Connecticut (1753), followed by Maryland (1778) with a state arbitration law. New York and Massachusetts adopted laws for industrial arbitration (1886). The Federal Mediation and Conciliation Service evolved from legislative action begun in 1913. (Private arbitration efforts date back to 1768 when the New York City Chamber of Commerce created a tribunal to adjust differences between those agreeing to arbitration. Arbitration Society of America was formed in 1922, later through mergers became the American Arbitration Association.)

The Fair Employment Practices Committee was created June 25, 1941, setting the stage for similar laws by the states. American Express Company began first retirement system in private industry (1875). Saturday half holiday was inaugurated at the Westinghouse air brake factory in June 1871. Ford Motor Company introduced the eight-hour day, five-day work week (1925). Charles E. Wilson (1886–1972), while president of General Motors (1941–53), devised the escalator wage formula, a cost of living pay plan. The union label was first adopted by the Cigarmakers Union (1874).

Federal troops were used for first time in a labor dispute January 29, 1834 to put down a "riotous assembly" of laborers building the Chesapeake & Ohio Canal near Williamsport, Maryland. The first American general strike began February 6, 1919, in Seattle when most unions and businesses protested elimination of the western cost of living differential by the U.S. Shipping Board; it lasted six days. The first modern sit-down strike occurred at a Hormel & Company plant in Austin, Minnesota, November 13, 1933.

12. Law

Notable Dates

Legal instruction began early in the colonies, with college teaching starting at King's (later Columbia) College in New York City (1755). The first law school was created by Tapping Reeve (1744–1823) in Litchfield, Connecticut; the first college level law school was created at Harvard (1817); the first law school to admit women was St. Louis Law School (now part of Washington University) (1869).

The first public defender office was created by Los Angeles County, June 11, 1913, and the first public defender was Walton J. Wood. The Legal Aid Society began as the German Society (1876) only providing aid to German immigrants. Later it was extended to all New Yorkers unable to afford legal help. It became the Legal Aid Society (1896) and branches opened everywhere. Another legal help society was the Bureau of Justice in Chicago (1888).

Various types of courts started in the early 1900s— night court, New York City (1907); domestic relations, Buffalo (1910); small claims, Cleveland (1913); small debtors, Kansas (1913).

The first all-female jury was ordered (1656) in Patuxent, Maryland, to try Judith Catchpole for murdering her newborn child. She was acquitted because there was not enough evidence.

The *American Law Journal* was founded in Baltimore (1808).

Notable Figures

Andrew Hamilton was the lawyer whose success led to the establishment of press freedom in the colonies. He defended Peter Zenger, who had been arrested (1735) for "seditious libel" in his newspaper. Zenger's original lawyers attacked the action and were immediately disbarred. Hamilton was retained secretly and was able to get Zenger acquitted.

George Wythe (1726–1806) was a pioneer law professor, teaching Thomas Jefferson in his chambers in Williamsburg. Through Jefferson's influence when he was Virginia's governor, Wythe was named professor of "law and police" at the College of William and Mary, the first chair of municipal law in an American college. He also taught John Marshall and Henry Clay.

James Kent (1763–1847) was the first professor of law at Columbia College (1793). He was named to the New York Supreme Court (1798), serving as chief justice (1804–14). He published the four-volume *Commentaries on American Law* (1830), the first major systematic work on Anglo-American law. Kent instituted the practice of written opinions. His *Commentaries* and decisions practically made him the creator of American equity law.

John Marshall (1755–1835) was Supreme Court chief justice (1801–35) and had a profound influence on American constitutional law and the establishment of judicial review. His important decisions established the fundamental principles for constitutional interpretation.

Joseph Story (1779–1845), a South Carolina justice, is considered one of the great American legal figures and his opinions helped establish the principles of American public and constitutional law.

Lemuel Shaw (1781–1861), chief justice of the Massachusetts Supreme Court (1830–60), helped mold common law to meet the needs of changing society, and his opinions deeply influenced commercial and constitutional law.

Christopher C. Langdell (1826–1906), dean of the Harvard Law School, revolutionized American teaching by using the case method.

Belva A. B. Lockwood (1830–1917) passed the bar (1873) after private tutoring and became one of the most effective advocates of women's rights. She drafted a bill which became law to give women equal pay for equal work in the civil service. She helped secure permission for women to practice before the Supreme Court and was the first admitted.

Esther H. Morris (1814–1902), who helped get the vote for women in Wyoming (1890), was the first American female Justice of the Peace (South Pass City, Wyoming, 1870–74).

Florence E. Allen (1884–1966) was the first woman to be elected to a state supreme court (Ohio, 1922) and the first woman to serve as a Circuit Court of Appeals justice (1934).

Caleb H. Baumes (1863–1937), a New York legislator, wrote the statute providing for life imprisonment for fourth felony conviction.

Ben(jamin B.) Lindsey (1869–1943) secured legislation (1899) to create the world's first juvenile court (Denver), serving as its judge (1900–27). In California (1939), he helped create a conciliation court for divorce cases susceptible to reconciliation and proposed a family court.

Ada H. Kepley (1847–1925) of Effingham, Illinois, became the first female law graduate, getting her law degree (1870) from Union College of Law, Chicago.

William H. Hastie (1904–76) was the first black judge on the U.S. Circuit Court of Appeals (1949). He also was the first black governor of the Virgin Islands (1946–49).

Philander Deming (1829–1915) taught himself shorthand and became a newspaper reporter. In November, 1865, he demonstrated the value of verbatim reporting in an Albany courtroom and was made official stenographer for the New York Supreme Court.

Sandra Day O'Connor (1930–) was the first woman named a justice of the Supreme Court (September 25, 1981).

13. Manufacturing

Manufacturing in the newly-settled American colonies began after the Revolution. The Du Pont family arrived in 1799 and built the first of its chemical plants (1802); iron making in all 13 colonies was established by 1780; glass making began in Jamestown soon after the first Virginia colonists arrived and later in Pennsylvania; marble quarrying began in Vermont (1785); the first American pottery began in Salem, Massachusetts (1641).

Industries which supported shipping flourished in the coastal towns— packing and bolting flour in New York City, tanning and currying of leather in Philadelphia, rum distilling in Boston and Newport, Rhode Island, sugar refining in New York City, Philadelphia, and Boston, and shipbuilding in Boston, Philadelphia, and Newport.

Armaments/Explosives

Many early settlers had weapons they brought with them to the New World. Then German craftsmen produced a new gun for American settlers, originally called the Pennsylvania rifle and later the Kentucky rifle.

The first American arsenal was at Springfield, Massachusetts. It was established in April 1794. At the start it took a month to produce 20 muskets, then completed 245 in the first year. Originally, the first weapon was the rifle, quickly followed by the cannon and machine gun. Then came the pistol. The production of rifles was sped up by Eli Whitney, best known for the cotton gin. Faced with financial problems because of litigation over his cotton gin patent, Whitney devised a system that set a pattern for rifle making and future industrial production. Whitney received a government contract (1798) to produce 10,000 muskets on the basis of a system he had developed to use interchangeable parts. He bought a plant near New Haven where the interchangeable parts were manufactured and assembled.

Early arms manufacturers were:

Eliphalet Remington (1793–1861) began making gun barrels in the early 1820s. He invented a lathe for making gunstocks and pioneered the cast iron drilled barrel. Remington moved into enlarged works at Ilion, New York (1828), and supplied rifles to the Army.

Thomas Blanchard (1788–1864) developed a lathe to turn gun barrels and improved the machine (1818) so that it could automatically duplicate any given pattern.

C. W. Morse developed a breech-loading system and produced a magazine rifle using metallic cases (1854).

Christopher M. Spencer (1833 —1922) patented a self-loading repeating rifle (1860) which was immediately adopted by the government and by the Civil War's end, 200,000 Spencer rifles had been produced.

John M. Browning (1855–1926), son of a gunsmith, made his first gun at 13 from scraps in his father's shop. He patented a breech-loading single-shot rifle (1879) that he sold to Winchester. Browning went on to design many types of machine guns and automatic rifles.

Oliver F. Winchester, a successful shirt manufacturer, became principal stockholder of a company that became the Winchester Repeating Arms Company (1866), turning out famous rifles.

John C. Garand (1888–1974) developed the M-1, the Garand rifle (1926), which became the basic shoulder weapon of American forces until 1957 when it was replaced by the fully automatic M-14.

In the field of artillery, the manufacture of cannon began in the early 1800s. Cyrus Alger, who organized the South Boston Iron Company, which became the largest in the United States, produced cannonballs for the War of 1812. He designed the first gun with a rifled barrel (1834). Gouverneur Kemble (1786–1875) built a foundry (1818) in Cold Spring, New York, which built the best American cannon up to then and was the chief supplier of Union Army artillery. Robert P. Parrott (1807–77) produced the first American rifled cast-iron cannon (1861), which was widely used in the Civil War. Benjamin Chambers Sr. patented a breech-loading cannon (1849).

Machine guns began to appear in the late 1800s. Richard J. Gatling (1818–1903) built and patented the first practical machine gun (1864) and it was officially adopted by the Army (1866). Hiram S. Maxim (1840–1916), who invented numerous things, developed a fully-automatic machine gun (1884), the first efficient gun of its kind. John T. Thompson (1860–1940) invented the submachine gun (the Tommy gun) (1915) and it was widely used in World War II. Other machine guns were developed by Charles E. Barnes, Benjamin Hotchkiss (1826–85), Melvin M. Johnson (1909–65) and Isaac N. Lewis (1858–1931).

Pistol manufacturers began with Simeon North (1763–1852), who first manufactured scythes and went into pistols (1799) after receiving a government order for 400. He improved the pistols and by 1813 was using interchangeable parts.

Samuel Colt (1814–62) conceived the idea of a revolver while working at sea and whittled one out of wood. He constructed two pistols (1831) and two years later he developed both a revolver and a pistol on the principle of a multi-shot weapon with a revolving barrel. He patented the first practical revolving firearm (1835).

Daniel B. Wesson (1825–1906) made a revolver similar to that of Colt but differing in its mechanism. Wesson sued Colt for patent infringement but lost. While working for an armaments maker, Wesson met Horace Smith (1808–93) and in their spare time they developed a repeating rifle (which they sold) and a revolver (1857) with a repeating action, firing cartridges. The weapon became very popular and it was adopted by the United States military.

Henry Deringer invented a short-barreled pocket pistol, which was known as the "Derringer."

Edward Maynard (1813–91) invented a system and mechanism for priming a gun by means of an automatically-fed tape on firing caps (1845).

Theodore Timby (1822–1909) invented the revolving gun turret which was not accepted until after it was used on the ironclad *Monitor* in its battle with the *Merrimac*.

John A. B. Dahlgren (1809–70) organized the first Navy ordnance workshop (1847) and developed a new 11-inch gun (1851).

Anson Mills (1834–1924) patented the woven cartridge belt (1866).

William Crozier (1855–1942) and Adelbert R. Buffington (1837–1922) invented the disappearing gun carriage (1896).

Ralph C. Browne (1880–1960) invented the electrical system used by the United States in the North Sea mine barrage in World War I.

John H. Hammond (1888–1965) invented a number of radio guidance systems (1912, 1914).

Land mines or "booby traps" were invented by Gabriel J. Rains (1803–81). He served with the Confederate Army and used the mines — shells with percussion fuses — in the roads to slow pursuers.

Pioneers in the development of explosives included Hudson Maxim (1853–1927), George M. Mowbray (1814–91), Paul A. Oliver (1830–1912), Beverly W. Dunn (1860–1936) and Egbert P. Judson (1812–93).

Maxim, brother of Hiram S. Maxim of machine gun fame, experimented with explosives, developing one that could propel a projectile through heavy armor plate and was 50 percent more powerful than dynamite.

Mowbray, an oil producer at Titusville, Pennsylvania, in the early 1860s, originated the use of nitroglycerin to shoot dormant oil wells. A depression (1866) forced the closing of his refinery and Mowbray concentrated on producing nitroglycerin, and became one of the largest producers. He demonstrated the value of explosives in tunneling and built a plant in Massachusetts to supply explosives for building the Hoosac Tunnel.

Oliver began making explosives after the Civil War and is generally credited with independently inventing dynamite and black powder. His successful plant was acquired by Dupont (1903).

Dunn invented a high explosive named after him — "dunnite" or "explosive D" — and Judson invented various explosives, including the first usable in railroad construction (1876).

Celluloid

John W. Hyatt (1837–1920) entered a contest to develop a substitute for ivory in billard balls. He won $10,000 for his product. In developing the prize-winning substitute, Hyatt discovered how to make celluloid, which he patented in 1870.

Chemicals

E(leuthere) I. Du Pont (1771–1834) and his family came to the United States (1799) and three years later built a plant near Wilmington, Delaware, to manufacture gunpowder. The company expanded into making many chemical and industrial products, including cellophane, neoprene and nylon. It became one of the world's foremost companies.

Herbert H. Dow (1866–1930) discovered and patented an easy, inexpensive method of extracting bromine from brine and founded a company in Canton, Ohio (1899), to produce bromine commercially. Later he formed a company to prepare chlorine from brine and Dow Chemical Company developed many other products from brine.

John Dwight and Company began commercial production of baking soda (bicarbonate of soda) (1846) in New York City.

The first commercial production of graphite occurred in Ticonderoga, New York (1840).

Arthur D. Little, a chemical engineer, developed processes for chrome tanning, electrolytic manufacture of chlorates, artificial silk, gas and petroleum. He supervised construction of the first American mill making sulphite wood pulp (1884).

Education

The first college civil engineering course was given (1819) by Norwich University (Northfield, Vermont), the first electrical engineering course at Cornell University (1883). The first engineering college was Rensselaer Polytechnic Institute in Troy, New York, which opened 1824.

Fasteners

Fasteners became very important in many manufacturing operations and began to be produced toward the end of the seventeenth century.

Jeremiah Wilkinson (1741–1831) of Cumberland, Rhode Island, developed a process to produce nails from a sheet of cold iron (1781), Ezekiel Reed patented a nail-making machine (1786) and Jacob Perkins (1766–1849) invented a machine to cut and head nails and tacks in one operation in about 1790, but litigation held up production of the machine for a decade.

Josiah G. Pierson of New York City patented a rivet-making machine (1794), Jesse Reed began manufacturing tacks in Connecticut (1807), Abel Stowell invented a screw-cutting machine (1809), and Aborn and

Jackson opened a factory for making screws (1810) at Bellefonte, Rhode Island.

William G. Angell (1811–70) developed an improved screw-making machine (1838), John I. Howe (1793–1876) invented a machine (1833) for making pins and Samuel Slocum (1792–1861) made a machine for making pins with solid heads three years later.

Walter Hunt, an inventor of several items, invented the safety pin (1849) and sold his patent rights for $400 so that he could pay a debt.

David Wilkins (1771–1825) patented a machine to make nuts and bolts (1798) and Micah Rugg, a blacksmith, received a patent (1840) for trimming the heads of nuts and bolts. Rugg and Martin Barnes founded a nut and bolt factory in Marion, Connecticut (1840).

Holmes & Hotchkiss in Waterbury, Connecticut, began manufacturing hooks and eyes (1836).

Brass buttons began to be produced by 1750 in Philadelphia; gilt buttons were made commercially (1802) by Abel Porter and Co. in Waterbury, Connecticut. The first cloth-covered buttons were made (1826) by Mrs. Samuel Williston in Easthampton, Massachusetts, employing many women in the work. Joseph S. Hayden (1802–77) and his father designed a machine to make cloth-covered buttons (1828).

The first factory to make vegetable ivory buttons was set up in Leeds, Massachusetts (1864); pearl buttons from shells of fresh water clams were made by John F. Boepple in Muscatine, Iowa, around 1890.

Whitcomb L. Judson of Chicago invented a hookless fastener for shoes in 1896 (two metal chains which could be fastened by a slider). The hookless slide fastener (zipper) was patented (1913) by Gideon Sundback (1880–1954) of Hoboken, New Jersey, who developed machines for its manufacture.

Among the leading names in locks is that of Linus Yale (1821–68), who brought out the monitor bank lock in the early 1860s, marking the transition to dial-operated combination locks. Yale patented the small cylinder lock with tumblers and operated with a key (1861).

James Sargent (1824–1910), a Yale employee who could pick any lock, developed a lock (1863) which he could not pick. He offered it to his employer, who rejected it, leading Sargent to form his own company. He perfected the first time lock (1873) which was installed at the First National Bank in Morrison, Illinois.

Glass

Among the first settlers in Jamestown, Virginia, were eight glass blowers. A glass factory, the first in the colonies, began production in 1608. The plant was destroyed by Indians (1722) and efforts to restore the plant failed because workers found it more profitable to grow tobacco.

Jan Smeedes opened a glass factory (1654) in New Amsterdam (New York City) which was followed the next year by Evert Duyckingk.

Caspar Wistar (1696–1752) operated the first successful glass works in New Jersey (across the river from Philadelphia) (1740), producing glassware and window panes. After Wistar died his son Richard (1727–81) operated the plant producing what is now called South Jersey glass.

Henry W. Stiegel (1729–85) had a successful iron business and then began glassmaking (1764) near Manheim, Pennsylvania. He imported a number of skilled glass workers from England. He concentrated on bottles and window panes, then table glass, which later became collectors' items.

John F. Amelung, a German immigrant, began a glass works near New Bremen, Maryland (1785), turning out some of the finest American engraved glass. He tried to establish self-sustaining communities and imported craftsmen, teachers and doctors.

Deming Jones (1790–1869) began producing pressed glass, also known as Sandwich glass (1827), in Sandwich, Massachusetts.

Other early glass producers included the Boston Crown Glass Factory, the first important window glass makers, founded in 1792. Thomas W. Dyott (1771–1861) operated a drug store in Philadelphia where he began merchandising patent medicines and became the nation's largest producer. The success of the medicine created a demand for bottles. Dyott bought the Philadelphia and Kensington glass works (1833) and became the nation's largest bottle producer.

Plate glass manufacture was begun about 1853 by James M. Richmond in Cheshire, Massachusetts. Ethan A. Hitchcock (1835–1909) established the first successful American plate glass factory in St. Louis (1874). Large scale plate glass production was begun by New York Plate Glass Company in Creighton, Pennsylvania (1883). It later became the Pittsburgh Plate Glass Company.

The first American stained glass was made (1844) by William J. Bolton (1816–84) and John Bolton (1818–93) for Christ Church in Pelham Manor, New York. Louis C. Tiffany (1848–1933) opened a factory (1878) to make stained glass by adding color while the glass was being made rather than coloring it after it was finished; he also shaped it while it was hot.

Michael J. Owens (1859–1923) built the first successful bottle making machine in Toledo (1893). The machine made 1,800 bottles an hour — a human glass blower could make only 25. Owens, who began as a coal shoveler in a glass works, worked his way up in the Toledo Glass Company (founded 1909) to plant superintendent and branch plant manager. After his invention, the company became the Libbey Owens Glass Company.

Irving W. Colborn (1861–1917) invented a sheet glass drawing machine (1902) and perfected it six years later to mechanically draw continuous sheets of glass.

Wire glass was invented by Frank Schuman of Philadelphia (1892).

Katherine B. Blodgett (1898–1979), a physicist, discovered (1939) a coating process to eliminate reflections on glass.

Iron/Steel

The first American iron works was built at Falling Creek, near Richmond, Virginia (1619), but lasted only a few years. Iron smelting was introduced in New England (1643) by Joseph Jenks (1602–83), who built an iron works using bog iron ore found near Saugus, Massachusetts. Blacksmiths were kept busy making felling axes, mattocks, wagon wheel rims and sleigh runners, chains and plows, and iron fittings for houses and ships.

Robert Bridges (d 1656) came to America in 1641 and took some samples of bog iron to England. He got 11 incorporators for "The Company of Undertakers for the Iron Works" to each put up 1000 pounds. Skilled workers were brought to the colony, the industry spread to near New Haven, Connecticut (1657), and Rhode Island (1675).

Abraham Darby, an English ironmaker, began producing iron in a blast furnace using coke rather than charcoal in Shropshire, England, in 1709. The first American iron blast furnace to use anthracite coal successfully was in Pottsville, Pennsylvania (1839). The first iron mill to puddle and roll iron was the Plumstock Rolling Mill in Fayette County, Pennsylvania (1817).

George Taylor (1716–81), who went on to the Continental Congress and was a signer of the Declaration of Independence, operated an iron furnace in Bucks County, Pennsylvania. The first steel was manufactured

(1728) by two Connecticut men — Samuel Higley of Simsbury and Joseph D. Dewey of Hebron.

Seth Boyden invented processes for making malleable cast iron and sheet iron (1826). In the following year, Cyrus Alger (1781–1865) organized the South Boston Iron Company, which became the largest of the time. An inventor, Alger also designed the first cylinder stoves and the first gun with a rifled barrel.

The Tredegar Iron Company in Richmond, Virginia (founded 1838) supplied the Confederate artillery during the Civil War.

Peter Cooper (1791–1883) founded the Canton Iron Works in Baltimore (1828) and its best customer was the newly-formed but foundering Baltimore and Ohio Railroad. Cooper built the first American steam locomotive ("Tom Thumb") (1830), enabling the railroad to continue using the existing tracks and helping promote the growth of railroads.

Abram S. Hewitt (1822–1903) helped organize Cooper Hewitt and Company about 1845 and invented the regenerating hot blast stove for blast furnaces which increased iron output significantly and reduced costs. His company made the first American steel (1870).

Alexander L. Holley (1832–82), while in England (1863), learned of the new Bessemer steelmaking process and purchased the American rights to the process. Within two years, he built a small plant in Troy, New York, and was turning out steel rails by 1867. Holley designed and built steel mills throughout the country, laying the groundwork for the American steel industry.

William Kelly (1811–88) operated the Suwanee Iron Works in Eddyville, Kentucky, and, to overcome charcoal shortages, he developed methods of heating pig iron. He came up with a process of shooting a blast of air through the molten metal (1851) but kept his process secret until the Bessemer method appeared in the United States. The Cambria Iron Works in Johnstown, Pennsylvania, used the Kelly method successfully.

Eventually the Kelly and Bessemer processes were combined forming the chief method of steelmaking until 1907, when it gave way to the open hearth method.

Andrew Carnegie (1835–1919) began as a telegraph operator, working up to division superintendent with the Pennsylvania Railroad. He formed the Keystone Bridge Company (1865), which became dominant in iron and steel making, and consolidated his holdings into the Carnegie Steel Company (1889). The company became part of the newly formed U.S. Steel Company in 1901.

U.S. Steel was first headed by Charles M. Schwab (1862–1939), who had been president of Carnegie. He left to become head of Bethlehem Steel Company (1903), of which he had bought control. Bethlehem was the outgrowth of Saucona Iron Company, founded in 1857.

Benjamin F. Jones (1824–1903) was a founder (1852) of the fore-runner of Jones and Laughlin Steel Company. He was one of the first to try to control all raw materials needed for iron and steel making by buying iron mines in the Lake Superior region and coal mines in Pennsylvania.

Henry J. Kaiser (1882–1967), a successful road and dam builder, became a shipbuilder in World War II. The steel demands of his shipyards caused him to construct the Pacific Coast's first steel mill (1942).

Other contributors to development of the American iron and steel industry include:

Elwood Haynes (1857–1925), who helped build an early automobile, discovered various alloys, such as tungsten chrome steel (1881), and patented stainless steel (1919).

Fred H. Daniels (1853–1913) made many improvements in the manufacture of steel and wire.

Hayward A. Harvey (1824–93) and Benjamin C. Tilghman (1821–1901) developed processes for hardening steel surfaces, such as for armor plates on ships.

Leonidas Merritt (1844–1926) discovered iron ore deposits in the Mesabi region of Minnesota in 1890.

Richard H. Rice (1863–1922) designed the first turboblower for American blast furnaces.

James Gayley (1855–1920) invented a bronze cooling plate for blast furnace walls (1891) and other improvements.

Leather

Leather tanning is usually credited to the Indians and the first known colonial tanner was Experience Miller, who came to Plymouth in 1623. Talmadge Edwards of Johnstown, New York, began leather tanning by an "oil tan" method (1810) and helped launch a prosperous glove industry.

Seth Boyden, who later succeeded in developing a process for malleable cast iron, developed a process for making patent leather (1819) and opened the first such plant in Newark.

Lumber

The need for lumber to build homes for the fast-growing population resulted in the early development of sawmills. It was the sawmill which built the colonies, thanks to the available timber and the presence of many swift streams.

The English had no sawmills but by 1611, a mill was constructed on the James River in Virginia by German craftsmen imported for that work. The Dutch did likewise when they arrived in the 1600s and by 1624 a sawmill built by Danish experts appeared in Massachusetts.

By 1700 nearly every town along a stream had a sawmill and they were quickly followed by grist mills. The first paper mill was established (1690) at Germantown, Pennsylvania, and textile mills in New England began flourishing in the 1780s.

William Monroe of Concord, Massachusetts, a cabinetmaker, established the first American pencil factory in June of 1812. He invented a machine that cut and grooved wooden slats precisely enough to make pencils.

Joseph Dixon (1799–1869), a self-taught chemist, opened a pencil and stove polish factory at Salem, Massachusetts (1827), and invented a process for producing colored inks.

(John) Eberhard Faber (1823–79) was born to a German family of pencil manufacturers and came to the United States in 1848. The next year he began to import and market pencils, then expanded to include stationery. He began to manufacture pencils (1861) and eliminated much manual labor with machines.

The indelible pencil was invented by Edson P. Clark of Northampton, Massachusetts (1866).

Peregrine Williamson of Baltimore patented a steel pen (1809) which was produced commercially by Richard Esterbrook (1813–95), who built a shop in Philadelphia (1858).

The first patent for a fountain pen was issued (1830) to D. Hyde of Reading, Pennsylvania, and John J. Loud of Weymouth, Massachusetts, patented a ball point pen (1888). Walter Hunt, a prolific inventor, devised a self-closing inkwell which later was used in postoffices.

The first practical fountain pen was perfected (1889) by Lewis E.

Waterman (1837–1901). It had to be filled with an eyedropper; lever filling was not available until 1913. Waterman perfected (1883) a method of using a hard rubber insert with tiny channels to control the flow of ink to the pen point.

The first American ink producer was Thaddeus Davids of New York City (1825).

The first American envelope manufacturer was a Mr. Pierson of New York City who made them in his little store on Fulton Street in 1839. Before that, letters were folded and addressed on the blank side.

A patent was issued to Jesse K. Park and Cornelius S. Watson of New York City for the first successful machine to make envelopes (1849). Dr. Russell L. Hawes of Worcester, Massachusetts, received a patent (1853) for an envelope folding machine and an improved envelope folding and gumming machine was patented (1898) by John A. Sherman (1823–1900) of Worcester, Massachusetts. An envelope with a window was patented by Americus Callahan of Chicago (1902).

Louis Prang (1824–1909) of Boston made the first engraved Christmas cards (1854) for export; they were first used in the United States in 1855. He began with sets of album cards (birds, flowers, animals), then Civil war scenes by Winslow Homer. He also printed advertising and visiting cards with floral designs and then seasonal greetings. Prang instituted design competitions (1880), a practice continued by other card makers.

Crude wood-cut valentines were produced in the 1840s by Robert H. Elton and Thomas W. Strong, a wood engraver and lithographer, of New York.

Valentines were first produced commercially in the United States (1847) by Esther A. Howland, realizing sales of $5,000 the first year. She organized an assembly line of young women to make the valentines.

Joyce C. Hall (1891–1982) began selling postcards while still in high school. He and a brother began a wholesale jobbing business in cards (1910) in Kansas City, Missouri; they soon added greeting cards. Hall bought an engraving plant (1916) to produce their own Hallmark cards, becoming the world's largest greeting card manufacturer.

Blotting paper was first made in New Haven by Joseph Parker and Son Company in 1856. Some had been imported earlier from England. Sand boxes were in general use before then.

Machinery/Tools

The manufacture of machinery and tools moved quickly to meet growing needs. The primary colonial hand tool was the English axe; the curve-handled axe did not evolve until the mid–1700s and the double-billed axe about 1800. The first axe manufacturing plant was opened in Johnstown, New York, by William Mann.

The first factory for making files by hand was Broadmeadow and Company in Pittsburgh (1829) and William T. Nicholson (1834–93) patented a file-cutting machine (1864) and began producing files by machine in Providence.

The first practical pipe or screw wrench was invented (1876) by Daniel C. Stillson of Somerville, Massachusetts, and Edward Ellsberg invented an underwater torch for cutting steel. David Melville invented a circular saw (1813) and Henry Disston (1819–78) began his saw-making plant in Philadelphia (1840).

Robert Hare (1781–1858) developed the oxy-hydrogen blowpipe (1801), source of the highest heat then known, and was able to fuse most refractory substances. This led to developing various illuminators.

Oakes Ames (1804–73) and his brother took over operation of the family shovel business (1844) and the Ames shovel was said to be "legal tender in every part of the Mississippi Valley."

Edward N. Hurley (1864–1933) originated and developed the American pneumatic tool industry.

The driving forces for the American manufacturing machines—motors and engines—date back to Thomas Newcomen (1663–1729), an English Baptist lay preacher who invented an atmospheric steam engine (1712), using cast iron cylinders.

The first steam engine was imported from England by Colonel John Schuyler (1753) to pump water out of his copper mine in North Arlington, New Jersey.

Oliver Evans (1755–1819) perfected machines for the textile industry and designed a flour mill (1785) with four stories of water-powered automated machinery to perform every step of the milling process. Millers refused to adopt the idea so Evans turned to making steam engines (1802) and a steam-powered dredge (1804) which operated on land and in water, predating the steamboat and steam automobile.

One of the first internal combustion engines was patented (1826) by Samuel Morey (1762–1843), who also patented a steam-operated spit and rotary steam engine in the 1790s.

Joseph Henry, the Smithsonian Institute's first secretary, combined a battery, an electromagnet and a commutator to build a continuously operating electric motor (1829). Thomas W. Davenport received the first American patent for an electric motor (1837) but could not get financial support for its production.

George H. Corliss, after devising various improvements on steam engines for his employer, set up his own plant (1848). The next year he invented the valve engine which regulated the amount of steam admitted into an engine cylinder in response to the load requirement. The Corliss plant constructed some of the nation's largest engines, including a 1600 horsepower engine that powered the machinery exhibits at the 1876 Centennial Exposition.

The Centennial engine was built by Corliss' plant superintendent, Edwin Reynolds (1834–1909), who built the first triple expansion pumping engine for a waterworks and patented a blowing engine for blast furnaces (1888).

Stuart Perry (1814–90) patented an internal combustion engine (1844) but was unable to get commercial acceptance.

Cornelius H. Delameter (1821–89) owned the Phoenix Foundry in New York City and helped John Ericsson (1803–89) build marine power systems and built the engines for the ironclad *Monitor* of the Union Navy and John F. Holland's first submarine.

George H. Babcock (1832–93) and Stephen Wilcox (1830–93) invented a steam engine, one of the first automatic cut-off engines. They patented a boiler (1867) which could handle high pressure and was safe to withstand explosions. They founded Babcock and Wilcox (1867) to manufacture boilers and steam engines.

George B. Brayton (1830–92) produced the first successful American internal combustion engine (1872). The engine operated on the two-stroke cycle principle and was used primarily for stationary purposes.

Nikola Tesla, an electrical engineer, discovered the rotating magnetic field to be an effective way to using alternating current. He adapted his discovery to an induction motor (1888), making possible the universal transmission and distribution of electricity.

The first diesel engine for commercial service was a two-cylinder 60 horsepower unit (1898) installed in the Second Street brewery of Anheuser Busch in St. Louis.

John F. Allen (1829–1900) invented the valve motion which made high speed steam engines possible. Charles G. Curtis (1860–1953) invented a steam turbine used in electric power plants and for marine propulsion.

Charles B. Richards (1833–1919) invented the first steam engine indicator suitable for use on high speed engines(1860).

One of the earliest and most significant contributions to American industry was made by Eli Whitney, who added to his cotton gin fame with another contribution. His gin was frequently pirated leaving him with financial problems so he bid on a contract to make muskets for the government. He was awarded a contract (1798) for 10,000 muskets and invented a jib for guiding operating tools. This made it possible to produce interchangeable parts, which he did successfully in making muskets at his New Haven plant.

Thomas Blanchard invented the stocking lathe (1818), actually a milling machine for turning irregular shapes in wood. Among his other inventions were a tack-making machine and a lathe for gun barrels.

Francis A. Pratt (1827–1902) and Amos Whitney, employees in an iron works, began doing machine work together in their spare time. Soon their spare time work grew so much they formed Pratt & Whitney Company (1865). They made machine tools that could turn out interchangeable parts for various products. One problem for using such parts was the lack of standard gauges. Pratt led the way to the development of the needed gauges.

LaVerne Noyes (1849–1919) invented numerous devices and machines of which the most important was the steel windmill ("air motor") and designed steel towers for the mills.

Alexander E. Brown (1852–1911) invented a hoisting, conveying machine to handle coal and ore at Great Lakes ports (1879). This made it possible to unload a 500-ton vessel in hours, rather than days, and led to larger vessels, going from 1,200 to 12,000 tons.

Ambrose Swasey (1846–1937) and Worcester R. Warner (1846–1929) founded Warner and Swasey (1881), manufacturers of machine tools and astronomical instruments (various large telescopes). Swasey invented a range and position finder.

Elijah McCoy (1843–1929), the son of slaves, pioneered the development of automatic machinery lubricators, which supplied oil intermittently from a cup, eliminating the need for stopping the machine. Machinists and engineers began to insist on this lubricator and it is believed the expression "the real McCoy" came from such insistence.

Joseph R. Brown (1810–76) and his father produced many tower clocks, automatic machines, milling devices and grinding machines. With Lucien Sharpe, Brown founded Brown and Sharpe Manufacturing Company (1853).

An improved gearing housing (journal box) was patented in 1831 by Isaac Babbitt but it received little attention. His recommendation that the box be lined with a metal composed of tin, antimony and copper — soon called Babbitt metal — became widely used.

Benjamin F. Sturdevant (1833–90), a shoe machine developer, noticed that the early buffing wheels created much dust and he developed a successful rotary exhaust fan (1867). The fan began to be used in many plants and fan manufacturing became a whole new industry.

Frederick W. Taylor (1856–1915) laid the foundation for scientific industrial management and introduced time-and-motion studies and systems for incentive pay. He studied the actual power of men and machines and the amount of work that could be expected from them, leading to stronger machines and fairer employee work loads.

Among the many other contributors to manufacturing were:

Edward G. Acheson (1856–1931) commercially produced silicon carbide crystals (carborundum), needed abrasives for manufacturing. This was second in hardness only to diamonds, which Acheson had been trying to reproduce.

James Bogardus (1800–74) invented engraving and die sinking machines.

Charles Brady King of Detroit patented a pneumatic hammer (1894).

John Stone of Concord, Massachusetts, patented a pile driver (1791).

Daniel Treadwell (1791–1872), who earlier had developed printing presses, designed rope making machinery (1831–35), which for some time produced all Navy rope.

William G. Otis of Philadelphia invented a steam shovel (1839) and it was first used in building the Western Railroad in Massachusetts.

Robert Fulton (1765–1815), remembered for his steamboat, patented a power shovel for digging canals.

Henry R. Worthington (1817–80) invented a direct-acting steam pump (1849) and the duplex steam feed pump ten years later.

Elihu Thomson of Lynn, Massachusetts, patented an electric welding machine (1886).

Yale and Towne Manufacturing Company produced the first crane (1883) for the Pittsburgh Bessemer Steel Company.

The first factory devoted exclusively to making machinists' tools was established (1838) in Nashua, New Hampshire, by John H. Gage.

Metals

Gold — John W. Marshall (1810–85) arrived in California (1845) and went to work for John A. Sutter (1803–80) to build a sawmill. Marshall was to supervise the mill and share its profits. He built the mill on the American River at Coloma and when it was finished it was necessary to deepen the tail race to permit the wheel to turn freely. In the deepening process, gold was discovered on January 24, 1848, and the rush began. The sawmill failed because the owners could not find laborers — all were busy looking for gold. The gold rush brought more than 200,000 persons to California in four years.

Silver and Copper — The first American copper mine was the Simsbury mine at Gramby, Connecticut (1705), and it was worked spasmodically until 1773. More copper was discovered in the 1850s in the Upper Peninsula of Michigan.

Marcus Daly (1841–1900) and three others began a silver mine in Montana which was not successful but led to the discovery of a major copper deposit (1866) and the development of the city of Anaconda.

Paul Revere (1735–1818), best remembered for his infamous ride, was a silver- and coppersmith. He cut many copper plates for prints and hardware for ships. Revere set up a copper rolling mill in Canton, Massachusetts (1800), to manufacture sheet copper which was used as sheathing for ships and the Massachusetts State House roof.

Meyer Guggenheim (1828–1905) entered the copper business (1888), founding the Philadelphia Smelting and Refining Company (1901), taking control of the combined firm.

Daniel S. Jackling (1869–1956), a metallurgist, revolutionized the industry by introducing the porphyry process to remove low grade copper ore.

Brass — The first brass foundry was opened (1645) in Lynn, Massachusetts, by Joseph Jenks, who was an early iron maker who prepared utensils and tools. Abel Porter and Company of Waterbury, Connecticut, began rolling brass (1802), the first to make brass by fusing copper and zinc.

Israel Holmes (1800–74) founded Holmes and Hotchkiss (1831) in Waterbury, Connecticut, the first American manufacturer of sheet brass and wire. Edwin Hodges developed brass wire in 1840.

Lead — Lead was mined and smelted as early as 1620 near Falling Creek, Virginia, to meet the demand for bullets and shot. An Indian massacre in 1622 ended that operation.

Moses Austin (1761–1821) operated lead mines in southwestern Virginia (1789) and went to Missouri (1796), where he founded the town of Potosi and successful lead mines. Moses Meeker (1790–1865) led 42 persons on an 89-day keelboat trip from Cincinnati to Illinois where he established a successful lead mine and smelter (1822). He also established a smelter in Wisconsin (1833).

Aluminum — Charles M. Hall (1863–1914) succeeded in separating a pure sample of aluminum from aluminum oxide by an inexpensive electrolytic process (1886) and was first to produce aluminum in commercial quantities (1888). His Pittsburgh Reduction Company became the Aluminum Company of America (Alcoa) (1907).

Other Metals/Minerals— Rogers and Burchfield opened a tin factory in Leechburg, Pennsylvania (1874). The first American commercial zinc plant was built (1858) in LaSalle, Illinois, by Frederick W. Mathiesen (1835–1918) and E. C. Hegeler. They added the first zinc rolling mill (1866).

Joseph Wharton (1826–1909), the only American producer of refined nickel, developed a process for making pure malleable nickel (1875). The nickel plating process was invented (1868) by William H. Remington of Boston.

The first sulphur deposit was discovered in Calcasieu Parish, Louisiana (1869).

Francis M. Smith (1846–1931) and William T. Coleman (1824–93) discovered the mineral from which borax is derived in Columbus, Nevada (1872). They gained control of the deposits and a virtual world monopoly; they later acquired more deposits in Death Valley, California.

The sluicing process for mining was perfected by E. E. Matteson.

Paper

The first American paper mill was built (1690) by William Rittenhouse (1644–1708) and five men at Germantown, Pennsylvania. Rittenhouse was the Mennonite pastor there and later (1703) became bishop. The paper was made by hand, each sheet separately, by pounding linen rags into pulp with stone mortars. The first American machine-made paper was produced (1817) by Thomas Gilpin near Wilmington, Delaware. He developed a machine to make a continuous sheet of paper.

John M. and Lyman Hollingworth of South Braintree, Massachusetts, received a patent (1843) for producing manila paper. The first toilet paper was produced (1857) by Joseph E. Gayetty in New York City.

William Goodale of Clinton, Massachusetts, invented a paper bag manufacturing machine (1859). Luther C. Crowell (1840–1903) developed a paper bag machine (1862) and perfected it to produce square-bottomed bags ten years later.

The first groundwood paper made from wood pulp is reported to have been in the mill of I. Augustus Stanwood and William Tower in Maine (1863). Four years later, a groundwood mill was established in Curtisville, Massachusetts.

Benjamin C. Tilghman developed a sulphate process for producing wood pulp for paper making (1867).

Corrugated paper was invented (1871) by Albert L. Jones of New York City and it was first manufactured by Thompson and Norris Company of Brooklyn. Corrugated paper boxes came into use about 1890.

Seth Wheeler of Albany produced the first perforated paper (1879). Crepe paper was first made (1890) by Charles T. Bainbridge's sons in Brooklyn.

Plastics

The first totally synthetic plastic was developed (1907) by Leo H. Baekeland (1863–1944). He called the hard, insoluble, acid-resistant malleable material "bakelite" and founded a company (1908) for its production. Earlier, he had invented a photographic paper (Velox) that could be developed in artificial light and that company was purchased by Eastman Kodak (1899).

Pottery

John Pride of Salem, Massachusetts, is believed to have produced the first American pottery — red earthenware — in 1641 and James Kettle turned out redware beginning in 1687 at Danvers, Massachusetts. The industry began (1838) in East Liverpool, Ohio, with an English potter, James Bennet. At about the same time, potteries were developing in Zanesville, Ohio, and Trenton, New Jersey.

Rubber

The first rubber company, Roxbury (Massachusetts) India Rubber Company, was founded in 1833 but had difficulty finding a market for its product. The early product had many faults—it softened with heat and hardened in the cold, it was odorous and it was easily destroyed.

Charles Goodyear (1800–60) opened a small retail outlet in Philadelphia for his father's hardware products and agricultural implements. He went bankrupt, spent ten years experimenting with rubber and patented a process for making useful rubber (1837). About 1838 he met Nathaniel M. Hayward (1808–65) who had invented a partial vulcanization process by treating rubber with sulphur. Goodyear acquired the patent. In 1839 Goodyear accidentally dropped some rubber mixed with sulphur on a hot stove and the rubber did not melt, but seemed greatly improved. Goodyear perfected the vulcanization process by 1844.

Benjamin F. Goodrich (1841–88) and a partner took over a rubber goods plant (1867) which became the B. F. Goodrich Company. Goodrich knew nothing about rubber but bought out his partner for $500. The company failed twice but, on the third try in Akron, it prospered. The company produced the first synthetic rubber tires (1940) and tubeless tires (1947).

A buggy salesman, Harvey S. Firestone (1868–1938) founded a company (1896) to sell rubber tires because he was convinced that all vehicles would eventually use such tires. He moved to Akron and formed the Firestone Tire and Rubber Company. Firestone patented (1903) a method of attaching tires to rims, began manufacturing tires and soon became a leader in the field. He introduced dismountable rims for quick replacement of a tire with a spare, and the balloon tire (1923).

Other rubber firsts include:

The principle of the pneumatic tire was patented by an Englishman Robert W. Thomson (1822–73) in England (1845), France (1846) and the United States (1847).

The first synthetic rubber was produced by Lucas P. Kyrides (1883–1947) and Richard W. Earle for the Hood Rubber Company in East Watertown, Massachusetts (1913).

Leverett Candee (1795–1863) began manufacture of elastic suspenders and the first rubber shoes (1842) in Hamden, Connecticut.

Thomas C. Wales of Dorchester, Massachusetts, patented "artics"—rubber, waterproof boots and gaiters (leggings) (1858).

The first rubber heels were made at Lowell, Massachusetts, by Humphrey O'Sullivan (1899).

Scales

The development of scales is associated with Thaddeus Fairbanks (1796–1886), inventor of the platform scale (1831). As manager of a mill where wagon loads of hemp had to be weighed, Fairbanks developed a platform on which hemp-loaded wagons were rolled and weighed.

Edward Canby of Dayton, Ohio, manufactured the world's first computing scale (1891). Allen DeVilbiss, Jr., of Toledo invented an automatic pendulum-type scale (1899) and organized a company which became the Toledo Scale Company.

Joseph Saxton (1799–1873) designed and built for the U.S. Mint the large standard balances used to verify weights in government assay and coinage offices.

Stone

Isaac Underhill began quarrying marble in Dorset, Vermont (1785), and the first granite was quarried (1820) for the Bunker Hill Monument.

The first practical stone crusher — and still in use — was built by Eli W. Blake (1795–1886) in 1858. Blake and a brother operated a firearms plant after the death of their uncle, Eli Whitney (1825). Blake opened a plant (1836) for producing domestic hardware.

John G. Leyner (1860–1920) perfected a compressed air rock drilling machine (1893) and improved it six years later. He developed a hollow drill (1902) through which air and water were forced to the bottom of a hole to expel rock drillings— popularly known as a jackhammer.

Albert Ball (1835–1927) developed a successful diamond drill channeling machine to quarry stone, especially marble (1868).

Textiles

While there were early American textile plants, the real beginnings of the industry go back to Samuel Slater (1768–1835) and Eli Whitney.

Important to the industry's success was the ability of Slater to remember enough of English textile machinery to make American duplicates offsetting the ban of exporting machinery from England.

The early mills included the first American cloth mill (1638) of John Pearson in Rowley, Massachusetts; the first worsted mill (1695) of John Cornish in Boston and the first calico printery of George Leason and Thomas Webber in Boston (1712). The Boston Sail Cloth Factory and the Hartford Woolen Manufactory, the first to be operated by water power, were organized in 1788.

After secretly leaving England because mechanics were not permitted to leave the country Samuel Slater arrived in America in 1789. He became a consultant to Almy and Brown, a Providence (Rhode Island) textile firm and reproduced from memory the design of a spinning frame invented by Sir Richard Arkwright. Slater traced the outlines of the machine parts on timbers and Sylvanus Brown (1747–1827) duplicated them in metal. Within a year, the machines were operating and the firm which became Almy, Brown and Slater, was the first American cotton mill.

At almost the same time, the Beverly (Massachusetts) Cotton Manufactory and a mill on James Island, near Charleston, South Carolina, came into being.

Cotton, the raw material for these and other mills, was difficult to get ready for use. Eli Whitney, a tutor to a Georgia family (1792), learned of the need for a device to remove seeds from short staple cotton. Within weeks he had developed a hand-operated cotton gin which, after some improvement, was able to clear 50 pounds of cotton daily. By 1795, the United States was exporting 40 times as much cotton as the year before. Whitney patented the gin (1794) but there were many infringements until the patent was upheld (1807).

Francis C. Lowell (1775–1817) established a cotton factory at Waltham, Massachusetts (1813), and made the necessary spinning and weaving machinery. It was the first mill in the world to process raw cotton into finished cloth under one roof.

Abbott Lawrence (1792–1855) and his brother, Amos (1786–1852), established textile mills in a town northwest of Boston, which later became Lawrence. Another brother, William (1783–1848), organized a company to manufacture woolen goods at Lowell, Massachusetts (1825).

Other developments in textile machinery and processes include: The first successful linen thread factory was established (1865) in Paterson, New Jersey, by William Barbour and Sons. The first cotton thread was made (1793) by Hannah Wilkinson Slater, wife of Samuel Slater, in Pawtucket, Rhode Island. The first silk thread was made (1810) by Rodney Hanks and his nephew, Horatio Hanks, at Mansfield, Connecticut. The first silk thread on spools was made by Merritt Heminway in Watertown, Connecticut (1849).

Jacob Sloat of Sloatsburg, New York, established a cotton twine factory (1839) and Arthur and John Scholfield began to produce broadcloth (1793), using a wool carding machine in a mill at Byfield, Massachusetts.

The first blanket factory was established (1854) in Maine by John H. Burleigh (1822–77), who later served in the House of Representatives. Thomas Goodall (1823–1910) began making horse blankets (1852) and after supplying the military in the Civil War opened a plant (1868) in Sanford, Maine, to produce all types of blankets.

Thomas R. Williams of Newport, Rhode Island, invented a process for making felt (1820) and Samuel L. Dana, a chemist, developed a system of bleaching cotton cloth and new ways of printing calico.

William Crompton (1806–91) patented the first successful power loom for making fancy cotton fabrics in the 1850s.

Calvin L. Goddard (1822–95) invented a machine (1866) to remove burrs which cling to wool and interfere with processing. Paul Moody (1779–1831) improved cotton spinning and weaving machines. John Good (1841–1908) developed machinery to make rope, which up to then was made by hand. The machinery included a breaker (1869) which drew flax and other fibers into slivers and became standard for the industry.

Egbert and Bailey of Cohoes, New York, manufactured the first power knitting machine (1830).

Silk culture in the United States began in Virginia (1623) and the state legislature called for the planting of ten mulberry trees for every 100 acres of property. Mulberry trees also were planted in South Carolina.

The first American silk mill was built (1810) for the Mansfield (Connecticut) Silk Company. Ward Cheney (1813–76) organized the Mt. Nebo Manufacturing Company, which he headed (1854–76). Jonathan H. Cobb (1799–1882) founded a silk factory in Dedham, Massachusetts (1837).

A patent for spinning artificial silk from cellulose acetate was issued to William H. Walker (1869–1934), Arthur D. Little (1863–1935), and Harry S. Mork. American Viscose Company began production in 1910.

14. Military

Air Force

The Army Balloon Corps was formed in 1861. The Army Balloon School was established April 6, 1917, by Major Albert B. Lambert in St. Louis. The Department of the Air Force began August 1, 1907, as the Aeronautical Division of the Army Signal Corps with an officer and two enlisted men to study the possible military uses of planes. By the end of World War I, the Division had 45 squadrons with more than 1,200 men. In May 1918, Congress created the Army Air service; it was renamed the Army Air Corps (1926) and became the Army Air Forces in World War II. The first Army parachute battalion was the 501st, organized at Ft. Benning, Georgia, October 1, 1940.

Army

The Continental Army was created June, 1775, when the Continental Congress formally accepted the forces defending Boston as the Army. Four days later, the Congress voted to raise ten companies of expert riflemen in Pennsylvania, Maryland and Virginia. The present Army marks this date, June 14, 1775, as its birthday.

The first Army unit to be formed was the Alexander Hamilton Provincial Company of Artillery of New York on January 6, 1776 (now known as Battery D, 5th Field Artillery). The first amphibious operation occurred August 29, 1776, when John Glover (1732–97) and his regiment saved 9,000 Continental Army men after their defeat in the Battle of Long Island by ferrying them across the East River to New York City in nine hours. Glover's unit also carried George Washington and his 2,400 men across the Delaware River December 25 to attack Trenton, New Jersey.

The Corps of Engineers was created March 6, 1802. Jonathan Williams (1750–1815) is known as the "father" of the Corps. He was the first to apply scientific engineering to military affairs and built Castle William on Governors Island in New York City.

The Army Medical Corps was organized April 14, 1818, with Joseph Lovell (1788–1836) as Surgeon General. The Army Ambulance Corps was established August 2, 1862, and was formally authorized by Congress March 11, 1864; both the Army Nurses Corps and Dental Corps were established in 1901. The Veterinary Corps was created in 1910.

The first cavalry unit was the Regiment of Dragoons, organized in August of 1833 at Jefferson Barracks, Missouri. The Signal Corps was created as a separate branch March 3, 1863.

The ROTC (Reserve Officers Training Corps) was created June 3, 1916, with the first units at Arkansas and Maine universities, St. John's College, Annapolis, Texas A and M, St. Thomas, St. Paul, Minnesota and The Citadel, Charleston, South Carolina.

The first armored force was created by Adna R. Chaffee (1884–1941) in 1928.

The Women's Army Auxiliary Corps (WAAC), later the Women's Army Corps (WAC), was created May 14, 1942 with Oveta Culp Hobby (1905–95) as director.

The Department of Defense was created by consolidating the War, Navy, and Air Forces departments into one agency September 18, 1947.

Marine Corps

The Marine Corps was created November 10, 1775, by the Continental Congress and formally established July 11, 1798.

Navy

The Navy was founded by the Continental Congress on October 13, 1775, commissioning Ezek Hopkins (1718–1802) as first commander of the fleet and authorized two cruisers.

Joshua Humphreys (1751–1838), who opened his own shipyard at age 25, became the foremost American marine engineer. He refitted eight small merchant ships for the Revolution. He submitted ideas for a U.S. Navy (1794). Congress asked him to prepare models for six frigates, which were built and made up the fleet which participated in some of the most memorable early American naval battles.

The Navy Department was created by Congress April 30, 1798, with Benjamin Stoddert (1751–1813) as the first Secretary (1798–1801).

The Navy Nurses Corps was created May 13, 1908, with Esther V. Hasson as first superintendent (1908–11). The Navy's women reserves (WAVES) was created 1942 with Mildred H. McAfee (1900–94), president of Wellesley College, as director.

The first Navy yard, the Portsmouth (New Hampshire) Navy Yard, was acquired in June of 1800 by purchasing 58.18 acres for $5,500. In the same year, the Navy built floating drydocks at Portsmouth and Pensacola, Florida.

The first American aircraft carrier, *Ranger*, was launched February 25, 1933, at Newport News, Virginia; a predecessor, the *Langley*, had been converted from a collier in 1922. The first atomic-powered carrier, the *Enterprise*, was launched in 1960.

The first American submarine, the *Turtle*, was developed by David Bushnell. It looked like the upper shells of two turtles and was a one-man vessel operated from inside and armed with a detachable gunpowder mine with an auger bit. The bit allowed the operator to attach the mine to the hull of an enemy ship below the water line. The *Turtle* was tried against the British in 1776–77 but the missions were unsuccessful.

Simon Lake (1866–1945), builder of marine machinery, constructed the gasoline-powered *Argonaut*. In 1897, it became the first submarine to operate successfully in the open sea. The Navy rejected Lake's vessel, which was purchased by several European countries.

The Navy purchased its first submarine April 11, 1900. Designed by John P. Holland (1840–1914), the vessel was equipped with an internal combustion engine and an electric motor.

Thomas Doughty, acting chief engineer of the Navy, invented the periscope (1864). Hyman G. Rickover (1900–86) was a leader in developing nuclear-powered submarines and other Navy vessels.

The world's first atomic-powered submarine, the *Nautilus*, was launched January 21, 1954, at Groton, Connecticut; the first ballistic missile submarine, *George Washington*, was launched June 9, 1959 at Groton.

Selective Service

The first conscription act was passed March 3, 1863, making all men 20–45 liable for military service which could be avoided by paying $300 or procuring a substitute to enlist for three years.

The Confederate Congress passed a bill for compulsory military service for all white men 18–35; amended in September to 18–45, and in February 1864 to 17–50.

President Wilson, on May 18, 1917, signed the Selective Service Act calling for the registration of men 21–30 for military service. An executive order in July called 678,000 registered men into the military service and a drawing a week later determined the date of service.

The first peacetime draft for military service was passed by Congress September 14, 1940, and more than 16 million men 21–36 registered on October 16, 1940. The draft age was lowered to 18 (November 13, 1942) with deferments limited to war industries, agriculture, hardship cases and the clergy. The draft law was amended December 22, 1941, extending service to men 20–44 and registration for men 18–64.

15. Music

American music is a mixture of music from many parts of Europe, the original home of many of the settlers, and from Africa, the homeland of many American slaves, who brought some of their music with them. There was very little original serious music in the early colonial days but it picked up in the early 1700s as a variety of musical instruments were imported.

The first formal concert was performed by painter Peter Pelham in Boston on December 30, 1731. Francis Hopkinson (1737–91) was the first noteworthy native-born composer. A signer of the Declaration of Independence, Hopkinson wrote the popular, "My Days Have Been Wondrous Free" (1759) and a first American music book, *Seven Songs for the Harpsichord.*

Brass Bands

The first American brass band was a group of fifes and drums organized when the Marine Corps was founded (1775). The fife and drum corps was the basis for the Marine Band which gave its first concert in Washington in 1800.

Patrick S. Gilmore (1829–92) introduced the new era of bands in the 1870s. He organized the National Peace Jubilee (1869) and the World Peace Jubilee (1872) in Boston. These spectaculars featured choruses of thousands of voices and large instrumental groups, including the "Anvil Chorus" with 100 firemen beating anvils to mark the rhythm. He also wrote the classic, "When Johnny Comes Marching Home Again."

John Philip Sousa (1854–1932) led the Marine Corps band (1880–

92), then formed his own band which toured successfully for 40 years. His talent for composing marches— about 140 of them — was unequalled.

Classical

Early composers of orchestral music were Edward A. MacDowell (1861–1908) and Charles W. Cadman (1881–1946). MacDowell, considered the foremost American composer (1880–1900) and the first American musician internationally acclaimed, composed many well-known songs ("The Rosary," "Mighty Lak a Rose") and the *Indian Suite* (1892) and *Woodland Sketches* (1896).

The New York Philharmonic Orchestra, oldest American symphonic organization, gave its first concert February 7, 1842, in the Apollo Rooms. The first chamber music organization was the Mendelssohn Quintet Club of Boston (1849).

The first symphony orchestra was the Collegium Musicum, Bethlehem, Pennsylvania. At the outset (1744), the orchestra had 14 members— four violins, two each of violas, flutes, trumpets and french horns, and a cello and double bass. The first college orchestra was founded at Harvard (1808).

Early American leaders of classical and semi-classical music were: Gottlieb Graupner (1767–1836) arrived in the United States (1792) and organized the Boston Phil-Harmonic Society, the first regular American concert orchestra (1810). He helped form the Handel and Haydn Society, one of the earliest choral groups (1815). Graupner is often referred to as the father of American orchestra music.

(C.F.) Theodore Thomas (1835–1905) began as a teenage violinist to supplement the family income, then joined chamber music groups. Thomas joined the Academy of Music Orchestra in New York City (1855) and became its conductor (1861). For the next 30 years, he conducted orchestras in and around New York City and did much to bring good music to more people. Thomas became conductor of the Chicago Symphony Orchestra (1891). The orchestra moved (1904) into Orchestra Hall, the first permanent auditorium for an American orchestra.

Leopold Damrosch (1832–85) founded the Oratorio Society of New York (1873), the New York Symphony Orchestra (1878) and produced the first music festival in New York City (1881), which drew 10,000 people. His son, Walter J. (1862–1950), pioneered radio concert broadcasting (1925) and children's music appreciation programs (1926). He conducted the New York Symphony for 30 years (1885–91, 1903–27).

Other noted symphony conductors were:

Serge Koussevitzky (1874–1951), Boston Symphony (1924–49), and founder of the annual Berkshire Festival (1934).

Eugene Ormandy (1899–1985), Philadelphia Symphony (1938–80).

Leopold Stokowski (1882–1977), conducted several orchestras, introduced modern music and the use of young and female musicians.

Arturo Toscanini (1867–1957), conductor of many orchestras including the NBC Symphony (1937–54), who exerted strong influence on musical performance standards.

Composers who influenced music with their innovations were Charles E. Ives (1874–1954), Arnold Schönberg (1874–1951), Edgard Varese (1883–1965) and John M. Cage (1912–92), probably the most radical and controversial modern American composer. Ives, a major innovator in twentieth century music, used polytonal harmonies and unusual rhythms; Schönberg abandoned the traditional tone system in favor of a 12-tone system; Varese, a leading experimenter, is considered the father of electronic music and the unconventional Cage made an indelible impression on twentieth century music. Two who achieved fame in classical circles with Negro spirituals and folk music were Harry T. Burleigh (1866–1949), baritone soloist at New York City's St. George's Episcopal Church (1894–1946), who composed and arranged spirituals, and Robert N. Dett (1882–1943), conductor/composer, who was the first to use Negro folk music in classical forms.

Among the leading classical instrumentalists were Louis M. Gottschalk (1829–69), one of the first American pianists to achieve international fame; Arthur Rubinstein (1889–1982), one of the greatest pianists and violinists Fritz Kreisler (1875–1962) and Jascha Heifetz (1901–87).

Education and Organizations

The St. Cecelia Society, perhaps the first American musical society, was formed in Charleston, South Carolina (1762). The New England Conservatory of Music, the oldest American independent conservatory, was founded in 1867. Composer William Billings (1746–1800) formed a singing school of 48 members (1774) which merged with the Stoughton Music Society (1786). (Billings is also credited with introducing the pitch pipe.)

Composer Lowell Mason (1792–1872) developed a system of music instruction for children and succeeded in introducing his methods in the Boston public schools (1837). The methods spread to many other schools. Mason organized the Boston Academy of Music (1833), which established a music school.

John K. Paine (1839–1906), an organist and composer, was the first American college music professor (Harvard 1875) and reportedly was the first to teach American music as art rather than a trade.

Hymns

Much of America's earliest music was hymnody. The first hymn book was *The Whole Booke of Psalmes* by Stephen Day. The book, issued in 1640, was generally known as *The Bay Psalm Book.*

The earliest known professional composer was Johann C. Beissel, the German founder of a religious and artistic society at Ephrata, Pennsylvania (1732). The principal vocation of the society was printing. Over the years, Beissel composed more than 1,000 hymns for the congregation of the Ephrata Cloisters and his hymns had a strong influence on later American hymns.

The first native-born professional composer was William Billings (1746–1800), who brought out the first of six church music collections, *The New England Psalm Singer* (1770). A choir member and music teacher, Billings wrote the first American war song, "Chester," widely sung by Revolutionary War soldiers.

Lowell Mason (1792–1872) was a prolific composer and adapter of hymns. Among his best known are "My Faith Looks Up to Thee" and "Nearer, My God, to Thee."

Samuel F. Smith (1808–95), a Baptist clergyman and editor, wrote the music for "America" ("My country 'tis of thee...") (1831) and an English professor, Katherine L. Bates (1859–1929) wrote the lyrics. Smith also wrote one of the best known hymns by an American — "The Morning Light Is Breaking."

Mahalia Jackson (1911–72) was the "queen" of gospel music, refusing to sing anything but religious songs.

Instruments

The first American musical instrument dealer was Michael Hillegas (1729–1804) in Philadelphia (1759). He later became a successful businessman and the first treasurer of the United States (1777–89). Instruments had been sold earlier (1716) at a dancing school in Boston.

The first American piano (spinet) was made (1769) by James Harris; another early piano maker was Benjamin Crehorne of Milton, Massachusetts (1803). A theater carpenter, Crehorne built string instruments and drums.

Jonas Chickering (1798–1853), an apprentice cabinet maker, undertook to repair the only piano in town. At 20, he began working for a Boston piano maker and helped form Stewart and Chickering (1823), which he headed from 1830, leading it to become one of the largest piano makers.

Henry E. Steinway (1797–1871) built a successful piano business in Germany (1820–48) but revolutions destroyed the business. He came to the United States (1851) and with his sons opened a piano shop in New York City two years later. Within a few years, the Steinway piano was a success.

Dwight H. Baldwin, a piano teacher, founded a piano manufacturing business in Cincinnati (1862). Valentine W. L. Knabe (1803–64) started as a repairman and began to manufacture pianos in Baltimore in 1840.

John McTammany (1845–1915), while fixing a music box, got the idea for a mechanical player piano and developed and demonstrated one in 1876. The music industry was opposed to the development but McTammany's 1881 patent was widely pirated and instruments were built and sold. McTammany won the legal battle and sold off his rights.

Wilcox and White Company began manufacturing a completely automatic player piano (1897).

The first American organ was built by Gustavus Hesselius (1682–1775) and installed in the Bethlehem (Pennsylvania) Moravian Church (1746). David Tanneberger (1728–1804) became the most expert and renowned American organ builder.

Emmons Hamlin (1821–85) worked in a melodeon (reed organ) factory and became partner with Henry Mason (1831–90) to form the Mason and Hamlin Organ Company (1854). The firm branched into piano making in 1882.

The first electric organ (1869), built by Hilborne L. Roosevelt (1849–86), was powered by storage batteries. Roosevelt opened a plant in New York City (1872), adding plants in Philadelphia and Baltimore. He built some of the largest church organs in the United States.

Laurens Hammond (1895–1973) invented and manufactured the first practical electric organ (1934).

Jacob Estey (1814–90) bought a small melodeon plant in Brattle-boro, Vermont (1850), and sold his products out of a wagon driving throughout New England and parts of Canada. The Estey Organ Company became the largest melodeon maker in the world by 1890, turning out 1800 a month.

Joshua C. Stoddard (1814–1902) of Worcester, Massachusetts, patented the steam calliope (1855) and organized the American Steam Music Company to manufacture calliopes for steamboats and circuses.

The first American carillon was installed in the belfry of the Old North (now Christ) Church in Boston (1745).

Wallingford Rieger (1885–1961), a leader in avant-garde music, helped develop a number of electronic instruments.

Jazz

An early jazz composer was Scott Joplin (1868–1917), a serious music student who played in the Maple Leaf Club in Sedalia, Missouri. A publisher heard him play a piano rag (1899) and gave him $50 and future royalties from what became "Maple Leaf Rag."

William C. Handy (1873–1958) specialized in writing blues—"Memphis Blues," which was written as a political campaign song (1911), "St. Louis Blues" (1914) and "Beale St. Blues."

Other early jazz composers include Buddy (Charles) Bolden (1868–1931), a cornetist and legendary founder of New Orleans jazz; Jelly Roll (Ferdinand) Morton (1885–1941), who wrote the "King Porter Stomp" and "Black Bottom Stomp," and Kid (Edward) Ory (1886–1973), a jazz musician who wrote "Muskrat Ramble."

Other early jazz bands and players include: Louis Armstrong (1900–71), who taught himself to play the cornet, then joined Kid Ory's band (1917) and later played with King (Joe) Oliver (1885–1938) and Fletcher Henderson (1898–1952). Armstrong formed his own band (1925) and did much to mellow the brass band sound of early jazz. Oliver began playing cornet in New Orleans jazz bands (1907), went to Chicago ten years later and took over the Creole Jazz Band, which became the first to make jazz recordings (1923).

Count (William) Basie (1904–84) was pianist with the Benny Moten band and after Moten died formed his own band (1935), which featured a "jumping" beat and Basie's piano.

Paul Whiteman (1891–1967), a symphonic viola player, developed "symphonic jazz" by combining blues and syncopated dance rhythms to be played by an orchestra. This gave jazz new style and form, which captivated large audiences. He gave his first formal jazz concert in New York City's Aeolian Hall (1924), featuring George Gershwin's "Rhapsody in Blue" with Gershwin at the piano.

Duke (Edward H.) Ellington (1899–1974), jazz composer and self-taught pianist, contributed many original jazz compositions, including "Mood Indigo" and "Black and Tan Fantasy."

Benny Goodman (1909–86), clarinetist with various groups, formed his own band (1934) and introduced "swing," which became immensely popular. He also developed a form of chamber jazz, using small combos.

Other contributors to the development of popular music include: Dave Brubeck (1920–), a pianist and leader in developing modern or progressive jazz; Bix (Leon B.) Beiderbecke (1903–31), legendary cornetist; Coleman Hawkins (1904–69), influential tenor saxophonist; Gene Krupa (1909–73), changed the drummer from timekeeper to soloist.

Charley Mingus (1922–79), great jazz bassist and the first to make the bass a solo instrument; Thelonius Monk (1917–82), jazz composer and pianist who helped develop "bop" with Hawkins; Dizzy (John B.) Gillespie (1917–92), and Charlie "Bird" Parker (1920–55); Sonny Rollins (1930–), jazz saxophonist who revived jazz improvisation.

The greatest woman blues and jazz singer was Bessie Smith (1898–1937), who received some training from her discoverer, "Ma" (Gertrude M.) Rainey (1886–1939), an early blues singer and Rome (Georgia) theater owner. Smith toured Southern bars and theaters and Columbia Records discovered her in 1923. Smith's first record, "Down-Hearted Blues," sold two million copies that year.

Music Publishers

The first music book by a native American was *Urania; or a Choice Collection of Psalmes-Tunes, Anthems, and Hymns* (1761) by James Lyon (1735–94). The first musical magazine was *American Musical Magazine*, published in New Haven (1786).

The first American music publisher was Moller and Capron of Philadelphia (1790). Two early major publishers were Oliver Ditson (1811–88) in Boston, who began, in 1835, what became one of the nation's largest music publishers, and Gustav Schirmer (1829–93), who worked his way into ownership of a publishing firm (1866), which became known worldwide.

Opera

The first opera performance in the colonies was Colley Cibber's *Flora* on February 18, 1735, in the Courtroom in Charleston, South Carolina.

The first American opera was *Tammany*, or the *Indian Chief* by James Hewitt (1770–1827) at the John Street Theater in New York City March 3, 1794. The first opera house in North America was the Theatre de St. Pierre, which opened in New Orleans 1791.

Early stock companies had regular performances, usually excerpts from different operas. A Spanish company starring Maria Mallibran gave the first American grand opera performance (1825) in its original language and form. After that, many European singers toured the country and cities began building opera houses.

The Metropolitan Opera House opened its $1,732,000 auditorium on Broadway and 34th Street, New York City, on October 22, 1883, with Gounod's *Faust*. Henry S. Abbey (1846–96) was the first manager of the Met (1883–84, 1891–96) and brought the best European talent to the United States.

Lillian Nordica (1859–1914) was the first American opera singer to win acclaim in Europe and was the most sought-after opera singer in the 1880–1910 period.

Popular Music

In colonial times, American songwriters borrowed from familiar English melodies and fitted them with homemade lyrics that expressed defiance of the mother country. The first such lyrics (1768) was "The Liberty Song" by John Dickinson (1732–1808) set to the music of William Boyce's "Heart of Oak." The song became an anthem of the Sons of Liberty. The most famous such song was "Yankee Doodle" which was sung by English soldiers to taunt the colonists. During the Revolution, the Americans appropriated the ditty and added new words.

One of the best known American composers of popular music was Stephen C. Foster (1826–64). While working as a bookkeeper in Cincinnati, he began his musical career with "O Susanna" and "Away Down South," written between 1846 and 1854. He went on to write such classics as "Old Folks at Home," "My Old Kentucky Home," "Camptown Races," "Old Black Joe," and "Beautiful Dreamer."

Septimus Winner (1827–1902) is credited with having written more than 200 volumes of music and instructions for various instruments. He also wrote a number of popular songs, including "Listen to the Mocking Bird," which he reportedly sold for $5. (In the next 50 years, 20 million copies of the song were sold.)

Carrie Jacobs Bond (1862–1946) wrote "I Love You Truly" and "A Perfect Day" but could not get the songs published. She organized a successful concert and formed her own publishing company. Charles Cadman, one of the first composers interested in Indian music and folklore, wrote "At Dawning" and "The Land of the Sky Blue Waters."

The minstrels were a source of much popular music and one of its greatest composers was James A. Bland (1854–1911), a banjo player with minstrel bands, who composed "Carry Me Back to Old Virginny," "Oh, Dem Golden Slippers," and "In the Evening by the Moonlight."

In popular, romantic music, one composer's name stands out — Irving Berlin (1888–1989), who grew up on New York's East Side and began work as a singing waiter. His first song, "Marie of Sunny Italy," was published in 1907 and he went on to write hundreds of popular songs, including "Easter Parade," "White Christmas," "God Bless America." He also pioneered in ragtime music with his "Alexander's Ragtime Band" (1911).

Among the popular dance bands were Guy Lombardo (1902–77) and Glenn Miller (1904–44). Lombardo formed his band (1920) in Canada, moved to the United States (1924), and the Royal Canadians became one of the most popular bands. Miller formed his band in 1937 and it quickly became the most popular band of the "big band" era.

Leadbelly (Huddie Ledbetter) (1888–1949) was one of the first black folk singers and master of the 12-string guitar. Pete Seeger (1919–), singer and composer, led the folk music revival of the 1940s and 50s.

Recorded Music

One of Thomas A. Edison's first inventions was the phonograph, which he patented in 1878. He invented the first record of vibrations which could be played back to reproduce sounds. He did little to exploit his invention because he was busy working on the electric light bulb and power systems.

Chichester A. Bell and Charles S. Tainter (1854–1940) improved on Edison's phonograph by cutting the sound track into wax rather than tinfoil (1885). Bell devised the turbulence amplifier and Tainter also invented such other sound recording devices as the Dictaphone.

Then came Emile Berliner, who patented a microphone (1891) and improved Edison's phonograph by discarding the cylinder and using a disc and needle moving horizontally across the disc. He called it a gramophone and patented it in 1887. Berliner than patented a flat phonograph record (1904) and developed a master disc from which copies could be made.

Stage Music

A major source of American popular music was— and remains— the Broadway stage musicals, operettas and light operas.

Victor Herbert (1859–1924), a cellist with many orchestras, wrote some of the most popular operettas—*Babes in Toyland* (1903), *The Red Mill* (1906), *Naughty Marietta* (1910), and *Sweethearts* (1913). Another noted composer was Sigmund Romberg (1887–1951), whose operettas included *Maytime* (1917), *Blossom Time* (1921), *The Student Prince* (1924), *The Desert Song* (1926) and *The New Moon* (1928).

Reginald DeKoven (1859–1920) established the style of American light opera, writing 20 such works, of which *Robin Hood* (1890) was the most successful.

Outstanding composers of Broadway musicals were Jerome D. Kern (1885–1945), Richard Rodgers (1902–79), Leonard Bernstein (1918–90) and Cole Porter (1893–1964), aided by such lyricists as Oscar Hammerstein II (1895–1960) and Lorenz Hart (1895–1943).

Kern wrote the music for 50 shows, including *Sunny* (1925), *Show Boat* (1927), *Music in the Air* (1932), *The Cat and the Fiddle* (1931), and *Roberta* (1933). Rodgers did *Jumbo* (1935), *Pal Joey* (1940), *Oklahoma* (1943), *South Pacific* (1949), *The King and I* (1951) and *The Sound of Music* (1959).

Bernstein, a noted conductor (New York Philharmonic) and composer of classical music, composed such musicals as *On the Town* (1944), *Candide* (1956), and *West Side Story* (1957), and Porter did *Anything Goes* (1934), *Red, Hot and Blue* (136), *DuBarry Was a Lady* (1939), *Panama Hattie* (1941) and *Kiss Me Kate* (1948).

16. Public Service

Firefighting

Gov. Peter Stuyvesant outlawed thatched roofs in New Amsterdam (1647), appointed wardens to inspect houses for fire safety. The next year, New Amsterdam prescribed fines for dirty chimneys, the fines to be used for purchasing hooks, ladders and leather buckets.

New Amsterdam created a fire watch of eight men (1658) and all adults were required to serve. The first American fire department was created 1659, equipped with 250 buckets, hooks and ladders imported from Holland. Each homeowner was taxed one guilder for each chimney to maintain the equipment.

New Amsterdam appointed two inspectors in each ward to check chimneys and hearths (1697).

The first fire engine built in the colonies was by Joseph Jenks of Lynn, Massachusetts (1654), and was designed to carry water in case of a fire — probably a water tank mounted on a cart. The first practical fire engine was built by Alexander B. Latta (1821–65) in Cincinnati (1852). Joseph G. Larned (1819–70) and Wellington Lee manufactured steam fire engines (1855) and later introduced a self-propelled steam fire engine.

Pennsylvania outlawed smoking tobacco on the streets (1696) with a fine of 12 pence for violators. The law also forbade storing more than six pounds of gunpowder within 52 yards of a dwelling.

Benjamin Franklin invented (1749) the lightning rod as a result of his kite experiments and had one installed on his house at 141 Market Street, Philadelphia.

The first fireboat was imported from England (1800) and used in New York City.

The first American fire insurance company, the Friendly Society for the Mutual Insurance of Houses Against Fire, was formed in Charleston, South Carolina (1735). Five years later fire destroyed half the city — and the company.

Another early fire insurance company was the Philadelphia Contributorship founded 1752, but it would not insure houses surrounded by trees. The Mutual Assurance Company was formed 1784 to insure houses that were surrounded by trees but had strict rules on tree trimming.

The first electric fire alarm system was invented by William F. Channing and Moses G. Farmer and installed in Boston (1851). Fire escapes were required in New York City (1860). Frank Grinnell, an engineer, patented a sprinkler system (1881) which was an improvement on the one invented by Henry S. Parmelee in 1874. Grinnell organized a merger of several companies (1893) into the General Fire Extinguisher Company. The fire extinguisher was patented by Alanson Crane of Virginia in 1863 and the Pyrene Manufacturing Company of Newark produced the first extinguishers (1905) using vaporized chemicals.

The National Board of Fire Underwriters was created (1866) to increase the public service activities of insurance companies.

The first American friction matches were made in Springfield, Massachusetts, by Daniel M. Chapin and Alonzo D. Phillips in 1834. Ohio C. Barber (1841–1920) organized the Barber Match Company (1862) which merged with other companies (1881) to form the Diamond Match Company. First book matches were produced by Diamond Match (1896) under a patent granted to Joshua Pusey of Linia, Ohio, in 1892.

Police

The first American police to have uniforms were those of New York City (1693) after the Council ordered they be provided "with a coat of ye city livery, with the badge of ye city armes, shoes and stockings...."

The first state police were the Texas Rangers (1835). New York City police created the first traffic squad (1850) — the Broadway Squad. The International Association of Chiefs of Police established the Bureau of Criminal Investigation (1896) in Chicago.

Allen Pinkerton (1819–94) became Chicago's first and only detective (1850) and later founded a major private detective agency.

The first practical use of fingerprints for criminal identification was made by New York State which began fingerprinting Sing Sing Prison inmates (1903). The next year, the warden of the federal prison at Leavenworth, Kansas, and the St. Louis Police Department began fingerprinting. All fingerprint collections were combined in 1924 by the FBI.

The first woman police officer was a Detroit policeman's widow, Marie Owen, in 1893; the first female detective was Isabella Goodwin in New York City (1912) and the first woman police chief was Dolly Spencer in Milford, Ohio (1914).

The first burglar alarm was installed by Edwin T. Holmes in Boston (1857). The alarm sounded when a door or window was opened, releasing a spring and causing a short circuit.

Postal Service

On November 5, 1639, the Massachusetts General Court ruled that all letters to and from England go to the home of Richard Fairfield, who would care for letters "brought from beyond the seas or to be sent thither." He would receive a penny for each letter.

The Virginia Assembly (1661) required planters to forward official mail from plantation to plantation until it reached its destination.

The first regular mail service began January 1, 1673, when a post rider began a monthly round trip from Boston to New York City. Pennsylvania established a postoffice in Philadelphia (1683) and the first postmaster was Henry Weldy, who was authorized to send mail weekly between Philadelphia and New Castle, Delaware.

Thomas Neale received a royal patent for 21 years on February 17, 1692, to establish colonial postoffices. There was a regular weekly post from Boston into New England (1707) and the middle colonies (not much farther than Philadelphia).

Benjamin Franklin was named Philadelphia postmaster (1737) and became co-deputy postmaster general of the British colonies in North America (1757). On July 26, 1775, the Continental Congress named Franklin head of the American postal system, a post he held until November 7, 1776.

The Federal Constitution gave Congress the right to establish post offices and post roads and it created the Post Office Department May 8, 1795. President Washington named Samuel Osgood (1748–1813) the first Postmaster General September 22, 1789. The Postmaster General became a member of the Cabinet March 9, 1829, and the Post Office Department an executive department June 8, 1872. The department was reorganized July 1, 1971 into the United States Postal Service.

The first post office building opened in Newport, Rhode Island (1830). Adhesive stamps were first used February 15, 1842, and their use became mandatory (1856). The first adhesive stamps (a five cent Benjamin Franklin and a ten cent George Washington) went on sale July 1, 1847. Perforated stamps were issued in 1857, books of stamps 1900 and rolls 1908. Stamped envelopes appeared in June 1853 and the first commemorative series (Christopher Columbus) in 1893. Free city delivery began in 49 cities (1863), was extended to cities of more than 50,000 population, and permitted in cities over 10,000 with postal receipts of $10,000 (1887). Residential mail deliveries were cut to once a day (1950). Rural free delivery began October 1, 1896, on three routes in West Virginia.

The first overland mail stage from San Francisco reached St. Louis October 9, 1858, after 23 days and four hours; the opposite stage left at the same time arriving in San Francisco October 10. The first Pony Express began April 3, 1860 between St. Joseph, Missouri, and Sacramento, California. It ended October 24, 1861, with the completion of the first transcontinental telegraph line.

The first airmail pilot was Earle L. Ovington (1879–1936), sworn in September 23, 1911, and service began May 15, 1918, between Washington and New York City. The first flight used War Department planes, with one plane flying from Long Island to Philadelphia and then a relief plane to Washington. The first flight took three hours 20 minutes and carried two sacks with 2,457 pieces of mail.

The first transcontinental airmail flight was February 22–23, 1921, from San Francisco to New York City, with actual flying time of 25 hours 16 minutes at an average speed of 104 miles an hour for the 2,629 miles.

The China Clipper left Alameda, California, November 22, 1935, to inaugurate transpacific airmail service and arrived in Manila seven days later. Transatlantic service began May 20, 1939, between New York City and Marseilles.

Private mail boxes—a series of numbered glass-front pigeon holes—were invented (1810) by Thomas Brown. The steel mail box was invented (1858) by Albert Potts of Philadelphia. Drive-up mail boxes to serve motorists in their cars began in Houston (1927). Mail chutes for high rise buildings began in the Elwood Building in Rochester, New York, (1883). The chute was invented by Architect Joseph G. Cutler, who called it the "letterbox connection." He and his brother formed a company to manufacture the chutes.

Parcel post service began June 1, 1913, throughout the country and an estimated six million parcels were sent the first day.

The Postal Savings System's first banks opened in 48 selected second class post offices June 3, 1911. The system ended in 1966. Money orders began November 1, 1864, registered mail 1855, special delivery October 1, 1885, special handling 1925.

The penny postcard was first issued May 1, 1873. V-mail began in 1943. Letter carrier uniforms were authorized in 1868. Postage meters went into use November 16, 1920. The idea originated in 1910 but was not approved until September 1920.

Water, Sewage

The first city to build a municipal water system was Boston (1652) and it consisted of a series of wooden pipes carrying water from springs to a reservoir. The first major water pumping plant to supply a city was installed in Bethlehem, Pennsylvania (1755), the water being pumped into a water tower.

Between 1837 and 1843, New York City's first aqueduct, Old Croton Aqueduct, was built — 43 miles long, supplying 95 million gallons daily. The New Croton Aqueduct, 25 miles long, was built in 1884–93, supplying 300 million gallons daily. The Catskill System was added (1907–17, 1927); it was 150 miles long, providing 555 million gallons daily. The final addition was the Delaware System. All four systems combined supply 1820 million gallons daily.

The first city water supplied by tunnel was the Chicago Lake Tunnel (1867), which ran 10,587 feet in Lake Michigan to an inlet crib. The first municipal water filtration system was built in Lawrence, Massachusetts (1893). The first city to fluoridate its water was Grand Rapids, Michigan (1945). The first practical sea water conversion plant opened 1961 in Freeport, Texas.

The first urban underground comprehensive sewage system began in Chicago (1856). The first separate sewage disposal system began in Memphis, Tennessee (1880). The first system using a chemical precipitation settling basin was in Worcester, Massachusetts (1890).

17. Publications

Books

Books were part of early colonial life. Some residents brought their libraries with them. By 1637, a "bookbynder" shop had opened in Boston and Hezekiah Usher began importing books (1647) to sell.

The Bay Psalm Book (1640) is generally considered the first book printed in the colonies. Puritan ministers Richard Mather, John Eliot and Thomas Weld (1585–1661) began the work (1636) with the idea of putting the psalms into verse suitable for singing at prayer meetings.

Early American authors include Capt. John Smith (1580–1631), with his several accounts of the Jamestown colony (1608, 1624) and an autobiography (1630) that established the legend of Pocahontas; Richard Rich, who made a round trip to Virginia (1609) and wrote *Newes from Virginia* (1610); Alexander Whitaker (1585–1616), with *Good Newes from Virginia* (1613) and William Byrd (1674–1744), a Virginia planter whose writings gave a highly detailed picture of life in the South.

New England was described by William Bradford (1590–1657) in his history of Plymouth Plantation; John Winthrop, first Massachusetts colonial governor, wrote an informative journal, published in 1790; Edward Johnson (1598–1672) wrote a New England history; Mary W. Rowlandson (1635–78), wrote of her 14-month imprisonment by Indians; Michael Wigglesworth (1631–1705), wrote the famous poem *Day of Doom*, and Cotton Mather, who became the most prolific and versatile prose writer of his time.

Other colonial writers were Daniel Denton (1626–1703) with his *Brief Description of New York* (1670); William Penn, who wrote about Pennsylvania (1681); Thomas Ashe wrote *Carolina* in 1682, and Nathaniel

Ward (1578–1672), pastor at Agawam (now Ipswich), wrote the *Simple Cobbler of Agawam* (1647), a satire on religion and politics in England and America.

Some of the early writers who helped lay the foundation for American literature:

William M. Brown (1765–93), author of the first American novel, *The Power of Sympathy*, published in January, 1789.

Cotton Mather's classic work *Magnalia Christi Americana* (1702), was an encyclopedic classic of the annals of New England. He turned out 459 books of essays, political fables, meditations and sermons, elegies and eulogies, tales of warfare and piracy, science and history.

Jonathan Edwards, a Puritan clergyman, was recognized as the first great American philosopher.

Samuel Sewall (1652–1730), who presided at the Salem witchcraft trials, wrote a three-volume diary which gave a vivid picture of the time.

Thomas Paine (1737–1809) gained fame with *Common Sense* (1776), originally a 46-page pamphlet urging an immediate declaration of independence. He later went on to write *The Crisis, The Age of Reason*, and *The Rights of Man*.

Jonathan Carver (1710–80), an explorer, wrote an early popular travel book — *Travels Through the Interior Parts of North America* (1778). It was the most popular, widely-read early American travel book.

Susanna H. Rowson (1762–1824) wrote the first American best seller, *Charlotte Temple* (1794) and Charles B. Brown (1771–1810) was the first American professional novelist and the first to gain an international reputation.

Parson (Mason L.) Weems (1759–1825) published the *Life of George Washington* (1800), which, after the fourth edition, carried the legendary cherry tree story. The book went through 29 editions.

Lydia Marie Child (1802–80), magazine editor, wrote practical books such as *The Frugal Housewife* (1829), which went through 21 editions in a decade.

Among the authors of children's literature were Clement C. Moore (1779–1863), a lexicographer whose 1822 Christmas gift to his children began with "'Twas the night before Christmas...." Others were Thornton W. Burgess (1874–1965), author of nature books; Samuel G. Goodrich

(1793–1860), who as "Peter Farley" published 116 educational books for children and Mary E. M. Dodge (1831–1905), who wrote *Hans Brinker; or The Silver Skates* and edited *St. Nicholas Magazine* (1873–1905).

Nature writers go back to Henry David Thoreau (1817–62) and his book *Walden* and John Burroughs (1837–1921), who established the nature essay as a literary form.

Short story writing dates back to Washington Irving (1783–1859), who began with a comic Dutch volume, *A History of New York*, followed by *The Sketch Book* (1820), which contained the memorable "Rip van Winkle" and "The Legend of Sleepy Hollow"; O. Henry (William S. Porter 1862–1910), who popularized the short story, and Bret (Francis B.) Harte (1836–1902), creator of the local color short story ("The Luck of Roaring Camp" and "The Outcasts of Poker Flat").

Essayists began with Ralph Waldo Emerson (1803–82), who served briefly as a Congregational minister and then turned to writing.

Mysteries started with Edgar Allan Poe (1809–49), whose talents included editing, poetry, the short story and mystery — he wrote "The Murders in the Rue Morgue" and many others after 1841. The "how to" books began with the most popular nonfiction book of modern times — Dale Carnegie's (1888–1955) *How to Win Friends and Influence People* (1936), which was translated into more than 30 languages.

Science fiction writers of note include Isaac Asimov (1920–92) and Robert A. Heinlein (1907–88). John W. Campbell, Jr. (1910–71), editor of *Astounding Science Fiction* (later *Analog*, 1937–71), exerted great influence in this field of writing and published most of the important writers.

The preparation of dictionaries began (1788) with William Perry of Edinburgh, who compiled the first American dictionary. Noah Webster began work in 1807 on the *American Dictionary of the English Language*, which came out in 1828 containing 1,939 pages and 75,000 definitions. Joseph E. Worcester (1784–1865), a serious competitor of Webster, issued a dictionary in 1860, the first to contain illustrations and synonyms and the first prepared by a large staff of experts.

The first American encyclopedia was the 13-volume *Encyclopedia Americana* issued between 1788 and 1797. An edition of the 18-volume *Encyclopedia Britannica* was printed in the United States in 1798.

American poetry dates back to Anne D. Bradstreet (1612–72), the first colonial woman poet, who produced *The Tenth Muse* (1650); Michael Wigglesworth, clergyman whose *Day of Doom* was a dramatic expression of the grim Puritan theology, and Edward Taylor (1654–1729), a minister and physician, who was the best colonial poet but his work was not published until 1939.

Then followed some of America's greatest poets: William Cullen Bryant, newspaper editor and writer of "Thanatopsis," the first poem to gain wide recognition, and "To a Water Fowl"; Henry Wadsworth Longfellow (1807–82), America's best known and best loved poet ("The Village Blacksmith," "Paul Revere's Ride," "Hiawatha"); Walt Whitman (1819–92), whose *Leaves of Grass* (1855) was probably the most influential single American volume of verse; Emily Dickinson (1830–86), considered America's greatest woman poet; Edwin Arlington Robinson (1869–1935), and Robert Frost (1874–1963).

The first American publishing enterprise was established 1638 in Cambridge and set a pattern which lasted many years. Once a press was set up, the owner usually first printed a book of local laws, then a newspaper, and in time a magazine and other books.

The first important American bookseller was Hezekiah Usher in Cambridge (1639). The first book entered for copyright was *The Philadelphia Spelling Book* by John Barry (1745–1803) on June 9, 1790. The first book fair was held June 1, 1802, in the Beaver Street Coffee House in New York City. The first book review editor was Sarah Margaret Fuller (1810–50) hired by the *New York Tribune* (1844) and the first book review section was issued October 10, 1896, by *The New York Times*.

Robert Bell (1732–84) began as a bookseller and auctioneer, then became a publisher issuing Thomas Paine's *Common Sense*. Isaiah Thomas (1749–1831), a co-founder of the anti-British journal, *Massachusetts Spy* (1770), became the leading publisher of his time putting out more than 400 books, including the first American Bible, the first American dictionary and more than 100 children's books.

Other early publishers were:

Brothers Dan (1771–1823), Ebenezer (1777–1858), and George Merriam (1773–1802) founded E. Merriam and Company (1798).

John (1797–1875) and James Harper (1795–1869) founded J. and J. Harper (1817), which became Harper and Brothers (1833).

William D. Ticknor (1810–64) founded a company (1831) which became Ticknor and Fields.

Joshua B. Lippincott (1813–86) organized J. B. Lippincott and Company (1836).

Charles C. Little (1799–1869), a bookstore clerk, and James Brown (1800–55) founded what became Little, Brown and Company (1837).

George P. Putnam (1814–72) began as a struggling salesman of American books in England, then founded G. P. Putnam and Sons (1866).

Charles Scribner (1812–71) founded the family publishing firm (1846).

In 1842, the first "paperbacks" appeared as supplements to newspapers, reprinting pirated copies of popular British novels. These were followed in the 1860s by the "dime novels."

Erastus F. Beadle (1821–94), a magazine publisher, joined with Robert Adams to form Beadle and Adams (1856) and began publishing dime novels (1860). The first such novel was *Malaeska* by Anne S. Stephens (1813–86), which was a tremendous success. The Beadle Dime Novel Series used a stable of writers and produced more than 1,800 books.

George Munro (1825–96), a Beadle employee, formed his own company (1863) and became one of the top five in the field for 30 years.

The Book of the Month Club, the first in the United States, was founded (1926) by Harry Scherman (1887–1969). The first selection was *Lolly Willowes* by Sylvia Townsend Warner. The Literary Guild was created (1927) by Harold G. Guinzburg (1899–1961) of the Viking Press.

Cartoons/Comics

Early American cartoons date back to Benjamin Franklin, who designed the "Join or Die" cartoon published in his *Pennsylvania Gazette* in May 1754, and Frank H. T. Bellew (1828–88), comic illustrator for *Harper's Magazine*, who drew the Uncle Sam cartoon which appeared in March, 1852, in the weekly *New York Lantern*.

One of the most influential cartoonists was Thomas Nast (1840–1902) of *Harper's Weekly* (1862–86). He introduced the donkey as the symbol of the Democratic Party (1870), the elephant for the Republican Party (1874) and the Tammany tiger.

The first newspaper cartoon strip, "Professor Tigwissel's Burglar Alarm," appeared September 11, 1875, in the *New York Daily Graphic*. James G. Swinnerton (1875–1974) created the cartoon "Little Bears" (1892) in the *San Francisco Examiner*, the first continuing characters to appear in a daily paper.

Richard F. Outcault (1863–1928) began his cartoon, "Origin of the New Species," in November 1894 in the *New York World*, which had new presses able to print color supplements. Outcault began his "Hogan's Alley," featuring the "Yellow Kid" (1895), then moved to the *New York*

Herald where he began his internationally-acclaimed "Buster Brown" cartoon (1902).

The *New York Journal* printed the first comic section (1896), a section of eight pages described as "polychromatic effulgence." Color comic books made their first appearance (1904) in New York City, reprinting cartoons from the daily papers.

Among the many notable cartoonists were: Fontaine T. Fox, Jr. (1884–1964), who did "Toonerville Trolley"; Rube (Reuben L.) Goldberg (1883–1970), creator of "Boob McNutt" and "Lala Palooza" cartoons but best remembered for his complicated invention cartoons; Bud (Harry C.) Fisher (1884–1954), creator of "Mutt and Jeff" (1908), the first comic strip produced six days a week and widely syndicated; George McManus (1884–1954), who began his "Bringing Up Father" (1912) with the most popular cartoon characters, Maggie and Jiggs.

Robert L. Ripley (1893–1949), a sports cartoonist with the *New York Globe*, in 1918 sketched some figures representing men who set unusual sports records, entitling it "Believe It or Not!" The response was immediate and he began using all sorts of bizarre facts, moving to the *New York Post* (1923) and syndication.

Elzie C. Segar (1895–1938) did the "Thimble Theater" comic strip (1919) featuring Olive Oyl and family, adding the character Popeye (1929); John Held, Jr. (1889–1958), did cartoons and illustrations depicting the 1920s jazz era; Milt(on A.) Caniff (1907–88) began "Terry and the Pirates" (1934) and "Steve Canyon" (1947); Al Capp (1909–79) started "Lil Abner" (1934).

Magazines

Magazines were the last of the print media to appear in the American colonies, starting in the 1740s. They were the outgrowth of the almanacs which began about 100 years earlier. The almanacs used features traditional in European almanacs which added bits of history, astrological prophecies and news.

The first American almanac was printed by Stephen Day, the first printer in the colonies—*An Almanac for New England for the Year 1639* by William Pierce, "mariner."

Nathaniel Ames (1708–64), a physician and innkeeper in Dedham, Massachusetts, published the *Astronomical Diary and Almanack* (1726–64), the standard New England publication. William Bradford, who later founded a New York City paper, published a single leaf almanac (1687) compiled by Daniel Leeds.

Benjamin Franklin's half brother, James, began the *Rhode Island Almanac* (1728) and Franklin's popular *Poor Richard's Almanac* began in 1733.

Nathan Daboll (1750–1818) began working on the popular *New England Almanac* (1770) and Robert B. Thomas (1766–1846) launched the long lasting *The Old Farmers Almanac* (1793).

The first magazine, *The American Magazine*, was issued February 13, 1741, by Andrew Bradford and John Webbe. Three days later, Benjamin Franklin issued his *General Magazine*. Both magazines folded within six months.

The first popular monthly magazine was the *Knickerbocker Magazine* (1833) and the first illustrated weekly, *Brother Jonathan* (1842). The first children's magazine, *The Juvenile Miscellany*, was founded (1826) by Lydia M. F. Child; an earlier publication, *Children's Magazine*, lasted only four issues in 1789. The first American women's periodical was the *Lady's Book* (later known as *Godey's Lady's Book*) (1830).

Many short-lived magazines came and went in the next hundred years. A brief flurry occurred before and after the Civil War, led by the *North American Review* (1815), *Harper's Weekly Magazine* and the *Atlantic Monthly* in 1857.

By 1900, ten cent magazines became popular —*McClure's*, *Colliers*, *Cosmopolitan*, and *Munsey's*— and great editors were in control. Edwin L. Godkin (1831–1902) at *The Nation*, Edward W. Bok (1863–1930) at the *Ladies Home Journal* and George H. Lorimer (1867–1937) at the *Saturday Evening Post*. Godkin founded *The Nation* (1865) and it quickly became the foremost review in the United States. He sold it to the *New York Post* (1881) and it became a weekly edition of the paper.

Cyrus H. K. Curtis (1850–1933) began the *Tribune and Farmer* (1879) and his wife contributed a woman's column which became the magazine's most popular feature. This led Curtis to found the *Ladies Journal* (later the *Ladies Home Journal*) (1883). Curtis invited Bok to edit the *Journal*, which he did for 30 years (1889–1919). Curtis formed the Curtis Publishing Company (1890), adding other magazines including the *Saturday Evening Post*, which he bought for $1,000 in 1897. (The *Post* began as a newspaper (1821), gradually changing to a magazine by 1871.)

Lorimer became literary editor of the *Post* (1898) and a year later editor-in-chief, developing the magazine into one of the leading periodicals of the time.

Frank A. Munsey (1854–1925) began the *Golden Argosy* for children (1882), later becoming the first successful all-fiction pulp magazine, *Argosy* (1896). He also founded *Munsey's Magazine* (1889), which led the world in circulation in 1907.

Samuel S. McClure (1857–1949), founder of the first American news syndicate (1884), established *McClure's Magazine* (1893), which became an important shaper of public opinion. The magazine carried the first so-called muckraking articles, such as those by Lincoln Steffens (1866–1936) and Ida M. Tarbell (1857–1944).

Gilbert H. Grosvenor (1875–1966) edited the *National Geographic Magazine* (1903–54), building it into a popular magazine with general articles and superior color photography.

John E. Johnson (1918–) began as an office boy (1936) in the Supreme Liberty Life Insurance Company. He worked his way through college, regularly buying stock in the company. He became the principal stockholder (1964) and later board chairman. As an early duty at the insurance company, Johnson began to prepare news of American blacks. This led him to found the *Negro Digest* (1942). Three years later he launched *Ebony*, which passed the million circulation mark by 1967, *Tan* (1950) and *Jet* (1951).

The first American humor weekly was *Puck*, which was edited by Henry C. Bunner (1855–96), from 1877 to his death. The paper became very popular.

Newspapers

The first American so-called newspaper was a broadside issued (1689) by Samuel Green of Cambridge called *The Present State of the New English Affairs*.

The first newspaper was issued by Benjamin Harris (1673–1716) in Boston on September 25, 1690, called *Publick Occurrences Both Foreign and Domestick*. The paper was suppressed four days after its issuance because it contained "Reflections of a very high nature; As also sundry doubtful and uncertain Reports…." Harris, who came to the United States in 1686, was a successful bookstore owner, published an almanac (1687), and the very successful school textbook, *The New England Primer*. His bookshop was a social and literary gathering place of Bostonians.

On April 24, 1704, the *Boston News Letter* (considered the first established paper) was issued by John A. Campbell (1653–1728), bookseller and postmaster. The paper was small, both sides of a 6½ by 10½ inch sheet, and never attained a circulation of more than 300. Campbell could not keep up with the demand for the paper and in 1722 turned it over to Bartholomew Green (1666–1732), his printer and son of Samuel Green. The paper, which lasted until 1776, gave much space to old foreign news and very little to local events. While Campbell had the paper he was replaced (1719) as postmaster by William Brooker, but Campbell refused to turn over the paper. Brooker then founded the *Boston Gazette* in December 1719. The paper's first printer was James Franklin (1697–1735), who had his 15-year-old half brother, Benjamin, as an apprentice.

James Franklin founded the *New England Courant* (1721), which was the first paper to cater to readers' likes and was not controlled by officials. Franklin attacked the stern discipline imposed by the clergy and the government, for which he was charged with contempt and jailed (1722). The *Courant* declined in popularity and James Franklin abandoned it (1726), founding the first Rhode Island paper, *Gazette*, in 1732.

Thomas Fleet (1685–1758) opened a print shop in Boston (1712) and founded the *Boston Evening Post* in August 1735.

Andrew Bradford (1686–1742), son of William (see below), and John Copson founded the first Philadelphia newspaper, the *American Weekly Mercury* in December 1719. A second paper, the *Universal Instructor in All Arts and Sciences and the Philadelphia Gazette*, was founded (1728) in Philadelphia by Samuel Keimer (1688–1739). Benjamin Franklin, who had become a Philadelphia printer working for Keimer, bought the *Gazette* (1729) and ran it successfully until 1748.

The first American daily newspaper, the *Pennsylvania Packet and General Advertiser*, was published in Philadelphia September 21, 1784, by John Dunlap (1747–1812), who began publishing it as a weekly in 1771.

William Bradford founded the first New York City paper (*New York Gazette*) November 8, 1725. Bradford, who helped found the first American paper mill in Pennsylvania (1690), was printer for the New York colony and the *Gazette* was the colonial government's organ.

John Peter Zenger (1697–1746) was induced to start the *New York Weekly Journal* (1733) in opposition to the *Gazette*. In 1734, he was arrested and charged with seditious libel. Zenger's attorney, Andrew Hamilton (1676–1741), argued that the matter printed was not libel but he was not permitted to prove the truth of the statements. So Hamilton asked the jury to act like free people and acquit Zenger, which it did.

New York State adopted a law (1805) guaranteeing freedom of the press and other states quickly followed. Papers sprung up in the other colonies— Maryland 1727, Rhode Island and South Carolina 1734, North Carolina 1735, Virginia 1736, Connecticut 1755, New Hampshire 1756, Georgia 1763, Florida 1783, Delaware, Vermont and Maine 1785.

The first newspaper west of the Appalachians was the *Pittsburgh Gazette* begun (1786) by John Scull (1765–1828) and Joseph Hull, who brought a press, type, ink, and paper over the mountains by pack horse. The first newspaper west of the Mississippi River was the St. Louis *Missouri Gazette* (1808), founded by Joseph Charles (1772–1834).

The first newspaper and publisher(s) (when available) in all 50 states:

Alabama —*Mobile Centinel* 1811 Samuel Miller and John B. Hood.

Alaska —*Esquimaux* (Point Clarence) 1866 John J. Harrington.

Arizona — The *Weekly Arizonian* (Tuboc) 1859.

Arkansas—*Arkansas Gazette* (Arkansas Post) 1819 William E. Woodruff.

California —*Californian* (Monterey) 1846.

Colorado—*Rocky Mountain News* (Denver) 1857 William N. Byers.

Connecticut —*Connecticut Gazette* (New Haven) 1755 Timothy Green.

Delaware —*Delaware Gazette* (Wilmington) 1785 Jacob A. Killen.

Florida —*East Florida Gazette* (St. Augustine) 1783 John Wells.

Georgia —*Georgia Gazette* (Savannah) 1763 James Johnston.

Hawaii —*Sandwich Island Gazette* 1836.

Idaho—*Golden Age* (Lewiston) 1862.

Illinois—*Illinois Herald* (Kaskaskia) 1814 Matthew Duncan.

Indiana —*Indiana Gazette* (Vincennes) 1804 Elihu Stout.

Iowa —*Dubuque Visitor* 1836 John King.

Kansas—*Kansas Weekly Herald* (Leavenworth) 1854.

Kentucky —*Kentucky Gazette* (Lexington) 1787 John Bradford.

Louisiana—*Moniteur de la Louisiane* (New Orleans) 1794 Louis Duclot.

Maine—*Falmouth Gazette* (Portland) 1785 Benjamin Titcomb, Jr., and Thomas B. Wait.

Maryland—*Maryland Gazette* (Annapolis) 1727 William Parks.

Massachusetts—*Boston News Letter* 1704 John A. Campbell.

Michigan—*Detroit Gazette* 1817.

Minnesota—*Minnesota Pioneer* (St. Paul) 1849 James M. Goodhue.

Mississippi—*Mississippi Gazette* (Natchez) 1799 Benjamin M. Stokes.

Missouri—*Missouri Gazette* (St. Louis) 1808 Joseph Charles.

Montana—*Montana Post* (Virginia City) 1864.

Nebraska—*Nebraska Palladium* 1854.

Nevada—*Territorial Enterprise* (Genoa) 1858.

New Hampshire—*New Hampshire Gazette* (Portsmouth) 1756 Daniel Fowle.

New Jersey—*New York Gazette* (published here during British occupation of New York).

New Mexico—*Santa Fe Republican* 1847.

New York—*New York Gazette* (New York City) 1725 William Bradford.

North Carolina—*North Carolina Gazette* (New Bern) 1755 James Davis.

North Dakota—*Ft. Union Frontier Scout* 1864.

Ohio—*Centinel of North-Western Territory* (Cincinnati) 1793 William Maxwell.

Oklahoma—*Cherokee Messenger* (Westville) 1844.

Oregon—*Oregon Spectator* (Oregon City) 1846.

Pennsylvania—*American Weekly Mercury* (Philadelphia) 1719 Andrew Bradford/John Copson.

Rhode Island—*Rhode Island Gazette* (Newport) 1732 James Franklin.

South Carolina—*South Carolina Gazette* (Charleston) 1732.

South Dakota—*Sioux Falls Democrat* 1858.

Tennessee—*Knoxville Gazette* 1791 George Roulstone.

Texas—*Telegraph and Texas Register* (San Felipe) 1835.

Utah —*Deseret News* (Salt Lake City) 1850.

Vermont —*Vermont Gazette* (Westminster) 1785 Timothy Green and J. B. Spooner.

Virginia —*Virginia Gazette* (Williamsburg) 1736.

Washington —*Columbian* (Olympia) 1852.

West Virginia —*Potomac Guardian* 1790 Nathaniel Willis.

Wisconsin —*Green Bay Intelligencer* 1833.

Wyoming —*Ft. Bridger Daily Telegram* 1863.

Newspapers developed steadily after the Revolution and between 1824 and 1890 the major metropolitan dailies and chains emerged. The greatest concentration was in New York City, including such papers as: *New York Sun*, the first penny daily, was founded by Benjamin H. Day (1810–99) on September 3, 1833. He set type, rewrote news from other papers, and lifted ads for a show of prosperity. He introduced the use of newsboys to sell the paper. Moses Yale Beach (1800–68) worked at the *Sun* and bought the paper (1838) by which time its circulation had grown to 30,000. His son, Moses S. (1822–92) took over (1852) and made numerous improvements.

New York Herald was founded by James Gordon Bennett (1795–1872) on May 6, 1835, with $500 and a willingness to do everything. He pioneered in presenting financial news, featured society news, used telegraph extensively, and established a string of reporters in Europe.

New York Evening Post was edited for nearly 50 years (1829–78) by William Cullen Bryant (1794–1878), best remembered as a poet ("Thanatopsis" and "To a Water Fowl").

New York Tribune was founded by Horace Greeley (1811–72) on April 10, 1841. Greeley was considered the greatest editor of his time and one of the great American moral leaders.

New York Times was founded by Henry J. Raymond (1820–69) and George Jones (1811–91) on September 18, 1851. Raymond and Jones, who worked together on the *Tribune*, created a paper unusual for its day as it strove for bipartisanship with an elevated tone and style. The *Times* was sold (1896) to Adolph S. Ochs (1858–1935), who had developed the *Chattanooga* (Tennessee) *Times* into a successful paper.

New York World was taken over (1883) by Joseph Pulitzer (1846–1911), who had succeeded in St. Louis. He set the pattern for modern papers by bringing together news, sports, women's pages, pictures and comics.

Outside New York City other important papers developed: *Baltimore Sun* was founded (1837) by Arunah S. Abell (1806–88), who, a year earlier, had become co-owner of a Philadelphia paper. Abell was a pioneer in systematic and speedy news gathering.

Springfield (Massachusetts) *Republican* began as a weekly (1824) with Samuel Bowles (1797–1851) the founder. It became a daily 20 years later and its success rested on a chain of local correspondents providing complete coverage of the Connecticut Valley.

Chicago Tribune was taken over (1874) by Joseph Medill (1823–99), who had operated papers in Ohio and gained gradual control of the *Tribune*. A similar approach led to control of the *Los Angeles Times* by Harrison G. Otis (1837–1917).

Des Moines (Iowa) *Register*, a family newspaper, was built up by Gardner Cowles (1903–85), who went on to buy the *Minneapolis Star*.

Michael H. DeYoung (1849–1925) and his brother, Charles (1847–80) developed a free theater program into a successful daily paper, the *San Francisco Chronicle* (1868).

William Randolph Hearst (1863–1951) took over his father's *San Francisco Examiner* (1887) and made it a success. He then went on to take over papers in New York, Chicago and Boston and other media properties including two news services, 24 other newspapers and 18 magazines.

Frank S. Gannett (1876–1957) founded a chain of 21 papers and Samuel I. Newhouse (1895–1979) built up a chain of 30 newspapers and several magazines.

Edward W. Scripps (1854–1926) and Milton R. McRae (1858–1930) formed the Scripps-McRae League of Newspapers (1895) which, over the years, developed into the Scripps-Howard chain (1922). The chain was run by Scripps' son, Robert P. (1895–1938) and Roy M. Howard (1883–1964).

There were many other contributors to development of the American press. In financial reporting were Charles H. Dow (1851–1902) and Edward D. Jones (1856–1920), who formed a financial information service (Dow Jones) which founded the *Wall Street Journal* (1889). Dow is credited with compiling the first average of stock prices, which developed into the Dow Jones industrial average.

Clarence W. Barron (1855–1928) took over Dow Jones and Co. (1901), the *Journal*, and founded his *Financial Weekly* (1921). Arthur Tappan (1786–1865), a successful silk merchant, founded the *New York Journal of Commerce* (1827).

The first important labor paper was the *Working Man's Advocate* founded (1829) by George H. Evans (1805–56). The paper ran sporadically until 1845.

The first American black newspaper, *Freedom Journal*, was published March 6, 1827, by John B. Russworm (1799–1851) and John Cornish but lasted only a year. The leading black paper, *Chicago Defender*, was first issued in May, 1905, by Robert S. Abbott (1868–1940).

Frank Leslie (1821–80) is considered the founder of American pictorial journalism. An engraver, he developed a technique to divide large illustrations into small blocks for speedier engraving. He founded *Leslie's Illustrated Newspaper* (1855) and later published weekly illustrated publications in other markets.

The forerunner of the news service was founded (1814) by Samuel Topliff (1789–1864), who ran a Boston coffee house and reading room. He gathered foreign news from patrons, which he sold to Boston, New York and Philadelphia newspapers.

Six New York City daily papers joined (1848) to pay for a telegraph relay of foreign news brought by ships to Boston. This became the New York Associated Press (1856) and the present AP (1892). The United Press was formed (1907) by Edward Scripps and two years later Hearst founded the International News Service.

The first regular newspaper column is usually credited to James M. Bailey (1841–94), owner and editor of the daily *Danbury* (Connecticut) *News*, who wrote humorous sketches of everyday events.

Other newspaper firsts: First color supplement—*New York World* (1893); first comic section—*New York World* 1894; first rotogravure section—simultaneously in seven papers (New York, Boston, Philadelphia, Chicago, Cleveland, St. Louis, Kansas City); first Sunday paper—*Baltimore Monitor* 1796; first crossword puzzle—*New York World* December 12, 1913 (prepared by Arthur Wynne); first newspaper editorials—introduced by Nathan Hale (1784–1863), nephew of the Revolutionary War hero and owner/editor, *Boston Daily Advertiser*.

Printing

The early American settlers brought with them the tradition of the printed word and it was not long after their arrival that printing began in the colonies. The first printing press arrived (1638) in Cambridge, Massachusetts. Within a year, an almanac — the early form of the magazine — appeared. The first American book was printed in 1640 and by 1690 newspapers emerged.

The first printing press in the colonies was set up (1638) in Cambridge by Stephen Day (1594–1668) with the backing of Rev. Jesse Glover. Day contracted with Glover in England to set up a press in the colonies. Glover died on the sea voyage and Day, with the help of Glover's widow, set up the plant in Cambridge. The initial output was the *Freeman's Oath* (January 1639), then an almanac, and the *Bay Psalm Book* (1640). Glover's widow married Henry Dunster, Harvard College president, and the Day shop eventually became the Harvard University Press.

Another Cambridge printing shop was that of Samuel Green (1615–1702) and Marmaduke Johnson (1630–74), which printed the first American Bible and an Indian translation by Rev. John Eliot.

Other early printers were William Bradford (1663–1752), who started in Philadelphia (1685) and later (1725) began a newspaper in New York City (the *Gazette*); William Nuthead (1654–95), a Jamestown printer who moved to Maryland (1685), and Thomas Short who began printing in New London, Connecticut (1709).

Isaac Doolittle of New Haven built the first American printing press as a commercial venture (1769). Francis Bailey (1735–1815) opened a print shop (1777) in Lancaster, Pennsylvania, where he published an almanac, then moved to Philadelphia where he printed the official copies of the Declaration of Independence, the Articles of Confederation and an edition of Thomas Paine's *Common Sense*.

When the Revolution started (1775) there were 50 printers in the colonies. The first successful American printer was Christopher Sower (1693–1785) in Germantown, Pennsylvania (1724). He imported a press and type from Germany, made his own ink and sometimes the paper. He printed a newspaper and almanac and many religious tracts.

A most famous press began operating about 1740 in Ephrata, Pennsylvania, under Johann C. Beissel, a founder of the Solitary Brethren of the Community of Seventh Day Baptists and a noted hymn writer. The first American improved printing machine (1816) was the Columbia press by George C. Clymer (1754–1834). Daniel Treadwell developed a treadle-operating printing press, eliminating the use of hand power and then a bed-and-platen press operated by steam (1822).

Richard M. Hoe (1812–86) patented the first rotary press, which began to be used at the *Philadelphia Public Ledger* (1847), revolutionizing newspaper production. Hoe then developed a rotary web perfecting press which fed continuous rolls of paper and printed on both sides in one operation (1871). The addition of a high speed folding apparatus four years later essentially made the present newspaper press.

The developers of printing type included:

Abel Buell (1742–1822) designed and produced the first American font of type (1769); William Church (1778–1863) patented a machine to automatically cast and compose type (1822) and Frederic W. Goudy (1865–1947) designed more than 100 type faces.

David Bruce, Jr., of New York invented an early automatic type caster (1838), the first great improvement over hand casting.

A key invention that helped make mechanical composition practicable was a pantographic punch-cutting machine by Linn B. Benton of Milwaukee (1884).

Ottmar Mergenthaler (1854–99) patented a linotype (1884) and it first went into use at the *New York Tribune* on July 3, 1886. The machine resulted in an upsurge in newspaper publishing. Tolbert Lanston (1844–1913) introduced the Monotype (1887), a composing machine especially suited to book publishing.

The introduction of lithography is credited to Bass Otis (1784–1861), a portrait painter and engraver, and Cephas G. Childs (1793–1871) in establishing its commercial use (1818). James A. Cutting (1814–67) and Lodowick H. Bradford, who headed a firm in Boston, produced the first American lithographic half tones (1850).

Alexander Anderson (1775–1870) made the first wood engravings in the United States (1794).

John C. Moss (1838–92) developed an early photoengraving process (1871) and was the first to establish a photoengraving business. Stephen H. Horgan (1854–1941) pioneered in developing photoengraving processes to make photo reproduction possible in newspapers (*New York Graphic*, 1880).

18. Religion

One of the declared purposes in settling Virginia was the propagation of Christianity among the "savages." This was followed and everyone was taxed to support the Anglican Church (Church of England).

New England was settled by separatists from the Anglican Church and by a large group who wanted to "purify" the established church. The early Puritans were strict and devout but they did not believe in religious tolerance, abusing Quakers and Baptists. The Middle Colonies were settled by Quakers, Calvinists, Lutherans, Mennonites and Moravians. The vast majority of the first settlers came to the New World for economic independence. A religious revival, the Great Awakening, occurred in the 1730s and 40s and did much to unify Americans before the Revolution.

The Anglican Church, which began with the settlement of Jamestown, Virginia (1607), was the official church in Virginia, Maryland, the Carolinas, and Georgia (and four counties in New York). In New England, the Puritans (Congregationalists) were in control except in Rhode Island. Nine of the original 13 states had an established church. The four that did not were Rhode Island, New Jersey, Delaware and Pennsylvania.

Anne Hutchinson (1591–1643) was banished from Boston for her independent beliefs (1637). She moved to Rhode Island the next year and then Pelham Bay on Long Island (1642), where she and most of her household were massacred by Indians.

The Continental Congress made the first formal provision for chaplains in the armed forces July 9, 1775.

Benjamin Hallett (1760–1849), shipowner, founded the Bethel Movement. He began by conducting services on his ship, which were announced by a special flag at the masthead. Services later were held in seamen's chapels in many ports. The Mariner's Church was built by the New York Port Society on June 4, 1820.

Elijah C. Bridgman (1801–61) was the first American missionary to China (1829).

Henry Ward Beecher (1813–87) was one of the most colorful and influential religious figures of nineteenth century America. He headed Plymouth Church in Brooklyn for more than 40 years (1847–87) and drew weekly crowds of 2,500.

Dwight L. Moody (1837–99), evangelist, brought about a revival of British and American Protestantism with his evangelistic trips to Great Britain and in the United States.

Billy (William A.) Sunday (1862–1935), a major league baseball player (1883–87), became a popular revivalist (1896).

The first religious service broadcast on radio was from the Calvary Episcopal Church in Pittsburgh January 2, 1921, by Station KDKA. Samuel F. Cadman (1864–1936), president of the Federal Council of Churches, was the first American radio minister (1928–36).

Baptists

The first Baptist church in the United States was organized in Rhode Island (1638) either by Roger Williams or Dr. John Clarke. Williams (1603–83) arrived in Massachusetts (1631) but his insistence on a church free of ties to any other church or government caused him constant trouble. He was convicted (1635) of venting "newe and dangerous opinions against the authoritie of magistrates" and was banished from the colony. He moved to Rhode Island where he founded the town of Providence, where church and state were separate. Williams distrusted some religions but defended their right to worship as they pleased. Clarke (1609–76), a physician, came to Rhode Island (1637) and became pastor of the Baptist church in Newport. He once stated that "a more flourishing Civill state may stand, yea, and best be maintained ... with a full liberty of religious concernments."

Massachusetts Bay General Court banished all Baptists from the colony (1644).

Denominational organization began with the Philadelphia Baptist Association, consisting of five churches (1707) and the denomination grew and weathered a number of splits. The major break came (1845) when 29 delegates from nine southern states met in Augusta, Georgia, and formed the Southern Baptist Convention.

Johann C. Beissel (1690–1768) split with the Dunkers and formed the Celibate Solitarity Brethren of the Community of Seventh-Day Baptists at Ephrata, Pennsylvania (1732). Beissel was well-known for his famous print shop and composition of more than 1,000 hymns, which influenced American hymnology.

Catholic

The first American Catholic parish was organized September 8, 1565, in St. Augustine, Florida. The first American convent was built (1727) in New Orleans and on January 31, 1752, a ceremony was held for the profession of Sister of St. Martha Turpin, the first American-born Catholic nun. The first Catholic church in the colonies was completed February 26, 1732, in Philadelphia.

An early American leader of the church was John Carroll (1735–1815), a Jesuit priest who studied overseas and returned to the United States in 1774. He served with Benjamin Franklin, Samuel Chase, and his cousin, Charles Carroll, in an unsuccessful effort (1776) to get Canadian help in the Revolution.

On June 9, 1784, Carroll was named superior of the U.S. Catholic missions and on September 14, 1789, he was named Bishop of Baltimore, the first American Catholic bishop. Carroll became the first American Catholic archbishop (1808).

He founded Georgetown College (now University) in 1789, the first American Catholic college, a seminary in Baltimore two years later, and laid the cornerstone for the first American cathedral — Cathedral of the Assumption of the Blessed Virgin — in Baltimore (1806).

The first American Catholic magazine was the French weekly, *Courier de Boston* (1789), which lasted only two months. The first in English was the *Michigan Essay* or *Impartial Observer* (1809).

John England (1786–1842), an outspoken militant priest in Ireland and Australia, was consecrated (1820) as bishop of the newly-created Charleston (South Carolina) Diocese. He organized churches, a school in the region and the first American Catholic newspaper, *U.S. Catholic Miscellany* (1822).

The first Catholic provincial council met in Baltimore (1829) and the first national council session was held there in 1852.

John McCloskey (1810–85) was named first rector of St. John's College (later Fordham) in 1841, then coadjutor bishop of New York and first Catholic bishop of Albany (1847). He became Archbishop of New York (1865) and four years later the first American cardinal.

St. Patrick's Cathedral in New York City was dedicated 1879.

John N. Neumann (1811–60) served as Bishop of Philadelphia (1852–60), established 100 parochial schools and a model seminary. He was beatified in 1963, canonized 1977.

Isaac T. Hecker (1819–88), a priest, helped found the Paulist Fathers (1858), the first American religious community or priests dedicated to conversion of non-Catholics. He served as its superior until his death.

The apostolic delegation was established in Washington January 14, 1893, by Pope Leo XIII and the first apostolic delegate was Archbishop Francisco Stolli.

An important legal victory was won for the church by Anthony Kohlmann (1771–1836), administrator of the New York Catholic Diocese (1808–14). He won a lawsuit which was brought against him to have him reveal information he had received in a confessional. This led to state legislation (1828) which protected the privacy of the confessional.

Congregational

The colonists arriving in New England (1620) were Puritans or members of the Congregational Church. The first arrivals were separatists who had left the Anglican Church. The second and much larger group arriving in 1630 were Puritans who simply wanted to purify the church. Their early leaders were the Mathers, John Cotton and Jonathan Edwards.

John Cotton (1558–1652) arrived (1633) and became the "teacher" of the Boston First Church, serving there until his death. As head of the Congregational Church, he was a man of great influence and popularity.

Richard Mather (1596–1669) became pastor of the Dorchester Church on his arrival (1635), remaining there for 34 years. He wrote the original draft of the Cambridge Platform (1649) which formulated the relations between church and state. Mather also was co-author (1640) of the *Bay Psalm Book*, the first American printed publication.

Increase Mather, son of Richard, served Boston's Second Church from 1664 until his death and also served as Harvard University president (1685–1701). While he did not speak out against the Salem witch-craft trials (1692), he later wrote *Cases of Conscience Concerning Evil Spirits*, which is credited with ending executions for witchcraft.

Cotton Mather (1663–1728), son of Increase, served the Second Church with his father (1685–1728). He was a prolific writer on a variety of subjects and his most celebrated work was *Magnalia Christi Americana* (1702), an ecclesiastical history of New England, which was considered the most important colonial literary and historical work of the time.

Jonathan Edwards (1703–58) served the Northampton (Massachusetts) Church from 1729 to 1750 when he was dismissed in a dispute over communion requirements. He was considered the greatest theologian of his time and his influence on religion gave a great push to the evangelical missionary movement of the time.

Horace Bushnell (1802–76), known as the "father of religious liberalism," tried to restore the truths of religion in terms of human experience. Washington Gladden (1836–1918) was called the "father of social gospel," applying religious principles to the current social problems.

Education

William Tennent (1673–1745), a Presbyterian minister, began to train young men for the ministry (1727). He built the "log college" on the Philadelphia-New York road (1736) for such training. Some of his students later established other learning centers in the colonies.

The first American theological school was founded by the Dutch Reformed Church in New York City (1784); it was moved (1810) to New Brunswick, New Jersey.

John M. Mason (1770–1829), a Presbyterian clergyman, founded (1804) what later became the Union Theological Seminary.

Henry Ware (1764–1845), a divinity professor at Harvard (1805–40), taught courses which led to the development of the Harvard Divinity School (1816).

General Theological Seminary was established (1817) in New York City. The first college to train Jewish men for the rabbinate was the Hebrew Union College in Cincinnati, opened in 1875. The Jewish Theological Seminary in New York City was established 1887.

Episcopal (Anglican)

The first Anglican service was held May 9, 1607, at Cape Henry, Virginia, and the first parish was established a month later (June 21) in Jamestown. The first Anglican service in New England was held in Boston's South Meeting House March 22, 1687 (Good Friday). Three days later, the Meeting House was established as the Anglican Church by Governor Edmund Andros.

While Virginia was the strongest supporter of the Anglican Church for 175 years of British rule, the Church never had a bishop in the colonies. As the movement for independence grew, the Anglican Church became linked with England and many patriots left the church. With the Revolution, all aid to the Anglican Church ended.

William White (1748–1836), rector of Christ Church, Philadelphia (1776–1836), led the move (1785) to Americanize the church by creating the Protestant Episcopal Church of America. He was named the first Episcopal Bishop of Pennsylvania (1787).

Samuel Seabury (1729–96) was consecrated November 14, 1784, as the first Bishop of the Episcopal Church in the United States (being in charge of Connecticut and Rhode Island).

An apparent split in the new Episcopal Church was averted when a convention (1789) united all branches of the church. White, who presided at the convention, was named presiding bishop (1795), a post he held until 1836.

The new united church consecrated its first bishop in 1790 — Thomas Clagett as Bishop of Maryland.

The Reformed Episcopal Church was formed (1893) after a protest in the Chicago diocese led by Charles E. Cheney (1836–1916). He was charged with heresy but a court ruled that the Christ Church property belonged to the parish, not the diocese. This led Cheney and George D. Cummins (1822–76) to organize the Reformed Church with Cummins as the first bishop.

Jewish

The first Jews to arrive in the United States were 23 who fled from Brazil (1654) and lived in New Amsterdam, where they formed the Shearith Israel Congregation (1655). These Jews rented a house in Beaver Street and created the first American synagogue (1682).

Gershom M. Seixas (1745–1816) became rabbi of the Shearith Israel Congregation (1766) and closed the synagogue during the Revolution rather than continue under British rule. He organized the Mikva Israel Synagogue in Philadelphia (1780) and re-established the New York City congregation in 1784. Seixas successfully challenged a clause in the Pennsylvania constitution (1783) which barred Jews from holding public office.

Isaac Leeser (1806–68), a rabbi in Philadelphia, was a pioneer in developing Jewish life in the United States. He founded and edited *The Occident and American Jewish Advocate* (1843–68).

The first Reformed Jewish congregation was established (1854) in Cincinnati by Isaac Mayer Wise (1819–1900), who also founded the Jewish rabbinical seminary (1875). The seminary graduated its first class of rabbis eight years later. Wise was the founder of Reform Judaism through the Union of American Hebrew Congregations (1873).

The United Synagogue of America, an association of more than 765 Conservative Jewish synagogues in the United States and Canada, was founded (1913) by Solomon Schechter (1847–1915). He came to the United States (1902) to serve as president of the Jewish Theological Seminary, which he developed into a foremost institution.

Stephen S. Wise (1874–1949) founded the Free Synagogue of New York (1907), serving as its rabbi until his death. An ardent Zionist, he founded what became the Zionist Organization of America (1898) and founded and headed the World Jewish Congress (1936).

Lutheran

Heinrich (Henry) M. Muhlenberg (1711–87), a founder of American Lutheranism, organized the United Lutheran Church (1748). Samuel S. Schmucker (1799–1873) helped found the General Synod of Lutheran Churches (1820) and was a founder of Gettysburg (later Lutheran) Seminary (1826), serving as its first professor and president (1831–34).

Carl F. W. Walther (1811–87) founded the Missouri Lutheran Synod (1847), bringing together scattered German Lutheran congregations, serving as its president (1847–50, 1864–78). He also helped found Concordia Seminary (1839), serving as its president (1849). Walther was called the "most commanding figure" in American Lutheranism in the nineteenth century.

Lars P. Esbjörn (1808–70) led a secession of Swedish Lutherans and formation of the independent Augustana Synod in 1860.

Mergers

Protestant churches over the years combined and merged to form new denominations. The Congregational and Christian churches merged July 1, 1932, and the Evangelical and Reformed Church was formed by the merger of the Evangelical Synod of North America and the Reformed Church June 26, 1934. The two merged groups—Evangelical/Reformed and Congregational Christian—combined July 4, 1961, to form the United Church of Christ. On September 27, 1985, the United Church of Christ declared its ecumenical partnership with the Christian Church (Disciples of Christ). The Unitarian and Universalist churches merged May 3, 1959.

The American Lutheran Church was formed January 1, 1961, by the joining of the Evangelical Lutheran and United Evangelical churches. The Lutheran Church in America began June 28, 1962, by the merger of the United Lutheran Church, the Augustana Evangelical Lutheran Church and the Finnish Evangelical Church. The two newly-merged churches then united January 1, 1988, to form the Evangelical Lutheran Church.

The Methodist Church was formed May 10, 1939, with the merger of the Methodist Episcopal Church, the Methodist Episcopal Church South and the Methodist Protestant Church. On November 16, 1946, the Evangelical and United Brethren Church was created by the merger of the United Brethren and Evangelical churches. Then the United Methodist Church was formed April 23, 1968 with the merger of the Methodist and Evangelical United Brethren churches.

The United Presbyterian Church in the United States was formed May 28, 1958, by the merger of the Presbyterian Church/USA and the U.S. Presbyterian Church. The Presbyterian Church/USA came into existence June 10, 1983, with the merger of the United Presbyterian Church in the USA and the Presbyterian Church in the U.S.

The first major merger of the Church of the Nazarene was in 1907 with the Pentecostal Churches of America; then it was joined in 1908 by the Holiness Church of Christ, and in 1919 several smaller churches joined and the present name was adopted.

Methodist

The first American Methodist clergyman was either of two Irish immigrants—Robert Strawbridge or Philip Embury. Strawbridge (d 1781) settled in Frederick, Maryland, about 1761 where he began preaching soon after his arrival. He built a log meeting house near his home and made preaching tours into Pennsylvania, Virginia and Delaware. Strawbridge did not cooperate with missionaries sent by John Wesley from England and administered the sacraments on his own authority. Embury (1728–73) began to preach in New York City (1766) as a result of a card game. Barbara Heck (1734–1804), called the "mother" of American Methodism, broke up a card game of her Irish countrymen, telling Embury he must preach to them or "God will require our blood at your hands." Embury began with a class of five in his home, the group grew quickly and the Wesley Chapel (the first John St. Church) was built in 1768.

Francis Asbury (1745–1816) came to the colonies (1771) as a missionary. When the Revolution broke out, all the missionaries except Asbury returned to England. He hid in Delaware until after the war. Sixty clergymen met in Baltimore at Christmas 1784 and formed the American Methodist Church with Asbury and Thomas Coke (1747–1814) as superintendents. Coke, who was in charge of missions, spent most of his time in England and Asbury assumed leadership of the growing church until his death under the title of bishop, which he assumed in 1785.

Like the Baptists, the dispute over slavery led to a major break. Representatives of 14 states met in Louisville in May, 1845, and organized the Methodist Episcopal Church, South.

The African Methodist Episcopal (AME) church was founded (1787) in Philadelphia by Richard Allen (1760–1831), a former slave who bought his freedom for $2,000. Allen joined the Methodist church at 17 and was licensed to preach at 22. Allen formed a church after he was asked to worship from the back of St. George's Methodist Church or the balcony and to take communion after white members. Allen's followers built their own meeting house in a converted blacksmith shop at Sixth and Lombard streets in Philadelphia (1793), the first Negro church in the colonies. Sixteen black congregations formed the AME denomination with Allen as first bishop (1816–31).

Mormons

Joseph Smith (1805–44) organized the Church of Jesus Christ of Latter-Day Saints (Mormon) in Fayette, New York, on April 6, 1830.

Smith reportedly had a vision which led him to a hill near Manchester, New York (1820), where he found golden plates on which was inscribed the history of the true church. Smith deciphered the inscriptions and published them as *The Book of Mormon* (1830).

Solomon Spaulding (1761–1816), clergyman, wrote *The Manuscript Found*, an account of the original work which supposedly had been dug up from an ancient mound. Later, it was charged that Smith had used this unpublished work in his book. The movement grew rapidly, moved to Kirtland, Ohio (1831), then to western Missouri (1838) where they were not welcome, and then to Nauvoo, Illinois. On July 12, 1843, Smith announced that a second divine revelation sanctioned the practice of multiple marriages (polygamy). (The practice was ended 1890 after Congress enacted the Anti-Polygamy Act.) In 1844, critics published a sharp attack on Smith in the local Nauvoo paper. Smith had the paper's press destroyed and expelled the editor. Smith and his brother, Hyrum, were arrested June 27, 1844, and that night a crowd broke into the jail and killed the Smith brothers.

Brigham Young took over the Mormon Church after Smith's death and led the people to Utah (1847–48). He planned settlements, organized emigrations from the East and Europe and sponsored educational institutions. Some groups refused to accept Young's leadership and formed the Reorganized Church of Jesus Christ of Latter-Day Saints with Smith's son, Joseph II, as their leader.

Soon after the Mormons settled in Utah, they began construction of the Mormon Temple, which was dedicated April 6, 1893, after 40 years construction.

Organizations

The first Bible society in the United States was organized in Philadelphia December 12, 1808, followed the next year by societies in Connecticut, Massachusetts, New York and New Jersey. The American Bible Society was organized by 35 societies on May 11, 1816, in New York City with Elias Boudinot (1740–1821), a former government official, as the first president.

The first Jewish fraternal society was B'nai Brith, organized in New York City (1843).

The Christian Endeavor Society was organized February 2, 1881, at the Williston Congregational Church in Portland, Maine, by its pastor,

Rev. Francis E. Clark (1851–1927). It became a world-wide organization with Clark heading the national and international bodies.

The Gideons was founded by the Christian Commercial Traveling Men's Association in Boscobel, Wisconsin (1899). Its members began placing Bibles in hotel rooms in October 1908, the first in Superior, Montana.

The National Council of Churches was formed by 29 major American Protestant and four Eastern Orthodox churches on November 29, 1950.

Other Denominations

Christian Science — Mary M. Baker Eddy (1821–1910) dated her discovery of Christian Science to 1866, after which she began a career of teaching and healing. She published the first of many versions of *Science and Health* (1875), claiming the mind is the sole reality and body infirmities can be cured by mental efforts. The Church of Christ Scientist was chartered August 29, 1879, and the first church was organized (1892) in Boston. The Christian Science Cathedral in Boston was dedicated June 10, 1906.

Evangelical — Jacob Albright (1759–1808) became a minister (1803) and four years later bishop of the "Newly-Founded Methodist Conference" which he had established. It evolved into the Evangelical Church.

Evangelical Lutheran — Elling Eielsen (1804–83) organized the Evangelical Lutheran Church of America (1846).

Mennonite — William Rittenhouse was first pastor of Mennonite settlers, who arrived in Germantown, Pennsylvania (1683), and became the first bishop (1703). Rittenhouse also built the first paper mill in the United States (1690).

Moravian — The first Moravian church was built in Savannah, Georgia (1735), and the first bishop (1736) was David Nitschmann (1696–1772), a Moravian missionary to the West Indies. At about the same time, Augustus G. Spangenberg (1704–92) arrived in the United States and worked for the church in Georgia and Pennsylvania. He founded the North American branch of the church, becoming bishop in 1744.

Seventh-Day Adventist — William Miller (1782–1849), a Baptist minister in Hampton, New York, predicted the Second Coming some time in the year between March 21, 1843, and 1844. At the end of 1843, he set the date for October 22, 1844, and when that didn't happen, the

Millerite movement ended. Millerites met in Albany in April 1845 in a "mutual conference of Adventists" and this ultimately led to the Seventh-Day Adventist Church.

Assemblies of God — One of the largest Pentecostal churches, the Assemblies of God was formed (1914) in Hot Springs, Arkansas.

Disciples of Christ (or Church of Christ) — Alexander Campbell (1788–1866) and his father, Thomas (1763–1854), were leaders of the Christian Association in Washington, Pennsylvania. They allied with Baptists (1812) to form the Disciples at Brush Run, Pennsylvania. The Baptists expelled the Disciples commonly called the Campbellites, who joined with disaffected Baptists, Methodists and Presbyterians (1832) and under the leadership of Barton W. Stone (1722–1844), formed the Disciples of Christ Church.

Shakers — Ann Lee (1736–84) joined the United Society of Believers in Christ's Second Appearing, commonly known as the Shakers (1758) in England. She began to preach a new gospel, opposing marriage and sexual relationships. She was considered the Shakers' leader and came to the United States (1774) with eight disciples. They formed a successful colony ("family") at Watervliet, New York, two years later. The first permanent colony was organized (1788) at New (later Mount) Lebanon, New York, and by 1826 there were 18 Shaker villages in eight states. They developed successful furniture making and other crafts which left a permanent influence on American crafts. The Shakers gradually disappeared as a religious sect.

Polish National Catholic Church — The church was organized March 14, 1897, in Scranton, Pennsylvania.

Church of the Nazarene — A group of small religious bodies merged October 13, 1908, at Pilot Point, Texas to form the church.

Universalist — John Murray (1741–1815) was shipwrecked off the coast of New Jersey (1770) and wound up in a small settlement called Good Luck, which needed a preacher. Murray preached his first Universalist sermon there September 30, 1770. He then settled in Gloucester, Massachusetts (1774), and five years later organized the Universalist Church of America. Various Universalists met in Philadelphia the next year and drafted their first denominational declaration of faith.

Church of the Brethren — Members came to Pennsylvania (1719) and the first church was organized in Germantown (1723).

Church of the United Brethren in Christ — The church was formed (1789) by Philip W. Otterbein (1726–1813) and Martin Boehm (1725–1812), both of whom were elected bishops of the new organization.

Christian Catholic Church — John A. Dowie (1847–1907) formed the church in Chicago (1896) and built Zion City, 40 miles north of Chicago. He was deposed shortly before his death by a revolt of his followers.

Quakers (Society of Friends) — The first Quakers arrived in 1656 in New England — Ann Austin and Mary Fisher — and they were imprisoned and deported. Some who came later were driven from town to town; four were hanged. Some Quakers found refuge in Rhode Island where there was religious freedom.

Jehovah's Witnesses — Charles Taze Russell (1852–1916) founded the International Bible Students Association (1872), which later became Jehovah's Witnesses. *The Watchtower*, a Bible journal, was founded in 1879.

The first B'hai house of worship was dedicated May 2, 1953, in Wilmette, Illinois; the denomination grew to nearly 100 assemblies.

The first Bohemian American church was the St. John Nepomuk Church in St. Louis (1855).

The first American Buddhist church opened July 15, 1904, in Los Angeles.

The first Greek Orthodox church in the United States was Holy Trinity in New Orleans (1867).

Swedenborgian (New Church) Temple was built in Baltimore (1799).

Church (later Churches) of God was founded (1830) by John Winebrenner (1797–1860).

Presbyterian

American Presbyterianism began with the arrival (1683) of Francis Makemie (1658–1708) in Maryland, which had issued a call for missionaries. On arriving from Ireland he founded the first Presbyterian church in Snow Hill, Maryland. With the help of two colleagues, he brought together churches from Maryland, Pennsylvania, New Jersey and Virginia into the first presbytery (1706), of which he was the first moderator.

Samuel Davies (1723–61) founded the Hanover Presbytery in Virginia and led a group in successfully opposing creation of an established state church. He was probably the greatest colonial preacher, becoming popular through the printing of about 20 editions of his sermons.

John Witherspoon (1723–94), a signer of the Declaration of Independence, organized the Presbyterian Church along national lines

(1785–89) and served as president of the College of New Jersey (later Princeton) (1768–94). The college closed during the Revolution and Witherspoon returned (1782) to reopen and rebuild the school.

James McGready (1758–1817) inaugurated the first revival camp meetings (1797–99) in his Logan County, Kentucky, churches and meetings were held throughout the West and South.

Lyman Beecher (1775–1863) served various Presbyterian churches and was the first president of Lane Theological Seminary in Cincinnati (1832–50). He was known for his fiery preaching against intemperance, Catholicism, religious tolerance and brought about passage of the blue laws.

Sheldon Jackson (1834–1909) was the foremost apostle of Presbyterianism in the United States and as missionary superintendent to the Choctaw Indians, he founded more than 100 churches in the West and Alaska.

Publications

John Eliot (1604–90), known as the "Apostle of the Indians," wrote an Indian translation of the Bible, the first Bible printed in North America (1663).

The first Bible printed in the United States (1782) was prepared by Robert H. Aitken (1734–1802). Aitken was a Philadelphia bookseller and printer.

The first American religious journal (1743) was *The Christian History*, a weekly; the first religious weekly newspaper was *The Religious Remembrancer* (1813), which became *The Christian Observer* (1840).

Religious Freedom

Rhode Island was declared a democracy by its General Court March 16, 1641, and adopted a constitution granting freedom of religion for all citizens.

The Presbytery of Hanover petitioned the Virginia Assembly about 1760 for religious liberty and the removal of taxes to support the Anglican Church. Virginia adopted a statute for religious freedom (January 16, 1786); it had been drafted by Thomas Jefferson in 1779.

Unitarian

Unitarianism came to the United States by way of liberal Christianity in the mid–1700s, when at least 20 Congregational ministers were preaching what was essentially Unitarianism.

The most prominent of them was James Freeman (1759–1835), who became the first American Unitarian clergyman November 18, 1787. A lay reader at New York City's King's Chapel, he was refused ordination as an Episcopal priest. After the Revolution, he revised the liturgy of the Episcopal service, was ordained a Unitarian minister by the senior warden of his church, and King's Chapel became the first American Unitarian church.

Other early Unitarian leaders were: Jonathan Mayhew (1720–66) of Boston's West Church was a well-known religious liberal and defended the liberal theories of government; Thomas Oxnard organized Unitarian congregations in Portland and Saco, Maine (1792), and William Ellery Channing (1780–1842), served the Federal Street Congregational Church (1803–42). He became a leader of Unitarianism and helped found the American Unitarian Association (1825).

Women

Through the years, women have played an important role in the development and growth of American churches.

Kateri Tekakwitha (1656–80), a Mohawk Indian Catholic known as the "Lily of the Mohawks," was the first North American Indian to be nominated for sainthood and was beatified (1939).

Ann Lee, mentioned earlier as the founder of the Shakers, was known as "Ann the Word" or "Mother Ann."

Elizabeth Ann Seton (1774–1821) founded the first American community of Sisters of Charity (1810), shaped American parochial education by founding a girls school in Baltimore (1809) and St. Joseph College at Emmittsburgh, Maryland (1810). She was the first native-born American to be canonized (1975).

Ann Ayres (1816–96) became the first American woman consecrated as a Protestant sister (Sisters of the Holy Communion).

Cornelia Connelly (1809–79), a Catholic nun, founded the Society of the Holy Child Jesus, an order for teaching English girls and later began a branch in the United States.

Antoinette L. B. Blackwell (1825–1921) was named pastor of the Congregational Church in South Butler, New York (1852), becoming the first formally appointed woman pastor.

Olympia Brown (1835–1926) became a Universalist minister (1863), the first American ordained woman.

Mary Baker Eddy, referred to earlier, was the founder of the Christian Science Church.

Celia C. Burleigh was the first woman ordained as a Unitarian minister (October 5, 1871) in Connecticut.

Francis Xavier Cabrini (1850–1917) came to the United States (1889), founded convents, schools, orphanages and hospitals. She was canonized (1946), the first American citizen so honored.

Katherine Drexel (1858–1955), philanthropist, founded the Sisters of the Blessed Sacrament for Indians and Colored People (1891). She was beatified in 1988.

The first Jewish woman cantor was Mrs. Sheldon (Betty) Robbins of Massapequa, New York, whose first service was held in Oceanside, New York, in 1955.

Barbara C. Harris, a black Presbyterian priest, became the first woman bishop in the Anglican/Episcopal Church January 24, 1989. She became suffragan bishop of the Boston Diocese.

19. Science

The pursuit of science in the colonies began early (1683) with the first scientific society, Boston Philosophical Society, founded by Increase Mather (1639–1723). Then Benjamin Franklin founded the American Philosophical Society (1743).

Studies of the sciences began early at various schools and in private efforts in astronomy, botany and physics. The American Association for the Advancement of Science was founded in 1848. The National Academy of Sciences was incorporated March 3, 1863, with physicist Alexander Bache (1806–67) as the first president. The National Science Foundation was created May 10, 1950.

The first American science magazine was the *American Journal of Science and Art* (1818); the first science newspaper was the short-lived *American Mechanic* in the 1830s, followed by the *Scientific American*.

Charles A. Spencer (1813–81) made the first American microscope (1838) and founded a company (1847) for its manufacture.

Anthropology

Pioneers in American anthropology were Lewis H. Morgan (1818–81) and Daniel G. Brinton (1837–99). Then came Melville J. Herskovitz (1895–1963), who made major contributions to the modern concept of culture; Earnest A. Hooton (1887–1954), who laid the foundation for physical anthropology and Margaret Mead (1901–78), psychological anthropologist.

Astronomy

The first American astronomer of note was John Winthrop (1714–79) of Cambridge, Massachusetts, who made sun spot observations (1739) and observed the transit of Mercury.

The first American scientific expedition (1761) was made to Newfoundland to observe the transit of Venus across the face of the sun. The trip was sponsored by Harvard University and Massachusetts, which also backed a trip by four Harvard professors and six students to Penobscot Bay to record an eclipse of the sun October 27, 1780.

David Rittenhouse (1732–96), a clockmaker and self-taught Philadelphia astronomer, built the first American orrery (mechanical model of the solar system) in 1767 and constructed a private observatory in Norristown, Pennsylvania, the next year. Rittenhouse is also credited with developing the first American telescope and being the first to use cross hairs in the scope. He invented (1785) a collimating telescope (which adjusts to the line of sight).

Amasa Holcomb (1787–1875) of Southwick, Massachusetts, built the first reflecting telescope (1826) after years of manufacturing compasses, scales, dividers and other instruments. Alvan Clark (1804–87) founded a firm in Cambridge to make the first American achromatic telescope lenses and built some of the world's largest.

Yale University's observatory, the first permanent American astronomy institution (1831), is still in existence. An observatory was built (1831–32) at the University of North Carolina in Chapel Hill but it was destroyed by fire (1838). Two observatories were begun in 1837 — Williams College and Harvard.

The United States Naval Observatory began as the Depot of Charts and Instruments (1830) and became a permanent observatory (1862). The Lick Observatory of the University of California was completed (1888) on Mt. Hamilton; the University of Chicago's Yerkes Observatory was established (1897) at William Bay, Wisconsin, and the Mt. Wilson Observatory was founded in 1904.

George E. Hale (1868–1938), director of Yerkes (1895–1905) and Mt. Wilson (1904–23), coinvented the spectroheliograph (1892).

William C. Bond (1789–1859), who had built his own observatory, was invited (1839) to bring his equipment to Harvard and was named astronomical observer. He supervised the construction of the Harvard Observatory (1843–44) and served as director until 1859. Bond was the first to photograph a star (Vega) (1850).

Lewis M. Rutherford (1816–92) built a small observatory (1856) in his garden in New York City. He built a camera with which he photographed the moon (1858). Rutherford developed a spectroscope with which he was able to photograph the solar spectrum.

Edward C. Pickering (1846–1919) pioneered in using photometric and spectroscopic techniques to measure the brightness of stars and photographed a solar eclipse at Mt. Peasant, Iowa (1869). Pickering directed the Harvard Observatory (1877–1919) and, with his assistant, Annie Jump Cannon (1863–1941), made a catalog of about 235,000 stars. Their spectral classification is now universally accepted.

Simon Newcomb (1835–1909) calculated the motions of the bodies in the solar system. A most far-reaching contribution was working with the British to inaugurate a unified system of astronomical constants which led to international cooperation.

John W. Draper (1811–82) made the first photograph of the moon (1840) and his son, Henry (1837–82), was first to successfully photograph the spectrum of a star (1872).

Samuel P. Langley, an aviation pioneer, did research which helped reorient astronomy from a geometrical to a physical basis. He invented the bolometer (1878) which permitted measuring the sun's energy output at any point in its spectrum.

Asaph Hall (1829–1907) discovered the two satellites of Mars (1877) and Percival Lowell (1855–1916), founder of the Lowell Observatory in Flagstaff, Arizona, made the mathematical study which led to the discovery of the planet Pluto by Clyde Tombaugh (1906–97) on February 18, 1930.

William W. Campbell (1862–1938), director of the Lick Observatory (1901–25) made the first accurate study of star velocities and Vesto M. Slipher (1875–1969), director of the Lowell Observatory (1926–52), discovered the rotation and extraordinary velocities of spiral nebulae.

Maria Mitchell (1818–89) was the first American woman astronomer and served 34 years as the first astronomy professor at Vassar. She discovered a new comet in 1847.

Edwin P. Hubble (1889–1953) demonstrated the existence of galaxies outside our own and Harlow Shapley (1885–1972), director of Harvard Observatory (1921–52), helped lay the foundation for the universe of galaxies.

Karl G. Jansky (1905–50) was the first to detect radio waves of interstellar origin which led to the science of radio astronomy and Gerard P. Kuiper (1905–73) is considered the founder of planetary astronomy.

Grote Reber (1911–), an amateur astronomer, built the first actual radio telescope in 1937.

Biology

Daniel Pease and Richard Baker, on January 7, 1848, succeeded in photographing the human gene during experiments at Southern California University.

James D. Watson (1928–70) and Francis C. H. Crook made a major scientific discovery (1953) in building a three dimensional molecular model of DNA.

Scientists at Merck Laboratories and Rockefeller University working independently synthesized an enzyme for the first time (January 16, 1968).

Botany

The first American botanist was John Bartram (1699–1777), who laid out the first botanic garden at 43d and Eastwick Streets in Philadelphia (1728).

Jane Colden (1724–66) was the first woman in the colonies distinguished as a botanist.

The first expedition to study and classify botanical species was made by Manassah Cutler (1742–1823), a Congregational minister. He was the first to prepare a systematic account of New England flora.

Humphry Marshall (1722–1801), a cousin of John Bartram, prepared *Arbustrum Americanum, the American Grove,* a catalog of American forest trees and shrubs (1785).

Frederick Pursh (1774–1820) came to the United States (1799) to manage a botanical garden near Baltimore. After managing other gardens near Philadelphia and New York City, he made a number of explorations and wrote the first complete flora of America north of Mexico (1814), which was the standard work for a generation.

Asa Gray (1810–88) was the nation's leading botanist of his time and his *Manual of Botany* was outstanding for more than a century.

Alva W. Chapman (1809–99), a Florida surgeon, was the pioneer investigator of Southern plants and his *Flora of the Southern States* (1860) was the only Southern botany manual for 50 years.

Chemistry

The first professor who taught only chemistry was Benjamin Rush (1745–1813). He lectured at the Philadelphia Medical School (1769) and wrote the first chemistry textbook (1770).

The first chemical society in the world was the Chemical Society of Philadelphia, founded 1792 by James Woodhouse (1770–1809). The American Chemical Society was formed in 1876.

Robert Hare invented the oxyhydrogen blow pipe (1801) and Samuel Hopkins of Philadelphia received the first chemistry patent for an improved potash kettle.

Benjamin Silliman, a leading developer of the Yale University Medical School, established science at Yale. He prepared hydrofluoric acid for the first time in the United States.

The first makers of synthetic dyes in the United States were Thomas and Charles Holliday, who began producing magenta and other coal-tar chemicals in Brooklyn (1864).

Oliver W. Gibbs (1822–1908), Harvard professor, laid the foundation for American chemistry, conducting researches into inorganic compounds, analytical methods and physiology.

James M. Crafts (1839–1917) was responsible for developing hundreds of new carbon compounds and Josiah Willard Gibbs (1839–1903), a mathematical physicist, laid the theoretical groundwork for thermodynamics and physical chemistry.

Ira Remsen (1846–1927) helped influence chemists for 30 years and, with a pupil, discovered saccharin (1879). He founded the *American Chemical Journal*, which he edited (1879–1927).

Thomas L. Willson began manufacturing carbide in Spray, North Carolina (1895).

Charles E. Acker (1868–1920) invented a process for producing caustic soda and chlorine from electrolysis of molten salt (1896) and Hamilton Y. Castner (1859–99) invented an electrolytic method of manufacturing caustic soda and chlorine from sodium chloride.

Herman Frasch developed a process for desulphurizing crude oils, which he sold to Standard Oil, and a hot water melting process of extracting sulphur (1891), thus helping to found the sulphur industry.

Samuel W. Parr (1857–1931) invented the calorimeter to determine the heat value of coal and other solids.

Herbert H. Dow developed a process for extracting bromine from brine. Charles H. Herty (1867–1938) invented a method of turpentine orcharding and developed a process for producing white paper from young Southern pines.

William J. Hale (1876–1955) patented processes for making phenol, aniline and acetic acid.

Richard B. Moore (1871–1931) supervised production of the first American radium salts and was an early advocate of using helium in balloons and dirigibles.

Irving Langmuir (1881–1957) made numerous discoveries—filling incandescent light bulbs with inert gases to prolong the life of the tungsten filaments, the nature of molecular films and the chemistry of surfaces. He developed a method (1946) to artificially produce rain by seeding clouds with dry ice.

Samuel C. Lind (1879–1965) invented the electroscope for radium measurements and originated the theory of chemical effects of radium rays. Frederick G. Cottrell (1877–1948) invented the electrostatic smoke (fume) precipitator.

Wallace H. Carothers (1896–1937) directed Du Pont research which led to the development of nylon (1935) and neoprene.

Harold C. Urey (1893–1981) discovered deuterium ("heavy hydrogen") and Melvin Calvin (1911–97) discovered the mechanics of photosynthesis.

Konrad E. Bloch (1912–) made important contributions to determine how cholesterol is synthesized in living organisms; Glenn T. Seaborg, pioneer nuclear chemist, helped discover transuranium elements 94 through 102 and Willard F. Libby (1908–80) developed the radio carbon dating technique to determine the age of organic materials (wood, charcoal, bone).

Geography/Geology

Simeon DeWitt (1756–1834) made maps for the Continental Army during the Revolution and then served 50 years as New York State surveyor general.

The first American geography book (1794) was *Geography Made Easy* by Jedidiah Morse (1761–1826), which went into 25 editions.

The first American geology book of importance was *Observations on the Geology of the United States* by William Maclure (1763–1840).

A famous team of English surveyors— Jeremiah Dixon and Charles Mason (1730–87)— began by determining the boundary between Maryland and Pennsylvania (1763–67) and the Mason-Dixon line became part of American geography and history.

Henry S. Tanner (1768–1858) issued a successful American atlas (1823), the first with maps using a scale. The five volume atlas was published over five years and ran through numerous editions.

Another outstanding figure in American geography was Samuel A. Mitchell (1792–1868), who prepared numerous textbooks and maps—*A New American Atlas* (1831) and *Traveler's Guide Through the United States* (1832).

Ferdinand V. Hayden (1829–87) pioneered geologic studies of the West and laid the foundation for the United States Geological Survey. Henry Gannett (1846–1914) was chief geographer for the Survey from 1882.

Physics

John Winthrop, an outstanding American scientist, established the first American laboratory of experimental physics (1746).

Josiah Willard Gibbs, Yale mathematical physicist (1871–1903), laid theoretical ground work for the theories of thermodynamics.

Two University of Chicago physicists and Nobel Prize winners were Albert A. Michelson (1852–1931) and Robert A. Millikan (1868–1953). Michelson worked on the speed of light rays and Millikan was first to isolate the electron and developed a theory of cosmic rays (later proved correct). Michelson was the first American to win the Nobel Physics prize (1907), Millikan in 1923.

Another University of Chicago physicist and Nobel laureate (1927), Arthur H. Compton, discovered the photon, a particle unit of light (1923).

John Bardeen (1908–91) shared two Nobel Physics prizes. He was the first to do so. One was for discovery of the transistor effect, shared with William B. Shockley (1910–89) and Walter H. Brattain (1902–88); the second was for a theory of superconductivity which he shared with Leon N. Cooper (1930–) and John R. Schrieffer (1931–).

Others who contributed to the development of American physics were:

Percy W. Bridgman (1882–1961) for work in thermodynamics of high pressure physics.

James A. Van Allen (1914–) discovered two regions of particles with high energy radiation that encircle the earth (the Van Allen radiation belts).

Charles H. Townes (1915–) co-invented the maser, used as radio frequency generators and sensitive amplifiers of faint radio signals. His work led to the development of laser beams by others.

Donald A. Glaser (1926–) invented the bubble chamber for tracking new particles and Carl D. Anderson (1905–91) discovered the positron, a subatomic particle (1932).

Psychology

The first psychological laboratory was established at Johns Hopkins University (1881) by Granville S. Hall (1846–1924), who also founded the first magazine on the subject, *American Journal of Psychology* (1887).

William James (1842–1910) set up a laboratory at Harvard and was a founder of pragmatism.

Joseph B. Rhine (1895–1980) founded modern parapsychology and coined the phrase extrasensory perception (ESP). John B. Watson (1878–1958) founded the behaviorist school of psychology (1913).

Lewis M. Terman (1877–1956) pioneered in measuring intelligence and achievement, developed the first intelligence test (the Stanford-Binet) and coined the term IQ (intelligence quotient).

The American Psychological Association was organized July 8, 1892, at Clark University.

Sociology

William G. Sumner (1840–1910) introduced the first university sociology course (1874) at Yale University. He wrote *Folkways*, a classic work on customs and mores, and *Science and Society*.

University of Chicago established the first academic sociology department (1893), headed by Albion W. Small (1854–1926). Two years later the university launched the first journal in the field, *American Journal of Sociology*, with Small as founder and editor (1895–1931).

Small, with Lester F. Ward (1841–1913) and Franklin H. Giddings (1855–1931), defined the nature and scope of sociology as a social science.

George H. Mead (1863–1931) provided the orientation for social psychology by his effort to show the human self arises in the process of social interaction.

William I. Thomas (1867–1947) and Robert A. Park (1864–1944) regarded cities as the natural laboratory for sociological research, with a wide variety of social processes.

Space

Rocketry and space exploration in the United States started with Robert H. Goddard (1882–1945), who began working on rockets (1908) and developed a two-step rocket (1914). He predicted the development of rockets (1919) which would travel to the moon and beyond. On March 16, 1926, he fired the first liquid-fueled rocket; three years later, the first rocket carrying instruments. Goddard received more than 200 patents which advanced rocketry.

Germany turned rockets into weapons (V2s) during World War II, after which German rocket experts were placed in American and Russian space projects. The Redstone engine, an adaptation of the V2, was used as the booster for the Jupiter C rocket that launched the first American satellite, the Explorer I, on January 13, 1958.

The National Committee for Aeronautics was created March 3, 1915, and its functions were transferred July 29, 1958, to the newly-formed NASA (National Aeronautics and Space Administration).

The first man-made contact with the moon occurred January 10, 1946, when a radar signal from a Signal Corps installation in New Jersey echoed from the moon in 2.4 seconds (477,714 miles round trip).

The Score satellite was launched December 18, 1956, and was the first to transmit voice messages from space; the unmanned Luna 2 spacecraft was the first to land on the moon (September 12, 1959). Luna 3 was the first to circle the moon and send back pictures of the far side.

In 1959 NASA announced the first seven men selected as astronauts and one of them, Alan B. Shepard, Jr. (1923–98), became the first American in space (May 5, 1961) when he rocketed 116.5 miles above the earth. John H. Glenn (1921–), another original astronaut, made the first American flight orbiting the earth three times February 20, 1962.

The first weather satellite, Tiros I, was launched April 1, 1960, and the first two communication satellites also went up in 1960 — Echo I on August 12 and Courier 1-B October 10.

Telstar I relayed the first transmission of television signals between Europe and the United States July 10, 1962, and Early Bird I, the first commercial satellite, was launched April 6, 1965. An unmanned satellite, Marine IV, photographed the surface of Mars November 28, 1964.

Edward H. White (1930–67) became the first American to "walk" in space June 3, 1965, but it was not until February 7, 1984, that an American astronaut, Bruce McCandless II, was the first to go into space with no ties to the spacecraft, using a powered back-pack for motive power.

Surveyor II made a soft landing on the moon January 9, 1968, and began sending back data and pictures of the moon's surface.

Then a space capsule, piloted by Neil A. Armstrong (1930–) landed on the moon July 20, 1969, and he became the first man to set foot on the moon. Astronaut Edwin "Buzz" Aldrin followed him on the moon's surface.

In the following years unmanned spacecraft have flown by Jupiter and Saturn, transmitting valuable data. The first manned space shuttle, the *Columbia*, successfully orbited the earth 36 times in April 1981.

Weather

Giuseppe Tagliabue (1812–78), from an Italian family of scientific instrument makers, came to New York City (1831) with a bellows, a bundle of glass tubing, a pan of tallow and less than $5. He began making thermometers and in the next 47 years became a leading American instrument maker.

Cleveland Abbe (1838–1916) began publishing daily weather bulletins September 1, 1869, while he was director of the Cincinnati Observatory. The bulletins, first of their kind, were based on telegraphed information from a chain of observers. This led to creation of the U.S. Weather Service on January 3, 1871. It later became the U.S. Weather Bureau in 1890, with Abbe as director until 1916.

James P. Espy (1785–1860), called the "Storm King," developed a theory on storms which proved to be correct.

Henry H. Clayton (1861–1946), a weather forecasting pioneer, made cloud studies which provided the first detailed information on atmospheric circulation over the United States. He was among the first to use kites to lift recording instruments (1894).

Zoology

Louis Agassiz (1807–73) founded Harvard Museum of Comparative Zoology (1859) and stimulated interest in natural history. George H. Parker (1864–1955) was one of the first American experimental zoologists.

20. Shelter and Domestic Furnishings

When the English colonists arrived in North America, their first concern was shelter from the elements. They put up tents, shacks or dugouts. The dugout was an opening in the side of a hill, over which they put a frame of saplings and branches, covered with wattles (poles intertwined with twigs and branches) and thatch daubed with mud.

The first permanent structures in New England and Virginia reflected the settlers English origin. In New York, most housing was of Dutch origin. The French along the Great Lakes and St. Lawrence and Mississippi rivers began with log forts, then proceeded to galleried wooden plantation houses. The Spanish, mostly in the Southwest, built along the style of the Indian pueblo, using stone and adobe.

New England houses were of split oak timber clapboards with an overhanging second story. The lack of thatching grass forced settlers to use wooden shingles for roofing. Many Southern houses were of brick. In the middle colonies, the Dutch built solid brick and stone houses, the Swedes built log cabins and then brick structures and the Pennsylvania Germans, buildings of heavy stone and wood.

Frequent fires hastened the use of stone for buildings and mortar was used for fastening. Good clay to make brick was abundant.

The important building on the farm was the barn, which was an American innovation. In England, farmers had a small cowhouse for milking, another building was used for threshing grain. The American barn was a combination structure to house livestock, store fodder and tools and thresh grain.

Architecture

Once the early colonists settled into regular work and home life they began to improve their modest houses and buildings. Many turned to the English Georgian architectural style which typically consisted of a central hall running from front to back of the house with two rooms on each side and an open staircase in the center.

The traditional fireplace in the common room (later called the kitchen), was of English origin. The common room, where all indoor work was done, became crowded as families grew, resulting in new, larger common rooms and additional living rooms.

After the Revolution, construction became more complicated and required architects as distinct from craftsmen. The houses ceased to be simple rectangles, windows grew in size, and ceilings were higher. Public buildings became more prominent.

Asher Benjamin (1773–1845), a noted architect, made a major contribution with his profusely illustrated guides—*The Country Builder's Assistant* (1797), the first American architectural book, and *The American Builder's Companion* (1806)—which greatly influenced American architecture.

Charles Bulfinch (1763–1844), the first American professional architect, designed the Massachusetts and Connecticut state houses and the Maine capitol. He served as an architect for the U.S. Capitol, designing the dome and rotunda.

William Thornton (1759–1828) furnished the Capitol's original design (1792) but he was not an architect so the plans had to be revised by Etienne S. Hallett (1755–1825). After a misunderstanding, Hallett was dismissed in 1794. James Hoban (1762–1831) supervised the start of Capitol construction and was succeeded by Benjamin H. Latrobe (1764–1820), who directed construction of the Capitol's south wing. Bulfinch succeeded Latrobe, who resigned in 1817, and oversaw completion of the Capitol by 1829. Latrobe supervised completion of the Virginia capitol designed by Thomas Jefferson and designed the first American Catholic cathedral in Baltimore. He is credited with professionalizing American architecture and engineering. Hoban designed the White House (1792), supervising its original construction and its reconstruction after the British burned it in 1814.

Robert Mills (1781–1855) served as architect of public buildings and designed the Treasury, Patent Office, Post Office and the Washington Monument. He founded the first architectural school in the 1830s in

Washington. This was followed by MIT (Massachusetts Institute of Technology) in 1868, Cornell in 1870, and University of Illinois in 1871.

The skyscraper, so much a part of the modern scene, did not appear until after Leroy S. Buffington of Minneapolis devised a method (1882) of supporting walls and floors on an iron frame. William L. Jenney (1832–1907) first applied the method three years later in the ten-story Home Insurance Building in Chicago, the first American tall building, lacking only a steel skeleton. The steel skeleton followed (1888) when architect William Holabird (1854–1923) and Wirt D. Walker designed the first office building with a complete skeleton construction, the Tacoma Building in Chicago. They also introduced the multiple deep basement.

Building Materials

After early construction in wood and stone, the development of new improved building materials followed rapidly. Bricks were used as early as 1611 in Virginia; the first brick building was erected (1633) in New Amsterdam (New York City). It was the residence of the Dutch governor. The first brick kiln was established in Salem, Massachusetts (1629). The first brick to withstand high heat was made in Mt. Savage, Maryland (1841).

Cement was first introduced in the United States (1870) when it arrived as ballast in English ships. The first Portland cement plant was built in Coplay, Pennsylvania (1871), by David O. Saylor, who perfected a process for making American cement. The European cement was considered superior until about 1897 when American cement surpassed the import. The first patent for prestressed concrete was issued 1888 to P. H. Jackson and the first concrete pavement was laid in Ohio (1892). The first major American prestressed concrete structure was a bridge in Philadelphia (1851).

Insulation and soundproofing began (1897) when Crystal Chemical Works of Alexandria, Indiana, started to manufacture rock wool insulation. The Armstrong Cork Company introduced insulating brick (1913) and a year later Carl G. Muench of St. Paul, Minnesota, invented insulating board. Emile Berliner (1851–1929) invented acoustic tile (1925). Glass wool and machinery for its manufacture were developed (1938) by (Russell) Games Slayter (1896–1964) and John H. Thomas of Newark, Ohio. Owens-Corning Fiberglass Corporation was founded to market the material.

Terra cotta was first manufactured (1853) by the noted architect, James Renwick (1818–95). Portland (Oregon) Manufacturing Company began to produce Douglas fir plywood in 1905.

Elevators/Escalators

Elevators date back to 1850 with the first machines only running between two floors. The first elevator, a platform type, was made (1850) by Henry Waterman for the Hecker and Brothers mill at 203 Cherry Street, New York City, to hoist barrels upstairs in the mill.

In 1852, Elisha G. Otis (1811–61) built a safety hoist for the bedstead factory where he was master mechanic. The next year he began manufacturing hoists with safety features. He demonstrated the safety publicly (1854) when he stood in a raised elevator, ordered the rope cut and the hoist did not fall. Otis installed the first passenger elevator in the E. V. Haughwout department store in New York City (1857). The Equitable Life Assurance Society Building, New York City, was the first office building with an elevator. The first hydraulic elevators were installed (1878) and the first electric elevator was installed (1889) by the Otis firm in the Demarest Building, New York City.

The first version of an escalator-type invention, or revolving stairs, was patented 1859 by Nathan Ames of Saugus, Massachusetts. The moving stairway, or the escalator, was invented (1892) by Jesse W. Reno (1861–1947). Otis, which acquired the rights, manufactured an escalator (1901), installed it in Gimbel's Philadelphia store.

Heating/Cooling

The heating of homes started with the fireplace as the primary source. The first manufactured cast-iron stove, produced in Lynn, Massachusetts (1642), had no grates and was simply a box. The first stove for heating was improved by Benjamin Franklin about 1744. It was first called the Pennsylvania fireplace, later the Franklin stove. John H. B. Latrobe (1803–91) invented a stove which fit into the fireplace — heating the immediate room and the one above it.

Zachariah Allen (1795–1882) invented the first hot air house-heating system (1821) and an automatic steam engine cutoff (1834). The first building heated by steam was the Eastern Hotel in Boston (1845).

John H. Mills designed one of the earliest steam heating systems, an overhead downfeed single pipe system (1877).

Cooling buildings began with John Gorrie (1803–55), a physician who treated victims of malaria and other fevers in rooms kept at low temperatures. Experimenting with means to achieve that cooling, he produced a machine (1842) that successfully cooled a room. By 1845, he gave up his medical practice, concentrated on cooling and developed a machine (1849) that produced ice. He received what was probably the first patent for a refrigerating device in 1851. Joseph McCreary of Toledo patented an air washer which cooled and humidified while cleaning the air (1897).

The birth of modern air conditioning is attributed to Willis H. Carrier (1876–1950), who built his first air conditioner (1902) to control humidity in a Brooklyn printing shop. He developed a central air conditioning unit of the air washer type (1906) and formed his development company (1915). Summer air conditioning started about 1920 with the advent of reliable refrigerating machinery. However, the 1930s depression and World War II delayed the emergence of air conditioning equipment until the late 1940s, when the demand became strong and new machines were developed.

Home Equipment

Home equipment developed slowly in the 1800s. One of the first mechanical washing machines was patented by Hamilton E. Smith of Philadelphia (1858). It required turning a crank to rotate paddles in a tub filled with water and clothes. The first electricity-powered machine was invented by Alva J. Fisher of Chicago (1910) and Howard Snyder invented an agitator-type washer 12 years later.

The first household refrigerator was invented (1803) by Thomas Moore of Baltimore. It consisted of two boxes, one inside the other, separated by insulation, with the food in the inner box. The first household gas refrigerator was marketed by Electrolux (1926).

George Hughes (1871–1944) built the first electric range using a wire resistor (1910), William S. Hadaway patented an electric stove (1896), Henry W. Seeley of New York City patented an electric flatiron (1882), and the General Electric Company patented an electric iron and toaster (1908).

A practical carpet sweeper was invented (1876) by Melville R. Bissell (1843–89). A suction-type vacuum cleaner was invented (1869) by Ives W. McGaffey of Chicago, and John S. Thurman of St. Louis invented the first motor-driven vacuum cleaner (1899). The Hoover Company introduced a rolling vacuum cleaner with a handle and dust bag (1907).

Another home equipment machine was the sewing machine. The early machines were those of Walter Hunt (1796–1859), inventor of many things, who developed a machine with a lock stitch (1834) but failed to patent it, and John J. Greenough of Washington, DC, who patented a sewing machine (1842). Hunt's machine was an important contribution because it showed that the machine need not imitate a hand operation.

Elias Howe (1819–67) patented a machine (1846) but could not get anyone to buy it. There were many infringements on his patent until it was finally upheld five years later.

Isaac M. Singer (1811–75) made numerous improvements on existing machines and created the first practical home sewing machine (1851). By the 1860s, Singer had become the world's leading sewing machine manufacturer.

The first patent for a practical chain-stitch single-thread sewing machine was granted (1857) to James E. A. Gibbs (1829–1902), who, with James Wilcox, marketed the Wilcox-Gibbs machine (1858).

Home Furnishings

Colonists brought no furniture with them. Individual cabinet makers began to operate about 1642, copying from the English, later adding Dutch and Pennsylvania German accents and influenced by some refugee French after their revolution.

Before 1750, most furnishings of the well-to-do were imported from England. By the time of the Revolution craftsmen began to take over. The first American efforts were simple in design and construction because of the limited skill of the craftsmen.

A major contribution to American craftsmanship was publication of Thomas Chippendale's *The Gentleman and Cabinetmaker's Directory* (1754).

Some of the better known early furniture makers were Scottish-born Thomas Affleck (1745–95), Jonathan Gostelowe (1744–95), Benjamin Randolph and William Savery (1721–87), all in Philadelphia, and John Goddard (1724–85) and John Townsend (1733–1809) in Newport, Rhode Island.

An early American furniture maker was Duncan Phyfe (1768–1854), a Scottish-born cabinet maker who helped create the Federal style. He opened a shop (1795) on Fulton Street in New York City where he employed more than 100 workers.

Other furniture makers of the period were Lambert Hitchcock (1795–1852), who built the first chair factory (1818) in Riverton, Connecticut; Levi Haywood, who invented various machines for chair making and Henry P. Kennedy, a Philadelphia upholsterer who patented a reclining chair (1841).

Box springs were first imported from France (1857) by James Boyle, a New York City bedding manufacturer. The folding bed was first manufactured in 1875–76 in Philadelphia by Hale and Kilburn Manufacturing Company and the Murphy door-bed began in San Francisco (1909).

Early colonists ate from pewter dishes as they did in England. Replacing them was too expensive so they began using poplar and soft white basswood for dishes—trenchers (flat plates), bowls, spoons and noggins (mugs). They had no forks and used either spoons or their fingers. Little pewter was made in the colonies before 1750; the earliest pewterers were those dealing in or repairing imported pewter.

Up to 1825, silverware in the United States was made only on special order. However, Jabez Gorham (1792–1869) felt there was a market and began to produce spoons, forks and later thimbles and other small items (1831). Isaac Babbitt (1799–1862), better known for his Babbitt metal, developed Brittania metalware (1824). After three years, he turned the plant over to his apprentices, and the firm became Reed and Barton, silverware makers.

Thomas Danforth (1703–86) opened a pewter shop in Norwich, Connecticut (1733), producing a large volume of pewter dishes, mugs, platters and basins.

Andre Duche succeeded in making porcelain by 1741. The first factory to produce domestic wares, including salt-glazed stoneware, was founded by John Norton in Bennington, Vermont (1793). The first quantity production was begun by William E. Tucker (1826).

Frederick G. Niedringhaus (1837–1922) began manufacturing tinware and formed St. Louis Stamping Company (which became National Enameling and Stamping Company). He developed a method of enameling steel plates, making cooking utensils cleaner and rust proof.

Timekeeping

Early developments in the field of timekeeping devices included a clock to strike the hours (1754) by Benjamin Banneker (1731–1806). Benjamin Hanks received a patent (1783) for a self-winding clock. Levi Hutchins of Concord, New Hampshire, made the first alarm clock in 1787.

Eli Terry (1772–1852) began making clocks (1794) in Plymouth, Connecticut. He patented an equation clock, showing both mean and apparent time (1797). He developed a "perfected wood clock" (1814) which dominated the market and reached production of 10,000 to 12,000 a year (selling at $15 each). Terry set up the first American clock factory in Plymouth, Connecticut (1800), using water power to drive his machines and was soon making 10 to 20 clocks at a time.

Simon Willard (1753–1848) patented his banjo-type clock in 1802.

Seth Thomas (1785–1859) helped change the clock making industry from small-scale craftsmanship to mass production. He began his career with Eli Terry (1807) and three years later he and Silas Hoadley bought out Terry. Thomas sold out to Hoadley and began his own plant (1812).

Chauncey Jerome (1793–1868) developed an inexpensive, accurate one-day brass movement clock (1838), which flooded the market. Hiram Camp (1811–93), a nephew of Jerome with whom he worked, went into business (1851) as the New Haven Clock Company. He bought out the failed Jerome company (1855) and the New Haven Company became the world's largest producer of inexpensive watches and clocks.

Aaron L. Denison (1812–95) and some friends built a clock factory in Roxbury, Massachusetts, where watches were made by machine (1849). The factory later became the Waltham Watch Company. Denison is generally credited with being the founder of American watchmaking.

Wall/Floor Coverings

Wall coverings started when Samuel Wetherill (1736–1816) began to manufacture white lead for paint (1790) and Adam Seybert (1773–1825) began to produce chlorides and red oxide pigment (1801). The Averill Paint Company in New York City began producing ready-mixed paint (1867) and the DeVilbiss Company of Toledo developed a paint sprayer (1909).

Moses Eaton (1796–1886) produced wall stencils which were in great demand until the use of wallpaper became general. Wallpaper was first manufactured by Plunkett Fleeson of Philadelphia (1739). Peter Force (1790–1868) patented a press to print wallpaper (1822).

Before rugs were woven by machines, the American settlers made floor coverings by knitting, crocheting or braiding thin strips of material in small squares and then sewing them together or by embroidering on a coarse-woven foundation. Hooking began around the turn of the eighteenth century and became very popular.

The first American carpet mill was founded by William B. Sprague (1773–1836) in Philadelphia (1791), producing Axminster rugs on hand looms.

Erastus B. Bigelow (1814–79) invented a loom for making lace and other figured fabrics (1837) and founded a factory (1843) in Clinton, Massachusetts, to make gingham. He developed machinery by 1851 to produce tapestry, velvet and Wilton and Brussells carpets. These machines revolutionized the industry and led to mass production.

Halcyon Skinner (1824–1900) designed a power loom to weave Axminster or tufted carpeting (1856).

Another floor covering, linoleum, was first manufactured (1875) by the American Linoleum Manufacturing Company in Staten Island, New York. Embossed inlaid linoleum was introduced by the Armstrong Cork and Insulation Company (1926).

21. Social Welfare

Early colonists followed the example of the English Poor Law, which placed emphasis on local responsibility and administration. One of the first acts toward charity was when Robert M. Hartley founded the New York Association for Improving the Condition of the Poor (1847). Between the Civil War and World War I rapid industrialization contributed to the growth of slums and the poverty of the immigrants and native workers.

Child Care

Massachusetts passed the first law regulating hours of labor by children in 1842—children under 12 could not work more than ten hours a day. Connecticut adopted a similar law for children under 14.

The first child hygiene bureau was established (1908) in New York City with Dr. Sara J. Baker (1873–1943) as director from 1908 to 1923. The bureau enabled the city to achieve the lowest baby death rate for any large American city.

The first kindergarten for crippled children opened at Alta Settlement House in Cleveland (1900). The same year, the first public school for cripples opened in Tilden School, Chicago.

Charles Burton made the first baby carriage (1848) in New York City. Protests were heard because people wheeling the carriages tended to hit pedestrians. Burton moved to England where his "perambulator" succeeded. The first American baby carriage factory, which became the F.A. Whitney Carriage Company, began in Leominster, Massachusetts (1858).

The first American baby show was held October 5, 1854, in Springfield, Ohio, with 127 babies entered, the winner being the ten-month-old daughter of William Ronemus of Vienna, Ohio. The first playground for children was created in Boston 1886.

The New York Children's Aid Society was founded in 1853 by Charles L. Brace (1826–90). The International Children's Welfare Congress met in Washington (1908) and the first White House Conference on Children (1909) recommended creation of a federal children's bureau.

Prominent in children's affairs were Arnold L. Gesell (1880–1961), psychologist who pioneered in scientific investigation of child development, and Dr. Samuel H. Durgin of the Boston Board of Health who inaugurated regular medical examination of school children.

Public and Private Organizations

Massachusetts led an attempt to improve the situation of its residents by founding a state board of charity and corrections (1863). Four years later there were 16 such boards and private charity organizations and social settlements began.

Among the earliest social settlements were Hull House in Chicago founded (1889) by Jane Addams (1860–1935) and the University Settlement established by Stanton Coit (1857–1944) and Charles B. Stover in New York City (1886).

Early charitable institutions were established by Elizabeth Ann Seton in 1797 (the Society for the Relief of Poor Widows with Small Children) and St. Joseph's House of Hospitality in the 1930s by Dorothy Day (1897–1980), who also founded the monthly *Catholic Worker.*

The first board of public welfare was created in Kansas City, Missouri (1910), and North Carolina and Illinois established state departments of public welfare (1917).

The Boys Club movement began in Hartford, Connecticut, with the founding of the Dashaway Boys Club which provided supervised after-school activities for underprivileged youth. The idea spread and 50 existing clubs joined to form what became the Boys Clubs of American (1906). The first girls club was formed in Waterbury, Connecticut (1864), to serve girls who had left home to work in mills and factories. The forerunner of the Big Brother movement was formed in Cincinnati (1903).

Daniel C. Beard (1850–1941) established the "Boy Pioneers, Sons of Daniel Boone" (1905), a recreational society with "forts" around the country. It merged (1910) with the Boy Scouts, founded in England. The first American troop was formed at the Central YMCA in Troy, New York (1911).

The Camp Fire Girls were organized by Luther H. Gulick (1892–1918) and his wife, Charlotte, at Lake Sebago, Maine (1910). Two years later Juliette G. Low (1860–1927) founded the first American troop of the Girl Guides (also founded in England) in Savannah, Georgia. The Guides became the Girl Scouts (1913).

Edward J. Flanagan (1886–1948), a Catholic priest in Omaha, Nebraska, began his Home for Homeless Boys with five residents in a rented house (1917). The next year it became the Father Flanagan Boys Home outside Omaha, developing into Boys Town (1922).

Dorothea L. Dix operated a school for young girls for 20 years. Once, while conducting a Sunday School class at a house of correction, she saw insane persons living in an unheated room. She began to campaign for separate facilities for the insane and convinced many states and foreign countries to improve their treatment.

Clara Barton (1821–1912) spent years helping wounded and missing soldiers in the Civil War and later in the Franco-Prussian War. She lobbied successfully to have the United States become a signatory to the 1882 Geneva Convention and organized the American Red Cross May 21, 1881. She served as president until 1904.

The Salvation Army came to the United States in March 1880 with the arrival of Commissioner George S. Railton and seven Salvation Army women in New York City. Ballington Booth (1859–1940) commanded the American Salvation Army (1887–96) but after an argument with his father, William, founder and head of the Army, Ballington resigned and founded the Volunteers of America. Evangeline Booth (1865–1950), sister of Ballington, took charge of the American Salvation Army (1904), serving as its head for 30 years.

Travelers Aid goes back to 1851 when Mayor Bryan Mullanphy of St. Louis endowed the society because of his concern over the problems of westbound travelers. There now are about 100 such agencies in the United States and Canada, serving as the National Travelers Aid Society, founded in 1917.

Public Opinion

Polling dates back to newspaper straw votes, the first being taken in 1824, and by 1900 many newspapers took straw votes on elections. Then magazines began polls, with the *Farm Journal* being the first in 1912.

From 1916 to 1936, the *Literary Digest* was foremost in the field, correctly forecasting election results. In 1936, the *Digest* mailed 20 million ballots to telephone subscribers and car owners and more than two million votes were tabulated. The result was a fiasco when it predicted Alf Landon would beat President Roosevelt — Landon carried only two states. By contrast other pollsters were correct in their predictions because they did a sampling of the voters.

George F. Gallup (1901–1984) conducted his first public opinion poll for the *Des Moines Register and Tribune* and discovered great popularity of pictures, resulting in the addition of a rotogravure section to the paper. Gallup founded the American Institute of Public Opinion in Princeton, New Jersey (1935).

The National Opinion Research Center, the first non-commercial opinion research agency, was established in 1941.

Women's Rights

The battle for equal rights— primarily for women — has been ongoing in the United States since the settlement of the colonies. One of the earliest examples dates back to 1647 when Margaret Brent (1600–71), a Maryland landowner — the first woman landowner in the colony — asked for a voice in the Assembly. She wanted two votes, one for herself as a landowner, the other as attorney for Lord Baltimore's estate. The colonial governor turned down the request.

From 1691 to 1780, women property owners in Massachusetts voted. In 1790, New Jersey revised its election law using the words "he or she" and women voted until 1807 when the right was limited to white males. The movement began in earnest in 1840.

Elizabeth Cady Stanton (1815–1902) went to a world anti-slavery convention where she met Lucretia C. Mott (1793–1880). They and other women were refused recognition at the convention because of their sex. They then decided to hold a convention of their own which occurred at Seneca Falls, New York, July 19–20, 1848, with 69 women and 32 men attending. Stanton drew up a bill of rights for the convention and a demand for women's suffrage, both of which were approved.

Sarah Margaret Fuller wrote an early plea for women's rights, *Woman in the 19th Century* (1845). She became a literary critic for the *New York Tribune* (1844) and two years later the first woman foreign correspondent. Another writer for the cause was Elizabeth Oakes Smith (1806–93) — *Woman and Her Needs*.

Amelia Jenks Bloomer began what was probably the first newspaper (*Lily*) edited entirely by a woman to carry stories about women's rights and temperance (1849). She is better remembered for her attempt to reform women's dress, wearing full cut trousers under a short skirt ("bloomers").

In 1850, the first national convention for women's rights was held in Worcester, Massachusetts.

Victoria Claflin Woodhull (1838–1927) and her sister began a stock brokerage firm (1868) with help from Cornelius Vanderbilt. They prospered and began publishing *Woodhull and Claflin's Weekly* advocating women's rights (1870). Woodhull became the first woman presidential candidate on the National Radical Reformers ticket (1872).

Congress held its first hearing on women's rights (1869) and appearing before the Senate committee were Susan B. Anthony (1820–1906) and Lucy Blackwell Stone (1818–93). The American Woman Suffrage Association was founded in 1869 and Anthony headed the group until 1892. Stone and her husband, Henry B. Blackwell, founded and ran (1870) the *Woman's Journal* for about 20 years. Mary A. R. Livermore (1820–1905), founded *The Agitator*, which after a few years merged with the *Woman's Journal*, which she edited for three years.

Anna Howard Shaw (1847–1919) served as a Methodist local preacher but was refused ordination because of her sex. She was ordained by the Protestant Methodist Church (1880) and five years late resigned to become active in the women's suffrage movement. She headed the American Woman Suffrage Association (1904–15).

Carrie Chapman Catt (1854–1947) was a high school principal in Mason city, Iowa, and became the first female school superintendent (1883). She headed the Women's Suffrage Association (1900–04, 1915–47).

Wyoming was the first state to give women the right to vote when it became a state in 1890. Fourteen others followed before national action occurred. A constitutional amendment to give women the vote was passed by the House of Representatives 274–136 on January 10, 1918, and 66–30 in the Senate on June 4, 1919. The 19th Amendment was ratified August 26, 1920, and the Supreme Court upheld its constitutionality February 27, 1922.

In more recent years, there was an active drive for an Equal Rights Amendment. Alice Paul (1885–1977) presented such an amendment before Congress (1923) but it failed to pass. It finally received congressional approval March 22, 1972, but ratification by the required 38 states failed when three state legislatures failed to approve before the June 30, 1982, deadline.

22. Sports

Soon after the arrival of settlers in the American colonies and after they had worked out caring for their basic necessities, they began to take up sports with which they were familiar. Among the earliest were horse racing, golf, billiards, bowling, cricket, sleighing and ice skating.

Horse racing in the colonies dates back to 1665 when an English colonel laid out a two-mile course on Long Island. Golfers were advised (1779) about the availability of golf clubs and societies were formed in Charleston, South Carolina (1786), and Savannah, Georgia (1795).

Billiard tables reportedly arrived with the Spanish in St. Augustine, Florida (1565), and bowling and ice skating were brought in by the Dutch when they occupied New York City in the 1660s. The first cricket match in the colonies is reported to have been held in New York City in 1751.

After the Civil War other sports began to grow; baseball, boxing, and, a little later, football and basketball.

Archery

The first American archery society, the United Bowmen of Philadelphia, was founded 1828. Modern archery began January 23, 1879, with the formation of the National Archery Association at Crawfordsville, Indiana, by eight archery clubs and the holding of its first tournament in Chicago (August 12–14, 1879) with 20 women and 69 men competing. Field archery was launched with the organization of the National Field Archery Association (1939), which held its first tournament seven years later in Allegan, Michigan.

Auto Racing

Automobile racing in the United States began November 28, 1895, when the *Chicago Times-Herald* sponsored a race in which 80 cars were entered but only six were able to start. The 52-mile race, which took eight hours, was won by J. Frank Duryea, an early automaker/racer. The first auto race on a track was held at the Rhode Island State Fair September 7, 1896, with six gasoline-powered and two electric-powered cars. The winner was an electric Riker with a speed of approximately 24 miles an hour. The pioneer auto races were the Vanderbilt Cup races of 300 miles which began in 1904 and ended in 1917. They were revived in 1936 and 1937.

On August 19, 1909, a group of automakers headed by Carl G. Fisher opened a dirt track in Indianapolis to test cars. It soon became a race track and the first Indianapolis 500 mile race was run May 30, 1911. Ray Harroun was the winner in 6 hours 41 minutes and 8 seconds, with an average speed of 74.7 miles per hour. NASCAR (National Association for Stock Car Auto Racing) was formed in 1947.

Badminton

The first American badminton club was organized in New York City (1878). Among the top American players were David G. Freeman of Pasadena, California, who began to play at 18 and was unbeatable in 1939–49, and Mrs. Judith D. Hashman, a former Baltimore school teacher, who won 32 American championships and ten All-England titles between 1954 and 1967.

Baseball

Often called the American sport, baseball's origin is generally credited to Abner Doubleday (1819–93), who served in the Mexican and Civil wars. He reputedly organized teams to play what became baseball around 1839 and according to legend laid out the first baseball diamond and established the rules of the game. The legend is firmly planted even though investigation showed baseball to be a variant of the traditional game of rounders, which was played early in the American colonies as town ball and under other names.

A book published in England (1744), *A Little Pretty Pocket Book*, described children's sports for each letter of the alphabet. The letter B was baseball and told how it was, and is, played. The book was reprinted twice in the United States (1762, 1787).

The Boys Own Book by William Clarke, published in London (1828), described the game of rounders which was played much the way baseball is played. There were many other references to the game in English literature.

Regardless of its actual origin, baseball has had a historic American career. The first recorded game was played in Hoboken, New Jersey, June 19, 1846, with the New York Knickerbockers, the first organized baseball team, losing 23–1 to the New York Club. The Knicks were organized September 23, 1845, by Alexander J. Cartwright, Jr. (1820–92), a New York City fireman, who introduced 90 feet baselines, nine man teams and nine inning games. In the second recorded game (1851), the Knickerbockers were the first to wear uniforms — straw hats, white shirts, and full length blue trousers. The first baseball enclosure was the Union Grounds in Brooklyn, which opened in 1862.

Harry Chadwick (1824–1908), known as the "father" of baseball, did much to ensure the game's growth by heading the rules committee of the National Association of Professional Baseball Players. He also began publishing an annual handbook (1869), which 30 years later became *Spalding's Official Baseball Guide*.

Henry (Harry) Wright (1835–95), an English-born cricket expert, came to Cincinnati and organized a baseball team (1866). Two years later, he reorganized it as a semi-professional team. The Cincinnati Red Stockings became completely professional (1869) and went on tour (the first to do so), winning 56 and tieing 1.

The National Association of Base Ball Players was formed by 16 clubs in New York City (1858). It became the National Association of Professional Base Ball Players (1871), including teams in Philadelphia, Boston, Chicago, Brooklyn, Cleveland, Rockford (Illinois), Troy (New York), Ft. Wayne (Indiana), Washington and New York. Five years later it became the National League of Professional Baseball Clubs. The league was formed February 2, 1876, with teams in Philadelphia, Hartford, Boston, Chicago, Cincinnati, Louisville, St. Louis and New York.

The American Association was formed 1882 and nine years later merged with the National League.

The American League was formed from the Western League January 29, 1900, by Ban (Byron B.) Johnson (1864–1931) but it was not recognized by the National League until 1903. The original American League teams were in Boston, Baltimore (moved to New York 1903), Washington, Chicago, Cleveland, Detroit and Milwaukee (moved to St. Louis 1902).

Recognition of the American League came with the first World Series (1903). Boston of the American League won four games, Pittsburgh of the National League, three. The Series, which was not played in 1904, was then played annually until 1994, when a strike of the players in August caused an early end of the season and cancellation of the Series.

Baseball entered a new era (1921) when it chose its first commissioner — Kenesaw M. Landis (1866–1944), a federal district judge. His hiring was made necessary by the "Black Sox" scandal (1919) when eight members of the Chicago White Sox were accused of "throwing" the World Series. A trial acquitted them on a technicality but the new commissioner banished them from the game. Landis ruled baseball with finality until his death.

Branch W. Rickey (1881–1965), a baseball executive with several clubs, made two unique contributions to the game. He introduced the minor league farm system and was the first to break the major league barrier against black players by bringing Jackie Robinson (1919–72) to the Brooklyn Dodgers in April 1947.

The popular game is replete with records and statistics and a few of the game's firsts are:

First professional league game was played May 4, 1871, at Ft. Wayne, Indiana, with the home team beating Cleveland 2–0.

First major league no-hit game was pitched by Joseph E. Borden of the Philadelphia Nationals against Chicago July 28, 1875. Then on May 2, 1917, opposing pitchers — Jim Vaughn of Chicago and Fred Toney of Cincinnati — each pitched nine no-hit innings; the Reds scored a run in the tenth to win.

Johnny Vander Meer (1914–97) of Cincinnati pitched two consecutive no-hit games in 1938 — one on June 11, the second June 15. Don Larsen (1929–) of the New York Yankees pitched the only perfect game (no hits, no base runners) in the World Series on October 8, 1956, beating Brooklyn 2–0.

The tradition of the president starting the baseball season by throwing out the first ball began with President Taft in 1910.

The first night major league baseball game was played at Crosley Field, Cincinnati, May 24, 1935, with the Reds beating Philadelphia 2–1. President Franklin Roosevelt pressed a button in Washington which turned on 363 lights on eight towers.

The first major league all-star game was played July 6, 1933, in Chicago with the American League winning 4–2.

Babe (George H.) Ruth (1895–1948), a great pitcher who became a homerun hitter, revolutionized and popularized the game. He set a season homerun record of 59 (1921), which he raised to 60 six years later. This record stood until 1961 when Roger Maris (1934–85) hit 61. That record stood until 1999 when Mark McGwire hit 70. Ruth's record career total of 714 lasted until April 8, 1974, when Hank Aaron (1934–) hit his 715th.

Lou Gehrig (1903–41), New York Yankees first baseman, set a record (1939) of playing in 2,130 consecutive ball games. The record stood until September 6, 1995, when Baltimore shortstop Cal Ripken, Jr. (1960–), played in his 2,131st game.

The Baseball Hall of Fame was established January 29, 1936, at Cooperstown, New York.

The cork center baseball was invented by Benjamin F. Shibe (1838–1922) of Bala, Pennsylvania in 1909. Frederick W. Thayer, captain of Harvard's 1878 baseball team, invented the catcher's mask. The first baseball glove was worn (1875) by Boston first baseman Charles C. Waite.

Basketball

Students at the International YMCA Training School in Springfield, Massachusetts, played the first official basketball game January 20, 1892. The game was invented by James Naismith (1861–1939), a teacher at the school. Luther H. Gulick, school physical training director, suggested to Naismith that he devise a game that could be played indoors during the winter. The first set of basketball rules was published in the YMCA newspaper, *Triangle*, on January 15, 1892.

Wesleyan University and Yale played the first intercollegiate game on December 10, 1896, in New Haven.

The professional game began (1898) when a Trenton, New Jersey, team rented an auditorium for $25 and paid each member $15. Trenton and the New York Wanderers were the first great professional clubs.

The first professional league, National Basketball League, was formed in 1898. The National Basketball Association (NBA) was formed (1949) by the merger of the National Basketball League and the Basketball Association of America (formed in 1946). A rival, the American Basketball Association, was formed in 1967 and merged with the NBA in 1976.

Bicycling

The first American bicycling organization was the Boston Bicycle Club founded February 11, 1878; the League of American Wheelmen, representing 28 clubs, was founded May 31, 1880.

The first international six-day races were held October 18–24, 1891, with only six of 30 starters finishing. The winner was William Martin, riding a "high wheeler." The first American six-day bicycle race was held in Chicago 1879.

The first intercollegiate race was held May 27, 1896, with Columbia University winning over four other schools.

Billiards

The first billiard table was brought to the American colonies (1565) by Spaniards arriving in St. Augustine, Florida.

Joseph N. White of New York City defeated George Smith of Watertown, New York, 500 to 484, in the first important billiards match on May 13, 1854, in Syracuse.

A billiard ball of composition material resembling ivory was patented by John W. Hyatt (1865). Hyatt won $10,000 in a competition for the new material.

The first national billiards championship was held in April of 1859 in Detroit with Michael Phelan of New York City defeating John Seereiter of Detroit.

Boating

The first American boat club was the Knickerbocker Boat Club of New York (1811). The same year saw the first recorded boat race in which

New York City's Whitehall ferrymen beat seamen from Long Island and Staten Island.

The Whitehall ferrymen defeated a British crew in a four mile race (1824) and the next year, 30,000 watched ferryboat men race for a $1,000 prize.

The first efforts to organize boat clubs occurred with the formation of the Castle Garden Club Association of New York (1834) and the Detroit Boat Club (1839).

The first intercollegiate eight-oared boat race was held August 3, 1852 on Lake Winnipesaukee, New Hampshire, with Harvard beating Yale and Brown. The National Association of Amateur Oarsmen, founded 1873, staged a regatta with 11 college crews the next year.

The first canoe club was the New York Canoe Club (1870) and the American Canoe Association was formed at Lake George, New York, ten years later.

The first motorboat races under organized rules were held June 23–24, 1904, by the Columbia Yacht Club on the Hudson River.

Among leaders in boating were James B. Herreshoff (1834–1930), inventor of the sliding seat for rowboats and racing shells and a fin keel for yachts; Gar(field A.) Wood (1880–1971), who popularized speedboat racing, and Ole Evinrude (1877–1934), developer of the first commercially successful outboard motor (1909).

Bowling

Dutch settlers in the 1600s brought the game of outdoor nine pins with them; it became very popular and was moved indoors. At one time, there were lanes in every block of Broadway in New York City between Fulton and 14th streets. The game came to be controlled by gamblers and nine pins was outlawed in New York and Connecticut. To get around the law, another pin was added. Several unsuccessful attempts to control the game were made between 1875 and 1890, then finally the American Bowling Congress (ABC) was organized September 8, 1895, followed by the Women's International Bowling Congress (WIBC) (1916).

The first recorded bowling match was held January 1, 1840, in the Knickerbocker Alley in New York City.

The game of duckpins (using shorter pins and smaller balls) was introduced in Baltimore (1900). Lawn bowling, like nine pins, began on the colonial greens and spread along the East Coast. The game died out in the 1800s, then Christian Schepflin of Dunellen, New Jersey, formed a club (1879) and interest was renewed. The American Lawn Bowling Association was organized in Buffalo 1915.

Boxing

The first American to shine in the ring was Bill Richmond (1763–1829) of New York City, the son of a Georgia-born slave, who knocked out a British champion in England (1805). He lost later in the year and never fought again in the United States.

The first recorded American championship fight was held in New York City between Jack Hyer and Tom Beasley. Hyer won, declared himself champion, then retired. Hyer's son, Tom, in the 1840s, was the first to be recognized as the American heavyweight champion.

John L. Sullivan reigned as champion (1882–92), the period which marked the beginning of organized boxing. Sullivan, who popularized the sport, was the last of the hardknuckle champions and was followed by a long line of champions.

Jack (William H.) Dempsey had an unprecedented popular following as champion (1919–26), losing only five of 69 bouts, two of them to Gene Tunney in 1926 and 1927. Tunney retired undefeated (1928). Other noted champions were Joe Louis, from 1937 to 1949, Rocky Marciano, from 1952 to 1956, Muhammad Ali, from 1964 to 1970 and 1974 to 1979, and Larry Holmes, from 1979 to 1985.

Tex (George L.) Rickard (1871–1929) became the first boxing promoter to stage fights which grossed one million dollars or more. The first such fight was the Dempsey-Georges Carpentier (1921) and then the Dempsey-Tunney fights.

The American Medical Association has called for an end to boxing (both amateur and professional) because of its danger to health.

Cricket

The first American cricket match was held May 1, 1751, in New York City with a city team meeting the Londoners. The Boston Cricket Club was the first American club (1809).

Croquet

The game was brought from England (1860) and became very popular. The National Croquet League was organized (1880) in Philadelphia with 18 teams, but it did not last long. The National Croquet Association was founded in 1950.

Curling

The first American curling club was the Orchard Lake Curling Club near Pontiac, Michigan, in 1831–32. The first national championship competition was held March 28–30, 1857, in Chicago with the Hibbing, Minnesota, club the winner.

Dogs (Racing, Trials, Shows)

The Tennessee State Sportsmen's Association put on the first public field trials for setters and pointers (1874).

The first important dog show was held at the Hippodrome in New York City May 8, 1877, by the Westminster Kennel Bench Show of Dogs.

The first dog race track was built by an Arkansas promoter, Owen P. Smith, at Emeryville, California (1920). The track was a failure because betting was not allowed. The racing moved to Florida where in 1926 the successful St. Petersburg Kennel Club opened its track.

The International Greyhound Racing Association was formed on March 3, 1926, with Smith as the first high commissioner.

Fencing

The Amateur Fencers League of America, organized 1891, staged the first competition the next year. The first intercollegiate competition was held in New York City (1894) with Harvard defeating Columbia and Yale.

Fishing

Fishing is one pastime in which a great many Americans indulge either as a sport or for food. It has been going on since the first settlers.

The more than 160,000 miles of coastal and inland waterways make fishing available to most residents.

The New York State Sportsmens Association held the first fly casting tournament in Utica, New York, in June 1861.

The first fishing magazine, *American Angler*, was issued October 15, 1881.

Football

Various games similar to soccer were played informally at some colleges. In 1820, Princeton students played a form of football called "ballown." Harvard banned such games on campus (1860), New Haven officials outlawed such games on the public green (1858).

Finally in 1867, a Princeton team played another team from the Princeton Theological Seminary. Then came the first intercollegiate game at New Brunswick, New Jersey, on November 6, 1869, with Rutgers defeating Princeton 6–4.

With the home team setting the rules, each team had 25 players in the first game and used a round rubber ball. A goal was scored when the ball was kicked between the goal posts and under the cross bar, rather than over. There was no running with the ball but it could be kicked or batted. A player could make a fair catch and get a free kick.

The following week they played at Princeton and used Princeton rules which required eight goals for a victory. Princeton won 8–0. The third game was cancelled by both school faculties.

Columbia began to play football in 1870, losing to Rutgers 6–3; then Yale two years later, beating Columbia 3–0. Then on October 18, 1873, the first football rules were drawn up by Columbia, Princeton, Rutgers and Yale. These four schools and Harvard, which lifted its ban (1871), formed the Intercollegiate Football Association (1876).

Walter C. Camp (1859–1925) is considered the "father" of American football. He played halfback for Yale and threw the first forward pass (1876) even though it was not legalized until 1906. Camp served as a member of the Intercollegiate Football Association rules committee for 48 years, helped create the scrimmage line, the 11-man team, signal calling and the quarterback position. He originated the rule that a team had to advance at least ten yards in four attempts or give up the ball. He began (1889) selecting annual All-American teams.

The first numerals on football uniforms were used by Pittsburgh University (1908).

One of the most successful users of the forward pass was Knute Rockne (1888–1931) when he starred on the Notre Dame team with Gus Dorais against Army (1913). Rockne went on to became a legendary coach at Notre Dame (1918–31).

Other noted coaches of the early years were Pop (Glenn S.) Warner (1871–1954), who coached 46 years and introduced the double wing formation, and Amos Alonzo Stagg (1862–1965), who coached 41 years and introduced the huddle, the shift, the man in motion, and the end-around play.

The first night football game was played September 29, 1892, at Mansfield, Pennsylvania, between Mansfield Teachers College and Wyoming Seminary. The teams played only one half, which lasted 70 minutes, and no one scored.

In the first college bowl game (1902) — the Rose Bowl — Michigan beat Stanford 49–0. The game did not become an annual event until 1916 and was later followed by many other bowl games.

The first professional football game was played (1895) in Latrobe, Pennsylvania, with the Latrobe YMCA defeating the Jeannette (Pennsylvania) Athletic Club 12–0. The winners paid quarterback John Brallier ten dollars to substitute for its regular quarterback.

The American Professional Football Association, forerunner of the National Football League (NFL), was formed September 17, 1920, with 11 teams. Jim Thorpe (1888–1953), an outstanding all-around athlete, was named first president of the Association. The original teams represented Chicago, Decatur and Rock Island, Illinois, Hammond and Muncie, Indiana, Rochester, New York, and Akron, Canton, Cleveland, Dayton, and Massillon, Ohio.

One of the founders of the Association was George S. Halas (1895–1983), who bought one of the original club franchises for $100 — the Staleys of Decatur. He moved the team to Chicago (1922), where the Bears have been ever since. The Association became the NFL (1922) and had a number of commissioners. Two of them served 42 years — Bert (de Benneville) Bell (1894–1959), who served 1946–59, formed a cohesive league, worked out successful television broadcasts of the games, and arranged the merger with the All-America Conference, and Pete (Alvin R.) Rozelle (1926–96), served 1960–89, helped the league grow from 12 to 28 teams, and led the merger of the NFL and American Football league.

The first Super Bowl game was played January 15, 1967, in Los Angeles with Green Bay beating Kansas City 35–10.

Fox Hunting

The first fox hunting club was the Gloucester Fox Hunting Club for residents of Philadelphia and Gloucester County, New Jersey, created January 1, 1767.

Golf

The first American reference to golf appeared April 21, 1779, in the *New York Gazette* with the following notice: "To the Golf Players: The season for this pleasant and healthy exercise now advancing, gentlemen may be furnished with excellent clubs and the veritable Caledonia balls by enquiring at the Printers."

There was a reference in the *South Carolina and Georgia Banner* (1793) about societies established in Charleston, reading "golf club formed 1786" and then listed the officers. Later notices referred to the 1794 anniversary dinner of the South Carolina Golf Club and the *Georgia Gazette* on September 22, 1796, announced the anniversary of the Savannah Golf Club. These were social organizations and did not survive the War of 1812. Probably the oldest American golf club was the Foxburg (Pennsylvania) Golf Club formed in 1885; then followed the St. Andrews Golf Club of Yonkers, New York (1888), and the Middlesborough (Kentucky) Golf Club (1889).

The first amateur tournament was held at the St. Andrews Club (1894) and the official open championship was played at the Newport (Rhode Island) Country Club the following year, with Horace Rawlins the winner. The women's amateur title was won by Mrs. Charles S. Brown.

The Intercollegiate Golf Association was established by Columbia, Harvard, Yale, and Princeton in 1897.

The first book on golf, *Golf in America*, was written by James P. Lee (1895). A steel shaft for a golf club was invented by Arthur F. Knight of Schenectady (1910) and the golf tee by George F. Grant of Boston (1899).

Some of the early giants of the game were three selected by sportswriters as the best of the 1900–50 era:

Walter C. Hagen (1892–1969), winner of the U.S. Open twice, British Open four times, and PGA (Professional Golfers Association) three times.

Bobby (Robert T.) Jones (1902–71), winner of the U.S. Open four times, British Open three times, U.S. amateur five times. He was the only player to win the open and amateur titles in both the U.S. and England in the same year (1930). Jones founded the annual Masters tournament (1934).

Gene Sarazen (1902–), winner of the U.S. Open twice, British Open and Masters once, and PGA three times.

More recently there have been such outstanding players as Ben (William B.) Hogan (1912–97), Jack Nicklaus (1940–), and Arnold Palmer (1929–).

Among the outstanding women players was Babe Didrikson Zaharias (1914–56), an all-around athlete and champion golfer.

Gymnastics

The first gymnasium to offer systematic instruction was the Round Hill School in Northampton, Massachusetts (1823). The first such college course was at Harvard (1826) and a women's college at Mt. Holyoke (1862).

The Cincinnati Turnegemeinde (1848) became the first gymnastic organization in the United States and the first national group, the Turnersbund, was created (1850) in Philadelphia by six gymnastic societies.

The first gymnastic book (1802) was a translation from the German — *Gymnastics for Youth.*

Robert J. Roberts, physical education director, Boston YMCA, invented the medicine ball (1895).

Handball

The sport was introduced to the United States in the late 1800s and the first international matches (1887) saw John Lawlor, the Irish champion, and Phil Casey, the American champion, meet for the world title and $1,000 with the best of 21 games the winner. Lawlor won six of the ten matches in Cork, Ireland, but Casey won seven straight in New York City. Casey retained the title until 1900.

The first national amateur handball championship was held in Jersey City January 7–8, 1897.

Hockey (Ice, Field)

Ice hockey began to be played in the United States in the early 1890s at St. Paul's School in Concord, New Hampshire, Johns Hopkins University in Baltimore, Yale University and in St. Paul, Minnesota. The first official league or association game was played between the St. Nicholas and Brooklyn skating clubs December 15, 1896, with St. Nicholas the winner 15–0.

The professional National Hockey Association was formed (1909) and the Pacific Coast Hockey League, including American teams, two years later. The National Hockey League (NHL) was established November 22, 1917, and included Boston (1924).

Field hockey was introduced to Americans (1901) by Constance M. K. Applebee of the British College of Physical Education and quickly became the most popular women's sport. The United States Field Hockey Association was formed (1922) to govern women's play; the Field Hockey Association of America to govern men's play (1930).

Horse/Harness Racing

The first organized horse racing began on Long Island (1665) when Colonel Richard Nicolls laid out a two-mile course on Hempstead Plains and called it New Market. The first thoroughbred race track was the Union Course on Long Island (1821).

New York State prohibited (1802) public horse races, permitting them only in private jockey clubs. The state legalized race track betting in 1887.

The first international horse race took place in England (1829) when the American horse *Rattler* beat the Welsh mare *Miss Turner* by nearly 60 yards.

The first running of the Belmont Stakes (1867) was won by *Ruthless*, ridden by J. Gilpatrick; the purse was $1,850. The first Preakness Stakes (1873) at Baltimore was won by *Survivor*, ridden by G. Barber. The first Kentucky Derby, run 1875 at Churchill Downs in Louisville, Kentucky, was won by *Aristide*; Oliver Lewis was the jockey.

The first steeplechase was held October 26, 1869, by the American Jockey Club at Jerome Park, New York.

The first horse show was held in Upperville, Virginia (1853); the first national show was held in Madison Square Garden, New York City October 22–26, 1883.

The first photo finish (electric eye) camera began operating January 16, 1936, at the Hialeah, Florida, race course. The first electric starting gate was invented by Clay Puett, who built a two-stall working model at Hollywood Park at Inglewood, California, May 8, 1939. A full-size gate was installed October 7 at Bay Meadows Race Track in San Francisco.

American harness racing dates back to 1788 when the English stallion *Messenger* was brought to the United States. *Messenger's* grandson, *Hambletonian*, foaled in 1849, and was the patriarch of the modern standardbred.

Trotting and pacing races were held in the mid-eighteenth century in Maryland and New Jersey and were very popular at county fairs. The first recorded trotting race was held in 1818 and about 1825 the first rules of harness racing were issued by the New York Trotting Club for use at the Jamaica track.

Horseshoe Pitching

The American Horseshoe Pitchers Association was organized (1914) in Kansas City, Missouri.

Hunting

The nation's historical attachment to guns has kept hunting a popular sport. Because of the danger of guns and the need to preserve many animal species, there has been careful regulation and licensing of the sport.

Lacrosse

This is the oldest organized sport in America. The Iroquois Indians in New York were playing the game before Columbus arrived. The game began to be played in schools, colleges and clubs in the 1840s.

The first international lacrosse match was played in Buffalo (1868) when a Canadian team beat an American squad. New York University, Harvard, and Princeton organized the U.S. Amateur Lacrosse Association (1877). Five years later, the three schools and Columbia formed the Intercollegiate Lacrosse Association.

The first women's lacrosse game was played (1814) at Sweetbriar College in Virginia.

Polo

The newspaper publisher, James Gordon Bennett, introduced polo to the United States on his return from England (1876). He brought back the needed equipment and had horses brought to New York from Texas. The first games were played at Dickel's Riding Academy at 39th Street and Fifth Avenue.

The first polo club, Westchester, was organized 1876 and the first match between American and English clubs was played in 1886.

The United States Polo Association was founded in 1890.

Racquetball

Racquetball, originally called paddle rackets, was created in the late 1940s by Joseph G. Sobek, a Connecticut tennis and squash teaching professional. The game was standardized by Robert W. Kendley, founder and first president of the U.S. Racquetball Association and the National Racquetball Club.

Shuffleboard

The game was introduced about 1913 at Daytona Beach, Florida. Representatives of the Florida clubs met (1924) and developed the modern form of the game.

Skating (Ice/Roller)

The Dutch brought ice skating and sleighing with them to the United States in the mid–1600s. Early ice skating clubs operated in Philadelphia (1849), New York (1863), and Boston (1912) and the first indoor ice skating rink was built in Madison Square Garden, New York City (1879).

The all-metal ice skate with screw clamps was developed by Everett H. Barney of Springfield, Massachusetts (1866).

Figure skating was influenced by Jackson Haines (1849–76), a ballet master who combined dance and skating. He put on exhibitions in the 1860s in the United States and Europe.

Dick Button (1929–) became the first American to win the men's world figure skating title (1948) and Tenley Albright (1935–), the first American to win the women's title five years later.

Speed skating began in the 1820s and Newburgh, New York, became the American headquarters for the sport. Charles June of Newburgh was considered the fastest for many years after 1838. The city also was the birthplace of the Donoghues—a father and two sons—who were the fastest in the world in the 1870 and 80s.

Roller skating was introduced to the United States by James L. Plimpton of Medfield, Massachusetts, inventor of the four-wheeled skate (1863). He organized the New York Roller Skating Association and built a rink in New York City the same year.

Skiing

Skiing was introduced to the United States by Scandinavian immigrants in the mid–1800s and began to gain popularity in the 1930s. Competitive skiing began in California in the 1860s. Early skiers had only bootstrap bindings so they ran only straight downhill courses.

The first American ski club was organized in Berlin, New Hampshire, and ten ski clubs comprised the Central Organization (1871) and the National Ski Association was founded in 1904.

The first steel ski jump was built (1908) at Chippewa Falls, Wisconsin, and the first rope ski tow was constructed (1934) at Woodstock, Vermont. The skimobile was invented (1937) by George Norton of Goodrich Falls, New Hampshire.

The Water Skiing Association was founded in 1939.

Soccer

Soccer was overshadowed in the United States by football until the 1960s and has since become popular in high schools and colleges and to some extent professional play. The game was brought to the United States by the British. The first intercollegiate football game (Rutgers v. Princeton, 1869) was more like soccer than present-day football.

The first American soccer game was played (1886) in New York City's Central Park. During the summer of 1994, the United States was host to the World Cup Games for the first time, increasing soccer's American popularity.

The U.S. Soccer Football Association was organized in 1913.

Softball

The game was invented (1887) by George W. Hancock of Chicago and originally used a broomstick for a bat and a boxing glove for the ball. The first indoor game was played at the Farragut Boat Club in Chicago November 30, 1887. The Amateur Softball Association of America was organized in 1932.

Sports Media

The first prize fight shown on film was Jim Jeffries against Tom Sharkey November 3, 1899, at the Coney Athletic Club.

The first radio sports broadcasts were: *baseball*— August 5, 1921, Pittsburgh against Philadelphia; *boxing*— September 6, 1920, Jack Dempsey against Billy Miske; *college football*— November 15, 1920, Texas and Texas A & M; *tennis*— August 4, 1921, Davis Cup at Sewickley, Pennsylvania.

First sports television shows: *baseball* (college)— May 17, 1939, Columbia and Princeton; *baseball* (major league)— August 26, 1939, Cincinnati and Brooklyn; *baseball* (World Series)—1947 New York and Brooklyn; *basketball*— February 28, 1940, Fordham and Pittsburgh; *boxing*— June 1, 1939, Max Baer and Lou Nova; *football* (college)— September 30, 1939, Fordham and Waynesburg; *football* (professional)— October 22, 1939, Brooklyn and Philadelphia; *hockey*— February 25, 1940, New York and Montreal; *tennis*— August 9, 1939, Eastern Grass Court championships; *track*— March 2, 1940, Madison Square Garden.

The Sportsman's Companion, the first important sports book, was published in 1783. Poultney Bigelow (1855–1954) founded *Outing*, the first American magazine devoted to amateur sports (1835).

Astro Turf, covering the baseball and football fields, was first used at a Providence, Rhode Island, private school (1964).

First Pendleton (Oregon) Round-up held in 1910; first rodeo held at Prescott, Arizona, July 4, 1888.

Squash

Squash rackets came to the United States in the late 1800s from England and was played here with some modifications. The U.S. Squash Rackets Association was formed (1920) and annual championships were held. Squash tennis was developed in the United States and is played primarily in New York City.

Swimming/Diving

The first American swimming school opened in Boston (1827).

The first American to swim the English Channel was Henry F. Sullivan of Lowell, Massachusetts (1923), doing so in 27 hours and 23 minutes. Gertrude Ederle (1906–), champion amateur swimmer and member of the 1926 American Olympic team, became the first woman to swim the Channel, doing so August 6, 1926, in (then) record time of 14 hours, 31 minutes.

Swimming at beaches is popular throughout the world but the United States was the first to use pools extensively.

The first American diving meet was held at University of Pennsylvania (1907). A member of the 1908 Swedish Olympic diving team, Ernest Brandsten, who became coach at Stanford University (1912), is credited with pioneering diving in the United States.

Tennis

Tennis began in the United States in 1874–75 but there is a difference of opinion about the originator. Mary E. Outerbridge had spent the winter of 1874 in Bermuda and saw the game being played by British officers. She returned with a net and some rackets and balls. Her brother, A. Emilius Outerbridge, helped lay out a court at the Staten Island Cricket and Baseball Club. At about the same time, James Dwight (1852–1917) and Fred Sears set up a court in Nahant, Massachusetts, where the first American tournament took place (1876).

The U.S. National Lawn Tennis Association (later becoming the U.S. Tennis Association) was organized in 1881. The first recognized American men's singles champion (1881–87) was Richard D. Sears (1861–1943); the first American women's singles champion was Ellen Hansel (1887).

There have been some dominant champions since those early years.

William A. Larned (1872–1926) and William T. Tilden (1893–1953) stood out among the men and Helen Wills Moody (1905–98), Billie Jean King (1943–) and Martina Navratilova (1956–) were women leaders.

Arthur E. Ashe, Jr. (1943–93), was the first black to win the United States men's singles (1968) and Althea Gibson (1927–) was the first black player to win at Wimbledon (1937).

Hazel H. Wightman (1886–1974) was the United States singles champion (1909–11, 1919) and donated a cup for international women's competition.

The first Davis Cup matches were held in Longwood, near Boston, August 8–10, 1900, with the United States winning three matches, the British none; one match was not played, one was not finished.

Professional tennis began in 1926 after a successful tour.

Track/Field

Amateur track and field competition began with the formation of the New York Athletic Club (1868). The Club staged the first American track meet November 11 of that year in a partly-completed, unroofed skating rink with a 220-yard track. The Club also conducted the first national amateur championships (1876).

The IC4A (Intercollegiate Association of Amateur Athletes of America) was organized (1876) and conducted college track and field championships. The organization became the National Collegiate Athletic Association (NCAA) in 1905.

The first annual marathon, the Boston Marathon, was won by John J. McDermott of New York City (1897).

Among the outstanding figures in track and field history were:

Jim (James F.) Thorpe, considered the greatest American athlete, who won the decathlon and pentathlon in the 1912 Olympics.

Babe Didrikson Zaharias, outstanding woman athlete, won gold medals for the javelin and 80 meters hurdles in the 1932 Olympics and was a great golfer.

Jesse Owens (1913–80) won four gold medals at the 1936 Olympics, setting three world records and sharing one in the relays.

Trapshooting

Trapshooting began in the 1830s with the formation of the Sportsmen's Club of Cincinnati, the Long Island Club, and the New York Sportsmen's Club. The first governing body of the sport was the Interstate Association of Trapshooters, which was succeeded (1900) by the American Trapshooters Association.

The evolution of targets for the United States followed the pattern of England — live birds, glass balls, and clay discs. George Ligowsky of Cincinnati developed the first successful clay targets and modern trap in the United States (1880).

The first Grand American trapshooting tournament was held on Long Island (1900) and the first national skeet shooting tournament was held at Solon, Ohio (1935).

Volleyball

The game was developed by William G. Morgan, physical education director of the Holyoke, Massachusetts, YMCA (1895). It was designed as an indoor sport for businessmen who found basketball too vigorous. The United States Volleyball Association was formed in 1928.

Yachting

The first boat built exclusively for sailing was the *Fancy* by Colonel Lewis Morris (1671–1746) of New York (1717); the second, the sloop *Jefferson* by George Crowninshield (1766–1817) of Salem (1801).

John C. and Edwin A. Stevens (1795–1868) of Hoboken were the first prominent yachtsmen in the New York area, building several boats in 1809 and 1816.

The New York Yacht Club was organized June 30, 1844, aboard the *Gimcrack*, a Stevens boat, marking the start of organized yachting. A great stimulus to American yachting was the victory over 17 British boats by the Stevens schooner *America* in a 53-mile race around the Isle of Wight, England, in 1851. This was the start of the America's Cup races.

23. Transportation

Automobiles

The American automobile industry is the outgrowth of bicycle and carriage manufacturing and the work of many engineers and mechanics in Europe and the United States in the late 1800s and early 1900s.

Steam technology was most advanced at the time but the size and weight of the vehicles and the relative complexity of steam power stimulated experimenting with other power sources. Among the earliest experiments in the United States were the men working with steam power — Oliver Evans built a steam-powered river dredge (1804) which he drove over land and in water under its own power, anticipating both the steamboat and auto. Other builders were Nathan Read of Salem, Massachusetts, and Apollo Kinsley of Hartford in the 1790s.

Thomas Blanchard, better known for inventing the lathe, built a steam auto (1825) but no one paid attention to it. Henry A. House (1840–1930) developed a horseless carriage (1866) powered by a 12 horsepower steam engine. George B. Brayton patented a two-stroke engine (1872) which had an electrical ignition. It was the first successful American internal combustion engine. He placed the one cylinder engine in a second-hand $70 carriage. A number of others built steam carriages— Sylvester H. Roper built one (1863) weighing only 650 pounds and achieved a speed of 20 miles per hour; John W. Lambert of Ohio City, Ohio, is credited with a combustion engine in 1890–91, and patents for three-wheeled carriages were issued to F. A. Huntington (1889), W. T. Harris (1835–1909) in 1893, Henry Nadig of Allentown, Pennsylvania (1899), and Gottfried Schloemer of Milwaukee (1890).

William C. Durant (1861–1947) and a friend, J. Dallas Dort (1861–

1925) organized the Durant-Dort Carriage Company in Flint, Michigan (1886), and it became the world's largest buggy maker. Durant bought the Flint Wagon Works (1904), which had the rights to an automobile developed by David D. Buick (1854–1929), who built his first cars in 1903. Durant organized the Buick Motor Company (1905), expanded the firm and acquired some smaller firms, consolidating them into the General Motors Corporation (1908). General Motors, in the next two years, added the Cadillac, Oldsmobile and Oakland companies. Durant was forced out of control of GM (1911) because of financial problems. He joined with racer/designer Louis Chevrolet (1879–1941) to form the Chevrolet Motor Company to compete with Ford. Chevrolet sold his rights to Durant (1915) and the new firm prospered so that Durant, with the help of the Dupont family, was able to regain control of GM (1916). Chevrolet was acquired by GM (1918). Durant was again forced out in 1920 because of economic problems. Alfred P. Sloan (1875–1966), president of United Motors Corporation when it became part of GM, served as GM president/chief executive officer (1923–37) and board chairman until 1966, leading the company to become one of the world's largest manufacturers.

Ransom E. Olds (1864–1950) invented a three-wheeled steam-powered vehicle (1886), a four-wheeled model (1893) and a gasoline-powered model (1895). He formed the Olds Motor Works the next year, which turned out six cars that year. His plant in Detroit burned (1902) and he built another in Lansing, Michigan, which, by 1904, was producing 5,000 Oldsmobiles. He left the company to form the successful Reo Motor Company. The 1902 fire made an important contribution to the industry because it forced Olds to subcontract for components of his cars, a practice that became standard in the industry.

Charles E. Duryea (1861–1938) went into the bicycle business in Springfield, Massachusetts, after leaving school and with his brother, J. Frank Duryea (1869–1967) developed a single cylinder, four horsepower gasoline engine (1891), small enough to be mounted in a carriage. Their car, the most advanced of the time, was successfully operated in April 1892 and appeared on the streets of Springfield on September 21, 1893. Frank drove an improved model November 28, 1895, to win the first automobile race, covering 54 miles in just under eight hours. The Duryeas formed their motor car company (1895), selling the first American-made commercial car the next year.

Elwood Haynes, working with Elmer and Elgar Apperson, produced a one-cylinder car July 4, 1894, in Kokomo, Indiana. They formed a company (1898) but the group split up (1908) over credit for the design of the car. Haynes continued car making until 1920 but his company was too small to survive.

Henry Ford (1863–1947) rose from machinist to chief engineer of Edison Illuminating Company in Detroit. He resigned (1899) to work on an automobile, having put together a tiny, tiller-steered quadricycle (1896). He founded the Ford Motor Company in 1903. Ford unveiled the Model T in October 1908, working on the premise that it was necessary to produce a car that would be durable in city and country, easy to handle and simple and inexpensive to maintain. The car captured a new market of auto buyers, who formerly were all sports and luxury-minded people. By the time the Model T series ended in 1927, more than 15 million had been made. Ford unveiled the conveyor belt assembly line (1913), which cut the time for assembling a car from 12½ hours to 93 minutes by 1914. The increased production dropped the price of the Model T from $850 to $310 by 1926. Ford also announced a $5 per eight hour day minimum wage as compared to the then current $2.40 for nine hours.

The Chrysler Corporation began soon after the Maxwell Motor Car Company went into receivership (1920). Walter F. Chrysler (1873–1940), president of Buick Motors (1916–20) who had resigned from GM, was named to supervise the reorganization of Maxwell and became president of the reorganized firm. He introduced a car of his own design (1924) with a high-compression engine, which was very successful and in the following year, the firm became the Chrysler Corporation. Chrysler bought Dodge Brothers Manufacturing Company (1928) primarily to acquire a large dealer organization and introduced the Plymouth to compete with Ford and Chevrolet.

A patent attorney, George B. Selden (1846–1922), played a vital role in the early days of the automobile. He received a patent (1895) which was based on drawings and a model, but not a finished car. The strength of the Selden patent led to formation (1903) of the Association of Licensed Automobile Manufacturers, which agreed to pay Selden a royalty of 1.25 percent of the retail price of all cars sold.

Ford fought against the royalty agreement and Selden successfully sued Ford in 1909, but the decision was reversed on appeal.

Other pioneer automobile manufacturers include:

Alexander Winton (1860–1932), a bicycle repairman and manufacturer in Cleveland, developed an experimental motor car (1896) and built two touring cars. He organized the Winton Motor Carriage

Company (1897) and introduced the use of spare parts and opened service stations to repair the cars. Winton pioneered in long distance driving, traveling from Cleveland to New York City (1898) and one of his cars was the first to cross the United States in 1903.

Francis E. Stanley (1849–1918) and his twin brother, Freelan (1849–1940), began as successful portrait photographers and then built one of the first successful steam motor cars— the Stanley Steamer (1897). One of their cars made the fastest one-mile run up to that time (1906)— slightly over 28 seconds.

James W. Packard (1863–1928) and his brother, William D. (1861–1923), were successful manufacturers of electrical equipment and built their first successful car in 1899. The Packard Motor Car Company, formed 1903, built the first air-conditioned car (1939).

Joseph S. Mack (1870–1953) and his brothers operated a wagon company and the first successful buses and trucks were turned out by them in 1900.

Clement Studebaker (1831–1901) built up the family wagon-making business with his brothers until it was the world's largest operation by 1897. Studebaker began experimenting with cars about then and the manufacture of electric automobiles began a year after his death, gasoline-powered cars in 1904.

John N. Willys (1873–1935) ran a bicycle manufacturing business in Elmira, New York, and expanded (1902) to include the sale of Pierce cars. Willys bought the Overland Automobile Company (1907) and changed it to Willys-Overland, which thrived until 1920.

Henry M. Leland (1843–1932) organized the Leland and Faulconer Manufacturing Company in Detroit (1890) and the Cadillac Motor Company (1904), then merged the two. He also founded the Lincoln Motor Company, which he sold to Ford. Leland refined and standardized parts to the point where in 1908 three of his Cadillacs were completely disassembled and the parts scrambled by Britain's Royal Automobile Club. The cars were put together using the parts interchangeably and the cars ran perfectly.

Henry C. Stutz (1876–1930) moved from making auto parts (1910) to automaking three years later. His first car competed in the first Indianapolis 500 race, finishing 11th. The Stutz Bearcat was very popular (1913–19) and a leader in racing.

Roy D. Chapin (1880–1936), an automobile pioneer, and Howard E. Coffin (1873–1937), founded the Hudson Motor Car Company (1909) with Chapin president (1910–23, 1933–36). Hudson produced the first sedan type car (1913).

In addition to the founders and heads of automaking companies, there were a number of very important contributors to auto components.

Charles F. Kettering (1876–1958) co-founded the Dayton Engineering Laboratories (Delco) which did much to develop improved auto electrical equipment and became part of General Motors. He became president and general manager of the GM Research Corporation (1925). Kettering had nearly 200 patents and designed the first practical electrical starter (1912), co-discovered the cause of engine knock, introduced ethyl gasoline (1922) and developed with Dupont chemists quick-drying lacquer finishes.

Frederic J. Fisher (1878–1941) was the principal founder (1908) and head of Fisher Body Company.

Henry Timken (1831–1909) was a successful carriage maker who invented a widely-used carriage spring (1877). He gave up carriage making to manufacture the springs. Timken introduced the tapered roller bearing (1898), which also became very popular.

Vincent Bendix (1882–1945) began producing auto starter drives (1912), which led to the automobile self-starter. The same year, he founded the Bendix Brake Company, which was the first mass producer of four-wheel auto brakes.

Henry D. Weed of Canastota, New York, invented tire chains in 1904.

Some firsts in automotive history:

American Automobile Association was formed in Chicago March 4, 1902, by representatives of nine automobile clubs.

First automobile trip across the United States began in San Francisco May 23, 1903 and ended in New York City on August 1.

Barney (Berna E.) Oldfield (1878–1946) because the first man to drive an automobile at 60 miles an hour June 15, 1903.

The first auto show was held in New York City's Madison Square Garden November 3–10, 1910, with 31 cars exhibited.

The first automobile accident occurred in New York City May 30, 1896, when a Duryea car driven by one Henry Wells of Springfield, Massachusetts, struck Evylyn Thomas, a bicycle rider. She suffered a broken leg and Wells spent the night in jail.

The first driver arrested for speeding was a New York City cab driver, Jacob German, on May 22, 1899, on Lexington Avenue for driving at "break neck speed" of 12 miles per hour.

New York was the first state to require license plates (1901); the fee was one dollar and the plates bore the owner's initials in three inch high letters. The first permanent plates were issued in Connecticut (1937).

New York was also the first to adopt speed limits (1904)—ten miles per hour in cities, 12 miles per hour in small towns, 20 miles per hour in the country.

Vermont required every moving automobile to be preceded by a mature individual carrying a red flag (1902).

The first driving school was established by the Boston YMCA (1903) to train chauffeurs, mechanics and prospective car owners.

The first drive-in gas station was opened by the Gulf Refining Company December 1, 1913, at Baum Boulevard and St. Clair Street in Pittsburgh.

The first public garage was established in Boston (1899) by W. T. McCullough as the Back Bay Cycle and Motor Company. The Park-O-Mat Garage, completely automatic pushbutton 16-story garage, opened in Washington (1951).

The first automatic parking meter was installed in Oklahoma City July 16, 1935.

The first automobile insurance policy was issued by Travelers Insurance Company (1898).

Installment buying of automobiles began 1910 and two finance companies were formed 1915 — Bankers' Commercial Corporation in New York City and Guarantee Securities Company, which bought consumers' installment notes from Willys-Overland dealers. The National Association of Finance Companies adopted minimum standards (1924) of one-third down payment for a new car, two-thirds for a used car.

Early buses were mounted on a truck chassis and the first vehicle with a specific bus chassis was built by the Fageol Safety Coach Company in Oakland, California (1922). The Yellow Bus Line began transcontinental bus service (1928); the trip took five days, 14 hours.

The first automatic toll collector was installed (1954) at the Union toll plaza on Garden State Parkway.

Aviation/Planes

Before the Wright brothers there were a number of others interested in and working on flying machines.

Augustus M. Herring (1867–1926), a mechanical engineering student, offered a thesis (1888)—"The Flying Machine as a Mechanical Engineering Problem." The thesis was rejected because the idea was considered unrealistic. He went to work for Octave Chanute (1832–1910), building and flying gliders, and for Samuel P. Langley (1834–1906), building light engines. He applied for a patent (1896) on a heavier-than-air powered flying machine, complete with sketches and plans. The patent request was turned down (1898) because the Patent Office required a working model and the examiner stated: "So far as the examiner is aware, no power-driven aeroplane has yet been raised in the air with the aeronaut or kept its course wholly detached from the earth for such considerable time as to constitute proof of practical usefulness."

Chanute, a civil engineer who built railroads and railroad bridges, turned to aerodynamics in his 60s. He built a camp on the dunes near Chicago, made about 2,000 glider flights, keeping detailed records. These records later helped the Wright brothers, a debt they publicly acknowledged.

Langley experimented for many years with small planes, one of them making a circular flight of three-quarters of a mile (1896). His were the first heavier-than-air powered flying craft. He built a full-scale machine with a gasoline engine and tried to launch it with a catapult from a house boat on the Potomac River near Washington. The catapult failed twice, the second time just nine days before the successful Wright brothers flight.

The Wrights—Orville (1871–1948) and Wilbur (1867–1912)—operated a successful bicycle manufacturing and repair shop in Dayton, Ohio, when they became interested in aviation. They wrote to the Smithsonian Institution (1899) for suggested reading material and were told of the work of Otto Lilienthal in Germany and Chanute. They studied the work of Chanute and developed a personal and technical relationship. Their first ambition was to build a man-carrying kite and settled at Kitty Hawk, North Carolina, on the advice of the Weather Bureau because of its steady sea breezes and sand dunes. They built a successful weight-bearing kite (1900), then a larger kite which failed. During the Winter of 1901 they built a crude wind tunnel in their bicycle shop. Their tests showed flaws in the data they had been using and they developed new data on airfoils (wings). They built a new glider on the basis of that data, made many successful flights, and then designed and built their own four-cylinder engine and propeller.

On December 14, 1903, Wilbur flew the plane, climbed too steeply and crashed after being aloft only three-and-a-half seconds. After repairs, Orville flew the plane December 17, stayed aloft 12 seconds and flew 120 feet. The brothers alternated in three flights that afternoon, the longest being Wilbur's 59 seconds and 852 feet. The test flights were greeted skeptically and only three American newspapers ran the story. The first complete account appeared in March 1904 in a magazine, *Gleanings on Bee Culture.*

The Wrights designed a new plane (1904), flying only about 45 minutes. Their third plane, the "Flyer," was built in 1905 and was really the first practical plane in history — it could bank, turn, circle and keep flying for a half hour at a time. The Wrights were granted a patent for a flying machine in 1906.

A rival appeared in the Aerial Experiment Association, financed by Alexander Graham Bell of telephone fame and headed by Glenn H. Curtiss (1878–1930), a bicycle/motorcycle shop owner and racer. Curtiss built an engine and motorcycle plant (1902) and raced motorcycles, setting a land speed record (1907). He became interested in aeronautics and built a dirigible for the Army. Curtiss then turned to airplanes and his first success was his "June Bug," which won a trophy for the first public flight of more than a kilometer (1908). He put pontoons on the plane and successfully demonstrated (1911) the first hydroplane. He built biplanes during World War I for American, British, and Russian aviation training and an NC-4 flying boat for the Navy (1918), which made a transatlantic flight. Curtiss also invented the aileron.

The 1910–11 period saw the setting of early aviation records — Walter R. Brookins set an altitude record of 6,175 feet, Curtiss won a $10,000 prize for flying the 152 miles between Albany and New York City in two hours 46 minutes, and Eugene R. Ely, a civilian, successfully landed a plane January 18, 1911, on the cruiser *Pennsylvania* in San Francisco Harbor and then took off from the vessel.

Among the early airplane manufacturers were:

Glenn L. Martin (1886–1955) built his first plane in 1909 and was the first to make an over water flight (Los Angeles to Catalina Island (1912). He built numerous planes in both world wars, including the first successful twin-engine plane and bomber.

Alexander P. DeSeversky (1894–1974), a Russian fighter pilot in World War I, formed his own company in the United States (1922) making important contributions to military aviation, including a bomb sight.

Leroy R. Grumman (1895–1982) founded Grumman Aerospace Corporation (1929) and designed fighter planes.

William P. Lear (1902–78) began as a manufacturer of navigational aids (1934) and turned to building small jet planes for private use (1962), becoming the leader in that field.

Anthony H. G. Fokker (1890–1939), a World War I German plane maker, came to the United States (1922) and developed the use of tubular steel and plywood in plane making.

John K. Northrop (1895–1981), an aircraft designer, formed the Northrop Corporation (1938).

William B. Stout (1880–1956) built the first American monoplane (1918) and the first American all-metal plane (1922).

Transatlantic flights began in 1926 when Charles A. Lindbergh (1902–74), an airmail pilot, was attracted by a $25,000 prize for the first such flight. With the help of St. Louis backers, he bought a plane which he flew in record time from San Diego to New York City (21 hours 20 minutes). Then on May 20, 1927, he made the 3,600 miles nonstop flight from Long Island's Roosevelt Field to Paris in 33½ hours.

Richard E. Byrd (1888–1957) flew over the North Pole May 9, 1926, with Floyd Bennett (1890–1928) as his pilot. They had planned to make the transatlantic flight but their plane was damaged and the flight was delayed until the end of June — a month after the Lindbergh flight. (The Byrd flight did not reach Paris as the plane landed just off the French coast.) On November 29, 1929, Byrd flew over the South Pole.

Amelia M. Earhart (1898–1937) was the first woman to fly the Atlantic — as a passenger in 1928, then she flew solo across the Atlantic May 22, 1932, in less than 15 hours.

Flying across the Pacific came later when Clyde Pangborn (1894–1958) and Hugh Herndon, Jr., flew nonstop in 41 hours 13 minutes from Tokyo to Wenatchee, Washington, on October 3–5, 1933. Earlier (1927), two Army Air Corps pilots flew from San Francisco to Honolulu.

The first round-the-world flight was completed September 28, 1924, when two of four Army Air Service planes landed at Seattle completing the flight in 175 days with 57 stops after takeoff.

Wiley Post (1898–1935) and his navigator, Harold Gatty, began a round-the-world flight June 23, 1931, finishing 8 days 15 hours 51 minutes later. Two years later, Post made the same flight alone in 7 days 18 hours 49 minutes. Howard Hughes (1906–76), industrialist/motion picture producer/aviator, made the round-the-world flight in 3 days 19 hours 14 minutes 26 seconds (1938).

A nonstop round-the-world flight without refueling was made by the "Voyager," piloted by Dick Rutman and Jeana Yeager; it landed December 23, 1986 — 9 days 3 minutes 44 seconds after takeoff.

Calbraith P. Rogers made the first transcontinental plane flight (1911), taking 84 days, surviving about 70 crashes in 82 hours of actual flying time. By contrast, two Army Air Corps pilots made the first nonstop transcontinental flight May 2, 1923, in 26 hours 50 minutes for the 2,516 miles.

The first transcontinental air service began in the summer of 1929. Passengers left New York City by train to Columbus, Ohio, then flew to Waynoka, Oklahoma, and completed the trip to Los Angeles by plane. The trip took 48 hours. This was shortened to 36 hours (1930) and the trip was all by plane with an overnight stop in Kansas City.

The first American jet flight occurred October 1, 1942, when a Bell XP-59A powered by two I-16 General Electric engines flew at Edwards Air Force Base. Air Force Major Charles E. Yeager (1923–) broke the sound barrier in a Bell X-1 rocket plane at Muroc, California, October 14, 1947.

Several important contributors to aviation development were manufacturers of components and engineers related to flying. Elmer A. Sperry (1860–1930) was a prolific inventor (400+ patents) and founder of eight companies, one of which built gyroscopic compasses and stabilizers. Charles E. Witteman built the first automatic pilot system (1918). Physicist Luis W. Alvarez (1911–88) and Lawrence Johnston devised a ground-controlled approach system that made possible all-weather aircraft landings (1940).

A full-scale wind tunnel for testing planes went into operation

May 27, 1931, at the Langley (Virginia) Research Center, site of the first wind tunnel (1923).

Amelia Earhart in the 1920s is probably the best known woman to have played a role in aviation, but there were others. The first woman aviator to make a public flight was Blanche S. Scott, a pupil of Glenn Curtiss. On October 23, 1910, at Ft. Wayne, Indiana, she flew across the field at a height of 12 feet. Harriet Quinby became the first American woman pilot on August 2, 1911. Ellen Church was the first stewardess, making her first flight May 15, 1930, for United Air Lines from San Francisco to Cheyenne. Jacqueline Cochran (1910–80), world's foremost woman pilot (1937–39), became the first woman to ferry a bomber to England in World War II. She organized and headed the Women's Air Force Service Pilots during the war.

The Army organized an aeronautical division in the Signal Corps August 1, 1907, with one officer, Captain Charles Chandler (1878–1939), and two enlisted men. He headed the first Army aviation school (1911–13) at College Park, Maryland. Benjamin D. Foulois (1879–1976), with eight pilots and one plane, established the Army "air force" (1910) at Ft. Sam Houston, Texas. He commanded an air squadron in the 1915 Mexican expedition and the American fliers in World War I.

The first aviation fatality occurred September 17, 1908, at Ft. Myer, Virginia, when a propeller blade struck an overhead wire. Lt. Thomas E. Selfridge, assigned by the Army to test the plane, was killed and Orville Wright seriously injured.

The Navy purchased its first aircraft from the Wright brothers August 2, 1909, for $25,000 plus a $5,000 bonus when the plane exceeded the 40 miles per hour specified speed.

The first aviation meet was held in Los Angeles (1910) and in the same year the first international air races were held at Belmont Park, New York.

Captain Albert Berry made the first American parachute jump (1,500 feet) March 1, 1912, at Jefferson Barracks in St. Louis. Jimmy (James H.) Doolittle (1896–1994), later a general who led the first raid on Tokyo (1942), made the first successful test of a blind instrument-controlled landing (1930).

The first aeronautical engineering course was given at Massachusetts Institute of Technology in 1913–14. The first government aviation training field opened at Rantoul, Illinois, July 4, 1917. The first flight training school opened in June of 1911 at College Park, Maryland; it moved two years later to San Diego.

Seasonal commercial air passenger service was launched with two daily round trips between St. Petersburg and Tampa (1914) for ten dollars a round trip.

The first in-flight movies (a newsreel and two cartoons) were shown October 8, 1923, by Transcontinental Air Transport.

Regular transatlantic passenger service began June 28, 1939, when a Pan-American plane with 22 passengers flew from Port Washington, New York, to Lisbon, Portugal.

The first helicopter of importance was demonstrated by Henry A. Berliner (1895–1970) at College Park, Maryland, June 16, 1922, to Aeronautics Bureau representatives. The first flight was December 19, 1928, at Willow Grove, Pennsylvania, by Harold F. Pitcairn (1897–1960), founder of Autogiro Company of America (1929).

The first successful helicopter was the VS-300 built (1939) by Igor I. Sikorsky (1889–1972), who flew the craft for 15 minutes on July 18, 1940. It was the first helicopter capable of sustained flight and satisfactory control. The first cross-country helicopter flight was 761 miles from Stratford, Connecticut, to Dayton, Ohio, in 16 hours 10 minutes of flying time over a four-day period in May 1942. The first nonstop transcontinental flight began August 23, 1956, in San Diego and ended 31 hours 40 minutes later in Washington. Helicopter passenger service was begun by New York Airways July 9, 1953, between LaGuardia and Kennedy airports. Commercial helicopter use began March 1946 when a Bell-47-B helicopter was licensed to the *New York Journal-American* for news coverage and photo delivery.

Balloons/Dirigibles

On October 6, 1873, W. H. Donaldson made the first attempt (unsuccessful) to fly a balloon across the Atlantic Ocean from Brooklyn. He bailed out near New Canaan, Connecticut. The first American balloon flight was made June 23, 1784, in Baltimore by 13-year-old Edward Warren in a balloon made by Peter Carnes (1762–1822). On July 14, Carnes tried to fly the balloon but it burst into flames.

Jean Pierre Blanchard (1753–1809), French balloonist, made a 15-mile demonstration flight January 9, 1793, from the courtyard of the Walnut Street prison in Philadelphia to near Woodbury, New Jersey, in 46 minutes at an altitude of 5,812 feet.

Charles F. Durant (1805–73), the first American professional balloonist, flew from New York City to South Amboy, New Jersey, September 9, 1830. Thaddeus S. C. Lowe (1831–1918), an early user of balloons for meteorological research, made his first flight in 1858. He served as chief of the Union Army's aeronautic section and made the first photos from a balloon.

The first American dirigible was built by Caesar Spiegler and made its maiden flight July 3, 1878, with balloonist John Wise (1808–79) at the controls. The Army bought its first aircraft, a dirigible, (1908) but only its manufacturer, Thomas S. Baldwin (1860–1923) could fly the machine.

Jean Felix Piccard (1884–1963) and his wife made a controlled balloon flight in 1934 from Michigan to Ohio at 57,979 feet.

Three Albuquerque, New Mexico, men — Ben Abruzzo (1930–85), Max Anderson, and Larry Newman — made the first balloon crossing of the Atlantic Ocean in August 1978, flying 3,107 miles from Presque Isle, Maine, to Paris in 137 hours six minutes. The first solo transatlantic balloon flight was made by Joe Kittinger September 14–17, 1984, from Caribou, Maine, to Italy.

Max Anderson and his son, Kris, made the first nonstop balloon flight across the North American continent May 11–14, 1980. Larry Newman, Ben Abruzzo, Ricky Aoki and Ron Clark made the first successful nonstop flight across the Pacific Ocean in November 1981.

Bicycles/Motorcycles

The first bicycles were imported from France (1819) and William K. Clarkson received a patent in June 1819 for an "improved currituck" (bicycle).

Pierre Lallement, a French mechanic who worked for the bicycle developer, Pierre Michaux, moved to Connecticut and patented the first American pedal bicycle in November 1866. Harry J. Lawson built a two-wheel bicycle (1879) driven by a chain mechanism attached to the rear wheels and called it a safety bicycle.

Albert A. Pope (1843–1909) began making bicycles in Hartford, Connecticut (1877), and was probably the founder of the American bicycle industry. His first cycles were manufactured for him by the Weed Sewing Machine Company (1878). Then he built a plant in Hartford, which by 1898 employed more than 3,000, turning out thousands of bicycles.

A two-wheeled steam-driven motorcycle was invented by William A. Austin of Withrop, Massachusetts (1868), but it had a limited traveling radius. The first practical motorcycle was built (1899) by Holley Motor Corporation. George M. Hendee, of Springfield, Massachusetts, began (1901) producing the "Indian" motorcycle which had a built-in gasoline engine.

The first motorcycle race was held July 4, 1914, in Dodge City, Kansas. Only half of the 36 starters were able to finish the 300 mile race.

Bridges

American bridges date back to Israel Stoughton (1603–45), who built one (1634) over the Neponset River from Milton to Dorchester, Massachusetts, and to the first stone bridge at Pennepecker, near Germantown, Pennsylvania, in 1697–98.

Samuel Sewell built a 270 feet wooden bridge over the York River at York, Maine (1761); the bridge was laid on upright piles hammered into the ground.

Enoch Hale built the first timber truss bridge over the Connecticut River at Bellows Falls, Vermont (1785), with two 180 feet long spans. James Finley built the first American suspension bridge at Uniontown, Pennsylvania (1796), with a 70 feet span between two towers over Jacob's Creek.

Louis Werwag (1769–1843) built his "colossus" bridge, a 340 feet span over the Schuylkill River at Fairmount, Pennsylvania (1812),and Erskine Hazard and Josiah White built the first iron wire suspension bridge (1816) over the Schuylkill River at Philadelphia. The suspension bridge was 408 feet long but it could only support six or eight persons at a time.

The first known American covered bridge was a 550 feet structure built (1805) over the Schuylkill at Philadelphia by Timothy Palmer (d. 1821).

Theodore Burr set a new pattern for wooden covered bridges (1815) with a record span of 360 feet in the McFall's Ferry Bridge. Ithiel Town (1784–1844), a noted architect, patented a widely-used design for a truss bridge (1820), building several such bridges.

John Snowden built the first cast iron bridge (1835), an 85 feet span over Dunlap's Creek at Brownsville, Pennsylvania; Earl Trumbull built the first iron truss railroad bridge (1845) at Manayunk , Pennsylvania, a 34.2 feet span for the Philadelphia and Reading Railroad.

Charles Ellet, Jr. (1810–62), built a suspension bridge across the Niagara River below the Falls (1847) and two years later built the world's longest suspension bridge — 1,010 feet — over the Ohio River at Wheeling, West Virginia, for the Baltimore and Ohio Railroad.

Daniel C. McCallum (1815–78) developed an arched truss bridge (1851) and the first bridge built across the Mississippi River was the railroad bridge connecting Rock Island, Illinois, and Davenport, Iowa, which opened April 21, 1855.

John A. Roebling (1806–69) was the first to manufacture wire rope (1841) in the United States and built the first American suspension aqueduct to carry a canal across the Allegheny River near Pittsburgh (1845). He built the first suspension bridge strong enough to withstand high wind and railway traffic — the Grand Trunk Bridge, an 820 feet span below Niagara Falls (1855). Roebling was named chief engineer for the proposed Brooklyn Bridge. He completed the design but died before construction began. His son, Washington A. (1837–1926), completed the bridge (1883).

James B. Eads (1820–87), who had gained prominence as inventor of the diving bell (1841) and builder of ironclad gunboats for the Union cause (1861), got into bridge building in a big way. Congress authorized a bridge over the Mississippi River at St. Louis calling for a 500 feet center span with 50 feet clearance. Most engineers said such a project was not possible but Eads proved them wrong. He completed the span, the first American bridge with steel and tubular steel arches, on July 4, 1874.

The first cantilever bridge was designed and built (1876–77) by Charles S. Smith (1835–86) over the Kentucky River near Harrodsburg, Kentucky.

Other notable American bridges are: Queensboro over the East River, New York City (1909), the first important double-deck span; International Peace Bridge, Buffalo (1927); George Washington Bridge over the Hudson River, New York City (1931); San Francisco-Oakland (1936); Golden Gate, San Francisco (1937); Thousand Islands over the St. Lawrence River (1938); Rainbow over the Niagara River, Niagara Falls (1941); Walnut Lane, Philadelphia (1950), the first notable American prestressed bridge; Chesapeake Bay Bridge near Annapolis, Maryland (1951); Mackinac Straits, Michigan (1958); Chesapeake Bay Bridge-Tunnel, 17.6 miles between Norfolk and the Eastern Shore of Virginia (1966).

Canals

A canal for creating water power to run a mill was dug (1639–40) at Dedham, Massachusetts. Some short canals were built early at South Hadley Falls on the Connecticut River, at Little Falls and Great Falls on the Potomac, and at Richmond on the James River.

The first American canal was the Santee (1800), connecting the Santee and Cooper rivers in South Carolina. The Middlesex Canal, the first extensive American canal, was started in June 1793 connecting the Merrimac River and Woburn, Massachusetts; completed 1808.

Work began July 4, 1817, on the Erie Canal, with groundbreaking at Rome, New York. It was completed October 26, 1825. Canvass White (1790–1834) walked more than 2,000 miles in England (1817–18) studying their canals before returning to supervise construction of the Erie Canal. He discovered (1817) that local lime rock could be converted into natural cement, eliminating the cost of importing cement.

July Fourth was a favorite day for other canal groundbreakings — 1825 at Newark, Ohio, for the 308-mile Ohio Canal between Cleveland and Portsmouth on the Ohio River; 1828 at Georgetown (now part of Washington, DC) for the Chesapeake and Ohio Canal, and 1836 when the State of Illinois began a canal to connect the Mississippi River and Lake Michigan.

The first Welland Canal connecting Lakes Erie and Ontario opened November 30, 1929.

Express Companies

Express companies made their first appearance in the United States at about the same time as the railroads.

William F. Harnden (1812–45) organized the first express service in February, 1839, between Boston and New York City. He made contracts with the Boston and Providence Railroad and the manager of a steamboat operating between Providence and New York to launch his service. After a few months, he hired others to carry packages and opened offices in Boston and New York.

Alvin Adams (1804–77) set up his express business in 1840 and during the next 20 years became a dominant figure in the field with a virtual monopoly in the East and South. Adams merged (1854) with the Harnden interests to form the Adams Express Company. They bought two found trip railway tickets from Boston to New York City. One day an Adams operator would start from each city, then return the next day, carrying valuables, securities and some bundles.

Benjamin P. Cheney (1815–95) began driving a stage at age 16 between Nashua and Exeter, New Hampshire, and formed Cheney and Company Express (1842), running between Boston and Montreal, using rail, boat and horses.

Ben Halladay (1819–87) began by getting a contract to supply the Army in the Mexican War. After the war, he bought surplus wagons and oxen from the Army to begin freight operation, then stage coaches. He expanded and improved operations over thousands of miles of routes throughout the West. Foreseeing the coming of the railroad, he sold out to Wells Fargo (1866).

Henry Wells (1805–78) and William G. Fargo (1818–81) established an express company operating between Buffalo and Detroit (1844). The service was expanded and with various partners operated from New York to St. Louis, and to Bangor, Maine. Wells and Fargo led a move (1850) to merge several lines into the American Express Company, with Wells as president, Fargo as secretary. The discovery of gold in California led to the formation of Wells Fargo and Company (1852) which developed a virtual monopoly west of the Mississippi. Wells headed American Express (1850–68), then Fargo was president to 1881.

Alexander Majors (1814–1900) started a freight moving business which operated from Independence, Missouri, to Santa Fe (1848) with six wagons and six teams. The firm expanded (1855) to include other partners and was the first to make regular wagon train trips. It later took over the stagecoach line from Ft. Leavenworth to Denver and on April 3, 1860, established the famous pony express carrying mail across the West in ten days. The glamorous express was a financial failure and lasted only 18 months.

Highways

The first American roads were Indian trails, many of which were used by the colonists. Some of the more noted trails were the Old Connecticut Path from the upper Hudson Valley near Albany to Boston; the Iroquois Trail which followed the Mohawk Valley to near Niagara Falls, and the Warrior's Path through the Cumberland Gap and Kentucky to the falls of the Ohio River.

Land travel increased in the early 1700s as Indian trails were gradually widened and vehicles began to appear. First came the chair, a two-wheeled, two-passenger, one-horse cart, and then the chaise, a two-wheeled carriage with a leather top.

As roads developed further, stagecoach and wagon transportation began. A hackney coach operated along the Bowery in New York City (1696) and stages ran from Boston to Newport, Rhode Island, by 1716. The first regular stage line between New York and Philadelphia began March 8, 1759, with the 90-mile jolting journey taking three days.

The best all-purpose vehicle was the Conestoga wagon developed by Pennsylvania Germans. A variation of the Conestoga wagon became the covered wagon or prairie schooner of westward migration. Conestoga wagons were in regular trade by 1717, handling fares to Philadelphia, returning to Lancaster County with trade goods.

Then came turnpikes (toll roads) built with private capital. The first of these (1785) connected settlements in the Blue Ridge Mountains with Alexandria, Virginia, and became known as the Little River Turnpike.

The first macadamized road in the United States was the Lancaster Turnpike between Lancaster, Pennsylvania, and Philadelphia, completed in 1785. The Federal Government began a road (1802) from the Tidewater of Virginia to the Ohio Valley.

The Cumberland Road, connecting Cumberland, Maryland, and Wheeling, West Virginia, was begun in 1811 and completed seven years later. It was extended to Vandalia, Illinois (1852), and became the main road for westbound settlers.

William Becknell (1796?–1865) organized an expedition (1822) with three wagonloads of goods and 21 men, which established the Santa Fe Trail from Franklin, Missouri, through the Cimarron Valley to Santa Fe, New Mexico. The first wagon train left Independence, Missouri, May 1, 1841, for California, arriving six months later.

The first coast-to-cast paved road was the Lincoln Highway between New York City and San Francisco. The first high capacity toll road was the Pennsylvania Turnpike, which opened (1940) between Harrisburg and Pittsburgh. It was so successful that other states followed. The most ambitious express highway system was the national interstate highway network authorized in 1944 with funding starting some years later. Congress authorized an additional $32.5 billion (1956) over 13 years to build 41,000 miles of highway.

Some miscellaneous facts about highways:

The Alcan Highway, 1,523 miles through British Columbia to Alaska, opened November 21, 1942.

The first road signs date back to 1704 when Maryland required that roads be marked with notches on trees — two notches for roads leading to courthouses, three to a ferry. United States route numbering began in 1924 with major routes retaining their identity across state lines. Highways running north-south have odd numbers, east-west even numbers.

The first electric traffic signals were installed August 5, 1914, at Euclid Avenue and East 105th Street in Cleveland.

Traffic lines to designate lanes were first painted on River Road near Trenton, Michigan (1911).

The first one-way traffic regulation (1791) was designed to avoid traffic jams at the John Street Theater in New York City before and after a performance.

New Amsterdam issued a regulation (1652) forbidding horses to be run or driven at a gallop in the city.

The first American road map was published (1789) by Christopher Colles (1739–1816).

The first taxicabs appeared in New York City (1907) when a fleet of "taximeter" cabs arrived from Paris.

Navigation

Thomas Godfrey (1704–49), a self-taught astronomer and mathematician, developed the Hadley quadrant (1730), a great step forward in navigation. The modern sextant is the direct descendant of the quadrant.

Nathaniel Bowditch (1773–1838), a self-taught mathematician, discovered many errors in a popular, standard navigation book and published a corrected American edition (1799). He published the *New American Practical Navigator* (1802), which became — and has remained — the "seamen's bible." He translated LaPlace's book on celestial mechanics with his commentary, regarded as a landmark in the development of American science.

Matthew F. Maury (1806–73), superintendent of the Navy Department of Charts and Instruments (1839–68), published the *Wind and Current Chart of the North Atlantic* (1847), which aided exploration. He organized world-wide gathering and collating of oceanographic data which led to charts for other ocean areas. He published the first modern oceanography work, *The Physical Geography of the Sea and its Meteorology* (1855).

Railroads

The first American primitive railroad was the inclined railway on the slope of Boston's Beacon Hill in 1795. Two other early forms of railroads appeared 1826 — a cable operated tramway made of grooved logs in Lewiston, New York (about 300 feet between the Niagara portage and lower Niagara River) and the Quincy (Massachusetts) Granite Railroad, a horse-drawn tramway running three miles from Quincy to the Neponset River.

The first true steam locomotive arrived from England in January 1829 — it was to be the first such locomotive to operate in the United States. The "Sturbridge Lion" was tried on a nine-mile track of the Delaware and Hudson Canal Company with the road's chief engineer, John B. Jervis (1795–1885), at the controls.

The imported locomotive proved to be too heavy for the tracks. Jervis then developed a locomotive (1831) which featured a leading truck and a set of small wheels on the front of the engine which were free to swivel, guide the locomotive, and enable it to reach speeds of more than 60 miles an hour.

A group of Baltimore businessmen met February 12, 1827, and 17 days later, the Baltimore and Ohio Railroad, the first American railway system, was chartered in Maryland and Virginia. Engineers and inventors were invited to develop a workable locomotive. Studies of the time showed that a steam locomotive could be operated for $16 a day compared with $33 for the same amount of work by horses.

Peter Cooper, operating a small foundry in Baltimore, put together a one-horsepower engine, the "Tom Thumb," dubbed a "tea kettle on a truck," which, on January 17, 1830, successfully ran on the existing tracks. Service began in May on the 13 mile trip between Baltimore and Ellicott Mills, Maryland. Although Cooper did not continue building locomotives, his "Tom Thumb" stimulated other engine builders and gave a strong impetus to the rapid growth of railroads. The new line was an immediate success and its southern and westward growth was rapid — Washington, DC (1835), Cumberland, Maryland (1842), Wheeling, West Virginia (1852), St. Louis (1857).

At about the same time, the South Carolina Canal and Railroad Company in February, 1829, developed a six mile stretch between Charleston and Hamburg. On Christmas Day 1830, it became the first American line to run scheduled passenger operations using a steam locomotive.

The B and O is often referred to as the American railroad "university" because of its many firsts—timetable (May 23, 1830), baggage car (1834), dining car (1843), iron boxcars (1844), electric locomotive in regular service (1895), streamlined passenger train (1900), air conditioned car (1930), completely air conditioned train (1931).

John Stevens campaigned vigorously for a railroad and although New Jersey and Pennsylvania (1823) granted him the first American railroad charter (1815), he could not get financial support. New Jersey again granted a charter to the Stevens family (1830) after it created the Camden and Amboy Railroad with Robert L. Stevens, John's son, serving as president and chief engineer.

Robert Stevens went to England (1830) to buy the best available locomotive. He knew that future trains would need much stronger, heavier rails and better roadbeds. He designed the first T-rail and the hood-headed spikes and metal plates needed to join the rails. He had discovered that rails laid on wooden ties over gravel provided a safer and more comfortable roadbed. The rails and locomotive, "John Bull," were made in England and a successful trial run was held November 12, 1831, at Bordentown, New Jersey.

The Camden and Amboy Railroad reached Perth Amboy in December 1832 and the new service gained immediate popularity, carrying 100,000 passengers the first year.

The Petersburg Railroad became the first American interstate railroad November 1, 1831, running from Petersburg, Virginia, to Blakely, North Carolina.

New York State was also interested in railroads. The Erie Canal was fine for freight but not suitable for passengers. The state's first chartered railroad, the Mohawk and Hudson (later part of the New York Central) made its first run between Albany and Schenectady. The trip was uneventful except that sparks from the wood-burning engine burned holes in the clothes of passengers in the open cars.

Philadelphia entered the railroad race (1832) with the start of the Philadelphia, Germantown and Norristown Railroad. An immediate benefit of this development was the entry of Matthias W. Baldwin (1795–1866) into locomotive building.

Baldwin was a machine and engine builder before concentrating on locomotives. Soon thereafter, he became a world leader in the field. He built one of the first locomotives (1832) for the new Philadelphia railway which could run at 28 miles per hour in fair weather. An 1832 advertisement stated: "On rainy days, horses will be attached."

Theodore Judah (1826–63) built the first railroad in California in the 1850s, the Sacramento and Folsom, after having built the Niagara Gorge Railroad in New York. Judah wanted to continue the Sacramento line through the mountains and on to the East. He spent years trying to convince others and finally interested four men — Charles Crocker (1822–88), a successful dry goods merchant; Leland Stanford (1824–93), a wholesale grocer and California governor, Collis P. Huntington (1821–1900), and Mark Hopkins, mercantile store partners in Sacramento.

The Civil War began and Judah died before the railroad could be started. The four men proceeded with the project, which received federal help, and Crocker was in charge of construction which began in 1863. The Central Pacific Railway was completed in 1869 with Stanford as president until 1893.

Meanwhile, the Union Pacific was heading west and it met the Central Pacific at Promontory Point, Utah, on May 10, 1869, to form the first transcontinental railroad.

Crocker also helped organize the Southern Pacific Railroad, which he headed from 1871 to 1884 when it merged with the Central Pacific.

Albert Fink (1827–97) was a construction engineer with the Baltimore and Ohio (1848–57) and the Louisville and Nashville Railroad (1857–75), where he rose to general superintendent. He supervised construction of the longest American iron railroad bridge (1852) at Fairmont, West Virginia, on the Monongahela River, using a truss of his own design. He is credited with founding the science of railway economics when in his annual reports he scientifically detailed the costs of transportation.

The problem of railroad safety occupied the attention of Lorenzo S. Coffin (1823–1915), Iowa state railroad commissioner (1833–38). He traveled freight trains finding a great many hazards, primarily in handcoupling and braking of cars. Coffin began a successful drive to have the activities done automatically as they were on passenger trains and accidents dropped by 60 percent.

Eli H. Janney (1831–1912) invented an improved automatic car coupler (1868) which became standard equipment. Ezra Miller (1812–85) patented a combined railroad car platform, couplers and buffer (1865) which was quickly adopted. William Robinson (1840–1921) invented a system of automatic electric signaling (1872), the basis for the modern automatic systems.

One of the great advances in passenger rail operations resulted from the work of George M. Pullman (1831–97). He and a friend remodeled two-day coaches into sleeping cars for the Chicago and Alton Railroad (1858). Pullman patented such special features as the folding upper berth (1863) and extendable seat cushions for the lower berth (1865). The first Pullman car, the "Pioneer," was built in 1865 and the Chicago and Alton Railroad discovered the wider new car required altering platforms, sheds, bridges and other facilities.

The Pullman Palace Car Company was founded 1867 and a dining car made its appearance in 1868.

Other accessories to railroad operations include:

The locomotive cowcatcher was invented (1833) by Isaac Dripps (1810–92); the locomotive electric headlight by Leonidas G. Woolley of Mendon, Michigan (1881).

Henry R. Campbell of Philadelphia introduced the eight-wheeled locomotive, with four leading wheels and four driving wheels (1836). It was not successful until Joseph Harrison, Jr. (1810–74), stabilized the suspension (1839) and it became standard on American railroads.

Asa Whitney (1791–1874) patented improved cast-iron railroad-car wheels and then formed a company (1849) to make them, becoming the largest firm of its kind.

The first railway car with a center aisle was introduced by the Baltimore and Ohio (1831); the first car with an observation dome by the Burlington (1945); first refrigerator car patent was issued (1867) to J. B. Sutherland of Detroit.

George Westinghouse invented an air brake (1869), making it possible for the engineer to brake an entire train at one time; he improved it and three years later it became standard equipment.

Other railroad facts: The first railroad for hauling freight was a tramroad (1809) which was operated by John Thompson and Thomas Leiper (1745–1825) to carry stone from Leiper's quarries for three-quarters of a mile in Delaware County, Pennsylvania. The road was replaced (1828) by a canal.

The first American railroad accident occurred (1832) near Quincy,

Massachusetts, when the cable on an incline snapped, the car went over the cliff, one person was killed.

The first railway tunnel opened between Johnstown and Hollidaysburg, Pennsylvania (1834).

The first railroad train crossed the Mississippi River April 21, 1855, on a bridge connecting Rock Island, Illinois, and Davenport, Iowa.

The first streamlined railroad was patented (1865) by a Unitarian minister, Reverend Samuel R. Calthrop (1829–1917); the "air resistor" train was tapered from the center to either end.

The first cog railroad was completed July 1869 by Sylvester Marsh (1803–84), a successful businessman who conceived the idea of a railroad to the top of Mt. Washington, New Hampshire. The railroad, built in 1866–69, cost $150,000 and Marsh had to invent and improve a cograil driving mechanism and braking system.

Massachusetts was the first state to create a board of railroad commissioners and a railroad law. Charles Francis Adams (1835–1915) was chairman of the first group and his reports led other states to create such boards.

A major problem for railroad travel in the 1870–80s was the difference in time. For example, there were 38 different times in Wisconsin and in the Pittsburgh area there were six. The railroads organized the General Time Convention (1883), which solved the problem by creating four standard time zones (November 18, 1883) to cover the entire country.

The first "piggy back" operation began January 5, 1886, on the Long Island Railroad when a produce train carried farmers' wagons, horses and drivers from Albertson Station to Long Island City, then by ferry across the East River to New York City.

George H. Daniels (1842–1908), general passenger agent of the New York Central, introduced the first American "red cap" service (1896), a small corps of attendants who helped passengers with their luggage.

Legendary railroad engineer Casey (John Luther) Jones (1864–1900) crashed his "Cannonball Express" into a stopped freight train near Vaughn, Mississippi, April 3, 1900.

The first electric passenger train was run experimentally by Thomas A. Edison (1930) from Hoboken to Montclair, New Jersey.

A federal Railroad Retirement Board was created August 29, 1935, to administer the railroad retirement and unemployment insurance programs.

A fully automatic freight yard was installed December 17, 1954, by the General Railway Signal Company in Gary, Indiana, for the Elgin, Joliet and Eastern Railroad. Radar and electronic circuits sorted and assembled freight cars by destination, weighed them automatically, and coupled them into trains.

The Pennsylvania, and Baltimore and Ohio railroads were the targets (1877) of the first major railroad national strike. The Pittsburgh freight yards were burned and looted. The strike was put down by the Army.

Tunnels

The first large tunnel was built between 1818 and 1821 as part of the Schuylkill and Susquehanna Canal in Pennsylvania (18 feet high, 450 feet long). The first railroad tunnel was started 1831 near Johnstown, Pennsylvania, by the Allegheny Portage Railroad — 902 feet long, completed 1834.

The Hoosac Tunnel, a 4.7 mile railway tunnel in Massachusetts, completed in 1857, was the first in which blasts during construction were set off electrically.

New York City began its water aqueduct system in 1837, building tunnels by the cut-and-cover method from Croton Lake to Murray Hill Reservoir, about 35 miles, and completed it in 1842. The city built the New Croton Aqueduct (1885–93), 33 miles long through rock at considerable depths. The Catskill aqueduct system was begun 1907, completed 1917. The Delaware aqueduct system began in 1937, delivering water through a concrete-lined pressure tunnel, the longest in the world; completed 1944.

DeWitt C. Haskins began excavating twin tunnels under the Hudson River (1879) and had completed 2,400 feet when a series of blowouts ended the attempt. This was the first time compressed air was used in a project and it blew a hole in the silt roof, flooding the tunnel and killing 20 workers. An effort to continue the tunnels in 1889–92 also failed. Finally the tunnels were completed (1907) as part of the Hudson and Manhattan Railroad tubes.

Alfred E. Beach, editor of *Scientific American*, developed a shield for tunneling under streets and rivers. Using this shield, Beach built a tunnel in New York City under Broadway, between Murray and Warren streets (1869). A car on tracks was driven back and forth in the tunnel using pneumatic power. Although the project was soon abandoned, it marked the start of underground transit in New York.

The first link in New York City's extensive underground transit system began in 1900. Some sections of the system followed streets and were built by the cut-and-cover method. Some subway tunnels under the East and Harlem rivers were put in place by digging a trench and sinking prefabricated tubes into them.

The first freight delivery tunnel system was put in operation in August 1906 in Chicago.

The Holland Tunnel under the Hudson River opened November 12, 1927; the Lincoln Tunnel under the Hudson consists of three tubes 1.6 miles long — the first opened 1937, the second 1945, the third 1957.

The East River Tunnel from New York City's Battery to Brooklyn opened January 9, 1908. The Brooklyn-Battery Tunnel, the longest in the United States — 1.7 miles — opened May 25, 1950, and cost $80 million to construct. Work began in 1940 but was interrupted by World War II; construction resumed in 1945. The length of the tunnel required a ventilation building at the halfway point.

Urban Transit

Public transportation in the cities began with horse-drawn vehicles and these were later improved by having the vehicles run on tracks.

The first street car company was the New York and Harlem Railway Inc. The company began with a horse-drawn streetcar designed and constructed by John Stephenson (1809–93), who went on to become the world's largest streetcar builder. The New York line began operating November 26, 1832, along Fourth Avenue from Prince to 14th Street. The fare was 12½ cents.

Moses G. Farmer began experimenting with electric railways (1845) and operated a car carrying two people in Dover, New Hampshire, but it did not attract support. A street railway line began operating in Louisville, Kentucky (1864).

The first successful substitute for the horse-drawn vehicle was the cable car, which used a steam-driven generator to run the cable attached to the cars. The first cable car was the Clay Street Hill Railroad in San Francisco, built and operated by Andrew S. Hallidie (1836–1900), a wire suspension bridge builder. The line, 2,800 feet long on a 307 feet high hill, began operating August 1, 1873.

Efforts to use overhead wires for power transmission to street railways were made by various developers.

The most successful was Frank J. Sprague (1857–1934), who installed the first successful street car system in Richmond, Virginia (1887). Sprague formed a company (1884) to build systems and developed a constant-speed electric motor which he used in Richmond.

Another overhead system was developed (1885) in Baltimore by Leo Daft, who used two overhead wires with a small carriage or "troller" (which later became "trolley") to gather the traction power. Charles J. Van Depoele (1846–92) developed a system in the 1880s similar to Daft's but used only one wire, with the rails serving as the return circuit.

An elevated street railway system began on Greenwich Street in New York City. Rufus H. Gilbert (1832–85) developed plans for an elevated railway and formed a company (1872). The Panic of 1873 delayed the start of operations until June 6, 1876, when the line began running from Trinity Church to 59th Street.

The first regular American bus service began on New York City's Fifth Avenue (1905) with an imported bus from London and the next year with a French double-decker bus.

An experimental pneumatic passenger subway, 296 feet long, was built under lower Broadway in New York City by Alfred E. Beach (1826–90), editor of *Scientific American*. A financial failure, the operation ended after a few years.

The first American subway built under city streets for transportation was the Tremont Street subway in Boston, which opened September 1, 1897. the first section of the New York City subway system opened 1904 from City Hall to 145th Street.

Two important accessories to public transportation were the coin fare box and transfers. Tom L. Johnson (1854–1911) invented the coin fare box (1869) for the Louisville Street Railroad. John H. Stedman of Rochester, New York, invented the street car transfer, first used in Rochester (1892).

Water

Most of the original transportation of the American settlers was by water and later by horse and carriage as roads and highways were developed.

Despite the many waterways, much travel was by land, mostly horseback, because settlers had little experience building or operating a boat.

The first water vehicles in the American colonies were probably the log raft and birch bark canoe, and, in the West, the bull boats, which were made of hides of male buffalo stretched over sampling frames.

The first ship built in America was the 30-ton pinnace, *Virginia of Sagadahoc*, built (1607) by members of an unsuccessful settlement at the mouth of the Kennebec river in Maine. The vessel took them back to England.

Shipbuilding was begun (1624) in Plymouth, Massachusetts, by an English professional shipbuilder but he died soon after his arrival in the colonies. Six shipwrights arrived (1629) with a supply of pitch, tar, cordage and sailcloth and built several small fishing vessels. Their first large ship, *The Blessing of the Bay*, was built for Governor John Winthrop, launched in 1631.

The shipyard, in a way, was the first American factory, requiring the assembly of many different materials and use of various skills.

Early vessels were designed to provide two-way travel on the rivers— the fore-and-aft rigged sailboats which went by many different names (pink, sloop, ketch, schooner, lighter, pinnace, shallop, pirogue) according to location, rigging, and shape of the hull. There also were pole boats for narrow or shallow rivers.

The Dutch on the Hudson River developed a sailboat called the Hudson River sloop, a 65–75 feet long vessel with much sail.

There were several early attempts to develop a motorized vessel.

William Henry (1729–86) tried to use a steam engine to propel a sternwheel steamboat (1763) but was unsuccessful. Nathan Read (1759–1849) patented a chainwheel method of ship propulsion (1791) but could not get financing to build a full-sized vessel. He also developed a steam boiler and steam engine.

James Rumsey (1743–92) developed a steam-powered motorboat which he unveiled December 3, 1787, on the Potomac River near Shepherdstown, West Virginia. The boat was propelled by jets of water forced out of the stern by a steam-operated pump, in what was probably the first jet-propelled vehicle. Although he received English and American patents, he could not get financial backing.

John Fitch (1743–98) received monopolies from several states to use their rivers and financial help from a group of Philadelphians to build a 45-feet steam-powered boat. He successfully demonstrated the first full-scale craft using steam-powered oars for propulsion on the Delaware River August 22, 1787, before delegates to the Constitutional Convention.

He built larger boats, one of which maintained a regular schedule between Trenton and Philadelphia (1790). Fitch received American and French patents but his fourth boat was wrecked in a storm and his backers deserted him.

Robert Fulton was a successful painter with a deep interest in vessels. He designed a small paddlewheel boat (1779) and while in France (1797) developed a submarine (the *Nautilus*). It was equipped with torpedoes, which he invented, and it sank a heavy brig in a demonstration. Fulton made a deal with Robert R. Livingston (1746–1813), the American minister to France, to build a steamboat with exclusive rights to sail on the Hudson River. Livingston provided the funds with which Fulton built and demonstrated a full-sized boat in France (1802). Fulton purchased a steam engine before returning to the United States (1806) to build the *Clermont*, 130 feet long and 16 feet wide. The vessel on August 17, 1807, completed a New York City–Albany round trip in 62 hours— sailing sloops ordinarily took four days. Fulton then built the *New Orleans*, which made the first steam voyage on the Mississippi River, sailing from Pittsburgh to New Orleans where it arrived on January 12, 1812.

(The first steamboat navigated the Missouri River in 1819, the first on the Great Lakes was the *Walk-on-the-Water*, which sailed from Buffalo to Detroit (1818) with 100 passengers.)

The first steam-propelled ferryboat was the *Juliana* which sailed between New York City and Hoboken, New Jersey, and was operated by John C. (1749–1838) and Robert L. Stevens (1787–1856) of later railroad fame. After the boiler gave out, the Stevens built the *Phoenix* which could not operate on the Hudson River because of the Fulton-Livingston monopoly. In June 1809, the *Phoenix* was the first steamboat to make an ocean trip, sailing from Hoboken on the Atlantic Ocean to Philadelphia on the Delaware River.

Many successful boat builders followed the early developers.

William H. Webb (1816–99) was the leading shipbuilder of the 1830–50 era, building transatlantic packets. He built a packet ship (1836) for the Black Ball Line and numerous warships for foreign countries.

John W. Griffiths (1809–82) created the first notable clipper sailing ship, the *Rainbow* (1845). Donald McKay (1810–80) built many record-breaking clipper ships, launching the first (*Stag Hound*) in 1850. William Cramp (1807–79) and his son, Charles H. (1828–1913), pioneered in steam and ironclad ship construction and developed the nation's largest shipbuilding company.

Alexander McDougall (1845–1923) developed the whaleback steamship (1881) and had numerous inventions in shipbuilding, ore and grain handling equipment, and dredging machinery. John Roach (1813–87) built marine engines and iron steamships, and was sometimes called the father of American iron shipbuilding.

John Ericcson was an independent engineer in London, where he switched to ship design. He was one of the first to place engines below the waterline and used a screw propeller rather than paddlewheels.

After building the first propeller-driven commercial vessel (*Novelty*) in 1837 he came to the United States where his propulsion system was quickly adopted. Ericsson built the *Princeton*, the first propeller-driven warship, and in 1861–62 built the ironclad *Monitor* of Civil War fame, which opened the age of modern warships.

Some miscellaneous items about water vessels:

William Raymond of Nantucket built the first lifeboat (1807) for the Massachusetts Humane Society. Joseph Francis (1801–93) invented the "unsinkable" rowboat (1819), then a wooden lifeboat (1838), which he strengthened with corrugated iron (1845).

Robert Gray (1755–1806) was the first American seaman to sail around the world (1790) and two years later discovered the Columbia River in the Northwest. His discoveries were the foundation for American claims to Oregon.

The first transatlantic sailing packet line (Black Ball) began operating between Liverpool, England, and New York City in January 1818; the first transatlantic steamboat (*Great Western*) sailed from New York to Bristol in 15 days in 1838.

Trade with China began as the *Empress of China* sailed from New York City on February 22, 1784, arriving in Canton August 30.

The first double-deck ferryboat, the *Bergen*, was launched October 25, 1888, to operate between Hoboken, New Jersey, and New York City; ferryboat operations between Staten Island and Manhattan began in 1905.

The first ferryboat built exclusively for motor vehicles began operating November 8, 1926, between New York City and Edgewater and Weehawken, New Jersey.

The first American submarine was built (1775) by David Bushnell (1742–1824). It resembled a turtle and was used unsuccessfully during the Revolution.

Alfred Guthrie (1805–82), an engineer, was responsible for the start of federal steamship inspection. He checked 200 vessels (1851) and charted their defects. Guthrie headed the federal inspection service, which he organized, for 30 years (1852–82) and it greatly reduced the number of ship explosions.

Napoleon E. Guerin of New York City invented the cork life preserver (1841).

The first American lighthouse was the conical tower built (1716) at the entrance to Boston Harbor on Little Brewster Island.

The world's first atomic-powered merchant ship, the *Savannah*, was launched July 21, 1959, at Camden, New Jersey.

Index

A.T. Stewart Company 35

Aaron, Hank 227

Abbe, Cleveland 207

Abbe, Robert 114

Abbey, Henry S. 158

Abbey, William F. 71

Abbott, Frank 99

Abbott, Jacob 63

Abbott, Robert S. 179

Abel, John J. 108

Abell, Arunah S. 178

Abruzzo, Ben 256

abstract paintings 17

Academy for the Education of Youth in Philadelphia 49

Academy of Natural Sciences 50

Academy of Sciences and Fine Arts 14

Acheson, Edward G. 139

Acker, Charles E. 202

actionmeter 18

Actors National Protective Union 85

Adams, Alvin 259

Adams, Robert 170

Addams, Jane 219

adding machines 27

Addison's disease 113

addressograph machines 26

Adirondack Cottage Sanitarium 115

Adlum, John 9

adult education 50

The Adventure of Harle-

quin and Scaramouche 81

advertising 22

aerial photographs 18

Affleck, Thomas 214

Agassiz, Louis 208

agricultural education 4

The Agricultural Museum 5

agriculture 3

Aiken, Howard H. 28

Aime, Valcour 96

air brakes 68, 266

air conditioning 213

Air Force 147

airplanes 250, 251, 252, 253, 254, 255

Aitken, Robert H. 195

Akeley, Carl E. 59

Alabama 83

Albee, Edward F. 86

Albert, Crane, Alanson 162

Albinus, C.F. 18

Albright, Jacob 192

Albright, Tenley 239

Alcorn Agricultural and Mechanical College 53

Aldrin, Edwin "Buzz" 207

Alexander, John 88

Alexander Brown & Sons 24

Alexander, Partridge, Alden 58

Alexanderson, Ernst F.W. 43

alfalfa 7

Alger, Cyrus 125, 132

Ali, Muhammad 230

Alice in Cartoonland 74

Allen, Florence E. 122

Allen, John 99

Allen, John F. 137

Allen, Richard 190

Allen, Zachariah 212

Allston, Robert F.W. 7

Allston, Washington 16

almanacs 171, 172, 179

An Almanac for New England for the Year 1639 171

alternating current 66, 67, 68, 69, 137

alternators 42

Altman, Benjamin 35

aluminum 141

Alvarez, Luis W. 253

ambulances 97

Amelung, John F. 130

American Academy of Arts and Sciences 50

American Academy of Dramatic Arts 85

The American Agriculturist 4

American Angler 232

American Association for the Advancement of Science 50

American Association of Public Accountants 22

American Association of University Professors 61

American Automobile Association 248

American baby show 219
American Bankers Association 25
American Cookery 90
The American Dictionary 61
American Economics Association 29
The American Farmer 5
American Federation of Teachers 61
American Forestry Association 12
American Foundation 110
The American Fruit Culturist 9
American Fur Co. 37
American Institute of Instruction 50
American Journal of Dentistry 99
American Journal of Science and Art 198
American Law Journal 121
American Library Association 58
American Literary, Scientific and Military Academy 58
American Lyceum 50
The American Magazine 172
American Mechanic 198
American Medical Association 100, 106
American Musical Magazine 157
American Ophthalmological Society 102, 106
American Philosophical Society 50
American Professional Football Association 233
American Red Cross 220
American Society for the Promotion of Temperance 89
The American Spelling Book 61
American Sugar Refining Company 96
American Tobacco Company 8
American Weekly Mercury 32

America's Cup 243
Ames, Nathan 171, 212
Ames, Oakes 136
amusement parks 73
Anderson, Alexander 181
Anderson, Kris 256
Anderson, Max 256
Andrews, Clark and Co. 71
Andros, Edmund 187
anesthetics 97, 99, 111
Angell, William G. 129
Angle, Edward H. 99
Anheuser, Eberhard 87
Anheuser Busch Brewing Company 87
animals 6
animated cartoon electric sign 23
animation 73, 74
Anthony, Susan B. 222
anthracite coal 65
anthropology 198
antibiotic 108, 109
Antioch College 53
Anti-Saloon League 89
Aoki, Ricky 256
appendectomies 111, 112
Apperson, Elgar 245
Apperson, Elmer 245
Applebee, Constance M.K. 236
Appleby, John F. 11
apples 9
Appleseed, Johnny 9
arades 81
archery 223
argonaut 149
Arithmetick Vulgar and Decimal 62
arithmometer 27
Arizona 83
Arkwright, Sir Richard 145
Armat, Thomas 78
armored cars 25
Armour, Philip D. 94
Armstrong, Edwin H. 43
Armstrong, Louis 156
Armstrong, Neil A. 207
Army 147
Army Ambulance Corps 148
Army Balloon Corps 147
art galleries 15
arthritis 113
artificial hearts 112
Asbury, Francis 190

"Ashcan School" 16
Ashe, Arthur E., Jr. 242
Ashe, Thomas 166
Ashmun Institute 53
Asimov, Isaac 168
Associated Actors and Artists of America 85
Association of American Painters and Sculptors 16
Association of Licensed Automobile Manufacturers 246
Astor, John Jacob 37
Astro Turf 240
astronomy 199
atomic bombs 71
Atomic Energy Commission 70
Atwater, Wilbur O. 4, 116
audion 42
Austin, Ann 194
Austin, Moses 141
Austin, William A. 256
auto bank 25
auto races 224
automobiles 244, 245, 246, 247, 248, 249
axes 136
Ayer, Francis W. 22
Ayer, James C. 109
Ayres, Ann 196

Babbitt, Isaac 139, 215
Babcock, George H. 137
Babcock, Stephen M. 9, 91
Babson, Roger W. 30
Babson Institute 30
Baby and Child Care 108
baby carriage 108, 218
Bache, Alexander 198
Bachrach, David, Jr. 18
badminton 224
Baekeland, Leo H. 142
Baer, Max 240
Bailey, Francis 180
Bailey, James A. 74
Bailey, James M. 179
Bailey, Liberty H. 4
Bainbridge, Charles T. 142
Baird, Bill (William B.) 81
Baker, Benjamin A. 83
Baker, Richard 201
Baker, Sara J. 218
Baldwin, Dwight H. 155
Baldwin, Frank S. 27

Baldwin, Matthias W. 264, 265
Baldwin, Thomas S. 256
Ball, Albert 144
ballet 75, 76
balloons 255, 256
Baltimore College of Dental Surgery 99
bananas 9
bands 151
Bank for Savings 24
Bank of America 25
Bank of North America 24
Bank of the United States 23
bank robberies 25
banking 23, 165
Banneker, Benjamin 216
barbed wire 12
Barber, Ohio C. 162
Barbour, Edmund D. 27
Barbour, William 145
Bard, John 100, 104
Bard, Samuel 100
Bard, William 32
Bardeen, John 204
barn 209
Barnard, Frederick A.P. 63
Barnard, Henry 55, 61
Barnes, Albert C. 109
Barnes, Charles E. 126
Barnes, Martin 129
Barney, Everett H. 238
Barnsdall, William 71
Barnum, P(hineas) T. 74
Barnum and Bailey Circus 74
Barron, Clarence W. 178
Barry, John 169
Barrymore, John 79
Barrymore, Lionel 79, 84
Barrymore, Maurice 84
Barton, Bruce 23
Barton, Clara 220
Bartram, John 201
baseball 224, 225, 226, 227, 240
Baseball Hall of Fame 227
Basie, Count (William) 156
basketball 227, 228, 240, 243
Bates, Katherine L. 154
Batten, Barton, Durstine and Osborne Inc. 23
batteries 69

Batterson, James G. 32
Battey, Robert 112
Baumes, Caleb H. 123
The Bay Psalm Book 154, 166
Beach, Alfred E. 268, 270
Beach, Moses S. 177
Beach, Moses Yale 177
Beadle, Erastus F. 170
Beard, Daniel C. 219
Beard, Thomas 41
Beasley, Tom 230
Beaumont, William 111
Beauregard, Pierre G.T. 33
Beck, Claude S. 111
Beck, Martin 86
Becknell, William 261
Bedford, Gunning S. 105
beds 215
Beecher, Catherine E. 63
Beecher, Henry Ward 183
Beecher, Lyman 195
beer 87, 88
Beers, Clifford W. 110
Beers, John H. 99
bees 9
Beiderbecke, Bix (Leon B.) 157
Beissel, Johann C. 154, 180, 184
Belasco, David 84
Bel Geddes, Norman 14
Bell, Alexander Graham 46, 47, 48, 251
Bell, Bert (de Benneville) 233
Bell, Chichester A. 160
Bell, Robert 169
Bellew, Frank H.T. 170
Bellows, George W. 17
Belmont, August 24
Bendix, Vincent 248
Benezet, Anthony 62
Benjamin, Asher 210
Bennet, James 142
Bennett, Elizabeth 111
Bennett, Floyd 252
Bennett, Hugh H. 13
Bennett, James Gordon 177, 238
Bennett, Jesse 111
Bent, Josiah 92
Benton, Linn B. 181
Benton, Thomas Hart 16
Benton, William 23
Benton & Bowles 23

Berkshire Agricultural Society 4
Berlin, Irving 159
Berliner, Emile 160, 211
Berliner, Henry A. 255
Bernays, Edward L. 36
Bernstein, Leonard 160
Berry, Albert 254
Berry, Marcellus F. 25
Berry, Martha M. 56
Bethune, Mary McLeod 63
Bethune-Cookman College 64
beverages 87
Bible 169, 180, 195
bicycles 228, 245, 246, 247, 249, 256
Bigelow, Erastus B. 217
Bigelow, Poultney 240
Biggs, Hermann M. 114
billiards 223, 228
Billings, William 154
binder 11
Bingham Library for Youth 57
biology 201
The Bird Catcher 75
Birdseye, Clarence 93
The Birth of a Nation 79
Bishop, Katherine S. 115
Bissell, Emily P. 115
Bissell, George H. 71
Bissell, Melville R. 213, 214
Bittner, John J. 114
bituminous coal 65
Black, Greene V. 99
Black, J.W. 18
Black, James 89
Blackton, Stuart 73
Blackwell, Antoinette L.B. 197
Blackwell, Elizabeth 100
Blackwell, Henry B. 222
Blair, James 52
Blake, Eli W. 144
Blake, Lyman R. 41
Blalock, Alfred 107
Blanchard, Jean Pierre 255
Blanchard, Thomas 125, 138, 244
Bland, James A. 159
Bloch, Konrad E. 203
Blodgett, Katherine B. 131
blood 98

blood transfusion 112
Bloomer, Amelia Jenks 39, 222
Blount College 53
Blow, Susan E. 60
Blue Backed Speller 61
Board of Regents 60
boarding school 63
boating 228, 229
Bobb, John S. 111
Boehm, Martin 193
Boepple, John F. 129
Bogardus, James 139
Bohune, Lawrence 103
boilers 137
Bok, Edward W. 172
Bolden, Buddy (Charles) 156
bolometer 200
Bolton, John 130
Bolton, William J. 130
Bond, Carrie Jacobs 159
Bond, Thomas 104
Bond, William C. 199
Bonwill, William C.A. 99
book reviews 169
bookmobiles 58
books 166
boot-stitching machines 41
Booth, Ballington 220
Booth, Edwin T. 84
Booth, Evangeline 220
Booth, John Wilkes 84
Booth, Junius B. 84
Booth, William 220
borax 141
Borden, Gail 91
Borden, Joseph E. 226
Borden Company 91
Boré, Jean Etienne 7, 96
Borglum, Gutzon 20
Borzage, Frank 81
Boston Cooking School 90
Boston News Letter 22, 25
botany 201
Botter, James 32
Boucicault, Dion 83
Boudinot, Elias 191
Bowditch, Henry P. 102
Bowditch, Nathaniel 20, 262
Bowker, Richard R. 58
Bowles, Chester B. 23
Bowles, Samuel 178
bowling 223, 229, 230

Bowser, Sylvanus P. 72
boxing 230, 240
Boy Scouts 220
Boyce, William 158
Boyd, William C. 98
Boyden, Seth 41, 132, 133
Boyle, James 215
Boylston, Zabdiel 104
Boys Town 220
Brace, Charles L. 219
Bradford, Andrew 172, 174, 176
Bradford, John 175
Bradford, Lodowick H. 181
Bradford, William 166, 171, 174, 176, 180
Bradley, Milton 76
Bradstreet, Anne D. 168
Bradstreet, John M. 28
Bradstreet Company 28, 29
Brady, Mathew B. 17, 18
Braidwood, John 55
brakes 248
Brallier, John 233
Brandsten, Ernest 241
brandy 87
brass 140
Brattain, Walter H. 204
Bray, John R. 74
Bray, Thomas 57
Brayton, George B. 137, 244
Brent, Margaret 221
bricks 211
bridges 76, 257, 258
Bridges, Calvin B. 111
Bridges, Robert 131
Bridgman, Elijah C. 183
Bridgman, Percy W. 204
Brill, Abraham A. 110
Brinks Inc. 25
Brinton, Daniel G. 198
Bronk, Detlev W. 109
Brooker, William 174
Brookins, Walter R. 251
Brooklyn-Battery Tunnel 269
Brown, Alexander 24
Brown, Alexander E. 138
Brown, Charles B. 167
Brown, Mrs. Charles S. 234
Brown, Ebenezer 40
Brown, James 169

Brown, Joseph R. 138
Brown, Nathan 35
Brown, Olympia 197
Brown, Sylvanus 145
Brown, Thomas 164
Brown, William 103
Brown, William M. 167
Brown Brothers Harriman & Co. 24
Brown University 53
Browne, Ralph C. 126
Browning, John M. 125
Brubeck, Dave 157
Bruce, David, Jr. 181
Bruce, Philip A. 82
Brush, Charles F. 67
Bryant, Billy 82
Bryant, Sam 82
Bryant, William Cullen 169, 177
Buell, Abel 181
Buffalo Eye and Ear Infirmary 106
Buffington, Adelbert R. 126
Buffington, Leroy S. 211
Buick, David D. 245
Bulfinch, Charles 210
Bull, Ephraim W. 9
bull boats 271
Bunner, Henry C. 173
Burbank, Luther 5
Burden, Henry 11
Bureau of Animal Industry 94
Bureau of Justice 121
Bureau of Labor 119
Burgess, Thornton W. 167
burglar alarms 163
Burleigh, Celia C. 197
Burleigh, Harry T. 153
Burleigh, John H. 146
burlesque 85
Burpee, Washington Atlee 13
Burr, Theodore 257
Burroughs, John 168
Burroughs, William S. 27
Burt, William A. 26
Burton, Charles 108, 218
Burton, William M. 72
bus service 270
Busch, Adolphus 87
buses 250
Bush, Vannevar 28
Bushnell, David 149, 274

Bushnell, Horace 186
Butler, Henry 82
Butler, Nicholas Murray 52
butter 10
Butterick, Ebenezer 39
Button, Dick 239
Byers, William N. 175
Byrd, Richard E. 252
Byrd, William 166

C.G. Glasscock Drilling Company 72
cable car 269
Cabrini, Francis Xavier 197
Cadman, Charles W. 152
Cadman, Samuel F. 183
The Cage 75
Cage, John M. 153
calculator 27
Calder, Alexander 20
California Electric Light Company 68
California Sugar Refining Company 96
Callahan, Americus 135
calliopes 156
calorimeters 202
Calthrop, Samuel R. 267
Camp, Hiram 216
Camp, Walter C. 232
Camp Fire Girls 220
Campbell, Alexander 193
Campbell, Henry R. 266
Campbell, John A. 173, 176
Campbell, John W., Jr. 168
Campbell, Thomas 54, 193
Campbell, William W. 200
canals 259
Canby, Edward 144
cancer 114
Candee, Leverett 143
Candler, Asa G. 88
candy 89
Caniff, Milt(on A.) 171
Cannon, Annie Jump 200
Cannon, Walter B. 109
Capp, Al 171
carbon transmitters 66
Carbutt, John 18
Carey, Henry C. 29
carillons 156
Carleton, Mark A. 6
Carlson, Anton J. 109

Carlson, Chester F. 28
Carnegie, Andrew 57, 132
Carnegie, Dale 168
Carnes, Peter 255
Carothers, Wallace H. 203
Carpentier, Georges 230
carpet 217
carpet sweepers 213
Carrel, Alexis 98, 112
Carrier, Willis H. 213
Carroll, Charles 184
Carroll, John 184
Carter, James G. 61
cartoons 170, 171
Cartwright, Alexander J., Jr. 225
Carty, John J. 44, 47
Caruso, Enrico 43
Carver, George Washington 5
Carver, Jonathan 167
Case, Jerome I. 11
Casey, Phil 235
cash registers 26
Cassatt, Mary 17
cast iron plows 10
Castle, Irene 76
Castle, Vernon B. 76
Castner, Hamilton Y. 202
Catchpole, Judith 121
Catt, Carrie Chapman 222
celluloid 127
cement 211
cereals 90
Certified Public Accountant 21
Chadwick, Harry 225
Chaffee, Adna R. 148
chamber music 152
Chambers, Benjamin, Sr. 125
champagne 88
Chandler, Charles 254
Chandler, Charles F. 107
Channing, William Ellery 196
Channing, William F. 67, 162
Chanute, Octave 250, 251
Chapin, Daniel M. 162
Chapin, Roy D. 248
Chaplin, Charlie 79
Chapman, Alva W. 201
Chapman, John 8
Chapman, Nathaniel 100
Chapman, William, Sr. 82

charity 219
Charles, Joseph 175, 176
Charlotte 220
Chase, Edna W. 39
Chase, Samuel 184
Chautauqua 50, 53
Chavez, Cesar 118
cheese 91
Cheever, Ezekiel 61
chemistry 202
Cheney, Benjamin P. 260
Cheney, Charles E. 187
Cheney, Ward 146
chess 77
Chevrolet, Louis 245
chewing gum 89
Chicago Board of Trade 30
Chicago Lying-In Hospital 102
Chicago Maternity Center 102
Chickering, Jonas 155
Child, Lydia M.F. 167, 172
Children's Bureau 120
Childs, Cephas G. 181
Chippendale, Thomas 214
chirographer 26
chiropracty 107
Chisum, John E. 6
chloroform 97
chop suey 94
The Christian History 195
Christmas cards 135
Christy, Edwin D. 77
Christy Minstrels 77
Chrysler, Walter F. 246
Church, Ellen 254
Church, William 181
Cibber, Colley 158
cider 87
cigar factory 8
cigar-making machine 8
cigarette tax 38
cigarettes 8
Cigarmakers Union 117
cigars 8
Cinerama 81
circus 74
Clagett, Thomas 187
Clark, Alvan 199
Clark, Edson P. 134
Clark, Francis E. 192
Clark, John B. 29
Clark, Ron 256
Clarke, John 183

Clarke, William 225
Clarke School for the Deaf 55
Clarkson, William K. 256
Classic and Comic Concert Company 75
Clay, Henry 122
Clayton, Henry H. 207
Clerc, Laurent 54
clocks 216
Cluett, Sanford L. 39
Clymer, George C. 180
coal gas 70
Cobb, Jonathan H. 146
Coca-Cola 88
Cochran, Jacqueline 254
coeducation 53
coffee 88
Coffin, Howard E. 248
Coffin, Lorenzo S. 265
Cohan, George M. 84
Cohn, Edwin Joseph 98
Coit, Stanton 219
Coke, Thomas 190
coke ovens 65
Colborn, Irving W. 131
Colden, Jane 201
Cole, Thomas 16
Coleman, William T. 141
collars 40
College of New Jersey 52
College of Philadelphia 52
College of Physicians and Surgeons 100
College of Physicians in Philadelphia 100
College of William and Mary 52
Collegiate School of Connecticut at Killingworth 52
Colles, Christopher 262
Colt, Samuel 126
Columbia University 4, 52, 63, 70
Columbus, Christopher 164
comic books 171
comics 171
Commentaries on American Law 122
commercial creameries 10
commercial mining 65
common rooms 210
Common Sense 167
community colleges 54

Company, John McLaughlin 76
The Compleat Housewife 90
comptometer 27
Compton, Arthur 70, 204
computers 28
Computing-Tabulating Recording Co. 27
Conboy, Sara A.M. 118
Concord grape 9
condensed milk 91
Conestoga wagon 261
The Congress Returns 75
Connecticut (later American) Asylum 54
Connecticut Society for Mental Hygiene 110
Connelly, Cornelia 196
Conrad, Frank 43
conservation 13
contact lenses 106
The Contrast 83
Cook, George C. 85
cookbooks 90
Cookman Institute for Men 64
Cooley, Denton A. 112
Coolidge, William D. 68
cooling 213
Cooper, Leon N. 204
Cooper, Peter 56, 132, 263
Cooper Union 56
Copley, John S. 15, 16, 17
copper 140
Copperthwaite & Sons 29
Copson, John 32, 174, 176
copying machine 28
Corcoran, William 15
Corliss, George H. 41, 137
corn 6
Cornell, Ezra 45
Cornell University 12
Cornish, John 145, 179
Corporation for the Relief of Poor and Distressed Presbyterian Ministers and of the Poor and Distressed Widows and Children of Presbyterian Ministers 31
Corson, Juliet 90
Cortelyou, George E. 120
Cosmopolitan Theater 23
Cotton, John 185
cotton 7, 145, 146

cotton gins 7, 138, 145
Cottrell, Frederick G. 203
Cournand, Andre F. 115
Cowan, Joshua L. 76
cowcatchers 266
Cowles, Gardner 178
Coy, George W. 48
crackers 92
Cradock, Mathewe 6
Crafts, James M. 202
Craigie, Andrew 108
Cramp, William 272
Crapaud, Johnny 76
Crehorne, Benjamin 155
cricket 223, 225, 230
Crile, George W. 112
Crisco 92
Crocker, Charles 265
Crocker, Francis B. 69
Crockett, Davy 83
Crompton, William 146
crops 6
croquet 231
Cross, Roy 72
crossword puzzles 76
Crowninshield, George 243
Crozier, William 126
Cudahy, Michael 94
Cudahy Packing Company 94
Culbertson, Ely 77
The Cultivator 5
cultivators 11
Cummins, George D. 187
curling 231
currency 29
Currier, Nathaniel 15
Curry, John Steuart 16
Curtis, Charles G. 137
Curtis, Cyrus H.K. 172
Curtis, John 89
Curtiss, Glenn 251, 254
Cushing, Harvey W. 112
Cushman, Charlotte 84
Cutler, Joseph G. 164
Cutler, Manasseh 201
Cutter, Charles A. 58
Cutting, James A. 181
cyclotron 70

Daboll, Nathan 172
Daft, Leo 67, 270
Daggett, Ezra 93
daguerreotypes 17
Dahlgren, John A.B. 126

Daly, Marcus 140
Damrosch, Leopold 152
Dana, John C. 58
Dana, Samuel L. 5, 146
Danforth, Thomas 215
Daniels, Fred H. 133
Daniels, George H. 267
Darby, Abraham 131
Dartmouth 52, 53
Davenport, Thomas W. 66, 137
Davey, John 13
David Groesbeck and Company 46
Davids, Thaddeus 135
Davies, Arthur B. 16
Davies, Samuel 52, 194
Davis, Henry G. 112
Davis, James 176
Davis, William 94
Day, Dorothy 219
Day, Stephen 154, 171, 180
Deane, Rev. Samuel 5
DeBakey, Michael E. 112
Decatur, Stephen 24
Deere, John 10
Deering, William 11
DeForest, Lee 42, 79
DeKooning, Willem 17
DeKoven, Reginald 160
Delafield, Edward 102, 106
Delameter, Cornelius H. 137
Delany, Patrick B. 46
Delaware and Hudson Canal Co. 65
DeLee, Joseph B. 102
delineator 39
Delmonico, Lorenzo 95
DeMille, Cecil B. 80
Deming, Philander 123
Deming, William C. 108
Dempsey, Jack (William H.) 230, 240
Demuth, Charles 17
Denison, Aaron L. 216
The Dental Art 99
dentistry 98, 99, 100
Denton, Daniel 166
dentures 99
Department of Labor and Commerce 120
Deringer, Henry 126
The Deserter 75
DeSeversky, Alexander P. 252

design 14
Desjardins, Alphonse 25
Dett, Robert N. 153
DeVilbiss, Allen, Jr. 144
Dewees, William P. 105
Dewey, John 56
Dewey, Joseph D. 132
Dewey, Melvil 58
DeWitt, Simeon 203
DeYoung, Charles 74, 178
DeYoung, Michael H. 178
diabetes 114
Diaghilev, Serge 75
diamonds 144
Dick, Albert B. 28
Dick, George F. 113
Dick, Gladys 113
Dickinson, Emily 169
Dickinson, John 158
Dickinson, Jonathan 52
dictionaries 168, 169
A Dictionary of the Photographic Art 19
digestion 111
Dilworth, Thomas 62
diphtheria 114
dirigibles 255, 256
dishes 215
Disney, Walt 74
dispensaries 101
Disston, Henry 136
Ditson, Oliver 157
diving 241
Dix, Dorothea L. 110, 220
Dixon, Jeremiah 203
Dixon, Joseph 134
Dodge, Mary E.M. 168
dog racing 231
dog shows 231
Doisy, Edward A. 116
Dole, John D. 93
Donaldson, W.H. 255
Doolittle, Isaac 180
Doolittle, Jimmy (James H.) 254
Dorais, Gus 233
Dort, J. Dallas 244
Doubleday, Abner 224
Doughty, Thomas 149
Douglass, William 106
Dove, Arthur G. 17
Dow, Charles H. 178
Dow, Herbert H. 128, 202
Dowie, John A. 194
Drake, Edwin L. 71
Draper, Henry 200

Draper, John W. 18, 200
Draper, Paul 76
drawing 14
Dressler, Marie 79
Drew, Charles R. 98
Drew, Georgianna 84
Drexel, Anthony J. 24, 56
Drexel, Katherine 197
Drexel Institute 56
Drexel, Morgan & Co. 24
dried milk 91
Drinker, Philip 103
Dripps, Isaac 266
Dryden, John F. 32
Duane, William 114
Dubos, Rene J. 108
Dubreuil, Joseph 7
Duche, Andre 215
Duck, Donald 74
duckpins 229
Duclot, Louis 175
Dufour, John J. 9
Duggar, Benjamin M. 108
Duke, Benjamin N. 8
Duke, James B. 8
Dummer, Jeremiah 15
DuMont, Allan 44
Dun, Robert G. 28
Dun & Bradstreet, Inc. 29
Duncan, Isadora 75
Duncan, Joseph Smith 26
Duncan, Matthew 175
Dunglison, Robley 103
Dunlap, John 174
Dunlap, William 83
Dunn, Beverly W. 127
Dunning, John Ray 70
Dunster, Henry 51, 180
Dunton, Jacob 109
DuPont, E(leuthere) I. 127
Durand, Asher B. 16
Durant, Charles F. 255
Durant, William C. 244
Durgin, Samuel H. 219
Duryea, Charles E. 245
Duryea, J. Frank 224, 245
Duyckingk, Evert 130
Dwight, James 241
Dwight, John 128
Dwight, Timothy 53
Dyer, E.H. 96
Dyott, Thomas W. 130

Eads, James B. 258
Earhart, Amelia M. 252, 254

Earle, Richard W. 143
earmuffs 39
Eastman, George 18, 19
Eaton, Amos 56
Eaton, Dorman B. 119
Eaton, Moses 217
Eckert, John P., Jr. 28
Eclectic Readers 62
Eddy, Mary M. Baker 192, 197
Eddy, Oliver T. 26
Ederle, Gertrude 241
Edison, Thomas A. 27, 28, 66, 68, 78, 79, 114, 159, 267
Edison and Thomas Houston Electric Company 66
Edison General Electric Company 66
Edison Lamp Works 66
education 49, 50
Edwards, Jonathan 167, 185, 186
Edwards, Talmadge 40, 133
Egloff, Gustav 72
Ehrlich, John 108
Eichelberger, Thomas 88
Eickemeyer, Rudolph 39
Eielsen, Elling 192
Einhorn, Albert 97
electric bells 67
electric fans 68
electric flatirons 68
electric irons 213
electric light sockets 68
electric meters 68
electric ranges 68, 213
electric stoves 68
electric toasters 68
electric typewriters 27
electrical vote recorders 66
electricity 66, 67, 68, 69, 137
electromagnets 67
elevated street railways 270
elevators 212
Eliot, Charles W. 51
Eliot, Jared 5
Eliot, John 166, 180, 195
Ellet, Charles, Jr. 257
Ellington, Duke (Edward H.) 157

Ellsberg, Edward 72, 136
Elssler, Fanny 75
Elton, Robert H. 135
Ely, Eugene R. 251
Emerson, Ralph 82
Emerson, Ralph Waldo 168
Emmett, Daniel D. 77
encyclopedias 168
Enders, John F. 108, 113
energy 65
engines 136, 137
England, John 184
English Classical School 60
English High School 60
engraving 15
Enterprise 149
envelopes 135
erector sets 76
Ericsson, John 137, 273
Erie Canal 259
Esbjörn, Lars P. 188
escalators 212
esophagotomies 113
Espy, James P. 207
Essays Upon Field Husbandry in New England 5
Esterbrook, Richard 134
Estey, Jacob 156
ethyl gasoline 72
Evans, George H. 179
Evans, Herbert M. 115
Evans, Oliver 136, 244
evaporated milk 91
Eve, Paul F. 111
Eveleth, J.G. 71
Every Man His Own Doctor; or, the Poor Planter's Physician 100
Evinrude, Ole 229
evolution 49
Ewell, Benjamin S. 52
experimental farms 4
explosives 127
exposure photometer 18
express service 259, 260
extinction light meters 18

F and J. Heinz Company 92
F.W. Woolworth Co. 37
Faber, (John) Eberhard 134
Fahlberg, C. 108

Fairbanks, John B. 26
Fairbanks, Thaddeus 144
Fairfield, Richard 163
fairs 4
fanning mills 11
fans 139
Fargo, William G. 260
farm machinery 10
Farmer, Fannie M. 90
Farmer, Moses G. 67, 162, 269
farming 3
Farnsworth, Philo T. 44
fasteners 128
The Father of an Only Child 83
Fay, Elijah 88
Federal Communications Commission 44
Federal Deposit Insurance Corp. 25
Federal Radio Commission 44
Federal Reserve System 24
Federalist Papers 36
Feke, Robert 15, 16
Felt, Dorr E. 27
female education 63
fences 12
fencing 231
Fermi, Enrico 70
Fernow, Bernhard E. 12, 13
Ferris, George W.G. 73
Ferris wheels 73
ferryboats 272, 273
fertilizer 12
Fessenden, Reginald A. 42, 43
Field, Marshall 34
Field, Stephen D. 46
Field, Palmer and Leiter 35
field hockey 236
Fields, Cyrus W. 46
figure skating 239
Filene, Edward A. 35
film strips 62
films 18
fingerprinting 162, 163
Fink, Albert 265
Finley, James 257
fire 162
fire extinguishers 162
firefighting 161
fireplaces 210

Firestone, Harvey S. 143
Fisher, Alva J. 213
Fisher, Bobby (Robert J.) 77
Fisher, Bud (Harry C.) 171
Fisher, Carl G. 224
Fisher, Frederic J. 248
Fisher, John D. 55
Fisher, Mary 194
fishing 231, 232
Fiske, Minnie Maddern 84
Fitch, John 271
Fitz, Reginald H. 114
Flagg, Josiah 98
Flaherty, Robert J. 80
Flanagan, Edward J. 220
flashing electric signs 23
flashlights 69
flatirons 213
Fleeson, Plunkett 217
Fleet, Thomas 174
Fleischer, Max 74
Fleischmann, Charles 92
Fletcher, Horace 116
Flexner, Abraham 101
Flexner, Simon 114
Floating Circus Palace 82
Floating Theater 82
floor coverings 217
flour 92
flushing toilets 107
Fokker, Anthony H.G. 252
Folmer, William F. 19
food preservation 92
football 232, 233, 239, 240
Force, Peter 217
Ford, Henry 246
forestry 13
Forrest, Edwin 83, 84
Forssmann, Werner T. 115
Foster, Stephen C. 158
Foster, Thomas J. 53
Foulois, Benjamin D. 254
fountain pen 134
Fowle, Daniel 176
Fox, Fontaine T., Jr. 171
Fox, William 80
Fox Film Corporation 80
fox hunting 234
Francis, Joseph 273
Francis Perot's Sons Malting Company 87
Franklin Bank 29
Franklin, Benjamin 3, 22, 24, 49, 50, 52, 57, 66, 104, 106, 161, 163, 164,

170, 172, 174, 184, 198, 212
Franklin, James 172, 174, 176
Franklin Theater 85
Frasch, Herman 72, 202
fraternities 54
Freeman, David G. 224
Freeman, James 196
Freeman, Walter 111
Freer, Charles L. 15
French, Augustus B. 82
frequency modulation 43
Frick, Henry C. 15
Friendly Society for the Mutual Insurance of Houses Against Fire 31
Froelich, John 11
Frohmann, Charles 84
Frost, Robert 169
fruit 8, 93
Fuller, Alfred C. 37
Fuller, Loie 75
Fuller, Samuel 103
Fuller, Sarah Margaret 169, 221
Fulton, Robert 139, 272
Funk, Casimir 115
furniture 214
Fussell, Jacob 91

Gage, John H. 139
Gaiety Theater 86
Gallaudet, Edwin M. 54
Gallaudet, Thomas H. 54
Gallaudet College 54
Gallup, George F. 221
games 76
Gannett, Frank S. 178
Gannett, Henry 204
Garand, John C. 125
Gardette, James 98
Gardiner, Maine, Lyceum 3
Garey, Thomas A. 9
Gas Light Company 69
gaslights 69, 70
gasoline tax 38
Gatling, Richard J. 126
Gatty, Harold 253
gauges 138
Gayetty, Joseph E. 142
Gayler, Charles 25
Gayley, James 133
Gaynor, Janet 81
Gehrig, Lou 227

General Electric Company 66
General Time Convention 267
Genin, John N. 39
The Gentleman and Gardener's Kalendar 13
geography 203, 204
Geography Made Easy 62
geology 203, 204
Georgetown 53
Georgia Female College 63
German, Jacob 249
German Mills American Oatmeal Company 90
German Society 121
Gershwin, George 157
Gesell, Arnold L. 219
Gesner, Abraham 72
Giannini, A(madeo) P. 24
Gibbs, James E.A. 214
Gibbs, Josiah Willard 202, 204
Gibbs, Oliver W. 202
Gibson, Althea 242
Gibson, Charles D. 15
Giddings, Franklin H. 205
Gifford, Samuel P. 109
Gilbert, Alfred C. 76
Gilbert, Rufus H. 270
Gillespie, Dizzy (John B.) 157
Gillette, William 84
Gilman, Daniel C. 53
Gilmore, Patrick S. 151
Gilpatrick, J. 236
Gilpin, Thomas 141
Gimbel, Isaac 36
Gimbel, Jacob 36
Gimbel's Department Store 36
Girl Guides 220
Girl Scouts 220
Gish, Dorothy 79
Gish, Lillian 79
Glackens, William J. 16
Gladden, Washington 186
A Glance at New York 83
Glaser, Donald A. 205
glass 130, 131
glasses 106
Glenn, John H. 206
Glidden, Carlos 27
Glidden, Charles J. 47
Glidden, Joseph F. 12
gliders 250, 251

Glover, Jesse 180
Glover, John 147, 148
gloves 40
Goddard, Calvin L. 146
Goddard, Robert H. 206
Godfrey, Thomas 83, 262
Godkin, Edwin L. 172
Godowsky, Leopold 19
gold 140
Goldberg, Rube (Reuben L.) 171
Goldberger, Joseph 115
Goldwyn, Samuel 80
golfing 223, 234, 235
Gompers, Samuel 117, 118
Gone with the Wind 80
Good, John 146
Goodale, William 142
Goodall, Thomas 146
Goodhue, James M. 176
Goodman, Benny 157
Goodrich, Benjamin F. 143
Goodrich, Samuel G. 167
Goodwin, Hannibal W. 19
Goodwin, Isabella 163
Goodyear, Charles 143
Gorgas, William C. 113
Gorham, Jabez 215
Gorky, Arshile 17
Gorrie, John 213
Gostelowe 214
Gottschalk, Louis M. 153
Goudy, Frederic W. 181
Gould, George M. 106
Graflex cameras 19
Graham, Everts A. 111
Graham, Martha 75
Graham, Sylvester 92
graham crackers 92
Grammar of the English Language 62
The Grange 5
Granger, Austin 40
Grant, George F. 234
Grant, William W. 111
grapes 9
Graupner, Gottlieb 152
Gray, Asa 201
Gray, Elisha 47
Gray, Robert 273
Gray, William 48
Great American Tea Company 37
Great Awakening 182

The Great Train Robbery 79
Greater Atlantic and Pacific Tea Company 37
Greeley, Horace 177
Green, Bartholomew 174
Green, Francis 54
Green, George F. 99
Green, Horace 113
Green, Samuel 173, 174, 180
Green, Timothy 175, 177
Green, William 118
Greenough, Horatio 19
Greenough, John J. 214
Greenwood, Chester 39
Greenwood, Isaac 62
Greenwood, John 98
greeting cards 135
Gregg, John R. 56
Grice, Charles C. 115
Griffith, D.W. 79
Griffiths, John W. 272
Grinnell, Frank 162
Gross National Product 30
Grosvenor, Gilbert H. 173
Groves, Leslie R. 71
Grube, Emil H. 114
Grumann, Leroy R. 252
Guerin, Napoleon E. 274
Guggenheim, Meyer 140
Guinzburg, Harold G. 170
Gulick, Luther H. 220, 227
Guthrie, Alfred 274
Guthrie, Samuel 97
gymnastics 235

H.J. Heinz Company 92
Hackett, James H. 84
Hadaway, William S. 68, 213
Hagen, Walter C. 234
Haines, Jackson 239
Halas, George S. 233
Hale, Enoch 257
Hale, George E. 199
Hale, Nathan 179
Hale, William J. 203
Hall, Asaph 200
Hall, Charles M. 141
Hall, Granville S. 205
Hall, Joyce C. 135

Hall, Samuel R. 61
Halladay, Ben 260
Hallam, Lewis 82
Hallett, Benjamin 182
Hallett, Etienne S. 210
Hallidie, Andrew S. 269
Haloid-Xerox Co. 28
Halsted, William S. 112
Hamilton, Alexander 24
Hamilton, Alice 111
Hamilton, Andrew 121, 174
Hamlin, Emmons 155
Hammer, William J. 66, 114
Hammerstein, Oscar, I 8
Hammerstein, Oscar, II 160
Hammond, George H. 94
Hammond, James B. 26
Hammond, John H. 127
Hammond, Laurens 155
Hanchett, M. Waldo 99
Hancock, George W. 240
handball 235
Handy, William C. 156
Hanks, Benjamin 216
Hanks, Horatio 146
Hanks, Rodney 146
Hannan, John 89
Hansel, Ellen 241
Hardy, James B. 111
Hare, Robert 136, 202·
harmonic telephones 47
Harnden, William F. 259
harness racing 237
Harper, James 169
Harper, John 169
Harper, William Rainey 53
Harrington, John J. 175
Harris, Barbara C. 197
Harris, Benjamin 173
Harris, Chapin A. 99
Harris, Elisha 107
Harris, James 155
Harris, W.T. 244
Harrison, Benjamin 33
Harrison, Elizabeth 61
Harrison, Joseph, Jr. 266
Hart, C.V. 11
Hart, Lorenz 160
Hart, Schaffner & Marx 39
Harte, Bret (Francis B.) 168

Hartford, George B. 37
Hartford Female Seminary 63
Hartley, Robert M. 218
Harvard, John 51, 57
Harvard Annex 63
Harvard University 14, 51, 52, 57, 102
harvesters 11
Harvey, Fred(erick H.) 95
Harvey, Hayward A. 133
Hashman, Mrs. Judith D. 224
Haskins, DeWitt C. 268
Hasson, Esther V. 149
Hastie, William H. 123
hats 39, 40
Havemeyer, Henry O. 96
Hawes, Russell L. 135
Hawkins, Coleman 157
Hawkins, Joseph 88
Hawthorne, Rose 114
Hayden, Ferdinand V. 204
Hayden, Horace H. 99
Hayden, Joseph S. 129
Hayes, Will R. 81
Haynes, Elwood 133, 245
Hayward, Nathaniel M. 143
Haywood, Levi 215
Haywood, William D. 118
Hazard, Erskine 257
health boards 107
Hearst, William Randolph 178, 179
heart surgery 107
heart transplants 112
Heath, John S. 11
heating 212, 213
Heck, Barbara 190
Hecker, Isaac T. 185
Hegeler, E.C. 141
Heifetz, Jascha 153
Heinlein, Robert A. 168
Heinz, Henry J. 92
Held, John, Jr. 171
helicopters 255
Heminway, Merritt 146
Hench, Philip S. 113
Hendee, George M. 257
Henderson, Fletcher 156
Henri, Robert 16
Henry, Joseph 45, 67, 137
Henry, O. 168
Henry, William 271

Henry Street Settlement 105
Herbert, Victor 160
heredity 111
Herndon, Hugh, Jr. 253
Herreshoff, James B. 229
Herring, Augustus M. 250
Hershey, Milton S. 89
Herskovitz, Melville J. 198
Herty, Charles H. 202
Hesselius, Gustavus 155
Hewitt, Abram S. 132
Hewitt, James 158
Hewitt, Peter Cooper 68
Heyl, Henry R. 78
high-frequency alternators 43
highways 260, 261, 262
Higley, Samuel 132
Hillegas, Michael 154
Hillman, Sidney 118
Hilton, Conrad N. 31
Hires, Charles E. 88
Hitchcock, Ethan A. 130
Hitchcock, Lambert 215
Hoadley, Silas 216
Hoard, William D. 10
Hoban, James 210
Hobby, Oveta Culp 148
hockey 240
Hodges, Edwin 140
Hoe, Richard M. 180
Hogan, Ben (William B.) 235
Hogg, George 36
Holabird, William 211
Holbrook, Josiah 50, 56
Holcomb, Amasa 199
Holland, John F. 137
Holland, John P. 149
Hollerith, Herman 27
Holley, Alexander L. 132
Holliday, Charles 202
Holliday, Thomas 202
Hollingworth, John M. 141
Hollingworth, Lyman 141
Holloman, R.G. 79
Holm, Hanya 75
Holmes, Edwin T. 48, 163
Holmes, Israel 140
Holmes, Larry 230
Holt, Henry 81
Homans, Sheppard 33
Home for Homeless Boys 220
Homer, Winslow 135

Hone, Philip 65
honey 93, 94
Hood, John B. 175
Hook, Albert H. 8
Hoosac Tunnel 268
Hooton, Earnest A. 198
Hoover, Herbert 44
Hopkins, Ezek 148
Hopkins, Mark 265
Hopkins, Samuel 202
Hopkinson, Francis 151
Hopper, Edward 17
Horgan, Gideon 11
Horgan, Stephen H. 181
Horlick, William 88
Hormel, George A. 93
hornbook 61
horse racing 223, 236, 237
horse shows 236
horseshoes 237
Horton, Valentine B. 65
Hospital for the Ruptured and Crippled 102
hospitals 101, 102
Hotchkiss, Benjamin 126
hotels 30, 31
Houdry, Eugene J. 72
House, Henry A. 244
House, Royal E. 45
houses 209
Houston, David H. 19
Howard, Roy M. 178
Howe, Elias 214
Howe, John I. 129
Howe, Lucien 106
Howe, Nathan 74
Howland, Esther A. 135
Hubbard, Gardiner G. 47
Hubbell, Harvey 68
Hubble, Edwin P. 200
Hubert, Conrad 69
Hudson River School 16
Huggins, Charles B. 114
Hughes, David E. 46
Hughes, George 213
Hull, Joseph 175
Humane Society 106
Hume, William 93
Humorous Phases of Funny Faces 73
Humphrey, Doris 75
Humphreys, Joshua 148
Hunt, Walter 40, 129, 134, 214
Hunter, Thomas 53
Hunter College 53

hunting 237
Huntington, Collis P. 265
Huntington, F.A. 244
Hurd, Earl 74
Hurley, Edward N. 136
The Husbandman's Guide 5
Hussey, Obed 11
Hutchins, Levi 216
Hutchinson, Anne 182
Hutchinson, Joseph C. 111
Hutin, Francisquy 75
Hyatt, John W. 127, 228
Hyde, D. 134
hydroelectric power 68
Hyer, Jack 230
Hyer, Tom 230
hymnody 154
hysterectomies 111

ice cream 91, 95
ice hockey 236
ice skating 223, 238
Illinois Wesleyan University 53
Illustrated Floral Magazine 13
illustration 15
Improve Mercantile Agency 28
"In God We Trust" 29
In Mizzoura 83
incandescent lamps 66
income taxes 38
incubator 108
Index to Periodical Literature 58
indigo 7
Industrial Schools 56
Infant School Society 60
Ingersoll, Charles 34
Ingersoll, Robert H. 34
inks 135
Inness, George 16
inoculations 104
Institute of Accountants and Bookkeepers 22
Institute of Accounts 22
insurance 31
internal combustion engine tractors 12
International Business Machine Company 27
International Children's Welfare Congress 219

International Foundation 110
International Harvester Company 11
International Institute of Agriculture 9
iron 131, 132, 133, 138
iron lungs 103
Irving, Washington 83, 168
Ives, Charles E. 153
Ives, Frederic E. 18
Ives, Herbert E. 44
Ives, James M. 15

J.P. Morgan Co. 24
J. Walter Thompson Company 23
jackhammers 144
Jackling, Daniel S. 140
Jackson, Abraham R. 102
Jackson, Andrew 20, 36
Jackson, Charles T. 97
Jackson, James 104
Jackson, Mahalia 154
Jackson, P.H. 211
Jackson, Sheldon 195
Jackson, William H. 18
Jacobi, Abraham 107
James, William 205
Janney, Eli H. 265
Jannings, Emil 81
Jansky, Karl G. 200
Jay, John 24
Jay Morris Concert and Olio Company 86
jazz 156, 157
The Jazz Singer 79
Jefferson, Joseph 83
Jefferson, Thomas 24, 122, 195, 210
Jeffries, Jim 240
Jenkins, Charles F. 44, 78
Jenks, Joseph 131, 140, 161
Jenney, William L. 211
Jerome, Chauncey 216
Jervis, John B. 263
Johns Hopkins Hospital 53
Johns Hopkins Medical School 101
Johns Hopkins University 53
Johnson, Ban (Byron B.) 225
Johnson, Edward 166

Johnson, Howard D. 95
Johnson, John E. 173
Johnson, Marmaduke 180
Johnson, Melvin M. 126
Johnson, Robert W. 109
Johnson, Samuel 52
Johnson, Samuel W. 4
Johnson, Tom L. 270
Johnston, James 175
Johnston, Lawrence 253
Jolson, Al 79
Jones, Albert L. 142
Jones, Benjamin F. 133
Jones, Bobby (Robert T.) 235
Jones, Casey (John Luther) 267
Jones, Deming 130
Jones, Dorothy 88
Jones, Edward D. 178
Jones, George 177
Jones, John 103
Jones, Robert E. 85
Joplin, Scott 156
Journal of Experimental Medicine 103
Juan, Don 79
Judah, Theodore 265
Judd, Orange 4
Judson, Egbert P. 127
Judson, Whitcomb L. 129
Julian, Percy L. 108
June, Charles 239
junior colleges 54
Juvenile Library 57

Kaiser, Henry J. 133
Kalmus, Herbert T. 80
Kantrowitz, Adrian 112
Kaye, Nora 75
Kearsley, John 101, 104
Keen, William W. 112
Keimer, Samuel 174
Keith, Benjamin F. 86
Keith, Minor C. 93
Kelley, Oliver H. 5
Kellogg, Will K. 90
Kelly, Howard A. 114
Kelly, William 132
Kemble, Gouverneur 125
Kendall, Amos 36, 54
Kendall, Edward C. 108, 113
Kennedy, Henry P. 215
Kenrick, William 9
Kensett, Thomas 93

Kent, James 122
Kent, Rockwell 15
Kepley, Ada H. 123
Kern, Jerome D. 160
kerosene 72
Kettering, Charles F. 248
Kettle, James 142
kewpie dolls 76
Keystone Company 79
Keystone Kops 79
kidney transplant 111
Kier, Samuel M. 71
Killen, Jacob A. 175
Kimball, Ernest 95
kindergartens 218
Kinematoscope 78
Kinetograph cameras 78, 79
Kinetoscope viewers 78
King, Billie Jean 242
King, Charles Brady 139
King, Charles G. 115
King, John 175
King, Richard 6
King's College 52
Kingsley, Elizabeth S. 76
Kinsey, Alfred C. 111
Kinsley, Apollo 244
Kittinger, Joe 256
Klieg lights 68
Kliegl, Anton T. 68
Kliegl, John H. 68
K-Mart 37
Knabe, Valentine W.L. 155
Knapp, Henry 39
Knapp, Seaman A. 5, 7
Knight, Arthur F. 234
knotters 11
Knowlton, Charles 105
Kodachrome 19
Kodak, Eastman 18, 28
Kohlmann, Anthony 185
Koller, Carl 97
Koussevitzky, Serge 153
Kreisler, Fritz 153
Kresge, S(ebastian) S. 37
Kress, Samuel H. 37
Krimmel, John L. 17
Kroc, Ray A. 95
Krupa, Gene 157
Kuiper, Gerard P. 200
Kuznets, Simon 30
Kyrides, Lucas P. 143

labor unions 117

laboratories 102
lacrosse 237, 238
Laemmle, Carl 80
LaFarge, John 16
Lake, Simon 149
Lallement, Pierre 256
Lambert, Albert B. 147
Lambert, John W. 244
Land, Edwin H. 19
Landis, Kenesaw M. 226
Landis, Merkel 25
Landon, Alf 221
Landreth, David 13
landscape painting 16
Landsteiner, Karl 98
Lane, John 10
Langdell, Christopher C. 122
Lange, Dorothea 18
Langley, Samuel P. 200, 250
Langmuir, Irving 203
Langstroth, Lorenzo L. 93
Lanston, Tolbert 181
Larned, Joseph G. 161
Larned, William A. 242
Larsen, Don 226
Lasky, Jesse L. 80
Lasky Feature Play Company 80
Lath, Julia C. 120
Latin Grammar School 49
Latrobe, Benjamin H. 210
Latrobe, John H.B. 212
Latta, Alexander B. 161
Laurent, Robert 20
law 121
Lawler, Richard H. 111
Lawlor, John 235
Lawrence, Abbott 145
Lawrence, Amos 145
Lawrence, Ernest O. 70
Lawrence, William 145
Lawson, Ernest 16
Lawson, Harry J. 256
Lazear, Jesse W. 113
lead 140, 141
Lear, William P. 252
Leason, George 145
leather 133, 134
Ledbetter, Huddie 159
Lee, Ann 193, 196
Lee, Ivy L. 36
Lee, James P. 234
Lee, Robert E. 20

Lee, Wellington 161
Leeds, Daniel 172
Leeser, Isaac 188
Legal Aid Society 121
Leigh, Douglas 23
Leiper, Thomas 266
Leiter, Levi Z. 35
Leland, Henry M. 247
LeMayeur, Joseph 98
Lemuel Shaw 122
Lenox, James 57
Lenz, Sidney 77
Leonard, Harry W. 66
Leslie, Eliza 90
Leslie, Frank 179
Levine, Philip 98
Levingstone, William 83
Lewis, Floyd J. 111
Lewis, Isaac N. 126
Lewis, John L. 118
Lexington School 55
Leyner, John G. 144
Libby, Willard F. 203
libraries 57
Library Journal 58
Library of Congress 57
license plates 249
Lichtenstein, Roy 17
The Life of an American Fireman 79
life preservers 274
Liggett, Louis K. 37
lighthouses 274
Ligowsky, George 243
Lilienthal, David E. 70
Lilienthal, Otto 251
Lincoln, Abraham 23, 46, 84
Lincoln University 53
Lind, Samuel C. 203
Lindbergh, Charles A. 252
Lindsey, Ben(jamin B.) 123
line photo-engravings 18
linoleum 217
Lippincott, Joshua B. 169
liquors 89
Little, Arthur D. 128, 146
Little, Charles C. 169
liver transplants 111
Livermore, Mary A.R. 222
Livingston, Robert R. 272
lobotomies 111
locks 129

Lockwood, Belva A.B. 122
Loeb, Robert F. 113
Loew, Marcus 80
Loewy, Raymond F. 14
lollipops 90
Lombardo, Guy 159
Long, Crawford W. 97
Longfellow, Henry
  Wadsworth 169
Longworth, Nicholas 9,
  88
Loomis, Mahlon 99
Lorimer, George H. 172
Loring, Edward G. 106
lotteries 33
Loud, John J. 134
Louis, Joe 230
Lovell, Joseph 148
Low, Juliette G. 220
Lowell, Francis C. 145
Lowell, Percival 200
Lubin, David 9
lubricators 138
Lucas, Eliza 7
Luks, George B. 16
lumber 21, 134
lung transplants 111
Lyon, James 157
Lyon, Mary M. 63

"Ma" (Gertrude M.)
  Rainey 157
MacDowell, Edward A.
  152
Macfadden, Bernarr A. 95
machinery 136
Mack, Joseph S. 247
Mackay, John W. 45
Mackaye, (James M.)
  Steele 85
Maclure, William 203
Macy, Rowland H. 35
magazines 170, 171, 172,
  173, 178, 220
mah-jongg 76
mail order 34
mail order seed business
  13
mail service 163
Majors, Alexander 260
Makemie, Francis 194
Mallibran, Maria 158
malted milk 88
Manhattan Project 71
Mann, Horace 53, 55
Mannes, Leopold 19

Mansfield, Richard 84
manufacturing 124
Mapes, James J. 12
marathons 242
marble 144
Marciano, Rocky 230
Marin, John C. 16
Marine Corps 148
Maris, Roger 227
Marsh, Charles W. 11
Marsh, Sylvester 267
Marshall, Humphry 201
Marshall, John 122
Marshall, John W. 140
Marshall Field and Com-
  pany 35
Martin, Glenn L. 252
Martin, Truman J. 32
Martin, William 228
Maryland Agricultural
  College 4
Mason, Charles 203
Mason, Henry 155
Mason, John M. 186
Mason, Lowell 154
matches 162
Mather, Cotton 104, 166,
  167, 186
Mather, Increase 185, 186
Mather, Richard 166, 185
Mathiesen, Frederick W.
  141
Matteson, E.E. 141
Matthews, John 88
Matthews, Thomas 77
Matzeliger, Jan E. 41
Mauchly, John W. 28
Maury, Matthew F. 262
Maxim, Hiram S. 126,
  127
Maxim, Hudson 127
Maxwell, William 176
Mayer, Louis B. 80
Mayhew, Jonathan 196
Maynard, Edward 126
Maywood, Augusta 75
McAfee, Mildred H. 149
McBurney, Charles 112
McCallum, Daniel C. 258
McCandless, Bruce, II
  207
McCay, Winsor 73
McCloskey, John 185
McClure, Samuel S. 173
McCollum, Elmer V. 115
McCormick, Cyrus H. 11

McCormick, Robert 10
McCormick, Stephen 10
McCoy, Elijah 138
McCreary, Joseph 213
McCrory, J.J. 37
McCullough, W.T. 249
McDermott, John J. 242
McDonald's 95
McDougall, Alexander
  273
McDowell, Ephraim 111
McElwain, William H. 41
McGaffey, Ives W. 214
McGready, James 195
McGuffey, William H. 62
McGwire, Mark 227
McKay, Donald 272
McKay, Gordon 41
McManus, George 171
McMillin, Edwin M. 70
McRae, Milton R. 178
McTammany, John 155
Mead, George H. 206
Mead, Margaret 198
Meany, George 118
meat 94
The Medical Repository
  102
Medical Society of Massa-
  chusetts 106
Medill, Joseph 178
Meeker, Moses 141
Mellon, Andrew S. 15
Melville, Bell, 46
Melville, David 69, 136
Menchey, Charles S. 91
Mendel, Lafayette B. 116
Mendez, Antonio 95
Menke, Ben 82
Menke, Bill 82
Menke, Charlie 82
Menke, Harry 82
Menninger, Charles F. 110
Menninger, Karl A. 110
Menninger, William C.
  110
Menninger Foundation
  110
Mercantile Agency 28
The Merchant of Venice
  82
Merchants' Vigilance
  Association 29
mercury vapor lamps 68
Mergenthaler, Ottmar 181
Merriam, Dan 169

Merriam, Ebenezer 169
Merriam, George 169
Merritt, Leonidas 133
Metamora 83
Metcalfe, Betsey 39
Metro-Goldwyn-Mayer
80
Metropolitan 39
Meyenberg, John B. 91
Meyer, Adolf 110
Michaux, Pierre 256
Michelson, Albert A. 204
Michigan Agricultural
College 4
Michigan State University
4
Mickey Mouse 74
microphones 160
microscopes 198
Middlebury Seminary 63
Middlesex Canal 259
Middlesex County Associ-
ation 50
Middleton, Peter 100
Midwest Institute 30
Mielziner, Jo 85
Milestone, Lewis 81
military schools 58
milk 9, 91
Miller, Ezra 265
Miller, Glenn 159
Miller, Lewis 50
Miller, Samuel 175
Miller, W.P. 11
Miller, William 192
Millikan, Robert A. 204
Mills, Anson 126
Mills, Clark 20
Mills, John H. 213
Mills, Robert 210
Milton Bradley and Com-
pany 76
mimeograph machines
28
Mingus, Charley 157
ministry 186
Minnes, Thomas S. 11
minstrel shows 77, 159
Miske, Billy 240
Mitchell, Maria 200
Mitchell, Samuel A. 204
Mitchell, Wesley C. 30
Mitchill, Samuel L. 4
Moana 80
mobile phones 48
mobiles 20

modern dances 75
Moller and Capron 157
money orders 165
Monk, Thelonius 157
Monroe, James 24
Monroe, Jay R. 27
Monroe, William 134
Monroe Calculating
Machine Co. 27
Montague, Hannah L.
40
Montague, Orlando 40
Montgomery Ward 34
Moody, Dwight L. 183
Moody, Helen Wills 242
Moody, John 25
Moody, Paul 146
*Moody's Analysis of Invest-
ments* 25
Moody's Magazine 25
*Moody's Manual of Rail-
roads and Corporation
Securities* 25
Moore, Clement C. 167
Moore, Richard B. 203
Moore, Thomas 213
Moor's Charity School 52
Morey, Samuel 136
Morgan, John 100
Morgan, J(ohn) P. 24
Morgan, Junius S. 24
Morgan, Lewis H. 198
Mork, Harry S. 146
Morphy, Paul 77
Morris, Anthony 87
Morris, Esther H. 122
Morris, Gouverneur 29
Morris, Lewis 243
Morris, Robert 24, 29
Morse, C.W. 125
Morse, Jedidiah 62, 203
Morse, Samuel F.B. 17,
45, 46
mortality tables 33
Morton, Jelly Roll (Ferdi-
nand) 156
Morton, William T.G. 97,
99
Moss, John C. 181
Moten, Benny 156
Mother Alphonsa 114
motion picture cameras
19
motion pictures 18, 62
motorcycles 251, 256, 257
Mott, Lucretia C. 221

Mount Holyoke Female
Seminary 63
Mt. Rushmore 20
Mt. Vernon School 63
movies 78
Mowbray, George M. 127
*A Muck Manual for Farm-
ers* 5
Muench, Carl G. 211
Muhlenberg, Heinrich
(Henry) M. 188
Mullanphy, Bryan 220
Munro, George 170
Munsey, Frank A. 173
murals 16
Murdoch, Frank 83
Murray, John 193
Murray, Lindley 62
Murray, Philip 118
museums 15, 59
music 151, 159
musical instruments 154
Muybridge, Eadweard 18,
78
"My Days Have Been
Wondrous Free" 151

N.W. Ayer and Sons Inc.
22
Nadig, Henry 244
Naismith, James 227
Nanook of the North 80
NASA (National Aeronau-
tics and Space Admin-
istration) 206
Nast, Thomas 170
Nathan, George Jean 85
National Academy of Sci-
ences 50
National Association of
Base Ball Players 225
National Birth Control
League 106
National Broadcasting
Company 44
National Bureau of Eco-
nomic Research 30
National Cash Register
Co. 26, 27
National Commission 110
National Congress of
Mothers 50
National Congress of Par-
ents and Teachers 50
National Deaf Mute Col-
lege 54

National Education Asso-
ciation 61
National Football League
233
National Grange of the
Patrons of Husbandry
5
National Hockey League
236
National Manufacturing
Co. 26
National Monetary Com-
mission 24
National Prohibition
Party 89
National Teachers Associ-
ation 61
National Women's Christ-
ian Temperance Union
89
natural gas 69
nautilus 149
navigation 262
Navratilova, Martina 242
Navy 148
Navy Nurses Corps 149
Neale, Thomas 163
Nelson, Christine K. 91
Nelson, Philip 54
neon tube advertising
signs 23
Neumann, John N. 185
neurosurgery 112
*New American Practical
Navigator* 262
*A New and Complete Sys-
tem of Arithmetic* 62
*New Dictionary of Medical
Science and Literature*
103
New England Asylum 55
The New England Farmer
5
New England Medical
College 101
New England Primer 61
*The New England Psalm
Singer* 154
*A New Guide to the
English Tongue* 62
The New Sensation 82
New York Academy of
Science 50
New York Association for
Improving the Condi-
tion of the Poor 218

New York Children's Aid
Society 219
New York City Normal
College 53
New York Clearing House
24
New York College of Den-
tistry 100
New York Cooking School
90
New York Eye Infirmary
102, 106
New York Fishing Co. 21
New York Historical Soci-
ety 15
New York Institute for the
Blind 55
New York Institution for
the Deaf 55
New York Knickerbockers
225
New York Life Insurance
and Trust Co. 32
New York Palace Theater
86
New York Prices Current
21
New York Public Library
57
New York State Agricul-
tural College at Cornell
4
New York State College of
Forestry 12
New York State Library
58
New York Stock Exchange
30
Newbold, Charles 10
Newcomb, Simon 200
Newcomen, Thomas 136
Newhouse, Samuel I. 178
Newman, Barnett 17
Newman, Larry 256
newspapers 173, 174, 175,
177, 178, 179, 180, 220,
222
Nicholson, William T.
136
nickel 141
nickelodeon 79, 80
Nicklaus, Jack 235
Niedringhaus, Frederick
G. 215
Nier, Alfred 70
Nijinsky, Vaslav 75

Nikolais, Alvin 75
Nitschmann, David 192
Nordica, Lillian 158
Normal and Industrial
Institute for Negro
Girls 64
Normand, Mabel 79
North, Elisha 104
North, Simeon 126
Northrop, John K. 252
Norton, George 239
Norton, John 215
Norwich University 58
Nova, Lou 240
novocain 97
Noyes, LaVerne 138
nuclear fission 70
nuclear power 70
Nuclear Regulatory Com-
mission 70
nursing 104, 105
Nuthead, William 180
Nutt, Emma B. 48
Nutting, Mary A. 105

oatmeal 90
Oberlin (Ohio) Collegiate
Institute 53
observatories 199, 200
obstetrics 105
oceanography 263
Ochs, Adolph S. 177
O'Connor, Sandra Day
123
Office of the Comptroller
of the Currency 23
Ogle, Henry 10
Ohio Institution for the
Blind 55
Ohio School of the Air 62
oil wells 71
The Old Farmers Almanac
172
Oldenburg, Claes 20
Oldfield, Barney (Berna
E.) 248
Olds, Ransom E. 245
oleomargarine 91
Oliver, James 10
Oliver, King (Joe) 156
Oliver, Paul A. 127
Oliver Co. 11
O'Neill, Rose C. 76
opalescent glass 16
opera 158
ophthalmology 106

ophthalmoscopes 106
Opie, Eugene L. 114
Oram, James 21
Ormandy, Eugene 153
Orpheum Circuit 86
orthodontia 99
Ory, Kid (Edward) 156
Osborne, Thomas B. 116
Oscars 81
Osgood, Samuel 163
Osler, William 103
Osteopathy 107
Osterheld, George 39
O'Sullivan, Humphrey 41, 144
Otis, Bass 181
Otis, Elish G. 212
Otis, Harrison G. 178
Otis, William G. 139
Ott, Fred 78
Otterbein, Philip W. 193
Out of the Inkwell 74
Outcault, Richard F. 170
Outerbridge, A. Emilius 241
Outerbridge, Mary E. 241
ovariotomy 111
Ovington, Earle L. 164
Owen, Marie 163
Owens, Jesse 243
Owens, Michael J. 131
Oxford Provident Building Association 24
Oxnard, Thomas 196

Packard, James W. 247
Packard, William D. 247
paddlewheel boats 272
Paine, John K. 154
Paine, Thomas 167, 169, 180
paint 216
painting 15
Palmer, Arnold 235
Palmer, Austin N. 56
Palmer, Charles S. 72
Palmer, Daniel David 107
Palmer, Potter 35
Palmer, Timothy 257
Palmer, Volney B. 22
Pangborn, Clyde 253
pants 40
Papanicolaou, George F. 114
paper 141, 142
paper bags 142

Paraf, Alfred 91
paralysis 114
parapsychology 205
A Parisian Romance 84
Park, Jesse K. 135
Park, Robert A. 206
Park, William A. 115
Parker, Charles W. 73
Parker, Charlie "Bird" 157
Parker, Francis W. 55
Parker, Joseph 135
Parmelee, DuBois D. 27
Parmelee, Henry S. 162
Parmly, Eleazar 98
Parr, C.H. 11
Parr, Samuel W. 202
Parrott, Robert P. 125
Parsons, Louella 81
Pastor, Tony (Antonio) 86
Patapsco Female Institute 63
patent leather 41
Patterson, John H. 26
Paul, Alice 222
Pavlova, Anna 75
Peabody, Elizabeth P. 60
Peale, Charles Willson 16, 17, 59
Peale, Rembrandt 69
Pearl, Raymond 111
Pearson, John 145
Pearson, Theodore 92
Pease, Daniel 201
Pease, W.H. 8
pediatrics 107
Pegram, George B. 70
Pelham, Peter 16, 151
pellagra 115
pencils 134
Pendleton, Edmund M. 12
penmanship 56
Penn, William 30, 87, 166
Penn State University 4, 12
Penney, J(ames) C. 34
Pennsylvania Academy of Fine Arts 14
Pennsylvania Agricultural College 4
Pennsylvania Company for Insurance on Life and Granting Annuities 31

Pennsylvania Hospital 104
Pennsylvania Rock Oil Company 71
Percy, Samuel K. 91
Perkins, George W. 33
Perkins, Jacob 128
Perkins Institution 55
Perky, Henry 90
Perrine, Henry 93
Perry, Stuart 137
Perry, William 168
Peter, Pelham, 15
petroleum 71, 72
Pfizer, Charles 109
pharmaceuticals 108, 109
Phasmatrope 78
Phelan, Michael 228
Phelps, Almira H.L. 63
Philadelphia Arcade 37
Philadelphia Dispensary 100
Philadelphia Medical Institute 100
Philadelphia Society for the Promotion of Agriculture 3
The Philadelphia Spelling Book 169
Phillippe, Don 93
Phillips, Alonzo D. 162
phonetic writers 26
Phonofilm 79
phonographs 160
photo-collotype process 18
photo journalists 18
photoelectric cells 69
Photographic Art Journal 19
photographic plates 18
photography 17
photostat 28
Phyfe, Duncan 215
The Physical Geography of the Sea and Its Meteorology 263
Physick, Philip S. 104
physics 204
physiology 109
Piccard, Jean Felix 256
Pickering, Edward C. 18, 200
Pickford, Mary 79
Pierce, William 171
Pierson, Abraham 52

Pierson, Josiah G. 128
Pike, Nicholas 62
Pillars of Fire 75
Pillsbury, Charles A. 92
pinball machines 76
Pinchot, Gifford 12, 13
Pinkerton, Allen 162
Pinkham, Lydia E. 109
Pitcairn, Harold F. 255
Pitts, Hiram A. 11
Pitts, John 11
Placide, Alexander 75
Plain … Remarks on the Treatment of Wounds and Fractures 103
Planned Parenthood Foundation 106
plant food 12
plastics 142
playgrounds 219
Playwright's Theater 85
Plimpton, James L. 239
Plotz, Harry 108
The Plough Boy 5
plows 10, 11
Plumbe, John 17
Plumbeotype 17
Pluto 74
plywood 212
Pocahontas 8
Poe, Edgar Allan 168
poetry 168
poets 169
polarized filters 19
polarized sunglasses 19
Polaroid cameras 19
police 162, 163
polio 113
Pollock, Jackson 17
polls 221
polo 238
Poole, William F. 58
Poor Richard's Almanac 172
pop art 17
pop sculpture 20
popcorn 90
Pope, Albert A. 256
Popeye 74
Porter, Abel 129
Porter, Edwin S. 79
portrait artists 16
portraiture 15
Post, Charles W. 88, 90
Post, Wiley 253
post service 165

Postal Savings Bank 25
Postal Service 164
Postal Telegraph 45
postcards 135, 165
Postum 88, 90
pottery 142
Potts, Albert 164
Pottsville (Pennsylvania) Miner's Journal 22
Powderly, Terence V. 117
The Power of Sympathy 167
Prang, Louis 135
Pratt, Charles 56
Pratt, Francis A. 138
Pratt, John 26
Pratt, Matthew 15
Pratt Institution 57
praxiscopes 18, 78
Prendergast, Maurice B. 16
Price, Edwin A. 82
Pride, John 142
Prince, William 13
The Prince of Parthia 83
Princeton 14, 52
The Principles and Practice of Medicine 103
Principles of Political Economy 29
Printer's Ink 22
printing 26, 174, 179, 180
printing presses 180
prohibition 89
promotion 36
Provident Hospital 102
Provident Institution for Savings 24
Provincetown Players 85
Prudden, Theophil Mitchell 108
Prudential Insurance Company 32
psychoanalysis 110
psychology 110, 205, 206
ptereotypes 26
publishing 169, 170
Puett, Clay 237
Pulitzer, Joseph 177
Pullman, George M. 266
Pupin, Michael I. 46, 103
puppetry 81
Pursh, Frederick 201
Pusey, Joshua 162
Putnam, Frederic W. 59
Putnam, George P. 170

Putnam, Herbert 58
Pynchon, William 94

quadruplex telegraphy 66
Quarterly Journal of Economics 21
Quinby, Harriet 254

R.G. Dun & Co. 29
racquetball 238
Radcliffe College 63
radio 42, 43, 62
railroads 263, 264, 265, 266, 267, 268
Railton, George S. 220
Rains, Gabriel J. 127
Rand, Remington 28
Randolph, Benjamin 214
Rauschenberg, Robert 17
Rawlins, Horace 234
Raymond, Henry J. 177
Raymond, William 273
Read, Nathan 244, 271
reapers 10, 11
Reber, Grote 201
Redfield, William C. 120
Reed, Ezekiel 128
Reed, Jesse 128
Reed, Luman 15
Reed, Walter 113
refineries 71
refrigerator cars 266
refrigerators 213
regenerative or feedback circuits 43
registered mail 165
religion 182, 197
religious freedom 195
The Religious Remembrancer 195
Remington, Eliphalet 125
Remington, Frederic 17
Remington, William H. 141
Remington Arms Co. 27
Remsen, Ira 108, 109, 202
Reno, Jesse W. 212
Renwick, James 212
respirators 103
restaurants 95
retirement 120
Reuther, Walter P. 118
Revere, Paul 140
Reynolds, Edwin 137
Rhine, Joseph B. 205
rice 7

Rice, Richard H. 133
Rice, Thomas D. 77
Rich, Richard 166
Richards, Charles B. 138
Richards, Dickinson W. 115
Richmond, Bill 230
Richmond, James M. 130
Rickard, Tex (George L.) 230
Rickes, Edward L. 116
Ricketts, John Bill 74
Rickey, Branch W. 226
Rickover, Hyman G. 149
Rieger, Wallingford 156
Riggs, John M. 99
Rillieux, Norbert 96
Ringling, Albert 74
Ringling, Otto 74
Ringling Bros. and Barnum and Bailey Circus 75
Ripken, Cal, Jr. 227
Ripley, Robert L. 171
Rittenhouse, David 199
Rittenhouse, William 141, 192
Ritty, John 26
Rivers, Thomas M. 111, 113
Roach, John 273
road maps 262
road signs 262
Robbins, Frederick C. 113
Robbins, Jerome 75
Robbins, Mrs. Sheldon (Betty) 197
The Robe 81
Roberts, Robert J. 235
Robinson, Bill 76
Robinson, Edwin Arlington 169
Robinson, Jackie 226
Robinson, William 266
Rockefeller, John D. 71
Rockefeller, John D., Sr. 36
Rockne, Knute 233
Rockwell, Norman 15
rodeo 240
Rodgers, John K. 106
Rodgers, Richard 160
Roebling, John A. 258
Roebling, Washington A. 258
Roebuck, Alvah C. 34

Roebuck, Sears 34
Rogers, Calbraith P. 253
Rogers, Harriet B. 55
Rogers, Henry H. 72
Rolfe, John 8
roller skating 239
rolling machines 8
Rollins, Sonny 157
Rollo 63
Romberg, Sigmund 160
Ronemus, William 219
Roosevelt, Franklin D. 25, 227
Roosevelt, Hilborne L. 155
Roosevelt, Theodore 76
Root, Amos I. 94
rope 146
Roper, Sylvester H. 244
Rorer, Sara Tyson 90
Rose, Rufus 81
Roswell Park 114
Rotch, Thomas M. 107
Rothko, Mark 17
Roulstone, George 176
rowboat 273
Rowell, George P. 22
Rowlandson, Mary W. 166
Rowson, Susanna H. 167
Rozelle, Pete (Alvin R.) 233
rubber 143
rubber shoes 143
Rubinstein, Arthur 153
Ruffin, Edmund 12
Rugg, Micah 129
rugs 217
rum 87
Ruml, Beardsley 38
Rumsey, James 271
Rush, Benjamin 100, 110, 202
Rush, William 19
Russ, John D. 55
Russell, Charles Taze 194
Russworm, John B. 179
Ruth, Babe (George H.) 227
Rutherford, Lewis M. 200
Rutman, Dick 253
rye 6

S & H (green) stamps 29
S. Wolcott, Alexander 18
Sabin, Albert B. 113

safe deposit vaults 25
sailboats 271
St. Ann's Church for Deaf Mutes 54
St. Denis, Ruth 75
St. Denis, Shawn 75
St. Joseph's House of Hospitality 219
St. Martha Turpin 184
sales taxes 38
Salk, Jonas A. 113
Salvation Army 220
Sanger, Margaret 105
Santee Canal 259
Saranac Laboratory 115
Sarazen, Gene 235
Sarg, Tony (Anthony F.) 81
Sargent, Franklin W. 85
Sargent, James 129
Sarnoff, David 43
satellites 207
Satterlee, Francis L. 103
Saturday Evening Post 15
Savery, William 214
sawmills 134
saws 136
Saxton, Joseph 144
Saylor, David O. 211
scales 144
Schechter, Solomon 188
Scherman, Harry 170
Schick, Bela 114
Schirmer, Gustav 157
Schloemer, Gottfried 244
Schmucker, Samuel S. 188
Scholfield, Arthur 146
Scholfield, John 146
Scholz, Roy P. 112
Schönberg, Arnold 153
Schrieffer, John R. 204
Schumacher, Ferdinand 90
Schuman, Frank 131
Schurz, Mrs. Carl 60
Schuyler, John 136
Schwab, Charles M. 133
science 198
Scopes, John T. 49
Scott, Blanche S. 254
Scott, Walter 95
Scribner, Charles 170
Scripps, Edward W. 178, 179
Scripps, Robert P. 178

Scull, John 175
sculptures 19, 20
Seaborg, Glenn T. 70, 203
Seabury, George J. 109
Seabury, Samuel 187
Seaman, Valentine 104
Sears, Fred 241
Sears, Richard D. 241
Sears, Richard W. 34
Second Bank 23
seed catalog 13
seed drills 11
seedlings 13
Seeger, Pete 159
Seeing Eye Dogs 55
Seeley, Henry W. 68, 213
Seereiter, John 228
Segar, Elzie C. 171
Seixas, Gershom M. 188
Selden, George B. 246
Selective Service 150
Selfridge, Thomas E. 254
Sellers, Coleman 78
Sennett, Mack 79
Seton, Elizabeth Ann 196, 219
Seven Songs for the Harp-sichord 151
sewage systems 165
Sewall, Samuel 167, 257
sewing machines 214
Seybert, Adam 216
Shallenberger, Oliver B. 68
Shapley, Harlow 200
Sharkey, Tom 240
Sharon Medical Society 106
Sharpe, Lucien 138
Shaw, Anna Howard 222
Shaw, Louis A. 103
Shawn, Ted 75
Shepard, Alan B., Jr. 206
Sherman, John A. 135
Shewing the Evil Tendency of the Use of Tobacco 8
Shibe, Benjamin F. 227
Shinn, Everett 16
Shippen, William 100, 104
ships 271
shirts 40, 41
Shockley, William B. 204
shoe stitching machines 41
shoes 41

Sholes, Christopher L. 26
Short, Thomas 180
shorthand 56
shovels 136
showboats 82
shuffleboard 238
Sibley, Hiram 45
Sicard, Stephen 75
Sidebotham, Thomas 24
signboards 15
Sikorsky, Igor I. 255
silk 146
Silliman, Benjamin 88, 202
Silly Symphonies 74
silver 140
Silverman, Sime 85
Simmons, Amelia 90
Simpson, George B. 68
Sims, James M. 102, 112
Singer, Isaac M. 214
skeet shooting 243
ski jumping 239
skiing 239
skimobiles 239
Skinner, Halcyon 217
Skinner, John S. 5
Skinner, R.C. 99
slapstick comedy 79
Slater, Hannah Wilkinson 146
Slater, Samuel 144, 145, 146
Slayter, (Russell) Games 211
sleeping cars 266
Slipher, Vesto M. 200
Sloan, Alfred P. 245
Sloan, John F. 16
Sloat, Jacob 146
Slocum, Samuel 129
Small, Albion W. 205
Smeedes, Jan 130
Smibert, John 15, 16
Smith, Bessie 157
Smith, Charles S. 258
Smith, Elizabeth Oakes 221
Smith, Francis M. 141
Smith, George 228
Smith, Hamilton E. 213
Smith, Hamilton L. 18
Smith, Horace 126
Smith, Hyrum 191
Smith, Capt. John 166
Smith, Joseph 190

Smith, Joseph, II 191
Smith, Owen P. 231
Smith, Samuel F. 154
Smithsonian Institution 67
Snelling, Henry H. 19
Snow White and the Seven Dwarfs 74
Snowden, John 257
Snyder, Howard 213
soccer 232, 239, 240
Society for the Relief of Poor Widows with Small Children 219
sociology 205
soft drinks 88
softball 240
Soliel, J.F. 18
sororities 54
Soule, Samuel W. 27
Sousa, John Philip 151
Sower, Christopher 180
space 206
Spalding, Lyman 103
Spalding's Official Baseball Guide 225
Spangenberg, Augustus G. 192
Spassky, Boris 77
Spaulding, Solomon 191
special delivery 165
spectroheliographs 199
speed skating 239
Spencer, Charles A. 198
Spencer, Christopher M. 125
Spencer, Dolly 163
Spencer, Platt R. 56
Sperry, Elmer A. 253
Sperry, Thomas H. 29
Sperry Hutchinson Co. 29
Spiegler, Caesar 256
Spock, Benjamin N. 107, 108
Spooner, J.B. 177
sports broadcasts 240
sports television 240
Sprague, Frank J. 270
Sprague, William B. 217
Spreckels, Claus 96
sprinkler systems 162
squash 241
The Squaw Man 80
Squibb, Edward R. 109
Staff, Charles 83

Staff, Mary 83
Stafford, John 55
Stagg, Amos Alonzo 233
stamps 164
Standard Oil Company of Ohio 71
Stanford, Leland 78, 265
Stanley, Francis E. 247
Stanley, Freelan 247
Stanley, William 69
Stanley Steamer 247
Stanton, Elizabeth Cady 221
Stanwood, I. Augustus 142
Starzl, Thomas E. 111
Statler, Ellsworth M. 31
steam calliopes 74
steam engines 136
steam tractors 11
Steamboat Willie 74
steamships 271, 272, 273, 274
Stedman, John H. 270
steel 132, 133
steel plows 10
steeplechase 236
Steffens, Lincoln 173
Steichen, Edward 18
Steinmetz, Charles P. 67
Steinway, Henry E. 155
Stephens, Anne S. 170
Stetson, John B. 40
Stevens, Edwin A. 243
Stevens, John 92, 264
Stevens, John C. 243
Stevens, Robert L. 264
Stevens, Uriah S. 117
Stewart, Alexander T. 35
Stieff, Richard 76
Stiegel, Henry W. 130
Stieglitz, Alfred 18
Stiles, Charles W. 111
Still, Andrew T. 107
Stillson, Daniel C. 136
Stoddard, Joshua C. 74, 156
Stoddert, Benjamin 149
Stokes, Benjamin M. 176
Stolli, Francisco 185
stone 144
Stone, Barton W. 193
Stone, John 139
Stone, John A. 83
Stone, Lucy Blackwell 222
Storer, Horatio R. 105

Story, Joseph 122
Stoughton, Israel 257
Stout, Elihu 175
Stout, William B. 252
Stover, Charles B. 219
stoves 212
Stowe, Calvin E. 61
Stowe, Harriet Beecher 61
Stowell, Abel 128
Straus, Isidor 35
Straus, Lazarus 35
Straus, Nathan 35
Straus, Oscar 35
Strauss, Levi 40
strawberries 9
Strawbridge, Philip Embury. 189
Strawbridge, Robert 189
street car transfers 270
street cars 269, 270
street lights 69
Strong, Thomas W. 135
Strowger, Almon B. 47
Stuart, Gilbert C. 16, 17
Stubblefield, Nathan B. 42
Studebaker, Clement 247
Sturdevant, Benjamin F. 139
Stutz, Henry C. 247
Stuyvesant, Peter 161
submarines 272, 274
subways 270
sugar 7, 8, 9, 95, 96
sugar cane 7
sugar mill 7
Sugar Refineries Company 96
sulfur mining 72
Sullivan, Henry F. 241
Sullivan, John L. 230
sulphur 141
Sumner, William G. 205
Sunday, Billy (William A.) 183
Sundback, Gideon 129
superheterodyne circuits 43
super-regenerative circuits 43
surgery 104, 111, 112
suspenders 143
Sutherland, J.B. 266
Sutter, John A. 140
sutures 112
Swasey, Ambrose 138

Swift, Gustavus F. 94
swimming 241
Swinnerton, James G. 170
switchboards 48
Sylvis, William H. 117
symphony orchestras 152
synchrotron 70
Szent-Györgi, Albert 115
Szilard, Leo 70

Tabulating Machine Co. 27
tabulating machines 27
Taft, William 226
Taggart, William H. 99
Tagliabue, Giuseppe 207
Tainter, Charles S. 160
Takamine, Jokichi 108
Tambo and Bones 77
Tanneberger, David 155
Tanner, Henry S. 204
tap dancing 76
Tappan, Arthur 178
Tappan, Lewis 28
Tarbell, Ida M. 173
Taussig, Helen B. 107
taxicabs 262
Taylor, Charles F. 103
Taylor, Edward 168
Taylor, Frederick W. 139
Taylor, George 131
Taylor, J.F. 18
teacher training 61
Technicolor 80
teddy bears 76
Tekakwitha, Kateri 196
telegraphs 43, 45, 46, 67, 164
telephones 46, 48
telescopes 138, 199, 201
television receivers 43
televisions 43, 44, 45
temperance 89, 92
The Ten Commandments 80
Tennent, William 186
tennis 240, 241, 242
Terman, Lewis M. 205
terra cotta 212
Terry, Eli 216
Tesla, Nikola 67, 137
textbooks 61, 62
textiles 144, 145
Thayer, Frederick W. 227
theater 82
The Theater Guild 85

thermometers 207
Thomas, Augustus 83
Thomas, (C.F.) Theodore 152
Thomas, Evylyn 249
Thomas, Isaiah 169
Thomas, John H. 211
Thomas, Robert B. 172
Thomas, Seth 216
Thomas, Terry. 216
Thomas, William I. 206
Thompson, Eliza Trimble 89
Thompson, James Walter 23
Thompson, John 24, 266
Thompson, John T. 126
Thompson, Lydia 85
Thompson, Mary Harris 101
Thomson, Elihu 69, 139
Thomson, Robert W. 143
Thoreau, Henry David 168
Thorn, George W. 114
Thornton, Grant 13
Thornton, William 210
Thorpe, Jim (James F.) 233, 242
three-dimensional photographs 19
threshing machines 11
Thurber, Charles 26
Thurber, Captain J. 7
Thurman, John S. 214
Tibbett, Jonathan 93
Ticknor, William D. 169
Tiffany, Louis C. 130
Tilden, William T. 242
Tilghman, Benjamin C. 133, 142
Tillie's Punctured Romance 79
Tilyou, George C. 73
Timby, Theodore 126
timekeeping 216
Timken, Henry 248
Timothy, O'Sullivan, 18
tin 141
tintype cameras 18
tires 143
Titanic 43
Titcomb, Benjamin, Jr. 175
Toastmaster 68
tobacco 8

tobacco shredding machines 8
toilet paper 142
The Toll of the Sea 80
Tombaugh, Clyde 200
Toney, Fred 226
tools 136
Topliff, Samuel 179
Toscanini, Arturo 153
Tower, William 142
Townes, Charles H. 205
track and field events 240, 242, 243
tractors 11
traffic lanes 262
traffic signals 262
transatlantic cables 46
transformers 66, 67, 69
trapshooting 243
traveler's checks 25
Travelers Aid 220
Travelers Insurance Company 32
Treadwell, Daniel 139, 180
A Treatise on the Human Teeth 99
The Tree Doctor 13
tree planting 13
tree surgery 13
triode electron tubes 42
Troy Female Seminary 63
Trudeau, Edward L. 115
Trudeau Sanitarium 115
Truman, Harry S 44
Trumbull, Earl 257
tuberculosis 114, 115
tubular fluorescent lamps 69
Tucker, William E. 215
Tull, Jethro 11
tunnels 268, 269
Tunney, Gene 230
Turner, Aaron 74
turnpikes 261
Tuskegee Institute 64
Tuskegee University 5
twine-binders 11
Tyler, Royall 83
typewriters 26, 27
typographers 26

Underhill, Isaac 144
Underwood, John T. 27
Underwood, William 92
Union Grounds 225

United Drug Company 37
United Fruit Company 93
United Shoe Machinery Co. 41
U.S. Soccer Football Association 240
United States Pharmacopeia 103
United States Volleyball Association 243
UNIVAC 28
Universal Pictures 80
universities 51
University Extension Division 51
University of Chicago 53
University of Maryland 4
University of Pennsylvania 50, 52
University of Tennessee 53
University of Toronto 12
Urania; or a Choice Collection of Psalmes-Tunes, Anthems, and Hymns 157
Urey, Harold C. 203
Usher, Hezekiah 166, 169

vaccinations 107, 108, 113
vacuum cleaners 214
Vail, Alfred L. 45
valentines 135
Van Allen, James A. 205
Van Buren, Martin 119
Van Camp, Gilbert C. 92
Van Depoele, Charles J. 270
Vanderbilt, Cornelius 222
Vanderbilt, Harold S. 77
Vander Meer, Johnny 226
Varese, Edgard 153
Variety 85
Vassar, Matthew 56
Vassar College 56, 63
vaudeville 85, 86
Vaughn, Jim 226
vegetables 9
veterinary medicine 115
Victor Animatograph Co. 19
Viets, Simeon 8
Vignes, Jean Louis 88
Vincent, John H. 50
vineyards 9

Virginia Minstrels 77
visible speech 46
vitamin deficiency 115
vitamins 115, 116
Vitascope 78
Vogue 39
volleyball 243

Wagner, John 87
Wait, Thomas B. 176
Waite, Charles C. 227
Waksman, Selman A. 108
Wald, Lillian D. 105
Wales, Thomas C. 41, 144
Walgreen, Charles R. 37
Walker, Francis A. 30
Walker, William H. 146
Walker, Wirt D. 211
wall stencils 217
Wallack, James W. 84
wallpaper 217
Walthall, H.B. 79
Walther, Carl F.W. 188
Wanamaker, John 35, 68
Ward, Lester F. 205
Ward, Nathaniel 166, 167
Ware, Henry 186
Warner, Harry 79
Warner, Jack 79
Warner, Pop (Glenn S.) 233
Warner, Sylvia Townsend 170
Warner, Worcester R. 138
Warren, Edward 255
Warren, John C. 104
warships 273
washing machines 213
Washington, Booker T. 63, 64
Washington, George 3, 16, 19, 74, 91, 98, 148, 163, 164
watches 216
water 270, 273
water skiing 239
water systems 165
Waterhouse, Benjamin 8, 104
Waterman, Henry 212
Waterman, Leontief, Wassily W. 30
Waterman, Lewis E. 134
Watson, Cornelius S. 134, 135
Watson, Elkanah 4

Watson, James D. 201
Watson, John 113
Watson, John B. 205
Watson, Thomas A. 47
Watson, Thomas J. 27
Watts, James W. 111
Wayland, Francis 53
weapons 124, 125, 126, 127
weather 207
weather satellite 206
Webb, William H. 272
Webbe, John 172
Webber, Thomas 145
Webber College for Women 30
Webster, Noah 61, 168
Weed, Henry D. 248
Weems, Parson (Mason L.) 167
Weidman, Charles 75
Welch, William H. 102, 103
Weld, Thomas 166
Weldy, Henry 163
Weller, Thomas H. 113
Wells, Henry 249, 260
Wells, Horace 97, 99
Wells, John 175
Werwag, Louis 257
Wesley, John 190
Wesley, Newton K. 106
Wesleyan 63
Wesson, Daniel B. 126
West, Benjamin 17
Western Union 45
Westinghouse, George 68, 266
Westinghouse Electric Corporation 68
Weston, Edward 18, 69
Wetherill, Samuel 216
Wharton, Joseph 141
Wharton School of Finance and Commerce 50
wheat 6
Wheeler, Schuyler S. 68, 69
Wheeler, Seth 142
Wheelock, Eleazar 52
Whelan, Israel 32
whiskey 87
whist 76
Whistler, James A.B. 17
Whitaker, Alexander 166

White, Canvass 259
White, Edward H. 207
White, Joseph N. 228
White, Josiah 257
White, William 101, 187
White House Conference on Children 219
Whiteman, Paul 156
Whitman, Walt 169
Whitney, Amos 138
Whitney, Asa 266
Whitney, Eli 7, 124, 138, 144, 145
The Whole Booke of Psalmes 154
Widows and Orphans Friendly Society 32
Wiener, Alexander 98
Wigglesworth, Michael 166, 168
Wightman, Hazel H. 242
Wilcox, James 214
Wilcox, Stephen 137
Wilde, Francis E.J. 23
Wiley, Rev. David 5
Wilkins, David 129
Wilkinson, Jeremiah 128
Willard, Emma H. 63
Willard, Frances E.C. 89
Willard, Simon 216
William College 54
William Penn Academy 52
Williams, Charles 47
Williams, Daniel H. 102, 111
Williams, Jesse 91
Williams, Jonathan 148
Williams, Roger 183
Williams, Thomas R. 146
Williamson, Peregrine 134
Willis, Nathaniel 177
Williston, Mrs. Samuel 129
Willson, Thomas L. 202
Willys, John N. 247
Wilson, Charles E. 120
Wilson, William B. 118, 120
Winchester, Oliver F. 41, 125
Wind and Current Chart of the North Atlantic 262
windmills 138

wine 88
Winebrenner, John 194
Winner, Septimus 159
Winslow, Edward 6
Winslow, Isaac 92
Winsor, Justin 58
Winthrop, John 8, 166, 199, 204, 271
Winton, Alexander 246
Wise, Isaac Mayer 188
Wise, John 256
Wise, Stephen S. 188
Wistar, Caspar 130
Wistar, Richard 130
Witherspoon, John 194
Witteman, Charles E. 253
Woman's Hospital of Illinois 102
Women's Army Auxiliary Corps 148
Women's Army Corps 148
women's rights 122, 221, 222
Wood, Gar(field A.) 229
Wood, Grant 16

Wood, James F. 97
Wood, Jethro 10
Wood, Walton J. 121
Woodhouse, James 202
Woodhull, R.S. 10, 91
Woodhull, Victoria Claflin 222
Woodruff, William E. 175
wool 146
Woolley, Leonidas G. 266
Woolworth, Frank W. 37
Worcester, Joseph E. 168
worker's rights 119
Worthington, Henry R. 139
wrench 136
Wright, Henry (Harry) 225
Wright, Orville 250, 254
Wright, Wilbur 250
Wrigley, William, Jr. 89
Wyeth, Andrew 17
Wyeth, Newell C. 15
Wynne, Arthur 76, 179
Wythe, George 122

Xerox Corp. 28
x-rays 68, 103, 109, 114

yachting 243
Yale University 52, 53, 88
Yale, Elihu 52
Yale, Linus 129
Ye Bare and Ye Cubb 82
Yeager, Charles E. 253
Yeager, Jeana 253
yeast 92
Young, Brigham 35, 191

Zaharias, Babe Didrikson 235, 242
Zenger, John Peter 121, 122, 174
Ziegfeld, Florenz 84
zinc 141
Zinsser, Hans 108
Zion's Cooperative Mercantile Institution 36
zoology 208
Zworykin, Vladimir K. 44